MARXIST-FEMINIST THEORIES AND STRUGGLES TODAY

MARXIST-FEMINIST THEORIES AND STRUGGLES TODAY

ESSENTIAL WRITINGS ON INTERSECTIONALITY, LABOUR AND ECOFEMINISM

Edited by Khayaat Fakier, Diana Mulinari, and Nora Räthzel

ZED

Marxist-Feminist Theories and Struggles Today was first published in 2020 by Zed Books Ltd, The Foundry, 17 Oval Way, London SE11 5RR, UK.

www.zedbooks.net

Editorial Copyright © Khayaat Fakier, Diana Mulinari, Nora Räthzel 2020

Copyright in this collection © Zed Books 2020

The right of Khayaat Fakier, Diana Mulinari, and Nora Räthzel to be identified as the editors of this work has been asserted by them in accordance with sections 77 and 78 of the Copyright, Designs and Patents Act, 1988

Typeset in Plantin and Kievit by Swales & Willis Ltd, Exeter, Devon
Index by ed.emery@thefreeuniversity.net
Cover design by Burgess and Beech

All rights reserved. No part of this publication may be reproduced, stored in a retrieval system or transmitted in any form or by any means, electronic, mechanical, photocopying or otherwise, without the prior permission of Zed Books Ltd.

A catalogue record for this book is available from the British Library

ISBN 978-1-78699-616-9 hb
ISBN 978-1-78699-615-2 pb
ISBN 978-1-78699-617-6 pdf
ISBN 978-1-78699-618-3 epub
ISBN 978-1-78699-619-0 mobi

For Cynthia Cockburn (24 July 1934–13 September 2019)
Our friend and colleague and a pioneer of Marxist Feminism

CONTENTS

Notes on contributors ix

    Introduction. 1
    Khayaat Fakier, Diana Mulinari, and Nora Räthzel

Part I: Conceptualising 7

1 Standpoint theory 9
   Cynthia Cockburn

2 Outside in the funding machine 22
   Gayatri Chakravorty Spivak

3 Contradictions in Marxist feminism. 27
   Frigga Haug

4 Ecofeminism as (Marxist) sociology. 40
   Ariel Salleh

5 The 'flat ontology' of neoliberal feminism 51
   Jennifer Cotter

6 The Byzantine eunuch: pre-capitalist gender category, 'tributary'
   modal contradiction, and a test for materialist feminism 70
   Jules Gleeson

7 Reading Marx against the grain: rethinking the exploitation of
   care work beyond profit-seeking. 88
   Tine Haubner

Part II: Production 103

8 Marx and social reproduction theory: three different
   historical strands. 105
   Ankica Čakardić

9 The best thing I have done is to give birth; the second is
   to strike 124
   Paula Mulinari

10 Women in small-scale fishing in South Africa: an ecofeminist
    engagement with the 'blue economy'. 144
    Natasha Solari and Khayaat Fakier

11 The 'crisis of care' and the neoliberal restructuring of the
    public sector: a feminist Polanyian analysis 167
    Rebecca Selberg

12 Gender regimes and women's labour: Volvo factories in Sweden,
    Mexico, and South Africa 187
    Nora Räthzel, Diana Mulinari, and Aina Tollefsen

Part III: Religions and Politics **209**

13 Religious resistance: a flower on the chain or a tunnel
    towards liberation? 211
    Gabriele Dietrich

14 A Marxist-Feminist perspective: from former Yugoslavia to
    turbo-fascism to neoliberal postmodern fascist Europe 231
    Marina Gržinić

15 Feminism, antisemitism, and the question of Palestine/Israel 249
    Nira Yuval-Davis

Part IV: Solidarities. **261**

16 Women in Brazil's trade union movement 263
    Patrícia Vieira Trópia

17 Argentinean feminist movements: debates from praxis 276
    Ana Isabel González Montes

18 Marxist feminism for a global women's movement
    against capitalism 296
    Ligaya Lindio McGovern

19 Marxist/socialist feminist theory and practice
    in the USA today 306
    Nancy Holmstrom

20 Solidarity in troubled times: social movements in the face of
    climate change 327
    Kathryn Russell

Index 350

NOTES ON CONTRIBUTORS

Ankica Čakardić, PhD, is an assistant professor and the chair of Social Philosophy and Philosophy of Gender at the Faculty for Humanities and Social Sciences, University of Zagreb. Her research interests include Social Philosophy, Marxism, Marxist feminism, Luxemburgian critiques of political economy, and history of women's struggles in Yugoslavia. She has edited two books on feminist epistemology (both in Croatian) and is currently finishing her book on the social history of capitalism and Marxist critique of the thinking of Hobbes and Locke. She is a member of *The Complete Works of Rosa Luxemburg* editorial board. She is a feminist and socialist activist.

Cynthia Cockburn was a feminist researcher and writer living in London, where she was active in Women in Black against War and the Women's International League for Peace and Freedom. She was a visiting professor in the Department of Sociology, City University London, and honorary professor in the Centre for the Study of Women and Gender, University of Warwick. Her last books, products of action-research on gender in processes of war and peace, are *From Where We Stand: War, Women's Activism and Feminist Analysis* (2007) and *Antimilitarism: Political and Gender Dynamics of Peace Movements* (2012).

Jennifer Cotter, PhD, is associate professor of English at William Jewell College. Her essays in feminism, materialism, and the (post)humanities have been published in *College Literature*, *Textual Practice*, *Nature, Society, and Thought*, *The Minnesota Review*, *Nineteenth-Century Prose*, *Lewą Nogą*, and *Das Argument*. She is co-editor of the book *Human, All Too (Post)Human: The Humanities after Humanism* (2016). She is currently completing a book on feminism and materialism in a time of biopolitics.

Gabriele Dietrich, PhD, is a retired professor in social analysis, having taught for 35 years in a Tamil-medium college in Madurai, South India. She is a naturalised Indian citizen and has worked with women's movements especially among unorganised sector workers. She has also been active with the National Alliance of People's Movements. Her PhD was in history of religions, at Free University Berlin

Khayaat Fakier, PhD, is a senior lecturer in the department of Sociology and Social Anthropology at the University of Stellenbosch, South Africa. She has authored and co-authored articles on social reproduction in journals such as *Antipode*, *International Journal of Feminist Politics*, and *Capital Nature Socialism*.

In 2014, she co-edited a volume titled *Socio-Economic Insecurity in Emerging Economies: Building New Spaces*.

Jules Gleeson is a gender historian, comedian, communist, and Londoner based in Vienna. Her published work addresses transfeminist ethics, gender abolitionism, effeminacy, intersex theory, embodiment struggles, and Byzantine monastic masculinities. She is co-editing a new essay collection, *Transgender Marxism*. She co-founded the Leftovers communist discussion group, and New Critical Approaches to the Byzantine World research network.

Ana Isabel González Montes, born in Argentina in 1954, is a social anthropologist specialised in human rights, gender and Indigenous Peoples rights. She was an associate professor at the Chair of Culture of Peace and Human Rights in the Faculty of Social Sciences at the University of Buenos Aires (2010–2018). She is a member of the Academic Committee of the Institute of Latin American and Caribbean Studies of the University of Buenos Aires. She was a UN official in the Peace Mission for Guatemala (MINUGUA), and worked as a UN official as coordinator of the field investigation and in the writing of the report *Guatemala Memoria del Silencio*, of the Commission for Historical Clarification of the Violations to Human Rights, which documented the genocide in that country (1997/1999). She was an official of the Human Rights Secretary of Argentina and of the National Institute against Discrimination, Xenophobia and Racism of Argentina (2003/2015). As an expert, she worked on the preparation of the National Plan against Discrimination (UN High Commissioner for Human Rights / Decree 1086/05). She was General Coordinator of the National Institute of Indigenous Affairs of Argentina (2000–2001). She has published numerous articles, in several languages, in the areas of human rights, women's rights and Indigenous Peoples, Guatemala and Central America. She has an extensive career and political commitment to the feminist movement, the human rights movement, and the popular movements of her country and the continent.

Marina Gržinić, PhD, is a philosopher, theoretician, and artist from Ljubljana, Slovenia. She serves as a professor and research advisor. Since 2003, she is professor at the Academy of Fine Arts in Vienna, Austria. She is research advisor at the Institute of Philosophy, Research Center of the Slovenian Academy of Science and Arts, Ljubljana, Slovenia. She publishes extensively, lectures worldwide, and is involved in video film productions since 1982. Selection of books: *New Feminism: Worlds of Feminism, Queer and Networking Conditions* (2008) (with Rosa Reitsamer), *Necropolitics, Racialization, and Global Capitalism: Historicization of Biopolitics and Forensics of Politics, Art, and Life* (2014) (with Šefik Tatlić), and *Border Thinking: Disassembling Histories of Racialized Violence* (2018).

Tine Haubner, PhD, studied sociology, psychology, and philosophy and is a researcher at the Department of Sociology at the Friedrich Schiller University,

Jena. Her research interests include the margins of working society such as informal and unpaid work, care and welfare, social inequality, and social theory.

Frigga Haug, PhD, is professor emerita in Sociology and Social Psychology, University for Economics and Politics, Hamburg. She was a visiting scholar in Denmark, Austria, Australia, Canada, USA. A founder of memory-work research, her early leadership in the field is reflected in *Female Sexualization: A Collective Work of Memory*. She is a member of numerous editorial boards, including a series on feminist crime and fiction, *Das Argument*, a journal for philosophy and social theory, and the *Historical Critical Dictionary of Marxism*, for both of which she is currently co-editor; she is also editor of the *Critical Dictionary of Feminism*, vols 1–3. Her research has ranged from automation and work culture to social science methodology and learning, to other areas of women's studies. Her most recent books are: *Rosa Luxemburg und die Kunst der Politik* (2007) (Rosa Luxemburg and the Art of Politics), *Die Vier-in-einem Perspektive. Politik von Frauen für eine neue Linke* (2008/2011) (The Four-in-One-Perspective: Women's Politics for a New Left), *Der im Gehen erkundete Weg. Marxismus-Feminismus* (2015) (The Path Explored by Walking: Marxism-Feminism), and *Selbstveränderung und Veränderung der Umstände* (2018) (Changing the Self, Changing the Circumstances).

Nancy Holmstrom, PhD, is a professor of philosophy emerita at Rutgers University in Newark. A lifelong socialist and feminist activist, she has published papers on core concepts in political philosophy, including freedom, exploitation, rationality, and human/women's nature. She has edited *The Socialist Feminist Project*, co-edited *Not For Sale: In Defense of Public Goods*, and co-authored *Capitalism for and against: A Feminist Debate*. She was a founding member of the board of directors of Left Forum, and is a member of the editorial board of *New Politics*. She believes that socialism is now an ecological imperative.

Ligaya Lindio McGovern, PhD, is professor of sociology and the major co-founder of the Office for Sustainability at Indiana University Kokomo. A recipient of a Fulbright Research Award in 2017, she conducted research on the impacts of extractive corporate mining on Indigenous men and women in the Philippines and its implications for an integrated framing of human rights and sustainability. With research and teaching interests on women/gender and globalisation, Third World development, social movements and social change, and sustainability she is author of *Filipino Peasant Women: Exploitation and Resistance* and *Globalization, Labor Export and Resistance: A Study of Filipino Migrant Domestic Workers in Global Cities*. A former director of Women's Studies, she co-edited *Globalization and Third World Women: Exploitation, Coping and Resistance* and *Gender and Globalization: Patterns of Women's Resistance*.

Diana Mulinari, PhD, is a professor in the department of Gender Studies, University of Lund. Her research interests are inspired by the traditions of Marxism, black and postcolonial feminist theory. Located within feminist sociology she explore topics such as gender and political identities, nation and ethnic belonging, racism, and Global North / Global South relations (with special focus on Latin America). Her most recent publications include: *Dreaming Global Change, Doing Local Feminisms* (2018) (co-edited with L. Martinsson), and 'Exploring Femonationalism and Care-Racism in Sweden', *Women's Studies International Forum* 68 (May–June 2018): 149–156 (with M. Sager).

Paula Mulinari, PhD, works as a lecturer and researcher at the Institution of Social Work at Malmö University. Her research has mainly been concerned with issues of labour market inequalities, especially in service and emotional work, and workplace resistance. Her most recent articles explore the struggles against austerity and racist politics within the public sector (2018), and the role of femonationalism in municipality labour market policy (2018).

Nora Räthzel, PhD, is senior professor at the University of Umeå, Sweden. Her main research areas are environmental labour studies, trade unions and the environment, working conditions in transnational corporations, and gender and ethnic relations in the everyday. Her latest publications are: '"You must aim high" – "No, I never felt like a woman": Women and Men Making Sense of Nonstandard Trajectories into Higher Education', *Gender, Science and Technology*, 10(1) (2018) (with Ana González Ramos), *Transnational Corporations from the Standpoint of Workers* (2014) (with Diana Mulinari and Aina Tollefsen), and *Trade Unions in the Green Economy: Working for the Environment* (2013) (co-edited with David Uzzell).

Kathryn Russell, PhD, is professor of philosophy emerita from the State University of New York College at Cortland, and an activist with the Tompkins County Workers' Center, the Coalition for Sustainable Economic Development and SURJ (Showing Up for Racial Justice). Anti-fracking action-research led to her article 'Will Fracking Bring the Soldiers Home?' *Peace Review* (2013). Other scholarship includes 'Feminist Dialectics and Marxist Theory', *Radical Philosophy Review* (2007), and 'A Value-Theoretic Approach to Childbirth and Reproductive Engineering', *Science and Society* (Fall 1994) reprinted in *Materialist Feminism: A Reader in Class, Difference and Women's Lives* (1997) (edited by Rosemary Hennessy and Chrys Ingraham).

Ariel Salleh, PhD, is a sociologist of knowledge with experience in water and mining politics, biodiversity conservation, and mothering. Her books include *Ecofeminism as Politics: Nature, Marx, and the Postmodern* (2017/1997), *Eco-Sufficiency and Global Justice* (2009), and *Pluriverse: A Post-Development Dictionary* (2019).

She is a founding editor of the journal *Capitalism Nature Socialism*, and has held teaching and research appointments at New York University, Friedrich Schiller University Jena, the University of Sydney, and Nelson Mandela University. www.arielsalleh.info.

Rebecca Selberg has a PhD in sociology from Linnaeus University. She is an assistant professor at the Department of Gender Studies, Lund University. Her research is focused on international working life studies, the political economy of care, and labour processes in paid care work. Recent publications include: 'Intersectional Directions in Working Life Research: A Proposal', *Nordic Journal of Working Life Studies* 3(3) (2013): 81–98 (with P. Mulinari), 'Nursing in Times of Neoliberal Change: An Ethnographic Study of Nurses' Experiences of Work Intensification', *Nordic Journal of Working Life Studies* 3(2) (2013): 9–35, and 'Vardagsrasism på sjukhuset', in *Ojämlikhet på arbetsplatsen* (edited by A. Neergaard and K. Boréus) (2019, forthcoming).

Natasha Solari is a graduate student in sociology and social anthropology at the University of Stellenbosch in South Africa. Her research focuses on women in small-scale and artisanal fishing and hones in on the contradictions between 'development' and ecology.

Gayatri Chakravorty Spivak, PhD, is a university professor, and a founding member of the Institute for Comparative Literature and Society at Columbia University in New York. She is director at elementary schools in Rashpur, Baidyanathpur, Langulia, Haripur, Tabadumra, and Shahabad near the Birbhum-Jharrkhand border where she also facilitates the will for a farmers' cooperative not imposed by benevolent feudal leaders. She has received honorary doctorates from the Universities of Toronto (1999), London (2003), Oberlin College (2008), Universitat Roveri I Virgili (2011), Rabindra Bharati (2012), Universidad Nacional de San Martin (2013), Universities of St. Andrews (2014), Paris VIII (2014), Presidency University (2014), Yale University (2015), and University of Ghana-Legon (2015). In 2012 she was awarded the Kyoto Prize in Thought and Ethics and in 2013 the Padma Bhushan. Among her books: *In Other Worlds: Essays in Cultural Politics* (1987, 2002); *Outside in the Teaching Machine* (1993, 2003); *A Critique of Postcolonial Reason: Towards a History of the Vanishing Present* (1999); *Our World* (2014).

Aina Tollefsen, PhD, is associate professor in the Department of Geography and Economic History at Umeå University, Sweden. She has researched processes of migration, return, and circulation as well as globalising working conditions. Her most recent publication is 'The Production of the Rural Landscape and Its Labour: The Development of Supply Chain Capitalism in the Swedish Berry Industry', *Bulletin of Geography. Socio-economic Series* 40(40) (2018): 69–82 (with M. Eriksson).

Patrícia Vieira Trópia, PhD, is professor at the Federal University of Uberlândia and permanent member of the PhD program in social sciences at the same university. She researches on trade unionism, gender, and social classes. She completed postdoctoral studies at the University Lumière Lyon 2, in France, under the supervision of Sophie Béroud. Her PhD in social sciences from Unicamp (University of Campinas, Brazil) (2004) is entitled 'The Impact of Neoliberalism on the Working Environment: A Study on the Metallurgists of São Paulo and the Força Sindical'. She is author of the book *Força Sindical: Politics and Ideology in Brazilian Syndicalism* (2009). She is the editor and author of the collection *Metallurgical Unions in Contemporary Brazil* (2012).

Nira Yuval-Davis, PhD, is professor emeritus, honorary director of the Research Centre on Migration, Refugees and Belonging (CMRB) at the University of East London. A diasporic Israeli socialist feminist, Nira has been active in different forums against racism and sexism in Israel and other settler colonial societies as well as in the UK and Europe. She has been the president of the Research Committee 05 (Racism, Nationalism, Indigeneity and Ethnic Relations) of the International Sociological Association, founder member of Women Against Fundamentalism and the international research network on Women in Militarized Conflict Zones, and has acted as a consultant for various UN and human rights organisations. She has won the 2018 International Sociological Association Distinguished Award for Excellence in Research and Practice. She has written widely on intersected gendered nationalisms, racisms, fundamentalisms, citizenships, identities, belonging/s, and everyday bordering. Among her books are: *Woman–Nation–State* (1989), *Racialized Boundaries* (1992), *Unsettling Settler Societies* (1995), *Gender and Nation* (1997), *The Warning Signs of Fundamentalism* (2004), *The Politics of Belonging: Intersectional Contestations* (2011), *Women Against Fundamentalism* (2014), and *Bordering* (Forthcoming). Her works have been translated into more than ten languages.

INTRODUCTION

Khayaat Fakier, Diana Mulinari, and Nora Räthzel[1]

The main intellectual experience haunting feminist scholars and activists working within the tradition of Marxist/socialist feminism today is the prevalence of crisis: the human crisis represented through an unprecedented increase of forced migration and widening gaps of inequality across and within countries North and South. The crisis of nature, visible in an ever-increasing number of natural catastrophes, which hit predominantly poor and vulnerable populations the hardest. The economic crisis analysed under the notion of 'financialisation', that is the pursuit of profit through financial transactions as opposed to investments in production processes. While vulnerabilities abound, the possibilities to care for those who are most vulnerable are decreasing, rather than broadening, a process analysed by feminist scholars as the crisis of care. Whether these crises have different causes and feed off each other, or whether they are seen as different facets of one and the same crisis is yet an open question to be explored. What we can observe though, is that they lead to the strengthening of religious fundamentalist, nationalist, racist, and misogynist movements across the globe, transcending the North–South divide.

To understand these crises and how to act against them, some Marxist-Feminists across the world decided to pick up the threads of their debates starting more than 40 years ago. Initiated by Frigga Haug with the Feminist Section of the Institute of Critical Theory in Berlin and supported by Canadian and US Marxist-Feminists with Sharzad Mojab, who were editing a book on Marxism and feminism[2] with Zed Books at the same time, Marxists-Feminists around the world came together to the first conference in Berlin, in March 2015.[3]

To everyone's surprise over 500 (mostly women) turned up wanting to hear and debate with what Marxist-Feminists had to say. The debates were engaged but also heated. Quite a number of participants thought that the Marxism-Feminism presented here was oblivious to the theoretical and political debates that had taken place since the heydays of Marxist feminism, namely during the resurgence of feminist movements across the world in the 1970s. They missed discussions of racism and postcolonialism, the inclusion of feminists from countries of the global South, they thought the critique of intersectionality did not do justice to the usefulness of the concept. However, there was a unifying conviction that these conferences should continue, and that the debate needed to be broadened in terms of issues covered, theoretical and political approaches, as well as geographically. In this spirit, the second conference was organised in Vienna by the team of *transform! Europe* and two colleagues living in Sweden and Spain, respectively. They made the effort to invite scholars and activists from every continent (a problem with limited resources) sending out an open call for papers to as many countries as possible.

The title of the second conference reflected the aim of pluralising the Marxist-Feminist debate: *Building Bridges – Shifting and Strengthening Visions – Exploring Alternatives*. Most of the results of this endeavour can be read in this anthology.

Again, over 500 participants visited the conference in Vienna, this time from 29 countries and covering a wide range of issues and theoretical approaches while defining themselves as Marxist or socialist feminists (https://marxfem conference.net/2016/11/22/writing-feminism-into-marxism/).

The third conference, in Lund, in October 2018, adopted a radically different format. While the conference in Vienna had broadened its range of contributors and perspectives, it was criticised for not leaving enough space for discussion. Thus, for Lund it was decided that the conference should feature only a few key-note speakers and a few panels and would otherwise consist predominantly of workshops, using methods that guaranteed the best possibility of participation. This decision led also to a further broadening of issues discussed within the frame of Marxist feminism (https://marxfemblog. files.wordpress.com/2018/07/program-marxfem-conference-2018.pdf).

Like the debates on Marxism-Feminism in general the conferences will continue. The fourth will be organised by a group of Catalan and Basque Marxist-Feminists and will take place in Bilbo/Bilbao[4] from 15th to 17th October 2020. It is their plan to include more Marxist-Feminist activists from outside academia, something that was suggested at the third conference.

The need for Marxist-Feminist analyses and practices

Feminist scholarship has increasingly returned to a Marxist/socialist tradition with a focus on capitalism as central to an understanding of gender inequality regimes globally. Marxism, and in its tradition of Marxist feminism, uses dialectics as a method to pursue the concrete study of societal relations and develops its categories from these analyses.

While at the first conference the question of how to define Marxist feminism was prevalent, the two following conferences seemed to take that answer for granted and contributors as well as participants were more interested in using Marxist-Feminist tools to analyse what they saw as the burning questions of our time: how to develop women's capacities to transform patriarchal capitalist societies (Haug), coalitions between workers' environmentalist and feminist movements (Russel, Holmstrom, Trópia), the rise of the right, of racist movements and state practices (Gržinić, Yuval-Davis), rethinking the position of women in the care sector (Haubner, Čakardić), women workers in industries, subsistence economies, and care (D. Mulinari, Räthzel and Tollefsen, Fakier and Solari, P. Mulinari, Selberg), gender performativity (Gleeson), women and religion (Dietrich), Marxist feminism and the new materialist feminism (Cotter), feminist movements in authoritarian states (González, McGovern) – to name only the contributions we were able to include in this anthology.

In this anthology, Cynthia Cockburn, who sadly died during the production of this volume, examines the history of Standpoint Theory from Marx to its usages in Feminist theorizations. She argues for its continuous usefulness in understanding new social movements. Gayatri Chakravorty Spivak makes us of aware that we are simultaneously within and outside the funding machine. As the difference between public and private breaks down, while trying to change the world we are always also complicit in its destruction. Frigga Haug examines the contradictions of Marxist-Feminist theory and practice, namely, that in order to create a new world and liberate themselves, women need to destroy the old ways of thinking and feeling, to which they are nonetheless emotionally and rationally attached. Kathryn Russel takes the reader through the challenges and dilemmas of forging solidarities between different social movements against climate change. Nancy Holstrom analyses the history and present state of Marxist/socialist feminist theories and movements in the United States arguing that theoretical diversity does not preclude practical solidarity. Patrícia Vieira Trópia provides a historical overview of the relationship between feminist activism and trade union organisation and renewal in Brazil, showing how the rise of women as members and decision makers connects in contradictory ways with the rise of CUT and the Lula and Rousseff presidencies. Marina Gržinić analyses political developments in Europe as forms of turbo-fascism and necropolitics, connecting Marxist analysis with Foucault's and Agamben's concepts of biopolitics, arguing that today politics have changed from making live and letting die to letting live and making die. Nira Yuval-Davis makes a strong case for socialist feminists to resist the identification of critique of the Israeli state and its politics against Palestinians with antisemitism. Tine Haubner argues that it is necessary to re-introduce the concept of exploitation into the social sciences, specifically into economic theories, since it is through this concept that we can understand how women in the care sector are exploited, even where profit-making is not at the centre. Ankica Čakardić revisits Marx's analysis of capital reproduction and feminist theories of social reproduction to argue that a unitary theory of the latter is decisive in order to analyse the social reality in a non-reductionist way. Nora Räthzel, Diana Mulinari, and Aina Tollefsen analyse the position of women in Volvo production plants in Mexico, South Africa, and Sweden, suggesting that the widening gap between working conditions in the North and the South can only be bridged by North–South and South–South alliances which retrieve women from their precarious location in globalised labour markets. Natasha Solari and Khayaat Fakier take their point of departure in the everyday life of women whose families and communities depend on their fishing skills and abilities. They explore the impact of neoliberal capitalism in vulnerable eco-systems and the strategies developed by women to protect the sea, their work, and their families. Paula Mulinari analyses a strike of railway workers in Sweden and shows that care and productive work cannot be assigned to different areas, but that caring for others at work and outside work is inextricably linked to forms in which paid employment is organised. While refuting the idea that unpaid care work is a space not subsumed under the logic of capitalism, she argues that resistance to this logic through caring for others can develop in all spheres of work, in paid employment as well as in the spheres of unpaid work within families and among friends. Rebecca Selberg explores the debates about care through the last decades and embarks on an analytical journey, exploring the power of creating a dialogue between the work of Nancy Fraser on the crisis of care and Michael Burawoy's understanding of the new phase of capitalism. Jules Gleeson provides a queer and postcolonial-inspired reading of the Byzantine Eunuchs, analysing not only their possible subject position within the gender and sexual order but their social location as contradictory subjects within a tributary mode of the pre-capitalist state. Gabriele Dietrich draws on Marx's writing on religion to focus on the radical positions of B.R. Ambedkar and Pandita Ramabai, who promoted religious conversion to avoid the oppressive Hindu caste system and its oppression of women. She argues that these positions needs to be protected in a violently, religious nationalist India, where feminists are securing secular spaces in their own faith communities and building links across widening religious rifts. Jennifer Cotter provides a solid challenge of the feminist new materialist and post-human school, emphasising their resistance to understanding the social through an analysis of capitalism as a totalising mode of organising the relations of production globally. Ana Isabel González Montes tells the story of the historical development of feminism in Argentina, characterising the history and present situation of Argentina in order to find the means to confront the challenges identified by feminist struggles today. Ligaya Lindio McGovern asks us to create a global Marxist-Feminist movement against capitalism. She demonstrates the prospects of such a perspective drawing on a Marxist-Feminist movement in the Philippines and a transnational women's movement, the International Women's Alliance, including individuals and organisations from all continents, which was founded in Montreal through the initiative of Filipino women.

As different as the usages and interpretations of Marxism-Feminism might be, in addition to Marx there are some towering historical figures to whose legacies we all keep coming back: Rosa Luxemburg, Flora Tristan, Clara Zetkin, Alexandra Kollontai, Raya Dunayevskaya.

The authors of this anthology pick up the insights of Marxist/socialist feminists in the conceptualisation of how labour, gender, class, and race relations are organised within capitalist relations of production. They further develop the pivotal contributions of Marxist-Feminists, Marxists and other feminists to understand capitalism as a societal formation, from intimate everyday relations to globalised power relations. The articles in the anthology also explore and challenge the tension between Marxist/socialist feminism and other critical theoretical traditions, intersectionality, queer theory, theories of care and social reproduction, as well as feminist ecology and analyses of gender relations at work. These tensions have often been exaggerated while their points of commonality have been underplayed. We suggest that it is fundamental to reframe the dialogue among and between these traditions for the future of feminist theory and feminist movements globally.

The variety of these contributions and their diverse approaches will beg the question of what Marxist feminism is supposed to be and do. Does it inscribe feminism into Marxism and/or vice versa? Does it add feminist theory to Marxist theory or does it integrate both theoretical approaches, thereby changing both of them? What kind of approaches can be further included to broaden the Marxist-Feminist perspective or can these approaches be successfully transformed by a Marxist-Feminist lens? As the editors of this anthology we do not see our task in defining Marxism-Feminism and creating borders around it to demarcate who is inside and who is outside.

Instead, this anthology attempts to show a spectrum of diverse understandings and usages of Marxist-Feminist frameworks. The authors in this anthology do not necessarily agree with each other's analyses, nor do we as editors agree with all the contributions in this book. However, we believe that in order for Marxist feminism to continue being a useful tool for the analyses, and, thus, for the struggles against today's relations of capitalist gendered and racialised exploitation and oppression we need a conversation between a variety of analyses and perspectives. What these diverse approaches have nevertheless in common is an understanding that for humanity to survive, we need to fundamentally transform the system of capitalism and its devastating globalised exploitation of humans and nature. This book, we hope, is only the beginning of a world-wide conversation among Marxist-Feminists and other feminists and Marxists about how to achieve this common goal.

Notes

1 These days the order of names has become so important for the development of our careers. We decided to use the 'traditional' format and list editors alphabetically. We have done so in acknowledgement and appreciation of each one of us investing the time available to us towards makings this a good book.

2 Mojab et al. published their book as *Marxism and Feminism* (Mojab, 2015). The organisation of the conference and the publication of the book were not related to each other. By coincidence, both initiatives

started more or less at the same time and then supported each other. However, this book and the two publications resulting from the first and second Marxist-Feminist conferences are not related to each other.

3 The book resulting from the conference in Berlin was titled *Wege des Marxismus-Feminismus* and edited by Frigga Haug and Ruth May (Haug and May, 2015). Funding was provided by the *Rosa Luxemburg Stiftung*, the *Institute of Critical Theory* (INKRIT), the organisation *transform! Europe*, and the German Party, *Die Linke*.

4 For further information please consult the website of all the conferences: https://marxfemconference.net.

References

Haug, F., May, R. (Eds.), 2015. *Wege des Marxismus-Feminismus*. Argument, Hamburg.

Mojab, S. (Ed.), 2015. *Marxism and Feminism*. Zed Books, London.

PART I

CONCEPTUALISING

1 | STANDPOINT THEORY*

Cynthia Cockburn

Standpoint theory is an epistemology, an account of the evolution of knowledge and strategies of action by particular collectivities in specific social relations in given periods. As a concept, standpoint derives from Karl Marx's exegesis of class relations in capitalism. The historical development of capitalism as a mode of production involved the disintegration of feudal hierarchies and their gradual replacement by a new class system. In the last few pages of volume three of *Capital*, Marx writes:

> We have seen that the continual tendency and law of development of the capitalist mode of production is more and more to divorce the means of production from labour, and more and more to concentrate the scattered means of production into large groups, thereby transforming labour into wage-labour and the means of production into capital. (Marx 1959: 885)[1]

Thus, though landowners remained in existence in the new era as a third class, it was the proletariat and the bourgeoisie – dynamic, mutually dependent, locked in antagonism – which were definitive of capitalism.

In his historical materialist analysis of capitalism, Marx stressed that the realities of life in the new mode of production shaped the consciousness of the individuals experiencing it. In *The German Ideology* he and Engels wrote: 'Life is not determined by consciousness, but consciousness by life' (Marx and Engels 1970: 47). Their distinctive understanding was that 'definite individuals who are productively active in a definite way enter into ... definite social and political relations' (ibid.: 46). They continue in this vein,

> The social structure and the State are continually evolving out of the life-process of definite individuals, but of individuals, not as they may appear in their own or other people's imagination, but as they really are; i.e. as they operate, produce materially, and hence as they work under definite material limits, presuppositions and conditions independent of their will. (Ibid.: 46)

So too do awareness, understanding and theory evolve. Individuals 'developing their material production and their material intercourse, alter, along with this their real existence, their thinking and the products of their thinking' (ibid.: 46).[2]

This theme in Marx's work was later developed by Georg Lukács. In *History and Class Consciousness*, Lukács addresses Marx's account of, as he

* This chapter was first published in *Marxism and Feminism*, edited by Shahrzad Mojab and published by Zed Books, 2015.

puts it, 'the special position of the proletariat in society and in history, and the standpoint from which it can function as the identical subject-object of the social and historical process of evolution' (Lukács 1968: 149).[3] He continues with a quotation from Marx and Engels' *The Holy Family*,[4] in which they represent the class relation as follows.

> The property-owning class and the class of the proletariat represent the same human self-alienation. But the former feels at home in this self-alienation and feels itself confirmed by it; it recognises alienation as its own instrument and in it possesses the semblance of a human existence. The latter feels itself destroyed by this alienation and sees in it its own impotence and the reality of an inhuman existence. (Cited in ibid.: 149)

As a consequence, Lukács himself continues, while class interests 'keep the bourgeoisie imprisoned within this immediacy', they force the proletariat to go beyond it, to become 'conscious of the social character of Labour'. It is 'only in the proletariat that the process by which a man's achievement is split off from his total personality and becomes a commodity leads to a revolutionary consciousness'. For the working class, therefore, recognizing the dialectical nature of its existence is, Lukács says, 'a matter of life and death' (ibid.: 164, 171). It necessarily pitches the class into struggle with its rulers. In this, the Marxian understanding of class standpoint can be heard to echo Hegel's account of the development of self-consciousness in which he employs the allegory of the 'master' and the 'servant', necessarily precipitated into existential conflict in which the stake is annihilation of self or other (Hegel 1977).[5]

One effect of class domination, therefore, is the emergence of a distinctive proletarian 'standpoint', or, as we might say today, a proletarian 'take' on life. What is more, because the view from below is capable of revealing 'the immanent contradictions' in the capitalist mode of production, the practical class consciousness of the proletariat has the revolutionary potential to disrupt the given structure, the unique 'ability to transform things' (Lukács 1968: 197, 205). Antonio Gramsci, also writing in the early twentieth-century tradition of 'Western Marxism', shared this understanding of class consciousness. Observing the capability of western European capitalist classes to sustain their rule over a potentially insurgent working class by hegemony – that is to say by culturally generated consent rather than coercion – he saw the potential for proletarian revolutionary thought to grow, find adherents among other elements in civil society, and eventually achieve counter-hegemonic capability, challenging the sway of ruling-class ideology (Gramsci 1971).[6]

The gendering of standpoint theory

Women do not feature in Marx's account of the creation of surplus value, the heart of his economic theory. Lukács and Gramsci for their part also seem to have conceived of the proletariat as male. They use masculine nouns and pronouns in referring to it, and rarely allude to female workers or female family members of male workers. In fact, the unthinking assertion of masculinity is sometimes so emphatic as to be laughable. Thus Lukács celebrating the proletarian achievement: 'From this standpoint alone does history really become a history of mankind. For it contains nothing that does not lead back ultimately to men and to the relations between men' (Lukács 1968: 186). Nonetheless, in the 1970s some feminist socialist thinkers began to see the usefulness of Marxist standpoint theory for understanding forms of thought emerging from women's exploitation and oppression in a patriarchal sex-gender order.

Dorothy Smith and Nancy Hartsock both began work on this theme in the 1970s, and published more substantial analyses in the following decade. In her major work *The Everyday World as Problematic: A Feminist Sociology*, Smith reprised the theme of earlier essays (Smith 1974, 1981), describing the 'brutal history of women's silencing' by authoritative male discourse. This marginalization of women's experience and thought she represented as part of 'the relations of ruling', a concept that, as she defined it, 'grasps power, organization, direction, and regulation as more pervasively structured than can be expressed in traditional concepts provided by the discourses of power'. It reflects, she says, 'the dynamic advance of the distinctive forms of organizing and ruling contemporary capitalist society, and the patriarchal forms of our contemporary experience' (Smith 1987: 3). Where was the sociology in which women would 'talk back' to power from the perspective of their everyday experience? Smith set out to make good the lack by creating 'a way of seeing, from where we actually live, into the powers, processes, and relations that organize and determine the everyday context of that seeing' (ibid.: 9). Referring explicitly to Marx's use of Hegel's parable of master and servant, Smith saw parallels between 'the claims Marx makes for a knowledge based in the class whose labour produces the conditions of existence, indeed the very existence, of a ruling class, and the claims that can be made for a knowledge of society from the standpoint of women' (ibid.: 79).

Similarly Nancy Hartsock, in an article on which she began work in 1978, brought a historical materialist approach to the understanding of 'the phallocratic institutions and ideology that constitute the capitalist form of patriarchy' (Hartsock 1985: 231).[7] She spelled out significant differences between men's and women's life activity. Where men have the singular role of producing goods, women as a sex produce both goods and human beings. Unlike those of men, women's lives are institutionally defined by the production of use-values in the home. She observed, therefore, that 'if life itself consists of sensuous activity, the vantage point available to women on the basis of their contribution to subsistence represents an intensification and deepening of the materialist world view available to the producers of commodities in capitalism, an intensification of class consciousness' (ibid.: 235).

Women's life activity, then, might be considered the source of a specific feminist standpoint. In proposing this, Hartsock spelled out some of the essential features of a 'standpoint' in Marxist theory. Material life, whether experienced by a given class or a given sex, both structures and sets limits on the understanding of social relations. In systems characterized by the domination by one group of another, the vision of each will be an inversion of that of the other. The view from above is likely to be both partial and perverse. Later, Hartsock would explain, 'By perverse I meant specifically both strange and harmful.'[8] On this reading, she concluded that women's lives surely 'make available a particular and privileged vantage point on male supremacy, a vantage point that can ground a powerful critique of the phallocratic institutions and ideology that constitute the capitalist form of patriarchy' (ibid.: 231). Most importantly, in Marxist theory, as Hartsock stresses, the standpoint of the oppressed group is an engaged vision, an achievement. It becomes available only through struggle. Finally, women's resistance to patriarchy, exposing the inhumanity of human relations, 'embodies a distress that requires a solution ... a social synthesis that does not depend on any of the forms taken by abstract masculinity' (ibid.: 246). Like the proletarian standpoint, it 'points beyond the present, and carries a historically liberatory role' (ibid.: 232).

Situated and plural knowledge

Recognizing 'standpoint' is to acknowledge that a plausible account of the world can be given from more than one positionality. In this spirit, a number of feminist theorists in the 1980s questioned the basis of knowledge claims (Rose 1983; Jaggar 1983; Harding 1986). Donna Haraway, addressing the multiplicity and diversity of feminist subjects and life experiences, developed the plural concept of 'situated knowledges' (Haraway 1988). She insisted on the embodied nature of all trustworthy seeing and knowing, dismissing 'unlocatable' knowledge claims as irresponsible. In particular, she stressed, one cannot expect to generate an understanding useful to subjugated groups from the universalizing standpoint of the master, 'the Man, the One God, whose Eye produces, appropriates, and orders all difference' (ibid.: 193). Diverse views from below, clearly rooted in life experiences, were a better bet for more reliable accounts of the world. 'The subjugated have a decent chance to be on to the god-trick and all its dazzling – and, therefore, blinding – illuminations. "Subjugated" standpoints are preferred because they seem to promise more adequate, sustained, objective, transforming accounts of the world' (ibid.: 191). 'Reliable', however, seemed to claim 'objectivity'. On what basis could partial and competing knowledges be considered objective? Haraway, and a little later Sandra Harding, reclaimed objectivity for situated knowledges. Harding had already contributed, in 1986, a major addition to feminist standpoint theory in her *The Science Question in Feminism*, in which she had savaged the androcentrism of the sciences and called for a feminist 'successor science' project (Harding 1986). Now she argued in defence of 'situated knowledges' that giving up 'the goal of telling one true story about reality' need not mean that 'one must also give up trying to tell less false stories' (Harding 1991: 187). Science had never been value-free, as scientists liked to claim. A stronger version of objectivity could be achieved by combining the standpoint from below with enquiry that was reflexive, by actors who named and clearly situated themselves, coming clean about power, interests and values, as informative about the subject and source of knowledge as about the objects of which they spoke.

Labour as Marxist-feminist problematic

Even within its own frame of reference, Marxist thought had clearly overlooked an important phenomenon. A distinctive feature of the division of labour is the sexual division of labour. This had been precisely Hartsock's project – to render an 'account of the sexual division of labour and its consequences for epistemology' (Hartsock 1985: 232). Capitalists reckon on, and profit from, both women's gendered disadvantage in the workplace and their unpaid labour in the home. This oversight has often enough been pointed out by women active in labour movements. It is possible, however, to represent the oversight as a shortcoming of socialist analysis, without positing a system of male supremacy in which men as men also benefit from women's labour. Lindsey German, for instance, dismissive of feminism as 'a limited political programme' (German 2007: 166), offers a thorough description of the position of women in capitalist labour relations while firmly rejecting the analysis of those feminist writers – she cites Heidi Hartmann (1981) in particular – who frame women's labour processes within patriarchal as well as capitalist relations. This, she writes, is 'an extremely partial reading' of women's history and a retreat from class analysis (German 2007: 154).

Other feminists challenging the gender blindness of Marxist thought have often tended, like Hartsock, to restrict their corrective analysis to labour processes and relations. Thus Heidi Hartmann, who, as Lindsey German noted, makes a cogent case for understanding patriarchy as a system of power relations distinct from, though deeply implicated in, the capitalist system of class relations, memorably defined patriarchy as 'a set of social relations which has a material base and in which there are hierarchical relations between men and solidarity among them which enable them in turn to dominate women'. Yet she continued immediately, 'The material base of patriarchy is men's control over *women's labour power*' (Hartmann 1981: 18, emphasis added). Elaborating on a point she had made two years earlier, that 'job segregation by sex is *the primary mechanism* in capitalist societies that maintains the superiority of men over women' (Hartmann 1979: 208, emphasis added), she writes:

> Job segregation by sex, by ensuring that women have the lower paid jobs, both assures women's economic dependence on men and reinforces notions of appropriate spheres for women and men. For most men, then, the development of family wages secured the material base of male domination in two ways. First, men have the better jobs in the labour market and earn higher wages than women ... Secondly ... women do housework, childcare, and perform other services at home which benefit men directly. Women's home responsibilities in turn reinforce their inferior labour market position. (Hartmann 1981: 22)

That many versions of feminist standpoint limit themselves to issues surrounding women's labour is in some sense a natural response to the fact that Marxist standpoint theory sees proletarian consciousness as resulting uniquely from the worker's experience of being forced to sell his labour power – something 'inseparable from his physical existence', as Lukács puts it – as a mere commodity (Lukács 1968: 166). Kathi Weeks' substantial recovery of feminist standpoint theory two decades after its founding moment is another case in which the analysis dwells on 'women's labouring practices' (Weeks 1998: 15). However, interestingly, she explicitly states that she does not propose 'labour as the fundamental source of women's oppression and the only site of feminist agitation'. Rather, the framing of this and earlier work (Weeks 1996) suggests a tactical choice, in the conflictual 1990s, to ground her argument in labour as a device for transcending the antagonism between modernism and postmodernism. Thus she writes:

> [I]f we take labouring practices, rather than signifying practices, as our point of entry into these configurations of gendered subjectivity, we can better account for the coercion under which gender is embodied; few would mistake labour for a practice that can be freely taken up or easily refused. Thus by privileging labour we are better able to keep sight of the constitutive links between systematic socioeconomic relations on the one hand and collective modes of practice and forms of subjectivity on the other. (Ibid.: 96)

Standpoint derived from other phases of life activity

Interestingly, Nancy Hartsock, at the start of the essay analysed above, seems to acknowledge a limitation implicit in her choice of focus. She writes: 'I argue that on the basis of ... the sexual division of labour, one could begin, though not complete, the construction of a feminist standpoint ...' (Hartsock 1985: 231). And indeed, some feminist thinkers did subsequently depart from the trope of 'work', the reiteration of the feminist standpoint's grounding in the exploitation of women's labour power and the struggle that evokes. They turned to other phases of women's lived experience to look for the emergence of feminist consciousness.

A highly innovative account came from Mary O'Brien, who, after many years as a practising midwife, turned academic and levelled her gaze on women's experience of conception, pregnancy and birthing. In *The Politics of Reproduction*, published in 1981, she suggested that an important impulse in patriarchy is control of offspring. Men's seed is alienated from them in copulation and conception. Women know their child as part of their own body, but if the man is to be sure of paternity, if he is to 'know' and appropriate the child, he must control the woman. In societal terms this requires cooperation between men. The biological process of reproduction, O'Brien argues, is a 'material substructure of history' necessarily giving rise to distinct forms of consciousness in men and women and accounting for systemic male supremacy as a historical phenomenon. Starting from this insight, she suggests, 'feminism must develop theory, method and strategy, and we must pursue this development from a fresh perspective, namely "the standpoint of women," women working from within women's reality' (O'Brien 1981: 188).

O'Brien is not the only feminist thinker to have noted that, while the subjection of the worker to the capitalist may hinge on labour and the working day, the subjection of women to men involves their whole being – physical, sexual, emotional, reproductive, aesthetic, relational – day and night. Others have looked to different aspects of oppression as potential sources of oppositional consciousness, feminist standpoints and movements. Towards the end of *The Science Question in Feminism*, published in 1986, Sandra Harding had already begun to question the singularity of 'the' feminist standpoint. It was the beginning of a period of postmodernist and post-structuralist emphasis on 'difference', on 'fractured identities' and 'hyphenized feminisms'. Socialist-feminism, radical-feminism, lesbian-feminism, black-Marxistfeminism, black-lesbian-socialist-feminism, radical-women-of-colour – these hyphenizations, Harding couldn't help feeling, bespoke 'an exhilaration felt in the differences in women's perceptions of who we are and of the appropriate politics for navigating through our daily social relations'. Standpoint epistemology, she feared, if it stressed a singular feminist standpoint, might be taken to devalue that exhilaration (Harding 1986: 163).

Two decades later she would edit a reader that responded to this doubt, drawing together multiple accounts of feminist standpoints (Harding 2004b). The volume reproduced an important essay by Patricia Hill Collins which argued that the thinking of black feminists, the 'outsiders within' US society, must be seen as constituting a special standpoint on self, family and society (Collins 1986).[9] And Maria Mies and Vandana Shiva contributed a chapter arguing that women of different racial, ethnic, cultural and class backgrounds, notably in the 'global South', have evolved a distinctive shared analysis in confronting the threat posed by capitalist exploitation to the natural environment and ultimately to human and other life on earth.

They represented this consciousness in terms of a rejection both of the Enlightenment notion that Man's freedom and happiness depends on 'his' eventual emancipation from Nature by the forces of reason and rationality, and of the Marxist concept of humankind's historic march from the 'realm of necessity' (i.e. the realm of nature) to the 'realm of freedom'. The feminist standpoint here takes the form of what the authors call the 'subsistence perspective' (Mies and Shiva 2004).[10]

Besides, by now it was no longer only diverse positionalities, in recognition of intersectionality, which were being proposed as sources of standpoints – it was also different phases of women's life activity. Another chapter in Harding's collection showed Sara Ruddick, for instance, arguing for maternal thinking, featuring 'preservative love', as generative of a feminist standpoint (Ruddick 1989).[11] In this vein, convinced by many years of empirical research in organizations of the women's peace movement, I entered this debate, proposing that the profoundly gendered phenomena of violence and war are significant features of women's 'life activity' and that resistance to them tends to generate a distinctive analysis. The social shaping of masculinity in patriarchy towards a readiness to prevail by use of force results in a marked predominance of men in violent criminality and in the ranks and commanding structures of armed forces. Women are a significant proportion of the victims of war and also experience gendered effects of militarization in everyday life in peacetime societies. I termed their critical analyses and mobilizations against violence and war a feminist anti-militarist standpoint (Cockburn 2007, 2010).

A further and somewhat startling Marxist-feminist innovation was that of Anna Jónasdóttir, who, in 1994, observed that we had been in error in so often reducing the 'material' in women's life experience to the economic. 'Work', she said, 'neither is nor ever can be life's only and total "prime want"' (Jónasdóttir 1994: 97). We were forgetting emotion. Empathy, attachment. In short, love. The activities around which the sexual struggle revolves, she maintained, are neither work nor the products of work, 'but human love – caring, ecstasy' (ibid.: 24). In making this case, Jónasdóttir represented herself as rendering reality 'from a standpoint best described as a certain kind of radical feminist stance' (ibid.: 17).

Women and men, Jónasdóttir believes, needing, seeking and practising love, 'enter into specific productive relations with each other in which they "quite literally produce new human beings."' Up to this point she was going no further than the 'conception and birthing' insight of Mary O'Brien, mentioned above. She went on to add, however, that women and men 'also produce (and reproduce) themselves and each other as active, emotional, and reasoning people' (ibid.: 63). It was in this process, she believed, that men became empowered. Adapting the Marxist theory of alienated labour, she suggested that:

men can continually appropriate significantly more of women's life force and capacity than they give back to women. Men can build themselves up as powerful social beings and continue to dominate women through their constant accumulation of the existential forces taken and received from women. If capital is accumulated alienated labour, male authority is accumulated alienated love. (Ibid.: 26)

Truth or power?

An informative exchange of ideas on standpoint took place in the feminist journal *Signs* in 1997. In an article entitled 'Truth and method: feminist standpoint theory revisited', Susan Hekman tackled several problems for standpoint theory raised by postmodernism. She remarked that 'among younger feminist theorists, feminist standpoint theory is frequently regarded as a quaint relic of feminism's less sophisticated past'. Its inspiration, Marxism, had been discredited in both theory and practice. Standpoint theory seemed to 'be at odds with the issue that has dominated feminist debate in the past decade: difference' (Hekman 2004: 225).[12]

Hekman's aim, however, was not to dismiss but to reinstate feminist standpoint theory, by stressing a plurality of standpoints. She proposed Thomas Kuhn's 'paradigm shift' as a conceptual device capable of giving feminist standpoint postmodernist credibility. The new rejection of the possibility of absolute truth, the substitution of a notion of multiple and relative truths, should be read as a paradigm shift in the sense Kuhn intended. For Hekman, the theory as proposed by Hartsock and Harding stalled on an illogicality she found troubling in Marxist thought more generally: social constructionist and absolutist conceptions of truth are in contradiction. She argued that the lifeworld, like every other human activity, is discursively constituted. A 'standpoint', therefore, cannot claim to express the 'truth' about 'reality' – it must be understood as one representation among others, political and value-laden, 'a place from which feminists can articulate a counterhegemonic discourse and argue for a less repressive society' (ibid.: 239).

Hartsock, Collins, Harding and Smith fiercely countered Hekman's 'Truth and method' article, arguing in the same issue of *Signs*[13] that she was mistaken in prioritizing the matter of 'truth': what is at stake in 'standpoint' is not truth but power. It is specifically about challenging, from the position of the marginal, silenced and subjected, the conceptual practices of power, the 'view from above'. Furthermore, the subjects posited by standpoint theory are not a ragbag collection of individuals. Rather, they are groups sharing an experience of subjection to and by power – capitalist power, patriarchal power, white power. Trodden down, and looking upwards to the systemic level, they find themselves an oppositional consciousness[14] that enables them to become a resistant, challenging collective subject (Hartsock 2004; Collins 2004; Harding 2004a; Smith 2004).

Hekman's article was symptomatic of a body of feminist work on standpoint that was to follow in the first decade of the new millennium, much of it detached from its roots in Marxist thought. Indeed, already in 2005, Michael Ryan's entry on 'Standpoint theory' in *An Encyclopedia of Social Theory* formulates it in its entirety as a product of feminist and 'multicultural' thought, without any reference to Marx or Marxism (Ryan 2005: 789). Prioritizing the issue of truth claims, many of these later authors found their primary inspiration less in Hartsock and Smith than in Donna Haraway's 'situated knowledges' mentioned above (Haraway 1988). Marcel Stoetzler and Nira Yuval-Davis, for example, proposed a strengthening of standpoint theory by the introduction of a concept of the 'situated imagination', in parallel with that of situated knowledge, arguing that it is only through a process of imagining that 'the transitions from positionings to practices, practices to standpoints, knowledge, meaning, values and goals, actually take place' (Stoetzler and Yuval-Davis 2002: 320).

A 2009 issue of *Hypatia* devoted to standpoint theory contained several articles in which the perspective of the social scientist, together with his or her problem in deciding how to evaluate competing truth claims, was largely substituted for the perspective of the feminist subject and her struggle to survive and thrive in capitalist patriarchy. Thus Janet Kourany tests standpoint theory against alternative methodological approaches in feminist studies, cautiously endorsing it as a usable academic resource despite the many questions she believes it leaves unresolved (Kourany 2009). Kristina Rolin problematizes the notion that the perspective of the disadvantaged is liable to be less partial and distorted than that of the powerful (the concept of 'epistemic advantage'). She proposes a lesser claim: standpoint theory may be understood as a resource for feminist epistemology and philosophy of science on the more modest ground that it simply 'urges feminist scholars to pay attention to relations of power as a distinctive kind of obstacle to the production of scientific knowledge' (Rolin 2009: 222). Joseph Rouse, in the same volume of *Hypatia*, traces the history of feminist standpoint theorization with the aim of moving 'beyond the constitutive tropes of standpoint theory' (Rouse 2009: 207). In doing so, he represents standpoints as competing knowledge claims generated by people 'as part of practical and perceptual interaction with one another in shared surroundings', without reference to power relations, subjugation or struggle. In historicizing standpoint theory, he notes that it dates back to the work of Smith, Hartsock and Collins, adding '*arguably ... even to Marx and Hegel*' (ibid.: 202, emphasis added). By the end of the first decade of the twenty-first century, it seems, Marx had become, to the generation of social scientists educated in 1990s postmodernism, an obscure figure, no longer one but two centuries back in time.

The flaccidity of these recent accounts signals an amnesia, a forgetting that a standpoint is, in Kathi Weeks' words, 'a project, not an inheritance'.

It is 'an ongoing achievement rather than a spontaneous attribute or consciousness ...' It is 'both a product and an instrument of feminist struggle' (Weeks 1998: 8). In other words, it is in, and of, movements of resistance and revolution. And in the meantime new political insurgencies have been occurring in the second decade of the twenty-first century, sparked by life experiences very different from those of the industrial working class as known to Lukács in the early twentieth century, and of the women of second-wave feminism, among whom Dorothy Smith and Nancy Hartsock lived and worked half a century later. The World Social Forum events have mobilized activists from a wide range of global movements. Billion Women Rise has precipitated women into street protests against male violence from New Delhi to Kinshasa and London. Occupy has brought young people of many countries into city encampments and has squatted outside banks to protest against financial crime and austerity policies. They call themselves the 'ninety-nine percent'. We have to probe deeper into the collective subjectivities emerging. Who are they? Who are we? We need to pay careful attention to the specificity of the power relations against which we are rising in rebellion, as one conjuncture gives way to the next. How do these systems intersect with and amplify each other? It is not in the analyses of academics, but in the voices, leaflets, placards and tweets of new historic subjects, sparked to consciousness by new scandals of subjugation and exploitation, that contemporary standpoints are being expressed. And it is in these movements that a deeper understanding of the value of standpoint theory for future transformative change is likely to be forged.

Notes

1 First prepared for publication by Frederick Engels in 1894 after Marx's death. As is well known, Chapter 50, entitled 'Classes', is a fragment, no more than a couple of pages in length, and was destined to remain unfinished.

2 Written in 1845/46, the full work remained unpublished during the lifetimes of its authors.

3 *History and Class Consciousness* was originally published in 1923. In this passage, Lukács is referring to Marx's *Critique of Hegel's Philosophy of Right*, published in 1843.

4 A critique of the Young Hegelians, first published in 1845.

5 Hegel's book was originally published in 1807.

6 *The Prison Notebooks*, written by Antonio Gramsci in prison in Italy between 1929 and 1935, were first published in the late 1940s.

7 Nancy C. M. Hartsock's article 'The feminist standpoint: developing the ground for a specifically feminist historical materialism' was first published in 1983, in Hintikka and Harding (eds), *Discovering Reality: Feminist Perspectives on Epistemology, Methodology, Metaphysics and Philosophy of Science*. It was reprinted as Chapter 10 in her *Money, Sex and Power: Towards a Feminist Historical Materialism* in 1985.

8 Hartsock in an interview with Thonette Myking (see Myking 2007).

9 Originally published as an article of the same title in *Social Problems* (1986), Collins' argument was spelled out at greater length in Collins (1991).

10 An excerpt from the introduction to their book *Ecofeminism* published in 1993.

11 This chapter was an excerpt from her book *Maternal Thinking*, published in 1989.

12 Hekman's article, which originally appeared in *Signs* in 1997, was later republished, along with those of its discussants, in a collection edited by Sandra Harding (2004b).

13 The references given here are to their articles as republished in a volume edited by Harding (2004b).

14 The phrase 'oppositional consciousness' was coined by Chela Sandoval, who, in a seminal article in the Harding (2004b) collection, elaborated 'a topography of consciousness that identifies nothing more and nothing less than the modes the subordinated of the United States (of any gender, race, or class) claim as politicized and oppositional stances in resistance to domination' (Sandoval 2004: 200). Her stress on subjection, power and the multiplicity of resistant standpoints was an important contribution to transcending the antagonisms into which postmodernism had cast standpoint theory.

References

Cockburn, C. (2007) *From Where We Stand: War, Women's Activism and Feminist Analysis*, London: Zed Books.

— (2010) 'Gender relations as causal in militarization and war: a feminist standpoint', *International Feminist Journal of Politics*, 12(2): 139–57.

Collins, P. H. (1986) 'Learning from the outsider within: the sociological significance of black feminist thought', *Social Problems*, 33(6): S14–32.

— (1991) *Black Feminist Thought: Knowledge, Consciousness and the Politics of Empowerment*, New York: Routledge.

— (2004) 'Comment on Hekman's "Truth and method: feminist standpoint theory revisited." Where's the power?', in S. Harding (ed.), *The Feminist Standpoint Theory Reader: Intellectual and Political Controversies*, London: Routledge, pp. 247–54.

German, L. (2007) *Material Girls: Women, Men and Work*, London: Bookmarks.

Gramsci, A. (1971) *Selections from the Prison Notebooks*, London: Lawrence and Wishart.

Haraway, D. (1988) 'Situated knowledge: the science question in feminism and the privilege of partial perspective', *Feminist Studies*, 14(3): 575–99.

Harding, S. (1986) *The Science Question in Feminism*, Milton Keynes: Open University Press.

— (1991) *Whose Science? Whose Knowledge?*, Milton Keynes: Open University Press.

— (2004a) 'Comment on Hekman's "Truth and method: feminist standpoint theory revisited." Whose standpoint needs the regimes of truth and reality?', in S. Harding (ed.), *The Feminist Standpoint Theory Reader: Intellectual and Political Controversies*, London: Routledge, pp. 382–91.

— (ed.) (2004b) *The Feminist Standpoint Theory Reader: Intellectual and Political Controversies*, London: Routledge.

Hartmann, H. (1979) 'Capitalism, patriarchy and job segregation by sex', in Z. Eisenstein (ed.), *Capitalist Patriarchy and the Case for Socialist Feminism*, London: Monthly Review Press, pp. 206–47.

— (1981) 'The unhappy marriage of Marxism and feminism: towards a more progressive union', in L. Sargent (ed.), *Women and Revolution: A Discussion of the Unhappy Marriage of Marxism and Feminism*, London: Pluto, pp. 1–41.

Hartsock, N. C. M. (1985) *Money, Sex and Power: Towards a Feminist Historical Materialism*, Boston, MA: Northeastern University Press, pp. 231–51.

— (1998) *The Feminist Standpoint Revisited and Other Essays*, Boulder, CO: Westview.

— (2004) 'Comment on Hekman's "Truth and method: feminist standpoint theory revisited." Truth or justice?', in S. Harding (ed.), *The Feminist Standpoint Theory Reader: Intellectual and Political Controversies*, London: Routledge, pp. 243–6.

Hegel, G. W. F. (1977) *Phenomenology of Spirit*, Oxford: Clarendon.

Hekman, S. (1997) 'Truth and method: feminist standpoint theory revisited', *Signs*, 22(21): 341–65.
— (2004) 'Truth and method: feminist standpoint theory revisited', in S. Harding (ed.), *The Feminist Standpoint Theory Reader: Intellectual and Political Controversies*, London: Routledge, pp. 225–42.
Jaggar, A. (1983) *Feminist Politics and Human Nature*, Totowa, NJ: Rowman and Allenheld.
Jónasdóttir, A. G. (1994) *Why Women are Oppressed*, Philadelphia, PA: Temple University Press.
Kourany, J. A. (2009) 'The place of standpoint theory in feminist science studies', *Hypatia*, 24(4): 209–18.
Lukács, G. (1968) *History and Class Consciousness: Studies in Marxist Dialectics*, trans. R. Livingstone, Cambridge, MA: MIT Press.
Marx, K. (1959) *Capital: A Critique of Political Economy*, vol. 3, London: Lawrence and Wishart.
Marx, K. and F. Engels (1970) *The German Ideology. Part 1*, ed. C. J. Arthur, London: Lawrence and Wishart.
Mies, M. and V. Shiva (1993) *Ecofeminism*, London: Zed Books.
— (2004) 'The subsistence perspective', in S. Harding (ed.), *The Feminist Standpoint Theory Reader: Intellectual and Political Controversies*, London: Routledge, pp. 333–8.
Myking, T. (2007) 'As we reoccupy Marxism as Feminism(s)', *Norsk filosofisk tidsskrift*, 42(4): 259–73.
O'Brien, M. (1981) *The Politics of Reproduction*, London: Routledge and Kegan Paul.
Rolin, K. (2009) 'Standpoint theory as a methodology for the study of power relations', *Hypatia*, 24(4): 218–26.
Rose, H. (1983) 'Hand, brain and heart: towards a feminist epistemology for the natural sciences', *Signs*, 9(1): 73–96.
Rouse, J. (2009) 'Standpoint theories reconsidered', *Hypatia*, 24(4): 200–9.
Ruddick, S. (1989) *Maternal Thinking*, Boston, MA: Beacon.
— (2004) 'Maternal thinking as a feminist standpoint', in S. Harding (ed.), *The Feminist Standpoint Theory Reader: Intellectual and Political Controversies*, London: Routledge, pp. 161–8.
Ryan, M. (2005) 'Standpoint theory', in G. Ritzer (ed.), *Encyclopedia of Social Theory*, vol. 2, London: Sage Publications.
Sandoval, C. (2004) 'U.S. Third World feminism: the theory and method of differential oppositional consciousness', in S. Harding (ed.), *The Feminist Standpoint Theory Reader: Intellectual and Political Controversies*, London: Routledge, pp. 195–209.
Smith, D. E. (1974) 'The ideological practice of sociology', *Catalyst*, 8: 39–54.
— (1981) 'On sociological description: a method from Marx', *Human Studies*, 4: 313–37.
— (1987) *The Everyday World as Problematic: A Feminist Sociology*, Milton Keynes: Open University Press.
— (2004) 'Comment on Hekman's "Truth and method: feminist standpoint theory revisited"', in S. Harding (ed.), *The Feminist Standpoint Theory Reader: Intellectual and Political Controversies*, London: Routledge, pp. 263–9.
Stoetzler, M. and N. Yuval-Davis (2002) 'Standpoint theory, situated knowledge and the situated imagination', *Feminist Theory*, 3(3): 315–33.
Weeks, K. (1996) 'Subject for a feminist standpoint', in S. Maksisi, C. Casarino and E. K. Rebecca (eds), *Marxism beyond Marxism*, London: Routledge, pp. 89–118.
— (1998) *Constituting Feminist Subjects*, Ithaca, NY: Cornell University Press.

2 | OUTSIDE IN THE FUNDING MACHINE

Gayatri Chakravorty Spivak

I am most grateful to be part of a comradeship with Frigga Haug that allows me to connect with this European Marxist-Feminist congress that strives to globality. I am a Europeanist and my task is to work with 'Europe'. After today's event, I have the honour of inaugurating the academic year at the ancient University of Coimbra, especially invited as a humanities teacher to speak to social scientists. Yesterday I received the news as I was chatting with the women who accompanied me to dinner that Portugal was one of the few states in the world going *upward* to liberate state policy! There are not too many states like that today in our world. This makes me particularly fortunate and particularly responsible.

You will see, I hope, that I have understood my brief here somewhat in the way that Portugal wished a paid humanities teacher among social scientists. Here I am among activists who are either non-academic or social scientists or yet performing artists, visual or otherwise.

As I mentioned in Berlin in May, my entire adult training into Marxism was under the wing of Samar Sen, developing a left-of-the-left critique of the parliamentary left. As the centre moved in India more and more to the right and alliance politics turned the parties of the left inevitably toward sometimes dubious moves to the right, even if only to retain their foothold, I have not been able to shake off the urgency of that training. That you will notice too.

And I know from the warmth of your reception that you will consider that critique legitimate and consider it with your customary gravitas.

From my old-fashioned task at Coimbra, I will go on to keynote the Open City Biennial in Barcelona. This is the new era of fully corporatised festivals whose subjects, deluded that globalised capital does only good, and the subject of victims of digital idealism think that the very powerful and wonderful digital resources that we have can actually be used well even if we ourselves are not epistemologically prepared, even if we have not been trained slowly as bodies are trained slowly in order to lift weight. It is a semi-deluded, semi-corporatised subject. And the object is the bemused underclass, even as Europe crumbles.

Add to this mixture of various Europes (minus Balkans and Sardinia most of the time) the event that I recently attended, an event at my own university entitled 'Europe Agora' – badly attended – where the general understanding was that the European left would rise or fall on the issue of migrants, and that the genuinely Marxist position on this issue would be resolved only if it were not in terms of culture (I confess I find that word quite frightening), nor in terms of racism, but in terms of redistribution. So that whether migrants are good or bad for us would not be decided in terms of our own class position, with the underclass bitterly resentful of competition, and the non-racist bourgeoisie benignly acknowledging the fact that they help the economy.

Although the gender division here, especially if the LGBTQ were considered, was not thought through, *mutatis mutandis*, it is undoubtedly something we should think about. And once we do, we are in the industrial and corporate machine. Because today, with increased privatisation and corporatisation, a redistributive program from the state must accommodate the workings of global capital much more than before. And, as many of us have been arguing recently, the distinctions between the public sphere and the private sphere are increasingly less clear outside the funding machine when we are obliged to be in the funding machine.

In the pre-globalised capital days, when the distinction between privatisation and nationalisation was clear, we were happy when we could say 'I got a government grant'. Clean, public. When I was in Sweden in 2015, the Director of the International Development Association of Sweden, SIDA, whose first degree was in theatre – with some training in the humanities – and who was just about to visit Burma to help digitise the government – had not *heard* of the Rohingyas.

Now in 2015, there was an immense lot of information available on the 'genocide' (although the name has only recently been accepted by the UN and the US Congress) of the non-Buddhist minorities by the Buddhist-majority government and military, with the full implicit sanction of the now-discredited Nobel laureate Aung San Suu Kyi. So, how do we assess the subjectship of digital idealism? And how to valorise the public sector? We must therefore remember that public and private help is not now something that we can very easily distinguish as in the old days. There is no public good.

I am *in* Europe even as I navigate my way through the United States daily. What makes my situation in the global more poignant is that, in between, since I use these invitations as instrumental to the visits to my schools, I have four days in a space about as remote from any kind of Europe that would think to involve me.

Let me quickly mention here the disappearance of the old one-on-one mud schools in China. I have been learning Chinese now for 12 years, and I used to go to these schools, hanging out. The teachers now lament the loss of the motivation toward socialism that they could teach. People of our kind and the authorities in China do not really know this group and how differently they feel. China is generalised all the time negatively in the United States, negatively in India because we are competitors, and also negatively in terms of what they're doing in Africa, and in terms of the Uygur Muslims of western China. But no one actually comes in to see the subaltern who represents China. This is a very serious question for me as well.

These folks are not really outside in the funding machine, they are working as hard as they can in the direction of social justice; but they are dependent nonetheless, those teachers, on the necessarily unacknowledged theft of surplus value.

In the late 1980s, after two miasmatic marriages lasting 21 years, I was able once again to pick up on the activist side of my Marxist-Feminist work. Just before this, through a classed metropolitan identity crisis, and a rediscovery of colonialism from a left US position, I had written such somewhat one-sided finger-pointing works as *Three Women's Texts and a Critique of Imperialism* and *Can the Subaltern Speak?* That period came to an end with a book called *In Other Worlds*.

And now, with institutional work and activist work coming together, I realised that in the current conjuncture left and right were bound together. They were complicit, folded together. Since then, I was no longer able to practise anything without acknowledging complicity. From the period of that change came a collection called *Outside in the Teaching Machine*, which gives me my title today, 'Outside in the Funding Machine'.

Today I am asking ourselves to learn the consequence of being *in* the funding machine: socially responsible, sustainabilising, etc., globalised capital, gaining fiscal advantages by top-down philanthropy practising corporatism – although we ourselves are *outside*. We do not practise it, but we are also inside. But most immediately we are subsumed – as one would say in strictly Marxist language.

Most immediately it is the conference circuit that has produced my words to you today. In June I was at a conference in Patna in Bihar, a state which adjoins my home state of West Bengal in India. The conference was called 'Karl Marx – Life, Ideas, Influence: A Crucial [*sic: she meant* Critical] Examination on the Bicentenary'. Now, I thought, since I never have time to read the elaborate programs etc., that I was going as a Bengali Marxist to the next state and for talking and strategising together. Lo and behold, I see that it was organised by something called the Asian Development Research Institute.

Much of the work of the Asian Development Research Institute is funded by Microsoft, which was then digitising the banks and the military in Myanmar, which was in turn genocidally engaged in ousting Rohingyas even as the world was busy investing in their new stock exchange.

I want to share something on what I said in Patna, because as a citizen there with more civil rights than anywhere else in the world, the nation-state-backed thoughts that come out, even as I'm perceived as global there, will apply to my effort to situate Europe, minus the Balkans and Sardinia.

I said to them: 'Think about regulating capital'. I argued there with urgency for long-term training in general capitalist realities and teaching even when groups and parties are engaged in immediate work.

I mention this because that is a remark which is quite often ignored. I quote here also a passage written for Occupy Wall Street, upon their request. Given Marx's unacknowledged humanism, I'm in other words urging that we should engage with Gramsci's suggestion that only training in epistemological performance would keep producing perhaps the will to social justice, generation after generation, without which the system would not stand, whatever state formation you bring in and whatever laws you make. Changing laws do not change minds. And law is not justice. This is something that you have to remember.

Here is a bit I wrote for Occupy, available in full in their journal *Tidal*, not *Tribal*: *Tidal!* In their journal *Tidal*:

> Without the general nurturing of the will to justice among the people, no just society can survive. The Occupy Wall Street movement must attend to education – primary through post-tertiary – at the same time as it attends to the uncoupling of the connection between specifically capitalist globalisation and the nation-state [because we were also talking about socialist globalisation]. This is an almost impossible task to remember, especially when there are such complex and urgent immediate tasks lined up! But it must be repeated: without this attention, there is no chance of survival – as we have seen in the case of the Soviet Union, China, and other post-revolutionary societies.
>
> Indeed, Mao Zedong tried to solve this problem by the once-and-for-all solution of the Cultural Revolution, whereby he simply reversed the hierarchy that inhabited Chinese society – only to prove that without the patient and continuous system of education, the mind of a people cannot be nourished, and without robust mental resources, we are at the mercy of brainwashing.[1]

The point of this education today is also to undo the nation-state and global binary in a sustained fashion. This is particularly important in the case of migration in extremis, but, since my topic is specifically outsidership in the funding machine, I will not expand it here. I will approach my topic through a related subject – human rights –outside in the funding machine.

One definitive characteristic of democracy, which all freedoms have to be bound to in order to be exercised, requires so much more imaginative training than the simple access to something called human rights, organised and supervised by the benevolent members of the ruling class upon those who have no way – in the current travesty of 'education' – of understanding and internalising the revolutionary historical burden the words 'human rights' carry. And a good bit of civil society work is dependent on endowment funding, inserted into the circuit of capital and the corporate funding; this includes gender work too, of course.

Hang out with the receivers of human rights to grasp what they're understanding. Unfortunately, I do. It's not unfortunate; it's very fortunate because of my work now for 40 years or with receiving communities. It's a small example, but it's an example. And, you know, I was just talking to the Columbia undergraduates, again by request: they wanted me to speak to them in what they call the Voting Week. It was almost impossible for them to understand the imperatives of the funding machine.

For the very poor people of the Tri-Continent as well as for the Euro–US beneficiaries, there is no way of internalising the subjectship of rights. The funders fund an activity described in English or the major European languages and in translations available only to the elites in the countries or migrant groups concerned.

So, when I was on the Committee on Values of the World Economic Forum – the custodians of the funding machine – the word 'dignity' was used all the time. And I would think: how do these subalterns understand the almost untranslatable word 'dignity'? The real problem with subalternity is it thinks that its wretchedness is normal. That's the thing. Just as we think this is normal. Just as anybody thinks. So, it's a situation where the idea 'human' is – first of all, let's forget the English word – not something that's so easily negotiable. And that's why it's something that, if you think about it, is an unwise thing to think about because it will make you sad. But if you acknowledge your limits, actually you forge a better practice.

And awareness sessions are zero! I can tell you, I have been at so many awareness sessions, I don't even know the count, and I have also seen the smiles and agreements. But the thing is, I'm the only one who's left behind after everybody has left. This is the policy of the millennially suffering – and in India we count in millennia – toward the benevolent ruling class, or malevolent ruling class: just smile and say, 'Yes, we agree!' The subaltern is not stupid.

In conclusion, three suggestions: as we use corporate funding, we acknowledge complicity, and make the regulation of globalising capital an important part of our agenda. And, as we necessarily abstract gender, in order to fight for equal rights within one nation-state, we acknowledge our class-epistemological discontinuity with the subaltern and attempt to access that damaged cognitive machine by learning from our mistakes that we discover by questioning those that we are 'helping'. Finally, attempt to produce the subjectship of 'human rights'. Here, the deep learning of languages might be necessary. The migrant European cannot be our irreducible native informant if we are forging global practice. It's not easy, changing the world, as we work outside (yet subsumed in) the funding machine. Thank you.

Note

1 http://interoccupy.net/blog/tidal-occupy-theory-occupy-strategy-available-for-download/.

3 | CONTRADICTIONS IN MARXIST FEMINISM

Frigga Haug

About the title

Thank you very much for giving me the space to go on working in the hope we could take up a transformation of society by means of connecting Marxism with feminism.[1]

My contribution by no means seeks to fulfil the expectation that the title promises, namely to find errors in Marxist feminism. It is not meant negatively, but, on the contrary, we perceive contradictions as possibilities for change. The approach is a dialectical one. The reference to dialectics as a method is not meant to produce some highbrow mystification but, with Marx, we use this method as one that 'in its comprehension and affirmative recognition of the existing state of things, at the same time also includes the recognition of the negation of that state, of its inevitable breaking up'; we use dialectics as a method which 'regards every historically developed social form as in fluid movement, and therefore takes into account its transient nature not less than its momentary existence; because it lets nothing impose upon it, and is in its essence critical and revolutionary' (Marx, 1998: 15). Thus, my contribution will be about showing and understanding how individual elements contradict each other through their real movement within society. To work out how this takes place is fundamental for us as feminists in our joint effort to develop our thinking and action.

Our theses: Marxist feminism as a transformative power

I want to recall the 12 *theses* proposed at the first two international Marxist-Feminist conferences (in 2015 and 2016), theses which we have changed through our discussions and which we still continue to review as a set of criteria against which we measure our projects in order to broaden our consensus; we want to critically continue writing these theses as a joint *manifesto* that is regularly developed further and elaborated.

At the beginning of our discussions we stated that to connect Marxism with feminism would change, enrich, and vitalise both. This talk about *contradictions within Marxist feminism* follows that path. In other words: I am discussing something that provides us with the hope that Marxist feminists represent a transformative force:

1. Marxism-Feminism represents two sides of a coin, but it must be added that this coin itself requires transformation. Feminist Marxism adheres to Marx's legacy, and thus to the significance of the analysis of work in the form of wage labour and as the driving force of the workers' movement. However, in the attempt likewise to put the remaining female activities at the centre of the analysis, Marxist feminism goes beyond the paralysing attempts to conceive domestic and non-domestic activities either as one and the same thing or, vice versa, as completely separate from each other (dual economy debate, domestic labour debate). Instead, it poses the fundamental challenge to occupy and further develop the concept of the relations of production to make it useful for feminist questions.
2. Here (as in Marx and Engels) two forms of production are assumed: the production of life and the production of the means of life. By analysing the two forms together it is possible to examine specific practices within each form and the way in which they interact. This opens up an enormous field of research, in which the different historically and culturally specific modes of domination can be investigated, as well as the possibilities for change.
3. It is clear that gender relations are relations of production, not an addition to them. All practices, norms, values, authorities, institutions, as well as language, culture, etc. are coded in gender relations. This assumption makes feminist Marxist research as fruitful as it is necessary.

Women as an illusionary commons

What is it about our project that gives us hope and what is our reason to argue, that we as Marxist feminists have nothing in common with the essentialist assumption that women are the 'better human beings', as the enemies of feminism maintain?

The practices attributed to women worldwide are those resulting from our actual care for life. This care is not only a biological necessity during the nine months it takes for a new human being to grow inside a woman's body, neither is it merely exercised during the phase of breastfeeding which (in most cases) provides the nourishment at the beginnings of life. Care for those growing up, for those who are ill or handicapped, for the elderly, in fact, for all those who would not be able to survive without support, is predominantly provided by women. Let's call these activities the *caring practices*. Marx and Engels have called the state an 'illusionary commons' because it appropriates people's communitarian practices, that is the practices that are necessary in order to create a community. They include mutual support, solidarity, the distribution of resources, caring for the members of the community who need support, etc. As the state appropriates and transforms these practices into state rules and regulations it alienates individuals from self-organised, horizontal relationships, through which the commons is created. The caring practices done (predominantly) by women can be seen as an anticipation of the re-appropriated commons. However, since they are carried out privately and at the expense of the full development of women's capacity, they remain an imagined or illusionary commons.

Caring practices will doubtlessly outlive all specific social formations and remain necessary within a transformed, non-capitalist society. Within capitalism, though, they are glorified through norms and values and ascribed to the female essence, constructing women as beacons of motherliness, helpfulness, and selflessness. They are perceived as being activated not only when they are paid for. If they become commodified they are badly paid, since, due to their closeness to women's everyday life, they appear as 'natural'. Currently these practices are at the centre of political struggles in Germany where our health system suffers from a crisis due to the lack of people in care jobs. To the degree to which these practices fill an entire life of unpaid work, they amount to a renunciation of a woman's personality, to self-sacrifice. The reward for this comes in the shape of societal respect that does not ask which price individuals have to pay for their selfless engagement. This moral appreciation includes simultaneously a denial of the kind of equality on which the exchange value of labour is based. For the individual women in different societies this simultaneity of moral appreciation and denial of equality manifests itself in myriad forms of marginalisation, non-recognition of women as human beings, and oppression to the point of rape and murder. Thus, reality provides quite an unreliable ground for our hope that caring practices might constitute the first steps towards an alternative society.

First contradiction

Consequently, one fundamental contradiction we are confronted with expresses itself in the fact that for women to become empowered, to become a transformative force, we would first have to get rid of the trained female virtues and practices. Like men, we would have to send ourselves into competitive fights or even revolutionary struggles. Women would have to adopt the modes of behaviour common in capitalism. However, it was precisely the transgression or contempt for these behaviours which were the reason to count on women as a transformative force in the first place. Brecht has repeatedly dealt with this contradiction in literary form (*The Seven Deadly Sins, The Good Person of Szechwan*), as has Heiner Müller (*Zement*, 2001).

In his piece *Zement* (*Cement*) Müller (2001) depicts in rough, broad-brushed images a revolutionary coming home as a husband who assumes his wife is his sexual possession, waiting for him, taking care of their child and the cosiness of their home but does not find her being this way. The woman is now an active revolutionary herself and has sent her child into a children's home because she could no longer afford the time to care for it. She has to care for the many hungry children in all those homes and not just for her own and therefore she is organising the women. The man insists on taking his own child out of the children's home, 'so that it doesn't snuff it' like the others. He wants to re-appropriate his home, wife, and child, but she withdraws: 'I was stupid. Our home was my prison' and finds freedom: 'I shed not a single tear for the ruins. My home is the executive committee, my work. I eat my meal there, in the canteen'. The property-relations have been radically changed and likewise their glorification.

Traditional feelings

There we are, a bit at a loss with our feelings that would like to agree. We are facing the debris of a long tradition of workers' struggles. The songs are still sung: *Brothers to the sun, to freedom ..., There stands a man like an oak ..., Awake, working man ..., This is how we stand, one brother for the other, filled with serious power ..., Who mines the gold? It's the working men, the proletariat,* etc. There are still pictures and symbols depicting the hard, clenched fists of working men.

Our feelings attempt to resist the desire to condemn as cruel and heartless the behaviour of the woman who sent her child to a children's home in order to be able to make revolutionary speeches. Only belatedly do we notice that such a condemnation stems from our unquestioning acceptance of a division of labour, where it is normal that within the context of capitalist competition those who win against others are seen as the best ones, while the strength of women, derived from those female practices which we wanted to use for the transformation of society, have been relegated to the shadowy realms of forgetfulness.

For the time being, we lack both the imagination and the strength of corresponding feelings as well as a theory to imagine and advocate a society in which a division of labour that distributes work so differently to the genders, generating different respective feelings, could be arranged in another manner. Said differently, we do not dare to think of the division of labour other than in binary oppositions, such as soft *or* hard, friendly *or* antagonistic, loving *or* hating. We need to work further on this problem.

Learning from Brecht

Bertolt Brecht is one of the poets feminists can learn a lot from, including, among other things, how to deal with contradictions. In his *Flüchtlingsgespräche* (*Refugee Conversations*) the worker Kalle provides the information that searching for a country which makes such 'terrible virtues as patriotism, thirst for freedom, kindness and unselfishness as unnecessary as shitting on your homeland, servility, barbarism and selfishness', increasingly requires the virtues which the revolutionaries had started out to get rid of: namely, 'extreme braveness, the deepest thirst for freedom, the greatest unselfishness, the greatest selfishness' (Brecht, 1982, 2019).

Brecht's statement baffles us in a number of ways. First because he places the attitudes that are usually ascribed to male heroes (patriotism and thirst for freedom) and those that are usually attributed to female heroines (kindness and unselfishness) side by side only to throw them all overboard. What he is looking for is a country where none of these virtues are required. In order for us to scrutinise our desires Brecht shows that it is not enough to simply negate them. Neither is it enough to throw overboard the despicable attitudes such as servility, barbarism, and egoism. If we want to reach the promised land namely socialism, where neither 'terrible virtues' nor vices, are necessary, some of these virtues and vices are even required in their extreme forms. We need a strong and egoistic desire to want socialism for ourselves, if we want to unleash the power necessary to overthrow the existing social order. Thus, the last of the solutions we know for dealing with this issue is also called into question, namely the differentiation between means and ends. This differentiation allowed us to think of the means as hard and difficult, to cover up all problems on the way to the end if only the goal remained untouched, shining brightly, kindly, and flawlessly.

To Brecht's unusual connection of selfishness and unselfishness we could add the connection of braveness with cowardice, or kindness with harshness in order to upset our usual ways of thinking and feeling. He shows us that in our search for the strengths of women as transformative forces we must put our own feelings and thinking up for discussion and change. This includes re-examining what is considered as weakness if we want to develop a new idea of what transformation could be. If we question what we are used to thinking of as belonging together, the space for doing the research needed to build the foundations for our politics broadens. We can think of all kinds of new alliances. What we are used to thinking of as solid ground becomes shaky, as we are forced to constantly doubt everything and to start from scratch again.

The second contradiction: construction and deconstruction

Those of us who are old enough to remember the years when the Second Women's Movement started will picture the many meetings and contemplate the never-ending stories of grievances that allowed us to become aware that what unified us as women, were our common experiences of oppression. The crucial turn that took place also internationally was triggered by the 'actor–victim thesis' (Haug, 1980). It was the appeal, made in one short essay, to take the road to liberation in a different way. Not to presume that an entire sex, that all women were mere victims of men, or of the conditions of life, but to presume that women as humans also produce their own lives. Therefore, the paths that lead to our oppression must have been taken ultimately by ourselves. This thesis triggered a fierce and hostile discussion (its most aggressive form taking place in the organisations close to the labour movement), which lasted for more than a decade and led to exclusions and new organisations, to the redefinition of what had previously been regarded as weakness and strength in both the women's and the worker's movements. Most of the newspapers, magazines, even institutions that were part of this controversy no longer exist. The debate is documented in my book *Der im Gehen erkundete Weg* (*The Path Is Found by Walking*) (Haug, 2015: 69–113).

For me this collision did not only lead to a personal crisis, but to the development of the actor–victim thesis into a research programme and method which I called collective memory work. It involved the socialist groups of the women's movement right from the start. It concerned everybody on their way towards the goal of women's liberation, no matter how vague their involvement and positions were. After the brief moment of shock in which we realised that women's politics could not mean liberating other oppressed women while the liberators themselves were already on the safe side of liberation. After realising that, like everyone else, we had arranged ourselves conveniently with our socialisation, had yielded to compromises, had constructed ourselves as subordinated beings, we started on a burdensome but nevertheless pleasurable path towards researching ourselves. We became subject and object of research simultaneously. The aim was to develop another concept of the subject. Two steps were necessary: first, to follow Althusser, who had already introduced a notion of the subject as subordinated, derived from its Latin root. Second, we needed to go beyond Althusser towards an understanding of a collective capacity to act. We began a productive struggle with many of our contradictory emotions: curiosity and shame, deception and revelation, love of truth and inclination to conceal, pain and joy. In short, we set out collectively to discover ourselves as historical beings, as part of history.

Memory work became a cultural practice for many. It was and is a method to improve women's capacity to act by tracing our self-construction and self-production, by learning about our self-subordination, about the paths not taken, about the search for the alternative ones that could have been taken. The second book, *Sexualisierung der Körper*, was published in English in 1983 as *Female Sexualization* (Haug et al., 1999). It paved the way for an international reception of this research method, which transcends the boundaries of disciplines by drawing on biography, language analysis, psychology, and politics while at the same time requiring the active participation of all group members. Of course, memory work never became mainstream in social sciences, which, anyway, cannot be accused of being a science of liberation. However, memory work has now been practised in 16 countries for almost four decades.

Entering history

Memory work can really be seen as a contribution to women entering history as *subjects*. We use this contested and tattered expression '*subject*' as a description of the necessary form in which women need to enter history: being responsible, not just subjected. In the many disciplines and mountains of accumulated knowledge we search for a language which allows us to feel that we might be meant. Literature as a condensation of experiences is such a storage room which we want to make use of. In her acceptance speech for the Büchner Prize (Büchnerpreisrede, 1980) (which I very much recommend you to read) Christa Wolf takes the audience on a brisk journey to a huge number of historical forms of femininity conveyed by literature. Rosetta is the name for the female persona in history,

> It is Rosetta's fate to live invisible to herself ... speechless, stripped of reality ... Her character is definable by what she is *not*.
> She lets her own history be taken away from her. Lets her soul be taken away. Her reason. Her humanity. Her responsibility for herself. Lets herself be married. Serves her husband. Gives him heirs. Is forced to believe that the pleasure he enjoys is denied to her forever.
> ...
> Rosetta lets her rights be taken away. Lets herself be forbidden to speak. Forbidden to grieve. To feel joy. To feel love. To work. To know art. She lets herself be raped. Be prostituted. Locked up. Driven crazy. In the role of Rose, she lets herself be worked to death, exploited; 'twice over', as the play says. Lets herself be forced to bear children. To abort children. Lets her sex be analysed away. Gets caught in the net of impotence. Becomes a nag. A whore. A vamp. A cricket. In the role of Nora, she leaves the Doll's House.
> At last – her name is Rosa now – she begins to fight. Then she is murdered, thrown into the canal. In persecution, her rights equal those of the man, who is oppressed and persecuted, too. (Wolf, 1995: 181)

I have quoted Christa Wolf at some length to give an idea of what we are able to gain from literature, but also to show the forms of femininity we might have swallowed without resistance, enjoying literature. To make us aware of the realities we might not have protested against seriously when compassion moved us to the wrong place and we wept tears of sympathy while anger and indignation would have been more appropriate. The references remind us of how much we have already accepted and where false emotions, false consideration, and false respect have prevented us from seriously considering other possibilities and alternatives. The question we ask in memory work is whether and how individuals might be able, with the help of the collective, to work themselves out of their old ways of thinking and feeling in order to enter uncharted territories.

We must recognise that we have not sufficiently considered and thought about the fact that a precondition of each process of renewal implies the destruction of the old and familiar, that each process of construction is at the same time one of a painful demolition, which we do not know how to handle.

Re-reading Marx and Luxemburg

We have to allow ourselves to take in and feel Marx's prophetic words more clearly, words that many of us know by heart. In the *Communist Manifesto* he writes,

> All fixed, fast-frozen relations, with their train of ancient and venerable prejudices and opinions, are swept away, all new-formed ones become antiquated before they can ossify. All that is solid melts into air, all that is holy is profaned, and man is at last compelled to face with sober senses, his real condition of life, and his relations with his kind. (www.marxists.org/archive/marx/works/1848/communist-manifesto/cho1.htm)

On closer reading one recognises that it is not the logic of an 'on the one hand and on the other hand' that is being used here but an internal connection: development requires breaking with the old form as a precondition for the new. In a similar way, Marx presents the introduction of science into production not as a mere impoverishment of workers, even though he characterises scientification as a complete separation of mental labour from manual labour, accompanied by the subjugation of the workers and the assignment of science to a 'numerically unimportant class of persons' (www.marxists.org/archive/marx/works/1867-c1/ch15.htm).

He derives his 'realistic' view from his analysis of the fate of labour, his historical-critical analysis of labour. He writes that the abstract category of labour, that labour as the point of departure of modern economy becomes a 'practical reality' only with the formation of bourgeois society (see: www.marxists.org/archive/marx/works/download/pdf/grundrisse.pdf). I am quoting this here, because it is of elementary importance for us to know how to deal with development, with contradictions, with crises and ruptures, how to use them as means of gaining knowledge, of enabling us to create theory, and to act practically. In *Capital* (especially in the chapter on 'Machinery and Modern Industry' in Volume 1) Marx elaborated in great detail that the workers became 'indifferent' towards the specific character of their work. This reduced them practically to mere owners of labour power to be spent. Earlier he uses the same term, 'indifference', to demonstrate the dynamics of a development which has to be understood as a movement. There he says,

> The fact that the specific kind of labour is irrelevant presupposes a highly developed complex of actually existing kinds of labour, none of which is any more the all-dominating one. The most general abstractions arise on the whole only when concrete development is most profuse, so that a specific quality is seen to be common to many phenomena, or common to all. (www.marxists.org/archive/marx/works/1859/critique-pol-economy/appx1.htm)

According to Marx, labour does not just mean that humans have to mediate their lives through non-human nature, but, more specifically, that the conditions under which this happens do not necessarily require domination but, on the contrary, enable horizontal forms of societalisation. The words he uses such as 'common' and 'common to all' could be interpreted as a foreshadowing of the commons. The optimistic expressions 'highly developed complex', 'none the all-dominating one', 'common to all' are embedded in a sentence with the ambiguous word 'indifference' as a subject. I call the clash of descriptions of misery with expressions denoting preconditions of a prospective commons the *arrangement of crisis*. Development is thought of as a break with old forms. People living in the old forms may be thrust into greater misery. But at the same time Marx insists on the old forms having prevented development. On the ruins of the old forms something better can be built. This construction is not deterministic. It leaves open whether people make use of the conditions and act constructively. Both Marx as well as Rosa Luxemburg see that if there is no intervention by the labour movement this very development will end in 'the destruction of the workers and the earth', 'barbarism and catastrophe'. Development as such is not the aspiration; on the contrary, the destruction of the old urges us to rethink our political goals and our political practices.

Once on track, one finds such an arrangement of problems at many decisive places in *Capital* and *Grundrisse*. Where he writes about the development of the forces of production Marx also mentions obstacles. One example is the case when the execution of a work task depends on specific human skills, another is the rules of the guilds which are 'shackles'. The 'traditional habit of clinging to a very definite kind of labour' hinders development. Marx writes in the same way about gender relations and their contradictions: 'custom, morality, family ties', the old social forms, appear as 'obstacles' while at the same time they are a protection for the individual: 'a last resort', they are 'the sole remaining safety-valve of the whole social mechanism' (Marx, 1998: 722). The effect of this safety-valve, of these protecting shackles is that liberation from them is lived as a catastrophe, like the breaking of dams. The break-up of the old forms creates tasks, the necessity to reorganise, conditions that need to be taken advantage of. The break-up is not in itself a liberation. This connection can also be found in Marx's *Capital*:

> However terrible and disgusting the dissolution, under the capitalist system, of the old family ties may appear, nevertheless, modern industry, by assigning as it does an important part in the process of production, outside the domestic sphere, to women, to young persons, and to children of both sexes, creates a new economic foundation for a higher form of the family and of the relation between the sexes. (Marx, 1998: 703)

At close reading it becomes obvious that Marx is arranging the categories in such a way that our spontaneous sympathy, our emotions, and our desires for the old forms are addressed. But what this then means is that our engagement for liberation includes a farewell to the old forms which have become dear to us, to traditions that have become part of who we are. Following these suggestions is extremely difficult and tedious, also because, along with today's adoration for everything new, spontaneous sympathy for the old ways, the old feelings and (especially family) values is part of the mainstream. But if we remain in the old forms we will not get rid of the contradictions. We do not seek to understand them only in order to comprehend the driving forces of our societies, but also because they are distressing. Marx writes as concisely as resolutely, '[T]he historical development of the antagonisms, immanent in a given form of production, is the only way in which that form of production can be dissolved and a new form established' (Marx, 1998: 701).

Rosa Luxemburg takes up and develops the constellation found in Marx which makes it possible to grasp the crisis as a chance for development.[2] She repeatedly uses the linguistic elements from the *Communist Manifesto* to demonstrate the catastrophe of war in an emphatic way. Thus, she writes in her brief text *Trümmer (Ruins)* (1914):

> But every war does not only destroy physical goods, not merely material culture values. At the same time, it is a disrespectful hustler against traditions. Old sanctuaries, venerated institutions, formulas trustingly repeated are thrown onto the same heap of ruins by its iron broom on which the remnants of shot cannons, guns, knapsacks and other war rubbish are lying. (Luxemburg, 2000: 10, translation: author)

In the emphatic introductory passages to *The Junius Pamphlet, the Crisis of Social Democracy* Luxemburg uses the following words to describe bourgeois society after the war:

> Business thrives in the ruins. Cities become piles of ruins; villages become cemeteries; countries, deserts; populations are beggared; churches, horse stalls. International law, treaties and alliances, the most sacred words and the highest authority have been torn in shreds. Every sovereign 'by the grace of God' is called a rogue and lying scoundrel by his cousin on the other side. Every diplomat is a cunning rascal to his colleagues in the other party. Every government sees every other as dooming its own people and worthy only of universal contempt. There are food riots in Venice, in Lisbon, Moscow, Singapore. There is plague in Russia, and misery and despair everywhere. (www.marxists.org/archive/luxemburg/1915/junius/ch01.htm)

But it is not this 'witches' sabbath' that she sees as the real 'catastrophe of world-historical proportions', but that, amid this anarchy, the 'International

Social Democracy has capitulated' (ibid.). What a call upon left politics and upon us today!

Provisional conclusions

The productive discussion of contradictions within Marxist feminism and the re-reading of Marx and of Luxemburg leaves us with wide-ranging new tasks for research. We have mostly been focusing on defining the institutional conditions and societal relations which have historically relegated women to the margins of society.

Up to now, we have used memory work to focus mainly on the ways in which we are complicit with the system and (re)produce ourselves as subordinated individuals. Our goal was to gain a general political capacity to act and to work collectively to develop a culture of change. This has been a very productive endeavour both for the individuals and for the respective collectives. A number of books and concrete knowledge about the processes of self-subordination were the outcome. In our view this went far beyond the postmodern statement issued later that women are 'a social construction'. Memory work comprises a school of language and writing, of perception, and at the same time, it is a method enabling us to trace the threads that have tied the individuals into the given societal forms and are now keeping them there.

But what follows from the contradiction that in order to transform society into a more human, alternative one, we need precisely those attitudes and practices on which the division of labour between the sexes is based causing the marginalisation of women and of those desired practices?

To build a socialist society, 'The female cook must run the state', Lenin once proposed. But Brecht objected that this 'obviously required another state and another female cook'. The attempt, at the beginning of the socialist experiment in the twentieth century, to socialise the caring practices as well, to turn the whole society into one single factory, did not lead to a humanisation of society.

The attempt to achieve gender equality under capitalist conditions by commodifying the hitherto unpaid caring practices conducted within the family, subjected them to labour struggles, strikes, and walkouts. This did unsettle family relations. The care crisis, which the state tries to tackle in the traditional capitalist way by importing people from poor countries, strikes in all social sectors: nurses, nursery school teachers, and teachers are all affected. On the one hand the crisis challenges the state, on the other, it is an incentive for capital to privatise these social services with the goal to reap profits from this previously unpaid work. This process is ongoing and it will certainly deepen the societal divide between the classes that can afford such private services and the majority of the population that is increasingly unable to afford them. This contradiction requires the conflict to be moved on to another level. The gendered division of caring practices needs to be overcome and caring needs to become a general practice exercised by each and every one. This in turn makes it obvious that waged labour needs to be reduced in order to give everybody enough time to engage in caring, friendly, loving practices and services to our fellow humans.

Discussing the second contradiction brought us an additional step further: we applied an abstract concept, that each process of construction implies a process of deconstruction, to our feminist questions. The obstinate survival of the family, a form which we know to reproduce women's repression, shows that it was not possible to simply abolish it. The production of life, the reproduction of the human species, we learned, could not easily be organised as a societal practice. This forces us finally to study the forces that stabilise our perseverance in these forms. We need to study the origins of our love for the familiar, for the old, even when these forms are already brittle, a mere debris of the old family forms. It seems that when society becomes a cold wasteland, individuals are the ones who guarantee the emotional stabilisation of the old as a last refuge.

If women's isolation is an obstacle to the unification that is necessary to bring about transformation and if individuals are emotionally tied to the old forms in highly contradictory ways, what we need to study is how the threads that keep individuals entangled in the old forms are tied together. We need to find out how those threads can be torn to pieces as well as explore the new forms that might already be lingering in the bosom of the old. In other words, we need to understand how the collective can become a new home challenging and replacing the private home that exists only at the expense of its members.

For the time being we think that the suggestion to organise struggles around the issue of time could be a way forward for the contradictions discussed here. I have called this suggestion the *Four-in-One-Perspective*. It proposes to overcome the divide between the unpaid work of producing life (termed reproduction) and the paid work of producing the means of life (termed production) while simultaneously allocating time for individuals to develop their capabilities, their artistic skills and to engage in politics. Four-in-One means that all individuals should be able and have the time to develop all four kinds of practices equally. Promoting this requires further research and an insightful political will.

Notes

1 I want to thank Hilde Grammel and Nora Räthzel for their help in translating my German text.

2 Given the critique of development theory and the critique of this critique I want to emphasise that in my understanding, development needs to be defined by those who want to bring about change within their own societies (see for example: Munck and O'Hearn, 2001).

References

Brecht, B., 1982. *Gesammelte Werke in 20 Bänden*. Volume 20: *Schriften zur Politik und Gesellschaft*. Suhrkamp, Frankfurt.

Brecht, B., 2019. *Bertolt Brecht's Refugee Conversations*. Edited by T. Kuhn. Bloomsbury, London.

Haug, F., 1980. 'Opfer oder Täter?' *Das Argument* 123(22): 643–649.

Haug, F., 2015. D*er im Gehen erkundete Weg: Marxismus-Feminismus*, German original edition, Berliner Beiträge zur kritischen Theorie. Argument, Hamburg.

Haug, F., Räthzel, N., Hauser, K., Nemitz, B., 1999. *Female Sexualization: A Collective Work of Memory*. Verso, London; New York.

Luxemburg, R., 2000. *Gesammelte Werke*. Volume 4: *August 1914 bis Januar 1919*, 6the revised edition. Dietz, Berlin.

Marx, K., 1998. *Capital: A Critique of Political Economy*, 1887th edition. ElecBook, London.

Müller, H., 2001. *Zement* in *Werke 4: Die Stücke* 2. Suhrkamp, Frankfurt.

Munck, R., O'Hearn, D. (Eds.), 2001. *Critical Development Theory: Contributions to a New Paradigm*, 2nd improved edition. Zed Books, London.

Wolf, C., 1995. *The Author's Dimension: Selected Essays*. University of Chicago Press, Chicago, IL.

4 | ECOFEMINISM AS (MARXIST) SOCIOLOGY[1]

Ariel Salleh

Realism, constructionism, and the humanity–nature question

The human relation to what is called 'nature' has become a focus of social thought in our time, with a new 'eco-politics' given over to it, and ecofeminists, eco-Marxists, social ecologists, and deep ecologists each offering unique conceptualisations. But conversation about the humanity–nature problematic seems to provoke both public confusion and intellectual hostility. Meanwhile, an insurgent globalising resistance to neoliberalism and its ecological crisis develops strategies across the humanity–nature interface with little help from sociological theory. However, one sociologist, Peter Dickens, has suggested that the difficulties people have in thinking about this connection result from the modernist industrial division of labour and its inevitable knowledge fragmentation. Like ecofeminists Maria Mies, Vandana Shiva, Mary Mellor, and Ariel Salleh, he argues that the marginalisation of lay and tacit forms of knowledge under industrialisation means that people lose a sense of their own organic nature, environmental abuse being an effect of this alienation (Dickens, 1995; Mies and Shiva, 1993; Mellor, 1997; Salleh, 1997).

The celebrated English sociologist Anthony Giddens also visits the topic of 'disembedding', attributing it to the phenomenon of globalisation (Giddens, 1991). But Giddens is generally optimistic, while Dickens sees the modernist division of labour alienating individuals and pulverising social relations. Like Marx, or really Alfred Sohn-Rethel, Dickens observes how abstract professional knowledges which inform modern labour processes become fetishised. And he cites the case of environmental economics here:

> ... attaching monetary value to environmental systems (or, more accurately, very limited parts of such systems) and abstracting them away from the processes involved in their production: not only the social and political processes involved [are externalised] but knowledge of the relations with the causal powers of nature engaged during their production. (Sohn-Rethel, 1978; Dickens, 1995: 142–143)

Moreover, under capitalism, such expertise is traded as a commodity, dislocated from its material source.

Before moving on to consider the subsistence alternative, it is worth noting that in making a claim for material grounding, Dickens himself draws on abstract knowledge, namely philosophic assumptions which combine critical realism and social constructionism in a dialectical way. Careful ecofeminist accounts of the human relation to nature likewise rely on this kind of explanation. Realism per se, posits nature as an expression of complex internal relations – some being general processes like thermodynamic principles, and others contingent factors like seasonal variability. A 'critical realism' accepts this, but on the understanding that a sui generis nature is mainly known through the medium of socially constructed languages – often elaborate disciplinary ones (Bhaskar, 1989). A critical realist approach to the humanity–nature question must be prepared to cross these socially constructed disciplinary boundaries – physics, biology, sociology. Moreover, it will track back and forth between degrees of abstraction within disciplines, namely the movement in sociology between individual and social structure.

Such an explanation articulates general processes and particular contingencies that converge in any concrete outcome, and forces at different levels of abstraction which actively determine that same conjuncture. Like dialectics, this kind of theory making relies on a notion of complex causality or overdetermination and it moves constantly between abstract and concrete forms. Such knowledge is described as tacit when the apprehension of internally related forces is not put into a language. Lay knowledge is often confused with tacit knowledge and it is sometimes said to remain concrete. But by my own ecofeminist conjecture, it is political interests which constrain the further articulation of lay knowledges.

The division between productive and reproductive labour

Despite an emphasis on the division of labour, Dickens's proto-ecofeminist sociology is inspired less by Durkheim than by Marx. Substantively, he treats nature as man's inorganic body and knowledge as rooted in practice; his object is to replace alienation with emancipation (Durkheim, 1964; Marx, 1973). Marxism identifies various forms of individual alienation and, at another level of abstraction, these can be read as contradictions or structural crises destabilising capitalist societies. The most often discussed contradiction occurs between social relations of production versus forces of production. For example, since profits are generated by labour, the displacement of jobs by new technologies may undermine future profits (Marx, 1981). Another contradictory moment occurs between conditions of production versus social relations of production. For example, since workers' health is often damaged by factory conditions and local pollution, this may undermine their future function as productive labour. Yet a further contradictory moment occurs between forces of production versus external nature. For example, since the material base of industrial provisioning is ecosystemic, damage by ongoing resource extraction may undermine the availability of future inputs.

An ecofeminist perspective is readily compatible with this materialist analysis, but it seeks to re-frame these contradictions using a different lens. In this respect, Maria Mies's work has been path breaking (Mies, 1986; Salleh, 1997, 1984). As a new social movement, ecofeminism privileges a politics of the body focused on sexuality, race, and environmental habitat. In this, it engages directly with the humanity–nature problematic. Marxist analyses of nature's commodification also deal with this interface, but there is a shift in ecofeminism away from production towards reproduction in its several senses. Since, as another English sociologist John Urry reminds us, the term reproduction may apply to biological processes, economic relations, or cultural practices (Urry, 1981). In its treatment of the divisions of labour by which humans negotiate their social relation with nature, Marxism is suggestive but not sufficiently explicit on the role of reproductive labour. This has led to confusing sociological claims like Jurgen Habermas's surmise that ecology and feminism belong to civil society and are therefore not class-based movements. Is class membership merely the prerogative of a privileged few (Habermas, 1989)?

Certainly Marxist sociologists like Sean Sayer accept class and gender as mutually determining categories.[2] But where exactly does gendered reproductive labour stand in the big picture? During the 1970s feminists engaged inconclusively with this question in what became known as 'the domestic labour debate' (Sargent, 1981). Ecofeminist thinking broadens that earlier emancipatory agenda by integrating ecopolitical concerns – equality, cultural diversity, sustainability. In fact, the constructionist aspect of ecofeminism interrogates the very foundations of historical materialism, with its supposedly transhistorical concepts of history, nature, and labour. Offering a transcendent critique, it asks whether there are not yet deeper causal structures, general processes, and particular contingencies, formative of older gender-innocent Marxist understandings. An ecofeminist lens addresses reproduction as a priori to production, and the implications of this flow on to Marxist concepts of class and contradiction.

Dialectical process: immanent and transcendent meanings

Ecofeminists view the humanity versus nature dualism, and the split between productive versus reproductive labours, as reflecting a profound alienation embodied in the social construction of masculine gender identity and the social construction of its thought products. With this gender critique, ecofeminism comes forward as a corrective transitional politics, appropriate to a certain historical conjuncture. It reads beneath the alienations which keep new social movements fragmented and single issue. And it invites ecopolitical activists and theorists of eco-Marxism, social ecology, or deep ecology to be more reflexive about how they absorb and reinforce profoundly gendered forms of alienation. In undertaking this task, ecofeminism becomes a sociology of knowledge.

The ecofeminist lens used in this paper develops the work of Maria Mies, Vandana Shiva, and some of my own earlier statements. It can be characterised as an 'embodied materialism' (Mies and Shiva, 1993).[3] It is 'materialist' in endorsing the basic tools of a Marxist sociology, and 'embodied' in that it sets out to re-frame that discourse by giving equal weight to the organically interrelated entities – man, woman, nature. Historically, these have been unequally valorised. In particular, the interests of male-dominated societies have been served by managing women's bodies as a 'natural resource'. That meant positioning the female sex 'somewhere between' men and nature in the order if things (Moraga and Anzaldua, 1981). This masculinist practice points to a fundamental structural contradiction in capitalism. A node of crisis not yet included in the conversations of political economy.

In unpacking the irrational contradiction which locates women, and usually indigenes, simultaneously within humanity and nature, the following ecofeminist deconstruction tacks between critical realism and social constructionism in a dialectical way. Dialectics provides a very helpful model for thinking about process and change (Ollman, 1992). In contrast to the static positivist 'cat is a cat' mindset, dialecticians trace the emergence and retreat of entities. This involves studying the interplay of meanings – immanent and transcendent, active and latent. For example, an activist or reader of ecofeminism as a transformative project will be aware that terms such as 'reason', 'women', etc. carry both an immanent, lay, ideological usage, and a transcendent, abstract, critical one. On the other hand, sometimes the abstract usage is ideological and the lay one fosters critique. As Ashis Nandy has written in the context of a postcolonial politics:

> I like to believe that each such concept in this work is a *double entendre*: on the one hand, it is part of an oppressive structure; on the other, it is in league with its victims. (Nandy, 1983: xiv)

Another illustration of immanent and transcendent meanings occurs in the analysis of ecofeminist politics This is because ecofeminists tread a zig-zag course between (1) their liberal and socialist feminist task of establishing the right to a political voice; (2) their radical and poststructuralist feminist task of undermining the very basis of that same validation; and (3) their properly ecological feminist task of demonstrating how most women – and thence men too – can live differently with nature. Now each phase of strategy implies different senses of woman, politics, nature, reason, and so on, but an understanding of context and intention makes clear which sense is active and which is latent. This dialectical openness or indeterminacy, indicates that ecofeminism is not an essentialist theory. That said, what Gayatri Spivak names a 'strategic essentialism' is sometimes relied on for pragmatic emphasis (Spivak, 1987).

Looking through an embodied materialist lens

But enough about words. Recalling Marx's eleventh thesis, Dickens urges:

> [The] insistence that changing our thought alone is sufficient to stop fragmentation and create an emancipated society misses the core underlying processes which cause the fragmentations. (Dickens, 1995: 107)

Social transformation requires both theory and praxis. This is why an 'embodied materialist' sociology grounded in reproductive labour is strong medicine for intellectual alienations and confusions of the industrial division of labour. For while industrialised productive labour is historically contingent, reproductive labour is necessary, integral, and attuned to general causal processes within the ecosystem. Many Indigenous Peoples actually use a single word for this humanity–nature nexus, a partnership of people in/with country.

Keeping focus for now on women and the modernist division of labour, it is plain that their relation to nature, and therefore to 'capital' and 'labour', is constructed, and constructs itself, differently to men's in several ways. A first difference involves experiences mediated by female body organs in the hard but sensuous labours of birthing and suckling. A second difference follows from women's historically assigned caring and maintenance chores that serve to 'bridge' men and nature. A third difference involves women's manual work in making goods as farmers, cooks, herbalists, potters, and so on. The fourth difference involves creating symbolic representations of 'feminine' relations to 'nature' – in poetry, in painting, in philosophy, and everyday talk. Through this constellation of lay labours, the great majority of women around the world are organically and discursively implicated in life-affirming activities, and they develop gender-specific knowledges grounded in this material base. As a result, women across cultures have begun to express political views that are quite removed from men's approaches to global crisis – whether these be corporate greenwash, ecological ethics, or socialism (see Salleh, 1994: 107).

There are elements of both realism and social constructionism in this description, and here another of Dickens's sociological perceptions coincides with ecofeminist reasoning:

> [T]he languages people use to understand nature and their relationships with it may be a product of people's innate causal powers to make sense of their circumstances. (Dickens, 1995: 12)

An acceptance of this judgement enables the practical experience and lay knowledge of workers outside the modernist division of labour to be taken seriously. More than this, it indicates that particular labour qualities inherent in what these workers do shape their skills and insights just as much as learned roles of socialisation do. There is an overdetermination, between bodily capacities, gender conditioning, and what these workers learn from their prescribed economic chores – that daily round of 'mediating nature' on behalf of men.

This lay knowledge defies conventional sociological stratifications of class and race, for women worldwide undertake reproductive labour – biological, economic, cultural – at some stage of their lives. But neither is ecofeminism 'sociobiological'; nor an argument that 'women are closer to nature' or 'better than men'; nor yet a celebration of 'the essential feminine' as superficial readers sometimes conclude. To amplify the argument for an embodied materialist perspective, and meta-industrial labour as a unique class location, I will visit three kinds of reproductive labour typically carried out by women – subsistence farming, housework, and parenting (see Salleh, 1997, 2000) In considering these exemplars, the reader should bear Marx's early anthropology in mind. As Dickens puts it:

> Human beings ... not only reach natural limits but make something new of themselves as a result of humanising nature. They realise new powers with which they were born but which they did not know they had. (Dickens, 1995: 104)

A classic statement of material agency in scientific complexity occurs in Vandana Shiva's study of Indian women subsistence farmers.

> It is in managing the integrity of ecological cycles in forestry and agriculture that women's [re]-productivity has been most developed and evolved. Women transfer fertility from the forests to the field and to animals. They transfer animal waste as fertiliser for crops and crop by-products to animals as fodder. This partnership between women's work and nature's work ensures the sustainability of sustenance. (Shiva, 1989)

In a parallel vein, German ecology activist Ulla Terlinden spells out the tacit dialectical epistemology behind domestic reproduction.

> Housework requires of women [or men] a broad range of knowledge and ability. The nature of the work itself determines its organisation. The work at hand must be dealt with in its entirety ... The worker must possess a high degree of personal synthesis, initiative, intuition and flexibility. (Terlinden, 1984: 320)

Contrast this total engagement with the fragmented industrial division of labour and the numb inconsequential mindset to which it gives rise.

Holding nature: the meta-industrial class and its vantage point

In discussing parental skills, US philosopher Sara Ruddick introduces a notion of 'holding' labour, which again embodies the principles of good ecological reasoning.

> To hold means to minimize risk and to reconcile differences rather than to sharply accentuate them. Holding is a way of seeing with an eye toward maintaining the minimal harmony, material resources, and skills necessary for sustaining a child in safety. It is the attitude elicited by world protection, world-preservation, world repair. (Ruddick, 1989: 79)

Paradoxically, while minimising risk, 'holding' is the ultimate expression of adaptability. As against the positivist separation of fact and value, space and time which marks science as usual, interconnectedness is commonsense in this mater/reality.[4]

Sociologist Barbara Adams offers yet another sensitive analysis of human engagement with the interlocking cycles of nature (Adams, 1998). When the material substrate of life is processed by manufacture and put up for a price, the socially contrived focus on 'things' misses the myriad of exchanges and reverberations which hold nature as matter together. Adams describes how people's sensitivity to nature's implicate timings is colonised by the clock of capitalist production and its administering state. Citizen consumers are disempowered by this one-dimensional landscape and are only able to grasp 'what is', in contrast to 'what can be' – in other words, appearance subsumes essence – the unrealised potential of nature.

Each of these ecofeminists describe a non-alienating way of objectifying natural human energies in labour. An embodied materialist sociology highlights the relational logic of this labour form and a sensibility that has been marginalised, censored, and repressed by the vanities of modernity. But metaindustrial labour as a general process of human partnership with nature is not necessarily gender specific. Rather, the gendering is an historically contingent aspect of industrialised societies. Conversely, ecological holding is found in both genders among Indigenous Peoples. By custom, Australian Aboriginal workers practice a kind of holding, nurturing sustainability as they move through country. Thus, the hunter gathering mode of production is really 'reproductive' in that it does not take more than it needs; does not splice and package land in legal title for fear of losing it. Rather, the seasonal walk is made in the knowledge that each habitat will replenish and provide again on the return (Bird Rose, 1996).

Self-managed Aboriginal provisioning generates lay knowledges that are not only environmentally benign, but creatively social. Besides subsistence, it fosters learning, participation, innovation, ritual, identity, and belonging. Indigenous Peoples are known to achieve a high quality of life with only three hours work a day. On the other hand, the engineered satisfiers of modern industrial societies like bureaucracies or cars, cost much time and energy, often sabotaging the very convenience for which they were designed (Max-Neef et al., 1991).[5] Reproductive labour is a metabolic bridging of human and natural cycles. But productive labours pursue a single goal whether in 'controlled' laboratory science, agribusiness, mining, or smelting. This instrumentalism collides with complex patterns of material exchange in nature leaving disorder.

To reiterate: in principle, holding labours transcend differences of class, race, gender, and age, though in practice, under modernity, they have become the province of low-status groups like women domestic caregivers, organic farmers, and indigenes. Each of these workers occupies an unspoken space in the industrial division of labour and in Marxism, its theoretical mirror. This is a remarkable sociological omission; but an especially salient one in today's ecological crisis. Meta-industrial provisioning, using simple ways of adapting nature to meet human needs, demonstrates an already functioning minimalist infrastructure, without ecologically damaging forces of production or socially oppressive relations of production. Meta-industrial labour literally embodies the precautionary principle – and increasingly applies it beyond home and neighbourhood to political action at large. Ecofeminists like Maria Mies, and others inspired by her sociological analysis, see our work as validating these already existing 'moral economies' as they start to challenge the depravities of neoliberalism.

Common objections from the modernist division of labour

Yet, for sociologists of 'ecological modernisation' like Arthur Mol and David Sonnenfeld, the exemplary properties of reproductive labour remain invisible (Mol and Sonnenfeld, 1999). For as noted earlier, the technologies which mediate daily needs in industrial societies numb people to their organic embodiment as nature. Sociologists, whose profession is both a cause and effect of modern knowledge fragmentation, may react especially negatively to an argument that challenges Durkheim's study of society sui generis. Others with a stake in the hegemonic division of labour, may be uncomfortable with the idea that lay knowledges carry any abstract significance. Objections to taking meta-industrial labour seriously may also come from Marxists and liberal feminist development theorists – each having tacitly evolutionist attitudes and a colonising commitment to Westernisation as progress.

But even Scott Lash's radically postmodern sociology of 'detraditionalisation' plays into this tendency (Heelas et al., 1996). To label meta-industrial labour 'traditional', is to lose sight of the fact that food growing and domestic maintenance are mediations of nature which will remain essential under any historically contingent mode of production. Again, ignoring the worker's necessary embodiment in a sustaining material ground, David Harvey maintains:

> For Marxists there can be no going back, as many ecologists seem to propose, to an unmediated relation to nature (or a world built solely on face to face relations), to a pre-capitalist and communitarian world of non-scientific understandings with limited divisions of labour. (Harvey, 1993: 42)

The linchpin of this assertion is the word 'unmediated'. And it reveals a typically modernist and masculinist idea of a somehow 'un-reproduced', autonomous labour, one that is inevitably technologised. Moreover, the tacit knowledges which enable the face-to-face reproductive sphere are reified by Harvey, and rejected as 'pre-scientific'.

Gender bias, in and beyond academic sociology, consistently diminishes the rationality of meta-industrial skills and insights. Unfortunately, in advanced industrial societies, middle-class women, even feminists enjoying professional status, may become complicit in this. Rewarded for adopting a dominant neoliberal or labourist sensibility and values, some women express contempt for the lot of subsistence farmers, mothers, and domestic workers, despite the fact that most of their sisters are 'unreconstructed' mediators of nature. Cecile Jackson's feminist critique of ecofeminism is a case in point. It fails to grasp the difference between an immanent 'here and now' discourse and a transcendent one. Thus she reads a layered ecopolitical argument about re-valorising exchanges between 'man, woman, and nature' through a narrow single issue lens focused on emancipation of women in modernist terms.[6] Jackson's pro-development line, like Harvey's, also relies on an idealised, unreflexive view of science, quite out of place in an era of exploitive free trade regimes and greenhouse pollution. In the words of German sociologist Ulrich Beck:

> Science has become *the protector of a global contamination of people and nature* ... [In] the way they deal with risks in many areas, the sciences have squandered *until further notice their historic reputation for rationality*. (Beck, 1992: 80, italics in original)

An inclusive participatory theory / strategy for global resistance

Progressive thinkers readily admit that in our century, the knowledge base and objectives of white middle-class male decision makers is largely what exacerbates environmental damage. But they are less clear about more positive human links with nature. This is where Dickens's sociological vision for moving beyond the modernist *impasse* again resonates with the ecofeminist project:

> Emancipation lies in linking dominant forms of abstract, explicit, global and expert knowledges to subordinated, concrete, tacit, local and lay understandings. (Dickens, 1995: 205)

The present essay joins meta-industrial skills and insights to abstract conceptualisations like sociology and ecology. But it also asserts that lay knowledge contains a rationality in its own right.[7] Nevertheless, as sociologists move towards inclusive theory, they will need care not to destroy this precious cultural diversity by semantic subsumption or repressive tolerance. For example, in Marx's materialism, 'humanising nature' means re-making it, whereas through an embodied materialism, nature is humanised in partnership.

In a time of powerful grassroots resistance to globalisation, an ecofeminist lens opens Marxist theory and strategy to knowledges from the widest possible base of political participation. And what is said of material production is applicable to theoretical production here.

> [T]he division of labour needs changing in such a way that people are given the opportunity to be involved in the creation of the product itself. (Dickens, 1995: 197)

Seizing the moment, ecofeminists point to an unformulated 'meta-industrial class' and a very specific humanity–nature contradiction in the late capitalist division of labour. In this dialectic, theory lags way behind practice: for exemplary moral economies and benign peoples' sciences already exist. The problem that besets hitherto existing sociology is that a theoretic reconfiguring of the historically deleted human identity with nature requires new modes of abstraction. My argument therefore, is that the nexus where reproductive labour and its knowledges mediate humanity and nature is the most promising vantage point for an ecologically literate sociology. At this site, ecopolitical strategies for ecology, feminism, postcolonial, and socialist movements can also find common ground.

Notes

1 This paper was first published in *Capitalism Nature Socialism* 14(1)(2003): 61–74, with thanks to Taylor & Francis for permission to reproduce it. The essay is based on ideas presented at the Conference of the International Sociological Association Research Committee on Environment and Society (RC24), Cambridge University, 5–7 July 2001.

2 Thus, 'the only way out of this impasse is to confront the intransitive and irreducible nature of each major structure of oppression in its own right, while realising that gender, division of labour, and class are constructed simultaneously and reciprocally' (Sayer and Walker, 1992: 40, quoted in Dickens, 1995: 70).

3 Although re-visioning political economy, the ecofeminist project is broader and more inclusive than the approach taken by eco-Marxist philosophers (see Benton, 1993; Hayward, 1995).

4 For an ecofeminist exploration of the semantics of mater/matrix/materiality, see Griffin (1979).

5 And further, as Dickens notes (1995: 123), even the US Department of Agriculture concedes that alternative biodynamic food production saves energy!

6 See Jackson (1995) and reply by Salleh (1996). Guha (1991) falls into the same trap as Jackson, criticising Shiva's analysis of the Chipko movement from a liberal feminist position, when Shiva's concern is a moral economy and a people's science.

7 Regarding knowledge theft in the ecological sphere. A case in point is biopiracy of the Indian neem tree by the US pharmaceutical W. R. Grace. Happily, ecofeminist Shiva and others succeeded in a court challenge to quash the patent. On repressive assimilation of radical ideas, see Marcuse (1972).

References

Adam, B., 1998. *Timescapes of Modernity: The Environment and Invisible Hazards*. Routledge, London.

Beck, U., 1992. *Risk Society: Towards a New Modernity*. Sage, London.

Benton, T., 1993. *Natural Relations, Ecology, Animal Rights, and Social Justice*. Verso, London.

Bhaskar, R., 1989. *The Possibility of Naturalism*. Harvester Wheatsheaf, Hemel Hempstead.

Bird Rose, D., 1996. *Nourishing Terrains: Australian Aboriginal Views of Landscape and Wilderness*. Australian Heritage Commission, Canberra.

Dickens, P., 1995. *Reconstructing Nature: Alienation, Emancipation, and the Division of Labour*. Routledge, London.

Durkheim, E., 1964. *The Division of Labour*. Free Press, New York.

Giddens, A., 1991. *Modernity and Self Identity*. Polity, Oxford.

Griffin, S., 1979. *Woman and Nature: The Roaring Inside Her*. Womens Press, London.

Guha, R., 1991. *The Unquiet Woods: Ecological Change and Peasant Resistance in the Himalaya*. Oxford University Press, Delhi.

Habermas, J., 1989. *The Structural Transformation of the Public Sphere*. Polity Press, Cambridge.

Harvey, D., 1993. 'The Nature of the Environment: The Dialectics of Social and Environmental Change'. *Socialist Register* 3: 1–51.

Hayward, T., 1995. Ecological Thought. Polity Press, Cambridge.

Heelas, P., Lash, S., Morris, P. (Eds.), 1996. *Detraditionalisation*. Blackwell, Oxford.

Jackson, C., 1995. 'Radical Environmental Myths: A Gender Perspective'. *New Left Review* (210): 120–140.

Marcuse, H., 1972. *One Dimensional Man*. Abacus, London.

Marx, K., 1973. *Grundrisse: Introduction to the Critique of Political Economy*. Pelican, Harmondsworth.

Marx, K. 1981., *Capital*. Penguin, Harmondsworth.

Max-Neef, M. et al., 1991. *Human Scale Development*. Apex, New York.

Mellor, M., 1997. *Feminism and Ecology*. Polity Press, Cambridge.

Mies, M., 1986. *Patriarchy and Accumulation*. Zed Books, London.

Mies, M., Shiva, V., 1993. *Ecofeminism*. Zed Books, London.

Mol, A., Sonnenfeld, D. (Eds.), 1999. *Ecological Modernisation around the World*. Frank Cass, London.

Moraga, C., Anzaldua, G. (Eds.), 1981. *This Bridge Called My Back: Writings by Radical Women of Color*. Kitchen Table Press, New York.

Nandy, A., 1983. *The Intimate Enemy*, Oxford University Press, Delhi.

Ollman, B., 1992. *Dialectical Investigations*. Routledge, New York.

Ruddick, R., 1989. *Maternal Thinking: Toward a Politics of Peace*. Beacon, Boston, MA.

Salleh, A., 1984. 'Deeper than Deep Ecology'. *Environmental Ethics* 6: 335–341.

Salleh, A., 1994. 'Nature, Woman, Labor, Capital: Living the Deepest Contradiction' in O'Connor, M. (Ed.), *Is Capitalism Sustainable? Political Economy and the Politics of Ecology*. Guilford, New York, 106–124.

Salleh, A., 1996. 'An Ecofeminist Bioethic and What Post-Humanism Really Means'. *New Left Review* 217: 138–147.

Salleh, A., 1997. *Ecofeminism as Politics: Nature, Marx and the Postmodern*. Zed Books, London and St Martins Press, New York.

Salleh, A., 2000. 'The Meta-Industrial Class and Why We Need It'. *Democracy & Nature* 6: 27–36.

Sargent, L., 1981. *Women and Revolution*. South End Press, Boston, MA.

Sayer, S., Walker, R., 1992. *The New Social Economy: Reworking the Division of Labour*. Blackwell, Oxford.

Shiva, V., 1989. *Staying Alive: Women, Ecology and Development*. Zed Books, London.

Sohn-Rethel, A., 1978. *Intellectual and Manual Labour*. Macmillan, London.

Spivak, G.C., 1987. *In Other Worlds: Essays in Cultural Politics*. Methuen, London.

Terlinden, U., 1984. 'Women in the Ecology Movement' in Altbach, E.. Clausen, J., Schultz, D., Stephan, N. (Eds.), *German Feminism*. SUNY, Albany, NY.

Urry, J., 1981. *The Anatomy of Capitalist Societies: The Economy, Civil Society, and the State*. Macmillan, London.

5 | THE 'FLAT ONTOLOGY' OF NEOLIBERAL FEMINISM[1]

Jennifer Cotter

After the 2008 economic crisis of capitalism, many feminists in the Global North are formally declaring their dissatisfaction with the 'poststructuralist fatigue' (Puar, 2013: 387) of the cultural turn and turning towards what Rosi Braidotti calls a 'new brand of materialism' (2013: 22) to explain the material contradictions of women's lives in capitalism now. The feminism of the 'cultural turn', which came of age with the rise of neoliberal capitalism and its marketisation, deregulation and 'free floating' currencies, taught an interpretive framework that served to normalise capitalism and adjust women to increased exploitation as wage-labourers by reducing material contradictions of gender, sexuality, and race to 'floating signifiers' and 'irreducible differences' and obscuring their dialectical relation to material relations of class and exploitation in production (Ebert, 2015, 2016). Now, in the wake not only of the *rise* but also the *crisis* of neoliberal capital, of austerity measures, increased exploitation, the commodification of all aspects of life, climate change and ecological disasters, and the resulting material inequalities and contradictions of women's lives under capitalism the 'textual approaches' to feminism are 'increasingly being deemed inadequate for understanding contemporary society' (Coole and Frost, 2010: 2–3).

Yet, what is rapidly becoming canonical in the Global North as the 'new material turn' in feminism is by and large updating an axiom that was central to feminism after the cultural turn: namely, that the feminist materialism of the future is a materialism without a dialectical critique of the relationship of gender and sexuality to class, labour, exploitation, and the mode of production. Instead, the 'new material turn' substitutes (post)humanist ontologies as the basis of materialist feminism now: from theories of 'new materialism' (Coole and Frost, 2010), to object-oriented feminism (Behar, 2016), performative metaphysics, and 'agential realism' (e.g. Barad, 2003), the 'matter of corporeality' (Grosz, 2017) in which the 'incorporeal' is inverted into the Deleuzian 'intensity' of the matter of the 'body', and new feminist vitalism (e.g. Hill, 2008), among others. In this view, what is needed in feminist analysis in the twenty-first century is a 'new ontology' of 'life as zoe' (Braidotti, 2013) or 'life itself' (Rose, 2016) that sees the autonomy and liveliness of matter, objects, and things as central to material reality. Rooted in the monist and vitalist theories of Spinoza, Bergson, and Deleuze among others, this view understands 'matter' to be constituted by an errant *élan vital* – an irreducible, capricious, vibrant, and radical alterity or 'surplus-life' (Cooper, 2008) – that is said to form the ontological basis of 'resistance' in a time of what Bruno Latour calls 'Dingpolitik' in which '*matter itself* is up for grabs' (2004: 14). On these terms, the material contradictions of gender, sexuality, and of women's lives are understood in terms of a 'flat ontology' of irreducible and contingent 'assemblages' (Deleuze and Guattari, 1987) of vitalist, 'auto-poietic', or 'self-producing' matter (Braidotti, 2013) that is autonomous from the dialectical praxis of labour and exists outside of any historical or social determination such as the mode of production. By embracing (post)humanist ontologies, new materialist feminism claims to offer a materialist feminism that confounds the 'binary' terms of dialectical and historical materialism and traverses binaries of gender, sexuality, race, and class and open us up to a radically new world 'devoid of dualisms' (Dolphijn and van der Tuin, 2012).

In this essay, I argue that, contrary to its claims, the 'new material turn' in feminism – by which I mean not only 'new materialist' feminism but the range of feminisms rooted in (post)humanist ontologies – does not 'traverse' binaries rather, it places class binaries, production for profit, exploitation, and the material contradictions these give rise to in ideological suspension. The so-called 'new ontologies' are ideological paradigms that bypass material relations of exploitation: more specifically, the dialectical relation of life, gender, sexuality, and reproduction to what Marx calls the 'ensemble of social relations' of production (1976b: 616). They offer a dehistoricised concept of material reality that addresses the material contradictions of life in capitalism – contradictions of life for women, for workers, for persons of colour, for other species and the environment – not through analysis of social structures with the aim of transformation, but through raising these contradictions to a new *metaphysical* level of abstraction that transcodes the historical and social laws of motion of capitalism into laws of nature and the ontological basis of objective reality as such. The 'new material' turn in feminism is a new idealism to crisis manage capitalism and adjust women to new imperatives to stave off declines in profit. As Julie Torrant argues in her critique of feminism's embrace of new materialism: 'Contrary to their self-representations, "new materialist" feminisms are disenabling forms of spiritualism that displace explanatory critique of the emergent material conditions [of capitalism] with strategies of enchanted affective adaptation' (2016: 97). More specifically, (post) humanist ontologies put forward a metaphysics of the market and 'exchange relations' in capitalism and, when used as the basis of feminism, at most offer a neoliberal feminism of market freedoms for women, such as the freedom to sell one's labour on the market for a wage and to be exploited, rather than freedom from exploitation. A telling sign of new materialism's embrace of neoliberal feminism is that it now literally embraces 'branding' and 'marketing' in the name of exploited women (Behar, 2016).

By contrast, what is needed now is what Teresa Ebert has called 'red feminism' (2015), which advances the understanding that freedom for all women, not just privileges for some, has a necessary dialectical and material relation to the abolition of wage-labour and capital relations, exploitation, imperialism, and the use of gender, sexuality, and cultural differences by global capital as 'instruments of labour' to raise or lower the rate of exploitation of the global workforces. What is needed, in other words, is a dialectical and historical materialist feminism that understands that capitalism at root requires the exploitation of the surplus-labour of workers in production as the source of profit and that 'gender', 'sexuality', and 'race' as material relations and sites of struggle and social transformation are not autonomous from the capitalist mode of production and its global division of labour and property relations. At the core of red feminism is the dialectical theory of the centrality of the materiality of labour as the means by which the world is transformed and transformable. It is 'by thus acting on the external world and changing it', as Marx writes, that humanity 'at the same time changes [its] own nature' (1976a). In grasping the revolutionary potential of labour, red feminism not only advances a revolutionary critique that uncovers the historical and social basis of the relation of gender to the exploitation of labour. It also explains why ending the exploitation of labour by capitalism is the necessary material basis for the collective transformation of human society from the accumulation of profit to the meeting of the needs of all.

Assembling the attack on dialectics

One of the central targets of new materialist feminism is a rejection of the development of dialectical and historical materialist feminist critique of capitalism. For example, Rosi Braidotti, whose writings have quickly become part of the canon of 'new materialist' and 'vitalist' feminism, rejects dialectics on the basis of what is by now the standard – or commonsensical – rejection: that it is 'too binary'. According to Braidotti, dialectical analysis is a method of analysis that *perpetuates* 'violent binary oppositions' in which 'difference or otherness [plays] a constitutive role, marking off the sexualized other (woman), the racialized other (the native) and the naturalized other (animals, the environment or earth)' (2013: 27). In other words, Braidotti equates and rejects historical materialist dialectical analysis and critique with classic Western metaphysical concepts of 'static binaries' and 'the negative dialectical processes of sexualization, racialization and naturalization of those who are marginalized or excluded' (2013: 28). New materialist feminism, therefore, claims that the central task of feminism is to 'overcome dialectical oppositions' by 'engendering non-dialectical understandings of materialism itself', which, so the narrative goes, 'results in relocating difference outside the dialectical scheme, as a complex process of differing ... based on the centrality of the relation to multiple others' (2013: 56).

Materialist dialectics, however, is not a theory of binaries in 'stasis' rather, it is the analysis of historically and socially produced, and therefore collectively transformable, material contradictions. Rather than taking 'what is' – existing conditions of life under capitalism – for granted as autonomous, self-evident, or 'static', materialist dialectics is an inquiry into the historical and material causes, i.e. *social* relations of production, behind immediate conditions and contradictions of life under capitalism. Materialist dialectics, Marx writes, 'is an abomination and a scandal to the bourgeoisie … because it includes in its positive understanding of what exists a simultaneous recognition of its negation, its inevitable destruction' (1976a: 103). In other words, the material contradictions of life produced under global capitalism in which a small fraction of society owns and controls the means of production and exploits the surplus-labour of the majority for profit, are material and objective contradictions but they are also social and historical and can be transformed. What Braidotti calls a 'negative dialectical process' that brings about 'sexualization, racialization, and naturalization of those who are marginalized and excluded' (2013: 27), when understood in dialectical materialist terms, is not the end of the dialectical turn 'because [dialectics] regards every historically developed form as being in a fluid state, in motion, and therefore grasps its transient aspect as well' (Marx, 1976a: 103). In materialist dialectics, there is also the 'negation of the negation': meaning that these are socially and historically produced, and therefore transformable, material contradictions.

Historical materialist dialectics is necessary for feminism in the twenty-first century because it examines the *historical* conditions that produce and bring about material contradictions, such as the social division of labour that produces 'sexualization' and 'racialization' and the wage-labour and capital – i.e. *class* relations – on which this division of labour is founded, as well as the development of material conditions which can lead to their collective transformation. As Eleanor Burke Leacock argues 'Marxist dialectics are used to describe processes as they unfold in the context of specific historical circumstances … in the *fully* structural sense of production relations' (1981: 213). The concept of 'dialectical opposition' or negation 'refers to an active process of transformation and the development of new forms' (1981: 219) that is not only necessary for understanding the historical conditions that give rise to 'the sexual division of labour itself [and] changes in its form and function' (1981: 215) but for understanding the material basis to change them. Dialectical materialism, in other words, is the theory of collective social transformation.

On the terms of anti-dialectical 'new materialism', however, 'dialectical oppositions' are regarded not as historical or material processes requiring transformation of social relations of production, they are regarded as artefacts of human correlationism, anthropocentrism, and 'human hubris' (Bennett, 2010) that obscure the diffuse, amorphous, radically contingent, and immanent material reality of which we are composed. At the core of new materialism is the revival of a *vitalist* and monist theory of ontology which is said to traverse binary oppositions. 'A "monistic universe"', Braidotti explains, 'refers to Spinoza's central concept that matter, the world and humans are not dualistic entities structured according to principles of internal or external opposition' (2013: 56). In advocating 'a monistic philosophy', Braidotti claims to 'reject dualism ... and stresses instead the self-organizing or (auto-poietic) force of living matter' (2013: 3). One of the implications of this view of 'auto-poietic' matter is that along with the rejection of dialectics, the new materialist and vitalist feminisms ideologically conceal the role of 'the dialectical praxis of labour' and the relationship of gender, sexuality, and race to the social relations of production in which labour is exploited. The 'problem' with dialectical and historical materialism, Jane Bennett claims in her book *Vibrant Matter* (2010), is its focus 'on collectives conceived primarily as conglomerates of human designs and practices' (2010: 1–2). According to new materialist feminists, Marxism, and therefore Marxist feminism and its understanding of the dialectic of gender and class and the revolutionary potential of labour, is simply another expression of dualism, 'anthropocentrism', and 'human instrumentality'. Thus, the new (post)humanist ontologies claim that feminism should not regard social existence as rooted in the 'social mode of production' and instead should see material reality as constituted by what Bennett, following Deleuze and Guattari (1987), calls a 'mode of assemblage', which she defines as 'ad hoc groupings of diverse elements, of vibrant materials of all sorts' (Bennett, 2010: 23). In non-dialectical assemblage theory material reality is seen as an aleatory and fragmented flow and temporary conglomeration of objects and social practices: '[w]hat it means to be a "mode"', according to new materialism, 'is to form alliances and enter assemblages: it is to mod(e)ify and be modified by others. The process of modification is not under the control of any one mode – no mode is an agent in the hierarchical sense' (Bennett, 2010: 22). In this view, material reality is made up of various conflicting, capricious, decentralised objects, things, in ad hoc local and micro assemblages outside of any structural relations or totalising mode of global social and economic relations of production – such as transnational capitalism – that determines social conditions of life.

This anti-dialectical theory of 'mode of assemblages' is, as Teresa Ebert remarks, 'a response to capital's need to block any understanding of social totality that brings to the surface the fundamental contradiction of the capitalist regime' (2015: 355), namely, that behind the exchange of commodities, including the exchange of labour-power for wages, is the theft of workers' surplus-labour in production. It produces an alienated consciousness that disappears the relation of exploitation of human by human that takes place behind the production, circulation, and conglomeration of 'diverse ... materials of all sorts' (Bennett, 2010: 23) and teaches the global workforces to instead look on capitalism and its requirements as 'self-evident natural laws' (Marx, 1976a: 899). When conceived of as 'assemblages' devoid of labour, material contradictions of gender, sexuality, race, and class are ideologically normalised and naturalised as the effect not of historically produced and therefore transformable social relations of production but as the effect of ontological conditions of life and 'being' as such what Elizabeth Grosz calls 'the precarious, accidental, contingent, expedient, striving, dynamic status of life in a messy, complicated, resistant, brute world of materiality' (2004: 2). In the face of 'assemblages' the only way for feminism to address the consequences of capitalism is to give up 'the aspiration towards cognitive and practical mastery over the world' (Frost, 2011: 78).

The opposition to 'dialectics' and dialectical materialism in (post)humanist ontologies, in other words, is an ideological opposition to the theory of collective social transformation; it is an opposition to the understanding that material contradictions of life under capitalism are not simply 'static binaries' but are the product of socially historically produced, and therefore, collectively transformable material relations of production. In place of collective social transformation, new materialism puts forward the theory of 'radical immanence'. The theory of 'radical immanence' is the understanding that already *within* the present there exists an 'other' future world – a radically immanent alternative world within – that is beyond binary opposition, exploitation, and capitalism but *without* the need to collectively transform the social relations of production founded on private property and to end exploitation.

For example, Rick Dolphijn and Iris van der Tuin, in their book *New Materialisms: Interviews and Cartographies* (2012), argue for a 'transversal' feminism of 'radical immanence' which 'traverses ... sexual dualisms' and provides 'a new way of mapping the relations between the sexes by moving beyond sex, sexual difference, and gender' (2012: 87) through what they call a 'performative ontology of sexual difference' (2012: 142). They argue that 'binary' sexual difference is 'nothing but a collective molar habit of mind' and that a post-binary society rooted in the vitalist 'sexual differing' of the performative body 'is not found in the future, but between the linguistic codes of sexual difference where it always already roams, materially and vitally' (2012: 156). In such a view there already exists a radically immanent vital ontology of differing within the body itself that is beyond sex, gender and other social binaries, and beyond material contradictions of class and exploitation. In this narrative 'sexual differing' and 'post-gender', 'post-race', and 'post-class' society is already here without social transformation of capitalism or, as Braidotti claims, 'We already live in permanent states of transition, hybridization and nomadic mobility, in emancipated (post-feminist), multi-ethnic societies' (2013: 184).

Feminism, in this view, can dispense with the collective social transformation and needs to give up the so-called 'negativity' of 'oppositional critique' for what Braidotti calls a 'life-affirming positivity' with 'the absence of any reference to negativity or violent dialectical oppositions' (2013: 56). By focusing on 'oppositional critique' and 'dialectical oppositions' such as the dialectical relation of gender and sexuality to class (i.e. the way in which gender and sexuality are used by capital to exploit surplus-labour), new materialism claims that we are constrained by the 'negativity' of the 'past' when feminism of the future must 'be indeterminate (infinite)' (Dolphijn and van der Tuin, 2012: 142). The call for 'the absence of any reference to … violent dialectical oppositions' (Braidotti, 2013: 56) is a way of marginalising oppositional critique aimed at social transformation. New materialist feminism is an ideological updating of neoliberalism and the argument that critique and transformation of capitalism is unnecessary for feminism and that the struggle for collective social transformation is an imaginary relic of the past. New materialism firmly recasts the feminism of the 'future' as a liberal feminism in which we all already have 'equal opportunity' for *differing* within capitalism and we just need to let go of our 'molar mental habits' and adjust our expectations to 'what exists' under capitalism as the basis of freedom.

To eliminate 'any *reference*' to 'violent dialectical oppositions' does not do away with material contradictions (i.e. 'binaries'), nor does it unleash the power of 'multiple others' as Braidotti claims. Rather, it actively suppresses, *from materialist feminist social theory*, the development of explanatory concepts with which to critique the material contradictions of gender and sexuality in capitalism, concepts that are needed for more effective collective transformation of the material relations in which women are exploited. This is because, contrary to the frame provided by new materialism and other (post) humanist ontologies, material contradictions of gender and sexuality are not simply artefacts of human correlationism projected onto an otherwise aleatory field of assemblages, rather, they are the effect of historical and material processes and contradictions in the social division of labour – of 'definite social relations' of production founded on exploitation (Marx 1986b: 29). Gender relations are a site of social struggle in capitalism because in class society gender is what Marx and Engels call an 'instrument of labour' which is deployed by capital to make labour 'more or less expensive to use' (1976: 491). Gender becomes historically useful to capital, as an instrument of labour, to raise or lower the *rate* of exploitation by, for example, organising workers into divided and competing labour forces which can be pitted against each other in order to divide class solidarity and cheapen the cost of labour. Marx (1986b) further elaborates on the way in which social differences such as 'gender' and 'age' are used as instruments of labour to naturalise the way in which capitalist development throws out of the workforce historically higher-waged workers and replaces them with 'fresh exploitable' workers at a cheaper rate. For example, as women, teenagers, and children have been drawn into the waged workforces of capitalism and more members of the family sell their labour for a wage and are exploited, rather than capitalism bringing about increased 'equality' and standard of living for all, capitalism proves 'Nothing more than that now four times as many workers' lives are used up as there were previously, in order to obtain the livelihood of one working family' (1986b: 47); in exchange for the same wage that capital used to pay one worker, it now gets the surplus-labour of multiple workers.

Put in other terms, 'gender', 'sexuality', 'age', 'race', and other social differences are not irreducible singularities that exist in accidental-acausal assemblages, rather they are 'instruments of labour' used by capital to normalise the lowering of the 'exchange-value' – i.e. the wages – of labour-power. In turn, they become ideological justifications for relative increases in the rate of exploitation because, by cheapening the cost of labour-power, they shorten the time the worker spends in the working day reproducing the value equivalent to her wages and increase the time the worker spends producing surplus-value. They, furthermore, are reproduced to provide a way to teach workers to interpret as natural the *social* division of labour and the way they are pitted in competition with one another by capital – a situation in which 'labourers compete not only by selling themselves one cheaper than the other, but also by doing the work of five, then ten, then twenty' (Marx, 1986b: 44). Gender, moreover, is also useful for capital as an instrument of labour by serving as a tool in controlling the rate of growth and development of the surplus-labour-producing population pushing and pulling women in and out of production and reproduction depending on the needs of capital. Cultural and discursive binaries are the outcome, at the level of ideas, of *material contradictions* in the social division of labour. They are the ideological translation of historically produced and therefore transformable social relations of exploitation into seemingly 'metaphysical' essences. However, without transformation of the material relations of production even 'post-binary' gender is not free from exploitation, but develops in relation to the need for capital to break down older, more rigid gendered divisions of labour to draw women into the workforce *en masse* as exploited producers of surplus-labour.

Rebranding capitalist ontology as feminist market freedom

The new '(post)humanist' ontologies are actually a metaphysics of the market. This is perhaps most strikingly apparent in the turn to object-oriented feminism, which transcodes the historical and social process of commodification – what Marx calls 'exchange-value' – into the essential and ontological basis of *Being* as such and, in doing so, represents exchange relations as a form of 'empowerment' for women. Similar to other feminisms that derive their understanding from (post)humanist ontologies, object-oriented feminism claims to break from the absorption of feminism into social 'constructionism', with its incessant focus on language and subjectivity, and to offer a more 'materialist' approach to feminism. Thus, Katherine Behar, in the Introduction to her edited collection *Object-Oriented Feminism* (2016), argues that feminism should be oriented around the understanding that 'the *impersonal* is political' in which 'the call for solidarity should be to rally around objects, not subjects' (2016: 7). This focus on 'objects, not subjects', Behar contends, 'promises a positive return to the 'real world' after a generation of feminist thought that has been accused of ascribing gender as a construct in language' (2016: 5).

What object-oriented feminism means by 'the real world', however, is what Behar and others call a 'flat ontology' – i.e. an ontology of 'objects in 'flat' or nonhierarchical arrangements' (2016: 10). This theory of materialism is drawn from object-oriented ontology's general assumption that the 'real world' is composed of an aleatory assemblage of objects, which are 'withdrawn' from each other and exceed any causal material relations, whether the dialectics of nature or the social relations of production. Thus, for example, object-oriented ontologist Graham Harman, in his essay 'The Road to Objects' (2011), claims that 'the real world is made up of individual objects that are withdrawn from all theoretical, practical, and even causal access' and that such objects always 'retain an unexhausted surplus deeper than our relation with' them (2011: 174). In this view, material reality is composed of objects that are unique and autonomous singularities. Moreover, as unique and autonomous singularities, object-oriented ontology claims that objects *ontologically* exceed any *material relations*. Harman claims that 'the failure of both theory and praxis to exhaust the things of the world', is not simply a limitation of human theory and practice, rather, it is an *ontological* limitation of reality: i.e. 'a limitation of relationality in general' and that 'relations … fail to [grasp] their relata' (2011: 174, 171).

In other words, according to object-oriented-ontology, the material world is composed of objects that ontologically exist as autonomous and irreducible singularities with no material relations of determination whatsoever, including labour relations and the social relations of production, and therefore they exceed any directed collective labour for social change. Rather than a more 'materialist' theory, object-oriented ontology is a ruling-class ideology – a commodity fetishism – that *disappears* the dialectical praxis of labour and the social relations of production into the free play of 'things' on the grounds that, as Harman puts it, 'every relation forms a new real object' (2011: 177). In the ruling-class 'logic' of object-oriented ontology all relations – including all humans and their production relations – are themselves objects such that the formation of new objects is a relation between objects, devoid of labour, and a relation is not a relation at all but a new object. This erases the material relations of production through which the 'unexhausted surplus' in objects is actually produced by the exhausted wage-labourer.

Behar (2016) claims that this kind of object-oriented theory 'stands to evolve feminist and postcolonial practices' because it 'extend[s] the concept of objectification and its ethical critique to the world of things' (2016: 8). What she regards as 'evolved' about object-oriented feminism is that rather than critique material relations in which people in general, and women in particular, are treated 'like objects', instead it proposes that all 'people are … objects *as such* from the outset' (2016: 8, emphasis added). For object-oriented feminism the basis of equality for all human and non-human 'others' is to regard all of reality to be composed of 'a pluralist population of objects, in which humans are objects no more privileged than any other' (2016: 5). According to this logic, if all are regarded as 'objects from the outset' no person or thing and no form of objecthood can be privileged over any others. Rather than arguing for transforming the social relations of production in which women are exploited and in which they are objectified and commodified, object-oriented feminism instead argues for 'equality' of all 'objects', human and non-human. At best this is a *formal* cultural equality of 'lifestyles', which is to say a cultural equality of 'styles' of consumption. For instance, while Behar references object-oriented feminism's claims to move beyond anthropocentrism and 'promote sympathies and camaraderie with non-human neighbors' (2016: 8), her main concern seems to be the 'exclusion' from feminism of 'sexual objects' and commodities, as well as visual imagery of sexual objectification and/or subjects who identify as 'sexual objects' – such as the 'Playboy bunnies' – on the grounds that all humans are 'objects from the outset' so no one form of objectification or object-status should be privileged over another.

Object-oriented feminism dehistoricises the 'commodification' of women and of sexuality and ideologically conceals its material basis in the *historical and social* development of commodity production and exchange relations and, ultimately, of modes of production founded on class and the exploitation of labour and production for private profit not collective need. Instead, it represents commodification in terms that translates capitalism into a law of nature. More specifically, in object-oriented thinking, the *commodification* – i.e. of humans, their labour, plants, animals, natural and manufactured objects, etc. – which is the social and historical effect of the capitalist mode of production, is *deconceptualised* and translated into a matter of 'objectification'. Then 'objectification' is understood as the status of being an object and as an ontological and elemental feature of all of material reality as such. By representing all of reality as ontologically composed by 'objects from the outset', object-oriented ontology abstracts 'objects' from any causal relations and disappears these causal relations into 'things' themselves. In the process of doing so, it ideologically transposes the material effects of what Marx calls the 'ensemble of social relations of production' in capitalism onto the ontological ground of 'Being' as such.

The commodification of women and of sexuality, however, is the historical and social effect of social relations of production founded on private ownership of the means of production, exploitation, and production for the profit of owners rather than the needs of workers. In her book *Myths of Male Dominance*, for example, Eleanor Burke Leacock (1981) demonstrates that the 'commodification of women' is neither the product of 'permutations of oppositions projected by the human mind', as in Hegel's dialectical idealism and more recent social constructionism, nor is it the product of universal ontological or existential conditions of life as such as in object-oriented feminism, rather, it is the effect of developments in the historical conditions and material relations of social production 'among people as they work under different constraints to maintain and reproduce themselves' (1981: 214). More specifically, the commodification of women in particular and of human life in general, is the effect and outgrowth of the general transformation of egalitarian societies based on collective production and use to class-based societies based on private property and commodity production and exchange. Through empirical studies of the transformation of dozens of egalitarian societies to private property relations and the relationship of the deterioration of women's social position to the rise of class and private property relations, Leacock demonstrates that,

> the process whereby exchange and specialization of labor beyond that by sex transformed goods (important for direct use) into commodities (important for exchange value) and concomitantly transformed relations among people from common production for cooperative use, to rivalry in production for accumulation and competitive exchange ... was decisive in the process through which egalitarian relations were undercut and virtually all women, along with increasing numbers of men, became themselves commodities. (1981: 216)

Gender and the commodification of women – of their bodies, sexuality, and of their labour – has a material and social history in the general development of social modes of production based on commodity production and exchange and the emergence of class relations in which social production is organised for the profit of *some* rather than the collective needs of all, i.e. in which some privately own and appropriate the products of social labour through exploitation.

Object-oriented feminism naturalises exchange relations and in doing so it conceals the necessary relationship of freedom of sexuality to the revolutionary project of freedom from exploitation and from the subordination of all social relations and conditions of existence to commodity relations (market relations) and production for profit. Instead, it substitutes for social transformation of capitalism the 'free play' of commodities and objects as a theory of emancipation for women. A telling example of object-oriented feminism's class-based politics is Behar's argument (2016) that object-oriented feminism 'takes [its] cue from OOO: it is a brand. As a brand, object-oriented ontology has leveraged a calculated posture of coolness to make waves among various communities' (2016: 6). Behar claims that, whereas 'the self- proclaimed radicality of OOO's discursive intervention was not matched by a radical politics ... OOF steps in, offering an alternative brand that is, following Haraway's vision, both a feminist practice and a multinational corporate strategy' (2016: 6). It is important to note that Behar reduces social theory and critique to a marketing strategy and market trend and is more concerned with the *exchange-value* of theory – its 'coolness' factor as a commodity – than with its *use-value* as a contribution to struggles for social transformation and the emancipation of women. This is a market feminism that represents 'multinational corporate strategies' and the subordination of all aspects of life to commodity production and exchange as a form of freedom and sexual 'empowerment' for women.

Object-oriented feminism equates freedom with 'market freedom', i.e. the freedom of exchange and the freedom to be exchanged. Instead of a theory for the material emancipation of women from exploitation and commodification, what object-oriented feminism offers is an ideological updating of liberal pluralism that, at its core, is a ruling-class theory of 'market equality'. This is market equality because, while it claims to advance the recognition of freedom, singularity, and individuality that has always been 'promised' by capitalism but in material reality is denied in capitalism, it accepts the equating of people and their labour with objects, including the objects that are the product of human labour. Yet, the equating of people and their labour with objects is enabled by historical and human social relations of commodity production and exchange in which the labour-power of workers is a commodity, like any other, to be bought and sold on the market for exploitation in production.

When object-oriented feminism claims that people are 'objects from the outset' on the grounds that all reality is composed of objects that exceed any relations, it conceals the *social and historical basis* of 'commodities' and 'commodity relations'. Objects – whether plants, animals, natural substances, or manufactured objects – become commodities only under specific historical and social relations of production in which use-values are produced for the purpose of their 'exchange-value' and 'exchange-value' is produced for profit. And, it is only under 'definite social relations of production' that 'labour-power is a commodity' like any other commodity on the market, 'which its possessor, the wage-worker, sells to the capitalist' (Marx, 1986b: 19). Moreover, workers sell their labour-power as commodities '*In order to live*' (1986b: 19, emphasis added). Workers, who own no commodity other than their labour-power, have no means under capitalism to live except to sell their life activity, that is, to 'sell themselves, and that by fractions' to capitalists, who privately own the means of social production (1986b: 20). Yet, far from being an eternal and natural ontological condition of Being as such 'labour-power was not always a *commodity* (merchandise)' (1986b: 19). The appearance of labour-power as a commodity on the market is not a natural, eternal, or ontological condition of Being as such, it is the product of historical and social relations of production in capitalism.

By naturalising the idea that humans and their social relations are 'objects from the outset', at most, object-oriented feminism takes the market logic of the ideology of exchange in capitalism in which the 'circulation or commodity exchange … is the very Eden of the innate rights of man' (Marx, 1976a: 280) and expands it into the value of all 'objects' whether human, including 'human others' or 'non-human neighbors'. Yet, ideology of exchange – i.e. the ideology of the market – is a ruling-class ideology that conceals that behind the so-called 'freedom' of the market, it is in the 'hidden abode of production' that the theft of workers' surplus-labour takes place, and when a worker brings 'their own hide to market' they have 'nothing else to expect but – a tanning' (1976a: 280). This is because exchange is *'the* [phenomenon] *of a process taking place behind it'* (Marx, 1986a: 186): that is, a process of exploitation in which, in the working day under capitalism, workers who do not own the means of production, spend part of the day producing the value in the form of commodities that is equivalent to their wages and means of subsistence (necessary-labour), and part of the day producing surplus-value which is appropriated by the owners for profit (surplus-value).

What is concealed by object-oriented feminism's celebration of a 'pluralist population' of objects is that behind the exchange relations of capitalism – behind objects and their exchange-value – is the theft of workers surplus-labour in production. While Behar in effect argues for the 'market equality' of the 'sexual object' or 'Bunny', her concept of 'freedom' has little to offer the vast majority of women in global capitalism who sell their labour-power as a commodity on the market and are exploited producers of surplus-value, including those who produce the global commodities that serve as the 'accoutrements' of sexual objects: from teenage girls who are the exploited wage-labour on cotton farms in Burkina Faso, to the girls and women who transform this cotton into cloth as the exploited wage-labour in India's textile mills, to those who cut and sew this cloth into lingerie as the exploited wage-labour in Sri Lankan garment factories subcontracted by Victoria's Secret (Simpson, 2011). By erasing the relationship of the oppression and exploitation of women to the social relations of production, this theory conceals that the producers of commodities, wage-labourers, are exploited and participates in mystifying the social and historical – and therefore collectively transformable – material relations in which women and girls have been drawn into the exploited waged workforces of global capitalism *en masse*. This is a theory for women who are part of a class that can revel in the pleasures of consumption and not a theory of emancipation for the majority of women in global capitalism who are exploited producers.

Against market feminism: the dialectics of red feminism

The 'return' to 'matter' in (post)humanist feminist ontologies is by and large a response, in *capitalist cultural* theory, to the *crisis* of capitalism. The so-called 'new material turn' in feminism is a new means of culturalising and spiritualising neoliberal capital in the wake of its global economic crisis. It is important to note that the 'economic' – and, therefore, 'matter' – is not only the focus of dialectical materialism it is also the focus of *capitalist* theory: it is a privileged category in neoliberal theory with its priority of economic reformism to stave off a crisis of profitability. Neoliberal theory, in its various forms, is only interested in economic and cultural reforms to remove the fetters *not* to human freedom, including freedom for women, but to *profit for capital*. The new (post)humanist ontologies are a *culturalising* of neoliberal economic theories; they contribute to producing a cultural intelligibility that ideologically updates the global workforces to adjust workers to new imperatives for profit in the wake of crisis. They do so by ontologising the exchange relations of capitalism as well as the economic crisis of profitability in capitalism as the metaphysical ground of objective reality as such.

'Life', in new materialist feminism, is *dehistoricised*. It is abstracted from historically produced social relations and structures of production and reproduction and is posited as a transhistorical, transsocial, metaphysical force. According to this logic, 'social totality' – the 'many determinations and relations' which dialectically constitute the social precisely in the sense that some elements *do* determine others (Marx, 1986a: 37) – are translated into relations without determination and thus beyond explanation or directed collective social change. This is the ideology of exchange in which:

> individuals appear to be independent ... appear to collide with each other freely, and to exchange with each other in this freedom; but they appear independently only to those who abstract from the *conditions*, the *conditions of existence*, in which those individuals come into contact with each other and these in turn ... appear, though produced by society, as it were, as *natural conditions*. (Marx, 1986a: 100)

In this view, social contradictions, inequalities, and differences in *historical* conditions of life that are the result of social relations of exploitation – of the class contradictions and a crisis of profitability in the mode of production founded on production for profit not needs – are ideologically, but *not materially*, dissolved, into the natural, the elemental, and the eternal.

While non-dialectical materialist feminisms represent themselves as unleashing the 'differences within' material reality, rather than what they contend is the exclusionary and totalising logic of class, the new (post)humanist ontologies upon which they are based represent capitalism as an invisible law of nature and translate violence and discrimination against the 'other' into an effect of a transhistorical irreducible ontology. (Post)humanist ontologies formally distance themselves from both the 'subjectivism' and 'constructivism' of poststructuralism, as Jaspir Puar does in her argument that intersectional theory has reached a 'poststructuralist fatigue' and needs to be updated with assemblage theory (2013: 387). Yet, this merely raises the logic of poststructuralism – and its reduction of material contradictions of gender, sexuality, and difference to 'irreducible signifiers' – to a new metaphysical level of abstraction by advocating the 'ontological irreducibility' of social contradictions (2013: 386).

Echoing Kimberlé Crenshaw's intersectionalist argument that 'discrimination' is like an 'accident [that] happens at an intersection' which 'can be caused by cars traveling from any number of directions and, sometimes, from all of them' (1989: 149), Puar contends that 'race, gender, sexuality are ... events, actions, and encounters, between bodies' in ontologically irreducible assemblages (Puar, 2013: 382). In the figure of assemblages, differences are collapsed into singularities without historical determination and material inequalities are the effect not of exploitation but of 'accident', 'indeterminacy', and 'unpredictability'. The systemic and structural violence against the other in capitalism is explained away as astructural, acausal, accidental. In such a view, material contradictions of gender, sexuality, race, and class are collapsed into a post-dialectical 'flat ontology' in which all are equally complicit in the inequalities generated within and beyond society, regardless of one's position in the global division of labour and social relations of production.

At *best* this logic culturally and ideologically updates, in a new (post) humanist rhetoric, a liberal feminist agenda of 'market freedoms' with its focus on equalising what Max Weber called 'life chances on the market' (2013: 91) by elimination of gender barriers in culture and the workplace that inhibit women's 'movement' or 'free flow' on the market and get in the way of women selling their labour-power for a wage or becoming managers on behalf of capital. Rather than working to eradicate *exploitation*, (post)humanist feminisms focus instead on 'discrimination' as an irreducible 'event' and, therefore, as an end in itself. However, discrimination cannot be ended *in itself* – that is, it cannot be ended *immanently* – *within* social relations of production based on exploitation and production for profit. It can be ended only from its *outside* by ending exploitation. Discrimination cannot be resolved immanently within capitalism because the social relations of production based on private ownership of the means of production and the theft of workers' surplus-labour for profit have become fetters to human freedom in general and fetters to the freedom of women in particular. Freedom for women comes not by *increasing* their 'life chances on the market' such as raising hourly wages but by ending wages – that is, ending wage-labour and capital relations – in which they are exploited as collective producers of surplus-labour. Gender discrimination is not the *root* cause of the situation in which women find themselves globally, rather, *exploitation* is. Gender discrimination is part of women's concrete reality because of the social relations of production founded on exploitation. Gender, as Delia Aguilar has argued, is a 'class-bound' issue with a dialectical relation to wage-labour and capital relations founded in the extraction of 'surplus-labour' (2004: 413). This is why the integration of women into the global waged workforces of capitalism – and the cultural and 'post-binary' adjustments to gender and sexuality that have been made within capitalism to accommodate this shift – have not emancipated women and brought about freedom from discrimination and inequality but, as a result of exploitation, have instead resulted in what Goretti Horgan, among others, calls the 'race to the bottom upon which global capitalism is founded' (2001).

Instead of providing means to understand, dialectically, the material contradictions in which women are situated today, (post)humanist feminisms instead assert that material reality itself is ontologically composed by crisis. On these terms the crisis of capitalism and the forced adjustment of the lives of millions of women to the dictates of production for profit are explained as the effect of an ontological condition of life as such or, as Lauren Berlant claims: 'we are all contingent beings, and life proceeds without guarantees' (2012: 166). Along similar lines Claire Colebrook claims, 'what is absolute is contingency' (2014: 74). Crises that have historical and social causes in the material contradictions of capitalism – in the declining rate of profit and the forcible extraction of social wealth from workers to stave off these declines – are dehistoricised and, to use Colebrook's language, are rendered as the 'infinite unfolded' or 'a different expression of a [infinite] whole that differs with each of its events of being expressed' (2014: 75). Or, in Braidotti's terms it is a vital life force that is unpredictable and precarious: 'Life', Braidotti argues, 'can be a threatening force, as well as a generative one' (2013: 112). Social crisis and contradiction, in this view, are ontological conditions of life – of the capricious life of zoe – as such. They are regarded as expressions of life's *eternal* unpredictability and 'infinite possibilities' (2013: 107). In the face of crisis, Braidotti argues that what we need is to embrace the 'exuberance of zoe' and privilege the affirmation of 'life' over the so-called 'thanatopolitics' or 'negativity' of dialectical materialist critique (2013: 107).

This offers a *class-based* feminism which advances the interests of a small class-fraction of women who have risen in the ranks of global capitalism and gained a greater share of the surplus-value produced by the majority and, therefore, see no need for developing a critique of relations of exploitation that can serve as a guide to the struggle for social transformation to emancipate women. The class logic of non-dialectical materialism is further evident in

Braidotti's concept of 'sustainable transformation'. What she means by a 'sustainable transformation' is not actually social transformation but endurance of and a positive affect within capitalism. More specifically, Braidotti argues that a sustainable ethics begins with a concept of 'a sustainable self that aims at endurance' (2010: 184). 'Endurance', she contends, 'means putting up with hardship and physical pain' (2010: 184). 'Sustainability', she continues, 'has to do with how much a subject can take. Ethics can be understood as how much bodies are capable of' (2010: 188). Braidotti argues, that 'For an ethics of sustainability, the expression of positive affects is what causes the subject to endure. Expression of positive affects is like a long-lasting source of energy at the affective core of subjectivity' (2010: 186). 'Survival', 'endurance', and 'putting up with hardship and physical pain', constant change, etc. are represented by Braidotti as forms of 'radical immanence' and the creation of another life, another world within and at the same time beyond capitalism. This is a politics which marginalises the necessity of collective transformation of the 'ensemble of social relations of production' and focuses on changing the *felt experience* and *affect* of individual women within capitalism in crisis. 'A radically immanent intensive body', Braidotti argues, is 'a portion of ... forces ... that is stable enough to sustain and undergo constant ... fluxes of transformation' (2010: 188).

However, this glosses over the historical and material relations in which the condition of survival to the next working day for increasing numbers of women around the world depends upon their ability to sell their labour-power to capital for a wage and thus become part of the logic of the capitalist working day. In doing so, new materialism dispenses with the necessity to critique and work to transform the material relations in which women are exploited. By arguing *against* the necessity of transforming material relations of exploitation and, at the same time, arguing for the 'endurance of pain and hardship' and 'expressing positive affect' within capitalism, monist feminism is, in effect, arguing for increasing the endurance of women workers and, therefore, increasing their productivity, within increased rates of exploitation in the existing relations of production. This is an austerity feminism that preaches on behalf of capital to the exploited women of the global workforces to get by on less, endure more, survive, and maintain a positive attitude under conditions of increased exploitation instead of working to struggle for social critique and transformation. In new materialism, conditions of dire need that are the effect of the structural crisis of capitalism are then presented as positions of 'creative radical alterity': 'precarious existence is not solely a negative phenomenon' because 'it gives space to women's creativity' (Fantone, 2007: 17). Such theories ideologically translate increased exploitation and the exigencies of austerity and capitalism in crisis into a new 'spiritual sublime'. In other words, the 'anti-dialectics' of (post)humanist feminism conceives of the 'reactivation' of feminism in terms of the neoliberal logic of irreducible singularities and translates living within the ruins of capitalism in crisis into an ontological and metaphysical condition of life as such at a moment when women have been pulled in and out of the workforces of capitalism as exploited producers to bolster the rate of profit.

In contrast to (post)humanist feminisms that return to 'matter' in order to ontologise capitalism, the Marxist-Feminist interest in 'material reality' and in the 'economic' is not to reify capitalism as a metaphysical basis of Being, but to abolish economic exploitation; to bring about freedom for women through freedom from exploitation for all. What is needed in feminism in the twenty-first century is critique that grasps that capitalism at root requires the exploitation of the surplus-labour of workers in production as the source of profit and that 'gender', 'sexuality', and 'race' as material relations, and sites of struggle and social transformation are not autonomous from the capitalist mode of production and its global division of labour and property relations. What is needed is a red feminism that advances the understanding that freedom for all women, not just privileges for some, has a necessary dialectical and material relation to freedom from class relations, exploitation, imperialism, and the use of gender, sexuality, and cultural differences by global capital as 'instruments of labour' to raise or lower the rate of exploitation of the global workforces. What is necessary more than ever today is a red feminism that advances a labour theory of gender, sexuality, and cultural difference rooted in Marx's labour theory of value and its dialectical critique of global capitalism.

Note

1 Portions of this essay have been excerpted and revised from: Jennifer Cotter, 'Feminismus, "Neuer Materialismus" und die Verabschiedung der Dialektik', ('Feminism, "New Materialism", and the Rejection of Dialectics') translated into German by Thomas Laugstien, *Das Argument* 325(60): 89–97.

References

Aguilar, D., 2004. 'Questionable Claims: Colonialism Redux, Feminist Style' in Aguilar, D., Lacsamana, A. (Eds.), *Women and Globalization*. Humanity Books, New York, 404–421.

Barad, K., 2003. 'Posthumanist Performativity: Toward an Understanding of How Matter Comes to Matter'. *Signs: Journal of Women in Culture and Society* 28(3): 801–832.

Behar, K. (Ed.), 2016. *Object-Oriented Feminism*. University of Minnesota Press, Minneapolis, MN.

Bennett, J., 2010. *Vibrant Matter: A Political Ecology of Things*. Duke University Press, Durham, NC.

Berlant, L., 2012. 'Post One' in 'Precarity Talk: A Virtual Roundtable Discussion with Lauren Berlant, Judith Butler, et al.'. *TDR: The Drama Review* 56(4): 163–177.

Braidotti, R., 2010. 'The Politics of Life as Bios/Zoe' in Smelik, A., Lykke, N. (Eds.), *Bits of Life: Feminism at the Intersections of Media, Bioscience, and Technology*. University of Washington Press, Seattle, WA, 177–192.

Braidotti, R., 2013. *The Posthuman*. Polity, Cambridge.

Colebrook, C., 2014. 'Disaster Feminism' in Blaagaard, B., van der Tuin, I. (Eds.), *The Subject of Rosi Braidotti: Politics and Concepts*. Bloomsbury, London, 72–77.

Coole, D., Frost, S. (Eds.), 2010. *New Materialisms: Ontology, Agency, and Politics*. Duke University Press, Durham, NC.

Cooper, M., 2008. *Life as Surplus*. University of Washington Press, Seattle, WA.

Crenshaw, K., 1989. 'Demarginalizing the Intersection of Race and Sex: A Black Feminist Critique of Antidiscrimination Doctrine, Feminist Theory and Antiracist Politics' in *The University of Chicago Legal Forum* 139. University of Chicago Press, Chicago, IL, 139–167.

Deleuze, G., Guattari, F., 1987. *A Thousand Plateaus: Capitalism and Schizophrenia*. Translated by Brian Massumi. University of Minnesota Press, Minneapolis, MN.

Dolphijn, R., van der Tuin, I., 2012. *New Materialism: Interviews and Cartographies*. Open Humanities Press, Ann Arbor, MI.

Ebert, T., 2015. 'Epilogue: Gender after Class' in Mojab, S. (Ed.), *Marxism and Feminism*. Zed Books, London, 347–366.

Ebert, T., 2016. 'The Poverty of the (Post) Humanities'. *Knowledge Cultures* 4(6): 25–54.

Fantone, L., 2007. 'Precarious Changes: Gender and Generational Politics in Contemporary Italy'. *Feminist Review* 87: 5–20.

Frost, S., 2011. 'The Implications of the New Materialisms for Feminist Epistemology' in Grasswick, H. (Ed.), *Feminist Epistemology and Philosophy of Science*. Springer, Dordrecht, 69–83.

Grosz, E., 2004. *The Nick of Time: Politics, Evolution and The Untimely*. Duke University Press, Durham, NC.

Grosz, E., 2017. *The Incorporeal: Ontology, Ethics, and the Limits of Materialism*. New York: Columbia University Press.

Harman, G., 2011. 'The Road to Objects'. *Continent* 3(1): 171–179.

Hill, R., 2008. 'Interval, Sexual Difference: Luce Irigaray and Henri Bergson'. *Hypatia* 23(1): 119–131.

Horgan, G., 2001. 'How Does Globalisation Affect Women?' *International Socialism* 92. http://pubs.socialistreviewindex.org.uk/isj92/horgan.htm. Accessed: 1 May 2012.

Latour, B., 2004. 'From Realpolitik to Dingpolitik: Or How to Make Things Public' in Latour, B., Weibel, P. (Eds.), *Making Things Public: Atmospheres of Democracy*. ZKM Center for Art and Media, Karlsruhe, Germany. Exhibition Catalog.

Leacock, E.B., 1981. *Myths of Male Dominance: Collected Articles on Women Cross-Culturally*. Monthly Review Press, New York and London.

Marx, K., 1976a. *Capital*. Vol. 1. Translated by Ben Fowkes. Penguin, New York.

Marx, K., 1976b. 'Theses on Feuerbach' in Marx, K., Engels, F., *The German Ideology*. Progress Publishers, Moscow, 615–617.

Marx, K., 1986a. *Economic Manuscripts of 1857–58. Marx–Engels Collected Works*. Vol. 28. International Publishers, New York.

Marx, K., 1986b. *Wage-Labour and Capital*. Edited by Frederick Engels. International Publishers, New York.

Marx, K., Engels, F., 1976. *Manifesto of the Communist Party. Marx–Engels Collected Works*. Vol. 6. International Publishers, New York, 477–519.

Puar, J., 2013. 'I Would Rather Be a Cyborg than a Goddess: Intersectionality, Assemblage, and Affective Politics'. *Meritum* 8(2): 371–390.

Rose, N., 2016. *The Politics of Life Itself*. Princeton University Press, Princeton, NJ.

Simpson, C., 2011. 'Child Labor Used in Victoria's Secret "Fair Trade" Products'. *Bloomberg News, Here and Now*, 15 December.

Torrant, J., 2016. 'Mind over Matter and Other Posthumanist Feminist Tales' in Cotter, J., DeFazio, K., Faivre, R., Sahay, A., Torrant. J.P., Tumino, S., Wilkie, R. (Eds.), *Human, All Too (Post)Human: The Humanities after Humanism*. Lexington Books, Lanham, MD, 95–114.

Weber, M., 2013. 'Class, Status, Party', in Lemert, C. (Ed.), *Social Theory: The Multicultural, Global and Classic Readings*. 5th edition. Westview Press, Boulder, CO, 90–97.

6 | THE BYZANTINE EUNUCH

Pre-capitalist gender category, 'tributary' modal contradiction, and a test for materialist feminism

Jules Gleeson

The gender position of eunuchs in the Byzantine Empire (and elsewhere) presents a challenge to existing schools of Marxist-Feminist history. At present, Marxist feminism is largely attempting to depart from 'dual systems' approaches to understanding patriarchy. What is lacking from these efforts is an appreciation of the complexity of pre-capitalist gender relations, and how these variations were entwined with the modal systems found prior to modernity. Pre-modern economic modes placed varied demands on the societies which sustained them, and were accompanied by a range of state formations – gender relations and household structure were responsively arranged to these demands, and must be understood for us to appreciate the full history of class societies.

As a medievalist, my contribution to this collection (and field) is from a member of a minority. As such, I'll begin by re-introducing some more familiar territory for Marxist feminists, before addressing the eunuchs as a particular feature of Byzantine gender relations (with particular reference to disputes *within* Marxist scholarship around the mooted 'tributary mode', and its distinctive imperial state). This essay aims to illuminate how each of these topics can benefit from integration with the other. Gender history of pre-modern eras can benefit from Marxist feminism, and considering pre-modern gender relations will certainly be necessary to resolve current debates over the 'patriarchy question'. If there is to be a 'unitary theory' of capitalist gender relations, pre-capitalist gender relations must be understood in their own terms, rather than with scholarly placeholders. Eunuchs enjoyed a contradictory position as subjects within the tributary mode, and as participants in the pre-capitalist state, which there have only been limited efforts to grasp. Marxist feminism at once provides a means to account for this complexity, and will fall short of its broader aims should it fail to.

If we are to succeed in meaningfully twinning gender liberation struggles, and the drive to surpass our current mode of production, the divisive relations (household and state) of any historical era can not be treated as truly bygone.

The systems debate: Arruzza's 'three theses' on gender and capitalism

In 2014, Cinzia Arruzza's 'Remarks on Gender' surveyed Marxist-Feminist literature to date (Arruzza, 2014). 'Remarks on Gender' used an exegetical style to tackle the still vexed question of 'patriarchy' (and whether Marxist feminists ought even speak of one existing today, if ever). Arruzza taxonomised previously existing Marxist scholarship on the 'patriarchy question' as divisible between three schools:

- *Dual (or Triple) Systems Theory.* Here, patriarchy and capitalism operate as historically interconnected systems, with dual system thinkers often proposing economic class existing alongside gender as a *'sex class'*. Both capitalism and patriarchy (and white supremacy, in many more recent accounts) serve as *'systems of oppression'*. Patriarchy predates capitalism and its logic has come into historical relationship, or entwinement, or consubstantiality, with capitalism. This school of thought has been advanced most famously by Christine Delphy (1980), Heidi Hartmann (1979), and Sylvia Walby (1990). Many variations of this position have been advanced, with structuralism's treatment of kinship and Lacan's theorisation of patriarchy and theorisation often drawn from as methodological troves offering external insights. For the most part, however, this strain of materialist feminism is based on Beauvoirean existentialism, focusing phenomenologically on gender as the relation of women/men as Other/Self.
- *Indifferent Capital.* This school asserts that capitalism has displaced patriarchy and interacts opportunistically with *race and gender*. Capital enjoys contingent use of gendered oppression, while pursuing its only intrinsic need: extraction of surplus value. This stance has been expressed more or less explicitly by many Marxist theorists, but was argued most clearly by the late Ellen Meiksins Wood (2015). In this view, patriarchy remains as a residual, rather than conditional feature of capital's dominance through coercion into the market, including the workplace. There is no *logical* basis within capitalism for gendered oppression, although it inherits and ideologically *naturalises* the hierarchies (racial and gender) it inherited. In this respect, capital's domination has in fact *opened* horizons for overcoming once sturdier patriarchal norms. Sexism and racism are historical features, not invariant pre-requisites for capital's intergenerational survival. Gender here appears as expedient and instrumental for the purposes of capital, historically rather than logically demanded by the system of capital.
- *Unitary Theory.* Arruzza's own position, this heavily informed by the work of Lise Vogel in her 1983 monograph *Marxism and the Oppression of Woman*, and subsequent work done to elaborate on the concept of *social reproduction*.[1] Unitary theorists hold there is no longer an autonomous *system* of patriarchy 'in capitalist countries' (Arruzza's words), even if gendered relations continue to pervade interpersonal interactions. Capitalism is a social order which extends beyond economic laws, and includes gender. Social reproduction of society (and its workforces) involves gender in a way that ensures the intergenerational reappearance of gender norms,

including (and requiring) the oppression of women. For as long as capitalist economies remain fuelled by labour power, the accompanying economic relations will require and direct women's oppression.

Although this goes largely unstated, this debate rests a lot on what form patriarchy (or patriarchal relations) took prior to capitalism. Implicitly, *each one of these views* seems to presuppose a pre-modern 'patriarchy', which either survived the development of capitalism as an 'autonomous' system (dual systems), or did not (unitary and indifferent). Variations on the '*Dual Systems*' thesis claim that patriarchy survived into capitalism as an autonomous system, whereas both the *indifferent* or *unitary views* of capital claim patriarchy-as-system was dissolved, subsumed, or otherwise exists only in a looser, non-autonomous form. In these discussions, there has been limited engagement in existing scholarship with the particular details of what a pre-capitalist patriarchal system looked like. Pre-capitalist societies are vaguely bracketed as 'agrarian' by 'Remarks on Gender', without further concrete division, or investigation. This elides considerable scholarly debate around relations in both modal or state formations, and gender relations, which prevailed in pre-capitalist class societies. It also seems to disregard non-class societies altogether, while occluding significant variations within pre-modern economies. (Whereas the Byzantine Empire strictly restricted commercial activity, for instance, its economy functioned quite differently from the rest of what would come to be known as 'Europe' or Anatolia, due to its centralised minting, tied up with continual operations of the imperial fisc.)

Arruzza herself (who when not writing Marxist feminism or organising the International Women's Strike, is a professional researcher of Platonism) is not to be blamed for this shared failing of the material she summarises.[2] Instead, it originates in the bulk of scholarship on the '*patriarchy question*', which was surely intended to address the circumstances which women faced today (or in the later twentieth century). The focus of these thinkers was on gender as a historical relationship which exists in the face of capital, in light of the capitalist context they worked against. While it is appropriate for political thinkers to confront the most pressing issues and strategic questions of the day, this will not suffice for a satisfying historical account. Pre-capitalist (or 'Tributary Mode') class economies will have to be examined for the fruitful materialist theorisation of gender as a historical particularity to continue.

In recent years, the existence of pre-modern societies without pervasively dyadic gender identification has been emphasised by postcolonial and decolonial activists and scholars. Marxist-Feminist theory can mutually benefit through theoretically including apparently non-dyadic gender forms, which at present seem to rarely appear in this field's work. At present, too much of Marxist-Feminist research literature risks establishing a normative account of gender, with the inevitable queer conflicts which arise in the face of such schematics thought through only post hoc (at best). A good corrective of this can begin with a concrete examination of the Byzantine eunuch.

Introducing Byzantine eunuchs

'The Byzantine Empire' is a term of convenience used by historians to discuss the Roman Empire between the re-founding of Constantinople by Constantine, and its eventual conquest by the Ottoman Empire almost ten centuries later.[3]

Other than during a brief interregnum of Western occupation between 1204 and 1261, the Byzantine state remained centred around Constantinople, easily one of the largest capitals across Eurasia. Eunuchs were a feature of imperial life throughout this history, particularly concentrated in positions reserved exclusively for them in the higher tiers of state administration. In a similar capacity (although in a 'racialised' fashion not yet present in the Byzantine Empire), courtly eunuchs later continued to serve the imperial court under the Ottoman Empire after their eventual conquest of Constantinople.

'Eunuch' (Greek: ὁ εὐνοῦχος, notably a masculine noun) was something of an umbrella term, most famously referring to Romans/Byzantines who had experienced a range of physically emasculating procedures (usually as boys). Procedures ranged from total excision of the male genitals, to (rarely, during the Byzantine period) the mere severing of the vas deferens. Castration itself was formally banned repeatedly under Roman Law, but continued as a *de facto* commonplace in the Empire's fringe territories. The procedure was largely performed on pre-pubescent boys, commissioned by slave traders or aspirational parents (adult castrations were very rare after Late Antiquity, with autocastration having been prohibited by the Early Church (see Hanson, 1966)).

The majority of eunuchs appear to have been emasculated as children. Both slave-traded eunuchs and the children of aspirational parents tended to originate in the imperial provinces, or beyond.[4] Less known (and in an indeterminate proportion of cases) the term also covered those 'born eunuchs' (Kuefler, 2001, 19): infants born with ambiguous genitals, who contemporary medicine would identify as those with intersex conditions.[5] It is impossible to estimate what proportion of eunuchs mentioned in our surviving sources were 'born', as opposed to those castrated: this is certainly not a topic on which historiographical authors were forthcoming with detailed speculation. Whatever the exact demographic composition, eunuchs as they appear in remaining sources are distinguished by liminality, and distinction within manhood. According to accounts by the Byzantines, eunuchs had distinctive appearances on both a physiological and a sartorial level (including lack of beards, tendency to be slender and tall, to specific courtly attire and attributed gendered mannerisms).[6] Eunuchs were often likened to angels (Hatzaki, 2009).

Existing scholarship on eunuchs: from telltale 'Oriental' figures, to gender construction

Western Byzantine scholarship until the mid-twentieth century was dominated by Orientalising tropes, which in this instance presented the Byzantine Empire as torn or in tension between the essential cultural forces of the Hellenic and the Oriental (given their heritage from the Classical era existing against theocratic dogmatic despotism). In this view, eunuchs were considered a telltale feature of the Byzantine Empire's 'Oriental' character by the Empire's earlier historians. To Enlightenment historians (most notoriously Edward Gibbon, who preferred an equally idealised vision of the rugged militarism of the West and Islamic East), the continued presence of eunuchs into the Ottoman Empire, and their parallel appearance in the imperial courts of China, made this something of an 'open-and-shut' case in terms of the Byzantine Empire being partially 'Oriental'. Even in scholarship from the earlier twentieth century, eunuchs could be portrayed in authoritative works as disfigured troublemakers, as this quote from Charles Diehl (1923: 756–766) shows:

> In this court full of eunuchs, women, and idle high dignitaries, there were intrigues incessantly and everywhere, alike in the Gynaceum, the barracks of the guards, and the Emperor's antechambers; every man fought for himself and sought to overthrow the reigning favourite, and any means were good, flattery or calumny, bribery or assassination. In dark corners was prepared the fall of the minister in power, nay even the fall of the Emperor himself.[7]

This attitude changed markedly in the second half of the twentieth century, when eunuchs were brought into more 'scientific' view, and unexamined reference to 'the Orient' came to be problematised by scholarship following Edward Said. Historically rigorous approaches to Byzantine eunuchs began in earnest with French scholar, Rodolphe Guilland, who in an array of papers in *Revue des études byzantines* meticulously examined evidence in surviving court records and imperial protocols for imperial courtly roles and other eunuch-reserved positions (Guilland, 1943, 1944, 1955; summarised and explored: Sidéris, 2003).

The prevalence of eunuchs was further historically investigated in Alexander Kazhdan and Michael McCormick's classic essay, 'The Social World of the Byzantine Court' (Kazhdan and McCormick, 1997). This essay included a statistical analysis of the prevalence of eunuch courtiers, showing that their numbers diminished with the rise of the Komnenoi dynasty (which nepotistically granted full-bodied males from their own lineage, and those in marriage alliances with them, choice administrative positions).

In the later twentieth and early twenty-first centuries, Shaun Tougher spent the better part of his career attempting a comprehensive working through of primary sources identifying eunuchs (Tougher, 1999, 2002, 2004a, 2004b,

2008, 2010, 2013, 2013, 2015). Finally, on the political level, the work of Judith Herrin on Byzantine empresses has demonstrated how those who secured power relied on eunuch courtiers to solidify their often tenuous position (Herrin, 2001, 2015; James, 2001).

There has been rather less theoretical work exploring and explaining how eunuchs were included in Byzantine society's gender relations, an upshot of the 'post-positivist' bent which shapes Byzantine studies more generally. In recent decades, however, theoretical accounts of Byzantine eunuchs have greatly improved, and begun to draw from cultural theory: Kathryn Ringrose's research considers eunuchs as an instance of 'gender construction', and as 'cultural mediators' (2003 and 1995). In Ringrose's account, eunuchs serve as a discrete gender category, relationally positioned as compared to Byzantine aristocratic men and women. Ringrose theorises eunuchs as 'socialised' into a gender via castration, attire, mannerisms, etc., resulting in them appearing as a distinct gender position. This view places eunuchs as part of social construction, in a relational view of eunuchs as defined by their place within the overall whole of Byzantine gender relations. Ringrose's account is compelling, if lacking both in historical materialist approaches (as outlined above), or the Butlerian 'performative' conception of gender.

Matthew Kuefler's *The Manly Eunuch* (2001) serves as a rare example of a fully theoretically informed conceptualisation of eunuchs as historical figures. While this monograph concerns the post-Roman West eunuchs, rather than the Byzantine Empire, it is still worth mentioning here given the rich methodological blend it deploys. Kuefler introduces gender as a dialectic, deploying Butler's performativity theory to present gender not as a set of fixed constructs or categories, but rather a field of continual contestation. Kuefler is closely informed by the materialist conception of gender elaborated by Raewyn Connell, who juxtaposed 'hegemonic' and 'insurgent' masculinities, in an attempt to provide a basis for the *multiplicities* always present in manhood's formation. Especially relevant for research into eunuchs, Connell's schema argues masculinity defines itself against effeminacy. In this view, it's easy to see that eunuchs could play an unsettling role (for male authors of Roman history), given their advanced social standing and ambiguous embodiment.

Eunuchs and class society

Eunuchs left us no confirmed material written by them first hand, meaning that the bulk of surviving written information about them was written by (full-bodied) males. Despite this 'speechless' quality, historical reconstructions of eunuchs in the Byzantine Empire have been possible given the prominent role they played in this literature society. Male authors, particularly in the empire's metropole, Constantinople, would have encountered eunuchs on an everyday basis, with their condition perhaps not unremarkable, but by no means exceptional. From this material, as well as architectural and art historical sources, we can determine the role of eunuchs in society requires examination of Byzantine society as a whole, and from this process of *salvage* we can draw conclusions about the developments within 'Byzantine patriarchy', if indeed such a term has much explanatory power. One approach is that of Charis Messis (2014), who has recently used a mixture of literary and historiographical sources to discern how eunuchs appear in the imagination of the Byzantines. Messis's gender historical approach uses the prevalence of male-written sources to focus on the eunuch as historical figure, rather than historical subject. A similar approach was taken by art historian Myrto Hatzaki, whose study of Byzantine beauty included a consideration of the eunuchs' perspective. From this view, eunuchs appear twinned with angels as a key instance of effeminated male liminality (Hatzaki, 2009: 86–115).[8]

Here, primarily for reasons of space and holding the attention of historical materialists, we will take a more institutional view. The privileged position enjoyed by eunuchs with relation to the Byzantine state ensured them an elevated role in the economic mode that prevailed across the imperial territories, just as their formal inability to found conventional patriarchal households ensured they had a more precarious (and unclear) relation to the core economic unit of this gender-divided class society.

Eunuchs and 'patriarchy' as a legal principle

While themselves existing in an unclear gendered state (at least for contemporary analysts), eunuchs were clearly excluded from a key dyadic convention: eunuchs were forbidden from marriage by Roman law (long predating the Empire's Byzantine phase), and given the formal centrality of biological reproduction in that institution, would have been a poor fit even without this legal restriction. They were, however, permitted to adopt following the reforms of Leo III to civil law in the 720s (in practice, adoption could include adult 'sons').

This left eunuchs males in grammatical terms, but rarely patriarchs in legal ones: their social and civic life did not include the normative opportunities to head a family that were available to lay men (including lower-ranking clergy). Eunuchs were in this respect non-viable heads of households in the conventional sense of the word, but still not altogether without opportunities for 'vertical' kinship. This is likely to have played some role in their formally granted advantages within the Byzantine state and its administration, which we will now briefly introduce.

Historical materialism and Byzantine history

In recent years, a range of historical materialist scholarship has provided accounts of Byzantine economic relations, and state. I will provide a brief overview of recent debates here.[9]

Marxist historical research has done much to improve on the classic work of Yugoslavian Byzantinist George Ostrogorsky, whose ambitious history of the Byzantine state was for many years one of the field's most popular works (Ostrogorsky, 1940/1951). This great work is now dated in various ways (its claims concerning the military-administrative reforms the Byzantine Empire underwent are accepted by no contemporary Byzantinists, and its account of Arab–Byzantine warfare especially features some strikingly dated Orientalism). Until the twenty-first century, however, the lack of introductory overviews of the Byzantine Empire written by professional historians ensured that this monograph was for many decades the closest the field had to a 'textbook'.

In the 1980s, Alan Harvey defended a conception of the Byzantine Empire as 'feudal'. As Harvey defined it, this was understood in terms of the peasantry being the economic base of the Byzantine 'social formation'. Although his Marxism remained a minority methodology among economic historians of the Byzantine Empire, Harvey was more broadly convincingly in arguing the case for economic expansion (from population size to surplus expansion) which began in the tenth century (Harvey, 1989). This argument has come to be accepted by the field's majority of non-Marxist scholars.

By the early 1990s (a uniquely unpromising juncture for Marxist theoretical research), John Haldon sought to replace the existing Marxist conception of pre-capitalist class societies in *The State and the Tributary Mode of Production* (1993).[10] Having previously defended (along with Harvey) a view of the Byzantine Empire as 'feudal' (Haldon 1985, 1989), Haldon's new formulation of the 'tributary mode' sought to retain the systemic explanation of Marxism, in new terms. A tributary mode economy as defined by Haldon is distinctive in two key ways: firstly that rents and taxes become modally undifferentiated, in a context where extraction of surplus is central to economic activity. Secondly, the state is obliged to fulfil the role of transcendent actor. Through comparative analysis Haldon considers instances where various pre-modern states (and periods of the Byzantine Empire) had achieved this more or less effectively.

In the 2000s, social historians Jairus Banaji (2007, 2010, 2015) and Peter Sarris (2006, 2009, 2010) researched the Late Antique and early Byzantine period (third–tenth centuries).[11] Banaji's research is particularly insightful concerning the varied means used by agrarian estate holders to maximise their exploitation, and has been particularly insightful in outlining how Byzantine monetisation allowed for hiring waged agricultural labourers. Sarris's research has often focused on the papyri documents left by the early Byzantine Empire's powerhouse economy in Egypt, and shares with Banaji a presentation of a proto 'proletariat' as an under-acknowledged but prominent feature of Byzantine economic relations. Sarris emphasises the formal continuity which existed between the ancient estate, and the Byzantine great estate until at least the tenth century.

More recently, Jairus Banaji has challenged John Haldon's definition of the tributary mode, preferring a more minimal conception to what he sees as the risk of formalism implicit in centring surplus extraction. Whereas Haldon follows from a methodological tradition that owes more to the aftermath of Western structuralism, Banaji sees the Byzantine Empire as an example of the differentiated labour deployment, which should be investigated through a theoretical framework continually responsive to empirical investigation. Banaji charges Haldon with lapsing into formalism, and overlooking the 'laws of motion' which Marx considered to govern each era. The subsequent debate between Banaji and Haldon is illuminating concerning both the nature and function of the Byzantine state and the motivation behind modal analysis itself.[12]

This brief survey has outlined a considerable body of Marxist history which surveys various facets of the Byzantine Empire. Regrettably, none of these figures have written a great deal on gender (although Haldon's edited collection *A Social History of Byzantium* contains essays on this theme).

Teasing out the contradictions: an imperial state

The Byzantine Empire was an imperial state: Constantinople served as a centre for tribute collection both from territory controlled by the imperial armies, and less reliably from neighbouring regions, in the cultural-economic orbit dubbed by Dimitri Obolensky the 'Byzantine Commonwealth' (the Macedonians, Bulgarians, Ukrainians, Montenegrins, Serbians, Moldovans, Belarussians, Rus', and Georgians).

Ideologically and practically, the Byzantine Empire centred stated legitimacy around the authority of the emperor as overseer of both tribute collection, and the wellbeing of the Empire as a Christian society. As a Middle Byzantine monk Kosmas Tzinzilokas wrote, while attempting to resolve disputes at Mount Athos on behalf of Emperor Constantine IX Monomachos (1045):

> The thoughts of a truly lordly and sacred emperor are deeply concerned not only with political matters and plans for the army, with turning back hostile peoples and enslaving enemies, with subjugating populous cities beneath his hand, but also with upholding especially the divine ordinances and the sacred canons. (Papachryssanthou, 1975; Thomas and Hero, 2010)

Eunuchs were ineligible as emperors, without exception. The same held true for men who had undergone other forms of mutilation (the one exception being Justinian II, who after being felled from the throne and mutilated returned with a silver nose, only to be dethroned once again, and beheaded). It seems that eunuchs were not appropriate as an embodiment of empire. In this respect, and given their aforementioned ineligibility to be direct partners to marriage alliances, eunuchs were reliable imperial administrative servants at least in the respect that they could not be direct claimants to the throne, nor develop the marital ties that were otherwise made heavy use of among the Byzantine ruling class.

Eunuchs and the state

The Byzantines did not conceive of themselves as having an 'economy' as such, with the word *oeconomia* instead meaning a ruling virtue best translated as 'discretion', or referring to household management.

Irrespective of this lack of theorisation immanent to their thinking, the Byzantine state was comparatively sophisticated next to most of its neighbours (other than the Persian Empire for its early history, and Caliphates for its later), featuring an administrative state apparatus including centralised minting of coins, centralised standards for commercial activity, and imperially overseen taxation of foreign traders. The role of the state shifted significantly in some ways throughout the empire's long history: until the loss of Alexandria (the 'workhouse of Europe') in 641, the state oversaw providing free daily bread to the inhabitants of Constantinople. But throughout its history, administering the imperial fisc ensured a structural tether between Constantinople as an economic centre and the agrarian estates of the provinces. The bureaucratic demands of the empire required a large civil service (the source of 'Byzantine' as a pejorative in modern parlance). Tasks would be overseen from a pool of educated members of the urban elite, to whom the emperor would extend formal titles that included responsibilities to his court. Within this system of imperially centred administration, eunuchs played a privileged role, with several prominent titles reserved for them, including that of chamberlain. Courtly eunuchs were not a consistently prominent feature across the empire's history, with their popularity declining with the rise of provincial dynasticism, then recovering for the final thirteenth to fifteenth century.

Eunuchs also served other gendered roles of state, most notably as generals – helpful for insecure emperors and empresses who could at least rely on not being directly deposed (Herrin, 2001).

Prejudice against eunuchs

Despite their prominence in the Byzantine state, there was no straightforward acceptance of eunuchs by Byzantine society. Despite their widespread employment in institutionally elevated positions, prejudices against them remained commonplace. Surviving written sources recurrently exhibit negative views of eunuchs, with Kuefler, Tougher, Sidéris, and Ringrose each noting how frequently jibes, negative insinuations, and dismissive comments appear in sources concerning eunuchs described by our historical sources.

Eunuchs were often presented as: unvirtuous, untrustworthy, libidinal, and immoral. Ringrose notes that eunuchs were often defined negatively, a flourish especially apparent in Greek (which uses an alpha prefix). For example, eunuchs might be described as unmanly (*anandros*). They were also more favourably characterised by some writers as filled with '*apatheia*', or without passion.

Despite this conventional disdain, eunuchs could serve male liturgical duties (performing the 'Divine Mysteries', or sacraments). That is, they ritually served male roles, and ones which were not permitted to women. Eunuch clergymen were found at all ranks, including patriarchs of Constantinople (Theophylact, tenth-century son of Emperor Romanos I). Tougher's work demonstrates the varied form these presumptions could take: with like features assumed by (male) authors being cast in an either positive or negative light. One limitation on establishing the extent of these sentiments is our surviving evidence includes no testimony written directly by a confirmed eunuch author. As such, we rely almost exclusively on full-bodied male authors for written sources, presumably resulting in a bias towards hostile (or insecure) reactions. Even explicit defences of eunuchs would draw on familiar tropes of their liminal state, attempting to reverse an understanding of effeminacy while accepting the basic terms of eunuch critics (Mullett, 2002).

In a classic article, the classicist and sociological historian Keith Hopkins compares eunuchs of the earlier Roman Empire to Jewish bureaucrats in the seventeenth- and eighteenth-century German states (Hopkins, 1963). While effeminated they could be formally and substantively advantaged by their particular social position, a source of resentment for those who didn't share this state. Similarly in the Byzantine context, Evelyne Patlagean explored eunuchs as liminal figures in hagiographic devotional fiction, sacral ambiguity (Patlagean, 1976). This *ambiguity* is shown, as in hagiography (writing about saints), a key genre for Byzantine cultural history. Until the Middle Byzantine era, one of the most commonplace *topos* (tropes) in these narratives was a female saint adopting the guise of a eunuch (appropriately beardless), in order to infiltrate an exclusively male monastery, and thus progress their career as a saint. As these narratives of virtuously effeminated women suggest, eunuchs were also found in many monasteries, with several existing solely for them – although certain banned them explicitly (Tougher, 2008). We'll turn to one episode where such a restriction met in conflict with the aforementioned high standing and state prominence of one Middle Byzantine eunuch, Symeon the Sanctified.

Symeon the Sanctified: state administration, gender transgression[13]

By the late 1070s, the eunuch Symeon had enjoyed service to his Emperor Nikephoros Botaneiates as a high-ranking administrator (*megas droungarios*).

Symeon arrived at Athos, perhaps at imperial request, with an entourage of three other eunuchs (Eusebios, Kandidatos, and Hilarion). Symeon, and particularly his young companions, caused offence at Athos shortly after their arrival in 1081 at the traditional annual meeting, for their 'arrogance' and beardless (*agenios*) appearance.

Beardless youths had been banned by John Tzimiskes in his foundational charter officially in the early 970s (with superiors forbidden to either permit eunuchs to join as brothers, or live in their monasteries' fields), then again by Constantine Monomachos's reforming intervention in 1054 (which had physically removed a group of eunuchs who had settled there since the first ban). This was in addition to a traditional ban of women, and explicit bans of female animals. Symeon and his trio of beardless (*agenios*) young men had attempted to entrench themselves in an exclusively male space. Much as with the 1054 episode, the eunuchs were once again expelled.

Having been ejected by Athos' monks, Symeon pleaded his case to the emperor, and was duly re-instated as superior, and returned his lands. Symeon's return was a lavish one, to the tune of 36 pounds of gold coin. By 1089, Xenophon's archives record it as having 14 plough teams including 100 horses and asses, 130 buffalo, 50 cows, and 2,000 goats and sheep in its vineyards, as well as donating estates beyond Athos itself (tethering the monastery to the process of surplus extraction that was the mainstay of the ruling class).

Rosemary Morris calls Symeon: 'a classic example of a refounder with obvious friends and patrons in high places'. We might add, an example of the value state service offered the effeminated in a tributary mode economy, and of imperial involvement in shaping the contours of the sacred.

As go eunuchs, so the world (the contradictory condition of effeminated manhood)

For the most part, Marxist feminism has failed to account for effeminacy, or explain it, besides the Gramscian investigations of Raewyn Connell (1995). Marxist feminism has also been commonly criticised for having little ability to grasp widespread gendered abuse (from rape and wife beating, to street harassment). Whereas many schools of feminism, and queer studies, have brought violence as delimiting gender normativity into view, at its worst Marxist feminism has sought to rationalise these contours as post hoc functions of economic imperatives. The castration of slaves and the sons of aspirational parents could fit easily into a model which emphasises cycles of regulatory violence as definitive to gender, and it remains for Marxist feminism to prove itself equally flexible. Another challenge has been posed by post/decolonial feminists, who've argued that dyadic gender was imposed across the world as a feature of colonial domination, with a Western model of differentiation only one feature of a thoroughgoing cultural imposition.[14]

I would suggest that the continued merit of materialist feminism rests in Marxism's unique emphasis on *contradictions*. So far, eunuch scholarship has largely not been able to present a satisfying answer to whether Byzantine eunuchs were men (with their male gendering on a linguistic, and often institutional basis, despite their unmistakable phenomenological particularity, and so many 'full-bodied' male authors feeling the need to depict them as effeminate, and unnatural). I would propose that a solution to this problem is neither possible nor necessary. Eunuchs were particularised as eunuchs through a mesh of contingency, convention, and custom, much like any other gender.

Marxist feminism may aid substantially in navigating between the Scylla and Charybdis of (defunct, yet still lingering) exotic Orientalist conceptions of eunuchs as a signifier of the despotic 'East', and the new challenge of an oversimplified account of gender history. A wholly abstracted view of pre-colonial gender relations risks the 'new exoticisation' of relegating eunuchs to being merely one pre-colonial 'third gender' among many (the Other to the Self of colonial gender dyadism). Eunuchs played an active role in sustaining and directing its imperial state. Through an approach which always keeps class in mind, we can best provide an account of these figures in their own right, navigating membership in class society and choosing within circumstances not of their own choosing, as did any other. Eunuchs are discontinuous with our own gender relations, while still quite relatable in this sense. Eunuchs deserve better than to be either overlooked as an integral feature of the Byzantine state, *or* treated as somehow exemplary of some pre-colonial radical freedom in gender relations.[15] They were actors in pre-modern class societies, both troubling (particularly to male authors) in certain contexts, and fully complicit in its day-to-day social reproduction.

The case for 'casting the net' into the pre-modern

To return to the systems debate and Arruzza's 'Three Theses': 'Dual Systems' or 'sex class' approaches sought to emphasise patriarchal relations as transhistorical. Both the 'Indifferent' approach of Meiksins Wood and 'Unitary' schools, as outlined and endorsed by Arruzza, are founded on the particularity of capital and its systemic domination – with gendered oppression as ad hoc, non-systemic, non-autonomous, and non-logical (even if structurally normalised by the demands of capital). Neither of these views of pre-modern gender relations can be verified without comparative examination of pre-modern historical periods.

Whatever conclusions are reached about gender's contemporary (capitalism entwining, or subsumed) form must not be based on a conflationary displacement of a unified 'patriarchal system' (or non-explanatory 'patriarchal relations') to societies formed around pre-capitalist modes. Is it analytically helpful to say that a 'patriarchal system' prevailed in the Byzantine Empire?

I'm going to offer a tentative 'no'. Or at least that the Byzantine tributary modal economy (however we define this) serves poorly as an example of a generic 'agrarian society' against which to juxtapose capitalist gender relations. Marxist feminism should take care to remain responsive to work into Byzantine literary, medical, and legal sources related to the experiences of women and private households, which have clearly challenged any straightforward assertion of consistent patriarchy as thoroughly binding juridical principle, or lived reality (Kaldellis, 2010; Laiou, 2011). This is not to deny that misogynistic gender ideals profoundly shape both the content and form of surviving Byzantine historiography (Fledelius, 1982; White, 2003; Markopoulos, 2004). Nevertheless, the complexity of the Byzantine state and its gender relations appears to be one case where attempts at systemic approaches to gender oppression might mislead, or at least brush over variations in development. Entrenched ideals must always be considered within the motion of historical experience (Mergiali-Sahas, 2000), with all the dissonance, mess, and contradictory features that characterise actual societies. A necessary predicate for historical materialist investigation is establishing what remains to be explained by our investigations, rather than simply assumed.

In the quite particular role they played in Byzantine statecraft (and the troubling way they appeared to contemporary male ruling-class authors), eunuchs are demonstrative of the contradictory variations thrown up by tributary mode societies, and must not be overlooked as historical subjects. Grasping the conditions of their lives (from formal privileges to oppressive conventions of contempt) will improve the grasp of Marxist feminism on gender more generally, and our theorisation of effeminacy (too often neglected), in particular. Historical materialism is well equipped to recover a history of eunuchs, and other non-dyadic actors. But this demands a wider comparative 'casting of the net' than previously existing historical theorisation of patriarchy has tended towards. To satisfactorily answer the question 'what has capitalism done to gender?' is one task required of historical investigations of how gender was marked out before it.

Notes

1 More recently a collection of essays: Bhattacharya (2017). The term was also explored from a wide range of angles in: *Viewpoint Magazine* 5: *Social Reproduction* (2015), published online: www.viewpointmag.com/2015/11/02/issue-5-social-reproduction/ See also: Lewis (2016).

2 More recently Arruzza has brought these fields together in a piece co-written with Aaron Jaffe (2018).

3 Certain scholars have adopted the term 'New Rome' for this state formation, in light of its population referring to themselves as Romans up until its final dissolution, but on pragmatic grounds I will retain 'Byzantine' as a term of scholarly convenience, with full apologies for any upset this anachronism causes to either the living or the dead.

4 This would continue to hold true of courtly eunuchs in the Ottoman period, see Toledano (1984).

5 The contemporary medical establishment, it should be noted, usually seeks to surgically eliminate these bodily

ambiguities in a procedure intersex activists term 'Intersex Genital Mutilation'. For more on this issue see my piece: Gleeson (2018). The contemporary intersex movement largely rejects the term 'conditions' as pathologising, we instead prefer to refer to 'intersex variations'. The contemporary plight of those born intersex is a worthy point for anyone prone to dismissing eunuchs as an exotic cultural 'Other' to consider carefully.

6 For an examination including analysis of a rare depiction of a bearded eunuch, see: Charles Barber (1997).

7 Orientalism as a feature of medieval Western historiography is considered in a paper by Shaun Tougher (2012).

8 See also on Byzantine angelology, Glenn Peers, *Subtle Bodies: Representing Angels in Byzantium* (2001) and Sidéris (2003).

9 For a more comprehensive view of Anglophone scholarship, see my forthcoming essay 'Byzantine Historiography, Byzantine Household'.

10 For much more recent reflections see Haldon (2013).

11 Sarris and Banaji also co-edited: *Special Issue: Aristocrats, Peasants and the Transformation of Rural Society, c.400–800, Journal of Agrarian Change* 9(1) (2009).

12 The debate as a whole can be found in: *Historical Materialism* 21(4) (2013). The essays addressed here are: John Haldon, 'Theories of Practice: Marxist History-Writing and Complexity' and Jairus Banaji, 'Putting Theory to Work'. Here we will use the tributary mode without committing fully to either Haldon or Banaji's definition of the term, especially as the two appear to be largely in accord by my reading (perhaps more so than Banaji might accept).

13 This brief recounting of a Middle Byzantine aristocrat (and eunuch) will add little to Rosemary Morris's comprehensive account of Symeon's subversive appearance at the monastic hub of Mount Athos (Morris, 2009 edition: Papachryssanthou 1986) But for our particular gender integrative purposes, he serves as an exemplary case for how gender normativity could be strained by those who had ascended to the heights of state administration.

14 This association of the dyadic genders with modernity/colonialism has become something of a 'common sense' or assumed base knowledge in certain critical circles. It was most concisely and rigorously advanced in Lugones (1997), which developed the framework of Quijano (2007). A similar argument was previously advanced concerning the African context by Oyewumi (1997).

15 For a detailed introduction to the risks of exoticising non-dyadic gendered subjects, see: Towle and Morgan (2002). While intended as an intervention to contemporary anthropology, many of the criticisms apply here, too.

References

Arruzza, C., 2014. 'Remarks on Gender'. *Viewpoint Magazine*. www.viewpointmag.com/2014/09/02/remarks-on-gender/.

Arruzza, C., Jaffe, A., 2018. 'Ancient Philosophy' in Diamanti, J., Pendakis, A., Szeman, I. (Eds.), *The Bloomsbury Companion to Marx*. Bloomsbury, London, 175–184.

Banaji, J., 2007. *Agrarian Change in Late Antiquity: Gold, Labour, and Aristocratic Dominance*. Oxford University Press, Oxford.

Banaji, J., 2010. *Theory as History: Essays on Modes of Production and Exploitation*. Haymarket Books, Chicago, IL.

Banaji, J., 2015. *Exploring the Economy of Late Antiquity: Selected Essays*. Cambridge University Press, Cambridge.

Barber, C., 1997. 'Homo Byzantinus?' in James, L. (Ed.), *Women, Men and Eunuchs: Gender in Byzantium*. Routledge, Abingdon, 185–199.

Bhattacharya, T. (Ed.), 2017. *Social Reproduction Theory: Remapping Class, Recentring Oppression*. Pluto Press, London; Chicago, IL.

Connell, R., 1995. *Masculinities*. University of California Press, Berkeley, CA.

Delphy, C., 1980. 'The Main Enemy'. *Feminist Issues* 1(1): 23–40.

Diehl, C., 1923. 'Byzantine Culture'. *Cambridge Medieval History*, 756–766.

Fledelius, K., 1982. 'Women's Position and Possibilities in Byzantine Society with Particular Reference to the Novels of Leo VI'. *Jahrbuch Der Österreichischen Byzantinistik* 32: 425–532.

Gleeson, J., 2018. 'Depathologising, Repathologising: The WHO's New Guidelines for Trans and Intersex Healthcare'. *Verso Books Blog*. www.versobooks.com/blogs/4136-depathologising-repathologising-the-who-s-new-guidelines-for-trans-and-intersex-healthcare.

Guilland, R., 1943. 'Les eunuques dans l'empire Byzantine. Etude de titulaire et de prosopographie Byzantines'. *Revue des études Byzantines* 1: 197–238.

Guilland, R., 1944. 'Fonctions et dignités des eunuques'. *Revue des études Byzantines* 2: 185–225.

Guilland, R., 1955. 'Études de titulature Byzantine: les titres auliques réservés aux eunuques'. *Revue des études Byzantines* 13: 50–84.

Haldon, J., 1985. 'Some Considerations on Byzantine Society and Economy in the 7th Century'. *Byzantinische Forschungen. Internationale Zeitschriftfür Byzantinistik* 10: 75–112.

Haldon, J., 1989. 'The Feudalism Debate Once More: The Case of Byzantium'. *The Journal of Peasant Studies* 17(1): 5–40

Haldon, J., 1993. *The State and the Tributary Mode of Production*. Verso, London.

Haldon, J., 2013. 'Theories of Practice: Marxist History-Writing and Complexity'. *Historical Materialism* 21(4): 36–70.

Hanson, R.P.C., 1966. 'A Note on Origen's Self-Mutilation'. *Vigiliae Christianae* 20: 81–82.

Hartmann, H.I., 1979. 'The Unhappy Marriage of Marxism and Feminism: Towards a More Progressive Union'. *Capital & Class* 3(2): 1–33.

Harvey, A., 1989. *Economic Expansion in the Byzantine Empire, 900–1200*. Cambridge University Press, Cambridge.

Hatzaki, M., 2009. 'Angels and Eunuchs: The Beauty of Liminal' in *Masculinity Beauty and the Male Body in Byzantium: Perceptions and Representations in Art and Text*. Palgrave Macmillan, New York, 86–115.

Herrin, J., 2001. *Women in Purple: Rulers of Medieval Byzantium*. Princeton University Press, Princeton, NJ.

Herrin, J., 2015. *Unrivalled Influence: Women and Empire in Byzantium*. Princeton University Press, Princeton, NJ.

Hopkins, K., 1963. 'Eunuchs in Politics in the Later Roman Empire'. *The Cambridge Classical Journal* 9: 62–80.

James, L., 2001. *Empresses and Power in Early Byzantium*. Leicester University Press, Leicester.

Kaldellis, A., 2010. 'The Study of Women and Children: Methodological Challenges and New Directions' in Stephenson, P. (Ed.), *The Byzantine World*. Routledge Worlds, Abingdon, 61–71.

Kazhdan, A., McCormick, M., 1997. 'The Social World of the Byzantine Court' in Maguire, H. (Ed.), *Byzantine Court Culture from 829 to 1204*. Dumbarton Oaks, Washington DC, 167–197.

Kuefler, M., 2001. *The Manly Eunuch: Masculinity, Gender Ambiguity, and Christian Ideology in Late Antiquity*. University of Chicago Press, Chicago, IL.

Laiou, A.E., 2011. *Women, Family and Society in Byzantium*. Variorum, London.

Lewis, H., 2016. *The Politics of Everybody: Feminism, Queer Theory and Marxism at the Intersection*. University of Chicago Press, Chicago, IL

Lugones, M., 1997. 'Heterosexualism and the Colonial / Modern Gender System'. *Hypatia* 22(1): 186–209.

Markopoulos, A., 2004. 'Gender Issues in Leo the Deacon' in *History and Literature of Byzantium in the 9th–10th Centuries*. Routledge, Abingdon, 1–16.

Meiskins Wood, E., 2015. 'Capitalism and Human Emancipation: Race, Gender and Democracy' in *Democracy against Capitalism Renewing Historical Materialism*. Verso, London, 264–283.

Mergiali-Sahas, S., 2000. *The 'Other Half', or Less Than That? Ideals and Realities in Women's Life in Byzantium*.

Hellenic Canadian Association of Constantinople, Toronto, Ontario Annual Lecture.

Messis, C., 2014. *Les eunuques à Byzance, entre réalité et imaginaire*. Centre d'études byzantines, néo-helléniques et sud-est européennes, Paris.

Morris, R., 2009. 'Symeon the Sanctified and the Re-foundation of Xenophon'. *Byzantine and Modern Greek Studies* 33(2): 133–147. Original Greek edition, Papachryssanthou, D. (ed.), 1986. *Actes de Xenophon (Archives de L'Athos)*. Lethielleux, Paris.

Mullett, M., 2002. 'Theophylact of Ochrid's "In Defence of Eunuchs"' in Tougher, S. (Ed.), *Eunuchs in Antiquity and Beyond*. Classical Press of Wales and Duckworth, Swansea, 177–198.

Ostrogorsky, G., 1940/1951. *The History of the Byzantine State*. Translated by John Hussey. Reprint edition: Rutgers University Press, New Brunswick, NJ.

Oyewumi, O., 1997. *The Invention of Women: Making an African Sense of Western Gender Discourses*. University of Minnesota Press, Minneapolis, MN.

Papachryssanthou, D. (Ed.), 1975. *Actes du Prôtaton*. Text and plates. Archives de l'Athos 7. Lethielleux, Paris.

Patlagean, E., 1976. *L'histoire de la femme déguisée en moine et l'évolution de la sainteté féminine à Byzance*. Studi Medievali 3e ser, Spoleto. Reissued 1981: Variorum Reprints, London.

Peers, G., 2001. *Subtle Bodies: Representing Angels in Byzantium*. University of California Press, Berkeley, CA.

Quijano, A., 2007. 'Coloniality and Modernity/Rationality'. *Cultural Studies* 21(2–3): 168–178.

Ringrose, K., 1995. 'Eunuchs as Cultural Mediators in Byzantium'. *Byzantine Studies Conference Abstracts of Papers* 21. Dumbarton Oaks, Washington, DC.

Ringrose, K., 2003. *The Perfect Servant: Eunuchs and the Social Construction of Gender in Byzantium*. University of Chicago Press, Chicago, IL.

Sarris, P., 2006. *Economy and Society in the Age of Justinian*. Cambridge University Press, Cambridge.

Sarris, P., 2009. 'On Jairus Banaji's Agrarian Change in Late Antiquity'. *Historical Materialism* 13(1): 207–219.

Sarris, P., 2010. 'Economics, Trade, and "Feudalism"' in James, L. (Ed.), *A Companion to Byzantium*. Blackwell, Chichester, 23–42.

Sarris, P., Banaji, J. (Eds.), 2009. *Special Issue: Aristocrats, Peasants and the Transformation of Rural Society, c.400-800, Journal of Agrarian Change* 9(1).

Sidéris, G., 2003. 'Le sexe des anges: la byzantinologie et les questions du genre' in Auzépy, M.-F. (Ed.), *Byzance en Europe*. Presses Universitaires de Vincennes, Paris, 217–233.

Thomas, J., Hero, A.C. (Eds.), 2010. *Byzantine Monastic Foundation Documents: A Complete Translation of the Surviving Founders' Typika and Testaments*. Dumbarton Oaks, Washington DC.

Toledano, E.R., 1984. 'The Imperial Eunuchs of Istanbul: From Africa to the Heart of Islam'. *Middle Eastern Studies* 20(3): 379–390.

Tougher, S., 1999. 'Ammianus and the Eunuchs' in Drijvers, J.W., Hunt, D. (Eds.), *The Late Roman World and Its Historian: Interpreting Ammianus Marcellinus*. Routledge, Abingdon, 64–73.

Tougher, S., 2002. 'In or Out? Origins of Court Eunuchs' in Tougher, S. (Ed.), *Eunuchs in Antiquity and Beyond*. Classical Press of Wales, Swansea, 143–159.

Tougher, S., 2004a. 'Holy Eunuchs! Masculinity and Eunuch Saints in Byzantium' in Cullum, P.H., Lewis, K.J. (Eds.), *Holiness and Masculinity in the Middle Ages*. University of Wales Press, Cardiff, 93–108.

Tougher, S., 2004b. 'Social Transformation, Gender Transformation? The Court Eunuch, 300–900' in Brubaker, L., Smith, J.M.H. (Eds.), *Gender in the Early Medieval World: East and West, 300–900*. Cambridge University Press, Cambridge, 70–82.

Tougher, S., 2008. *The Eunuch in Byzantine History and Society*. Routledge, Abingdon.

Tougher, S., 2010. 'Cherchez l'homme! Byzantine Men: A Eunuch Perspective' in Stephenson, P. (Ed.), *The Byzantine World*. Routledge, London, 83–91.

Tougher, S., 2012. 'Eyeing up Eunuchs: Western Perceptions of Byzantine Cultural Difference' in Lambert, S., Nicholson, H. (Eds.), *Languages of Love and Hate: Conflict, Communication, and Identity in the Medieval Mediterranean*. Brepols, Turnhout, 87–97.

Tougher, S. 2013, 'The Aesthetics of Castration: The Beauty of Roman Eunuchs' in Tracy, L. (Ed.), *Castration and Culture in the Middle Ages*. Boydell & Brewer, Rochester, NY, 48–72.

Tougher, S., 2015. 'Eunuchs in the East, Men in the West? Dis/unity, Gender and Orientalism in the Fourth Century' in Dijkstra, R., Poppel, S. Slootjes, D. (Eds.), *East and West in the Roman Empire of the Fourth Century: An End to Unity?* Brill, London, 147–163.

Towle, E.B., Morgan, L.M., 2002. 'Romancing the Transgender Native: Rethinking the Use of the "Third Gender" Concept'. *GLQ: A Journal of Lesbian and Gay Studies* 8(4): 469–497.

Walby, S., 1990. *Theorizing Patriarchy*. Basil Blackwood, Oxford.

White, L., 2003. 'The Ideology of the Feminine in Byzantine Historical Narrative: The Role of John Skylitzes' Synopsis of Histories'. PhD thesis, University of Manitoba.

7 | READING MARX AGAINST THE GRAIN

Rethinking the exploitation of care work beyond profit-seeking

Tine Haubner

Introduction

When it comes to exploitation a strange disparity occurs: while social movements, NGOs, and activists constantly talk about and denounce exploitative relationships around the globe, social scientists have been avoiding the term for more than three decades. There are at least three possible explanations for the academic downfall of the concept. Exploitation still serves as a normative notion – it is either a dead classic of inequality research or a negative example of misdirected theory building in outdated Marxist economics. This means exploitation is, on the one hand, still at the heart of 'social critique' (Boltanski and Chiapello, 2003: 380) and is therefore suspected to be more a term of political jargon than an instrument of proper social analysis. On the other hand, the concept of exploitation's close association with the labour theory of value resulted in a huge loss of significance in the social sciences following the academic demise of Marxist social theory and the economic turn towards marginalism.

In the context of its reception in economics from the 1960s to the 1980s, exploitation has largely been reviewed with regard to its mathematical quantifiability and accuracy of econometric measurement (Crocker, 1972), while leaving aside any implications for social theory (Steedman, 1981; Morishima, 1973; Samuelson, 1971). Because exploitation has often been received – both within and outside Marxist debates – as a 'technical' (Steedman, 1981: 17) quantitative concept for the explanation of profits in industrial capitalism, one tightly linked to the labour theory of value, the downfall of the term exploitation began when economists started to massively question the validity of this theory. Since then, neither the labour theory of value nor exploitation has played any serious role in economic theory, inequality studies, or social science in general. Hence, the concept of exploitation had largely disappeared from social science by the 1980s and was virtually extinct after the collapse of actually existing socialism and the interlinked image loss of academic Marxism. Ever since, it has led only a reduced life as a metaphor of outrage or, at best, a phenomenon of moral philosophy (see for example McLaughlin, 2008; Parijs, 1984). Since then 'rent-seeking', 'closure', and 'exclusion' have replaced exploitation as far more popular and accepted sociological mechanisms of social inequality. These notions not only claim to reflect current social developments of late capitalist societies better than exploitation (like long-term unemployment or the link between inequality, education, and discrimination; see Parkin, 1974; Kronauer, 2010) but to also be free of theoretical burdens such as the labour theory of value (Sørensen, 2000).

Another reason for the academic demise of exploitation is its narrow conception within Marxist theory itself. The concept's origin in the field of Marxist economic theory also worked to limit its claim and context of validity because exploitation often served as a model to explain profits reserved for 'productive' industrial wage labour as the only source of surplus. This focus on profit-seeking becomes specifically problematic for understanding the increased exploitation of less profitable and even unpaid domestic, subsistence, or care work within the context of the ongoing crisis of social reproduction (Jürgens, 2010), global care chains (Hochschild, 2001), national care regimes (Daly, 2000), and private households.

Although exploitation has vanished from the academic ground, I will suggest that this concept needs to be revitalised due to its unique sociological meaning. Only exploitation describes a specific social relation wherein someone takes advantage of another by appropriating their labour (see also Wright, 1989: 77; Wertheimer, 1996: 10). Terms like rent-seeking, closure, or exclusion have proven unsuccessful substitutes because they do not intend to grasp this specific meaning at all but silenced it for decades. Neither closure, rent-seeking, nor exclusion grasp the aspect of appropriating labour power when relating benefits and disadvantages of different persons (see for example the critique of Parkin by Barbalet, 1982). Although the 'marriage' between not only Marxism and feminism but of the labour theory of value and unpaid (care) work has often been an 'unhappy' one (Hartmann, 1997: 97), I will show that a feminist perspective on the labour theory of value can help to understand the exploitation of less profitable and even unpaid care work on highly state-regulated care markets. My contribution consists of four parts: firstly, I will discuss the classic Marxian concept of exploitation and its narrow economic reception. Secondly, I will examine some feminist interventions in this context, focusing specifically on the relation between domestic labour and the labour theory of value. Thirdly, I will explore some possibilities to think about 'unproductive' work with the help of Marxist terms proposed by feminist contributions. Lastly, I will introduce a way of rethinking exploitation in relation to elderly care work within state-regulated 'quasi-markets'.

The Marxian concept of exploitation

The term 'exploitation' was first elevated to a powerful analytical-scientific term within the work of Marx (Berger, 1994: 736). Marx himself used the term inconsistently in various ways to describe strategic political opportunities, extractivism, or colonialism. In sum, he did not use different concepts of exploitation like Buchanan for example claimed (Buchanan,

1979: 122) but developed the term exploitation (like other concepts in his work) on different levels of abstraction: Firstly, Marx and Engels articulated in *The German Ideology* (Marx and Engels, 2004: 110) a basic understanding of the 'exploitation de l'homme par l'homme', put simply as 'I derive benefit for myself by doing harm to someone else'. Subsequently, Marx expanded this basic meaning of the term to analyse historical class societies and to understand how the private appropriation of socially produced surplus ('Mehrprodukt') took place. Thus the general historical conditions for an exploitative social order are: firstly, a societal level of productivity that allows for surplus; secondly, the fact that one class is in control of the means of production, leading to the exclusion via power of proletarianised non-owners; thirdly, a specific historical relation of exploitation characterised by the appropriation of socially-generated surplus value by the respective ruling class.

Marx's usage of the term 'exploitation' varies, and his value-theoretical elaboration of its meaning for capitalist society is given only in *Capital*. Following Marx, as a feature of all previous class societies (Marx and Engels, 1969: 26), exploitation occurs not only within capitalism. Besides that, Marx distinguishes exploitative relations not only with a historical focus. He also differentiates between forms and agents of exploitation within a given social structure (Marx, 1959: 446). Furthermore, he distinguishes 'primary' from 'secondary' exploitation – the former referring to the relationships between workers and capital, the latter referring to relationships between workers and members of other fractions of the bourgeoisie, such as landlords (Marx, 1959: 454). Finally, terms like 'surplus product' also feature in Marx's analysis of pre-bourgeois relations of production and exploitation, although he fundamentally applies his value theory only to capitalist exploitation. This indicates that, for Marx, exploitation occurs not only within capitalist societies and is not only relevant in relation to the assumptions of value theory. Finally, it is not meant only as an explanation of how capitalist profit is generated.

Though Marx used exploitation to describe every class society in history, his value-theoretical concept of capitalist exploitation in particular became especially well known. Following Marx, capitalist exploitation is conceptualised as a real existing paradox, namely a difference based on the exchange of equivalents. In essence, capitalist exploitation for Marx denotes the appropriation of a specific difference in value, namely the difference between the value of labour power as a commodity and the value embodied in commodities as products of labour. Accordingly, surplus value occurs within the formally free exchange of the commodity of labour power and is legally appropriated by the owners of the means of production. Because only labour power creates more value than is needed for its own reproduction, this very special commodity is the real source of profits. It is exchanged according to its 'exchange value' and creates surplus. The institutional context Marx had in mind when he spoke about capitalist exploitation was primarily the industrial production of goods and 'productive' wage labour (Marx, 1887: 359). As a consequence, only productive labour that creates surplus has been considered by many Marxists to be capitalistically exploited.

Although Marx himself never thought that the capitalist exchange of equivalents could develop without removing people more or less violently from their land, economic dependence, and the compulsion of the working class, many Marxist and non-Marxist economists understood his idea of capitalist exploitation mainly as a quantitative model to explain the generation of profit in free competitive markets. For example, in 1986 the Analytical-Marxist economist John Roemer asked: 'What economic institutions appear to be necessary for one producer to appropriate the labour of another? As has been discussed, Marx's task was to construct a theory of exploitation that was operative even when a coercive institution of labour exchange was absent' (Roemer, 1986: 84). Here, exploitation is understood as a concept that deals with the exchange of commodities on free competitive markets that are in principle independent from discrimination or coercion. Not only Roemer but many Marxists even today think of capitalist exploitation as something exclusively reserved for the profit-driven and allegedly non-coercive capitalist exchange of commodities deriving only from 'productive' industrial labour on free markets (see for example Berger, 2009: 115). Because Marx in his late economic works somehow assumed an ideal-typical capitalism in accordance with the law of value (Gerstenberger, 2017: 14), within many Marxist debates about exploitation, the influence of power relations, discrimination, and devaluation have not received appropriate attention. Marxist-Feminist debates have sought to remedy this gap by placing exactly these missing links at their centre.

Domestic work and the labour theory of value

The aforementioned narrow understanding of capitalist exploitation was prominently attacked in the context of the 'domestic labour debate' among Marxist feminists in the 1970s and 1980s. Here, feminist approaches to exploitation provided at least three important insights. First, they understood capitalism, as Federici writes, as a 'heterogeneous combination of different types of labour and exploitation' (Federici, 2012: 40). While Marxists often assumed that wage labour would become the dominant means of utilising labour power worldwide, feminists stressed the persistence of supposedly pre-capitalist forms of labour like slavery or subsistence farming. The exploitation of 'productive labour' in the industrial workplace thus still coexists with the exploitation of economically 'unproductive' care work, for example in private households. Neither form of exploitation is secondary or less important for capitalism. Feminist approaches, like the 'subsistence approach' of Maria Mies, Veronika Bennholdt-Thomsen, and Claudia von Werlhof referred to the fact that, on a global scale, industrial wage labour was a minor form of labour compared to the huge amount of subsistence farming (Werlhof et al., 1983). Secondly, by demonstrating the importance of unpaid domestic work for capitalist accumulation, feminists have broadened our understanding of exploitation so that it can no longer be reduced simply to the exploitation of wage labour. Thirdly, feminist approaches systematically took into account the importance of discrimination and exclusion of socially vulnerable people like women, Indigenous People, and migrants. By doing so, they exposed the economic meaning of power relations in contrast to Marxist positions that treated capitalism as in principle independent of violence, power, and discrimination. The term exploitation has therefore been understood rather differently by feminist approaches to the concept. To give one example, the already mentioned 'subsistence-approach' emphasised the violent and predatory character of exploitation by focusing on the subsistence farming of rural peasants in the so-called 'Third World' (Werlhof, 1981: 204; Mies, 2009: 268), in contrast to Marx, who assumed that violence would not vanish but in the long run be decreasingly used as a means of capital accumulation (Marx, 1887: 523). Hence, whether one looks only at paid industrial labour (and its presumed historical generalisation) or at unpaid domestic and subsistence work has important implications for different understandings of exploitation and capitalism.

Within the debate about domestic work initiated in the US during the late 1960s (Haug, 2015; Dalla Costa and James, 1972; Folbre, 1982, Haug and Hauser, 1984), feminists not only indicated that capitalism systematically exploits domestic and subsistence work around the globe, but also disputed whether exploitation of the non-commodified, unpaid domestic work done by housewives could even be grasped using the labour theory of value. Feminist approaches dealing with unpaid domestic and subsistence labour indeed must come into conflict with the Marxist labour theory of value, as it does not take these forms of uncommodified work into account. By using the labour theory of value, Marx's 'ultimate aim' was 'to lay bare the economic law of motion of modern society', i.e. the capitalist mode of production, carried out via the value-theoretical and intrinsically critical reconstruction of these 'laws of motion' (Marx, 1887: 7). Feminist critiques of Marx were therefore forced to either abandon Marx's labour theory of value, or to read it against the grain by widening the concept of exploitation to include 'unproductive' and mostly unpaid labour such as care, domestic, and subsistence work. Linked to this were key questions such as if domestic work lowers the value of male labour power as a commodity, or whether domestic work produces value itself and could therefore actually be defined as 'productive'.

Marx did not reflect upon the exploitation of unpaid care work. Even though he wrote 'The owner of labour power is mortal' (Marx, 1887: 121) and focused on the reproduction of labour power, he equated the reproduction of labour power with the production of goods consumed by the workforce. According to Marx, the costs of reproducing labour as a commodity constitute a package of several commodities necessary for reproducing labour power at a given social reproductive scale. When writing about the 'given quantity of the means of subsistence' (1887: 121), he thus left unpaid reproductive work such as the preparation of purchased foods and other care work required unmentioned. Thus, what Marx did not mention was the unpaid domestic work of women that reproduces the most valuable commodity in capitalist societies: namely labour power itself, in the form of producing and reproducing new workers (Neusüß, 1985). Thus, the importance of unpaid domestic work for the reproduction of labour power – and by that the exploitation of 'unproductive', uncommodified labour as constitutive of capitalism – was not taken into consideration (Marx, 1887: 359).

This missing link became one of the central issues of Marxist-Feminist debates about the labour theory of value and the importance of domestic work for capital accumulation. While some feminists have regarded this blind spot as proof of Marx's androcentric narrow-mindedness (Werlhof, 1981), others argued that his aim was the value-theoretical reconstruction of capitalism's laws of motion from the perspective of capital (Beer, 1983). Following the second interpretation, the absence of unpaid care work in Marx's analysis is not rooted in misjudgement but is rather inherent to capital's consistent ignorance of social reproduction in general. One prominent example here is the controversy between German feminists Claudia von Werlhof and Ursula Beer in the early 1980s. According to Werlhof, representing the Bielefeld subsistence approach, both the unpaid subsistence work of peasants in the 'Third World' and the domestic work of housewives around the globe are indeed important unpaid sources of capitalist profits. But this so-called 'colonial-rent' or 'women's rent' is not only a valuable part of profits. According to Werlhof it is even the main source of profit within capitalism (Werlhof et al., 1983: 154). In contrast, Beer argued that because unpaid (domestic) work is disregarded by capital, the labour theory of value does not apply in this instance either (Beer, 1983: 29ff.). Beer also argued that Werlhof had not been able to prove that domestic labour really lowers the value of labour as a commodity.

Feminist efforts to understand the meaning of unpaid 'unproductive' labour in capitalism via Marxian notions and the labour theory of value often led to a controversial question: could these notions be applied more generally to contexts that actually lie beyond their scope, or would such applications inevitably overstrain them (Barrett, 1980)? The question of whether Marxian theory could help explain the economic importance of domestic labour or if it rather contributed to ignoring it further divided feminist debates, finally leading to a stalemate. While some blamed Marx for his male bias (Vogel, 1973: 24), others suggested taking Marxian methodology into account before reaching a final decision (Beer, 1983).

Either Marx's methodology had been misunderstood by some who blamed him for his blind patches or those who prevented anything from touching

Marx did not accept what was not theoretically developed by him. Looking back, none of these two positions turned out to be much help for further theoretical development. But what has since remained clear is that domestic labour is of central importance for capitalist accumulation because care work in the first place produces the very foundations of capitalist society, in particular because it reproduces labour power as the only source of surplus. Whatever side one falls on in this debate, we can learn from the blind spots of the labour theory of value that domestic work is the devaluated and made-invisible foundation of capital accumulation. From this perspective, Marx's reconstruction of the economic law of motion shows at least that care work as an 'unproductive' and narrow profitable kind of work is structurally crisis ridden under capitalism. From this perspective, the ignorance of the labour theory of value towards care work issues reflects the ignorance and devaluation of care work within capitalism. Thus Marx's ignorance towards care work tells us much about the inferior status of care work within societies geared for profits and economic growth.

Profit-fixation in Marxist-Feminist debates: a way out

The labour theory of value has remained a central problem for Marxist-Feminist debate about domestic work. Because Marx's usage of the labour theory of value mainly seeks to explain firstly how labour is divided and secondly how labour is exploited to create profits in capitalist societies based on the exchange of goods, domestic work always had to be grasped in relation to (male) wage labour to achieve the status of exploitation in the strictly Marxian sense. This poses the fundamental question of the relationship between reproductive domestic labour and capitalist production. By many feminist thinkers in the debate, domestic work was understood to be capitalistically exploited only because it produced something considered to be really exploited, namely industrial male labour power (Komlosy, 2012). The productivity of unproductive work therefore had to be proven, at least indirectly. Although the debate targeted Marxism's fixation with profit and aimed at criticising the theoretical narrowness and absence of care work within Marxist thinking, the debate itself finally concentrated on questions about domestic work and labour theory and did not care much about the division of labour within families, elder care, or child care (Molyneux, 1979: 21; Folbre, 1982). The central focus on 'reproduction' has therefore to be taken seriously as the focus on the reproduction of 'productive' wage labour. This fixation itself is highly associated with the Marxist concept of capitalist exploitation and its one-sided economic reception. Yet while domestic work actually lies beyond the scope of the labour theory of value, I argue that it is nevertheless possible to illustrate the economic meaning of domestic work by way of this theory. But this is only possible if we tweak the notion of surplus value. In this sense, the Austrian sociologist Rainer Bauböck has demonstrated the possibility of applying value theory to unpaid domestic work (Bauböck, 1988). He claimed that by expanding both, domestic and subsistence production, capital manages to find a third way, in addition to the relative and absolute increase of surplus value, to indirectly lower the value of labour power:

> Exploitation in the sphere of production is the surplus of time extended over the amount of labor-time necessary in order to produce the goods and services contained in the value of labor power as a commodity. By analogy, an exact definition of exploitation in domestic and subsistence work could be: ... Exploitation in the reproduction of labour power is the surplus of the performed labor for all goods and services that are necessary to reproduce labor power for the capitalist labor market beyond the labor time incorporated in the value of labor power as a commodity. (Bauböck, 1988: 13–14, my translation)

Thus, according to Bauböck, Marx erred with his assumption that 'the labour-time requisite for the production of labour power reduces itself to that necessary for the production of those means of subsistence, in other words, the value of labour-power is the value of the means of subsistence necessary for the maintenance of the labourer' (Marx, 1887: 121). In order to verify this claim, Bauböck uses socially necessary labour time as a yardstick for comparing 'abstract' wage labour and 'concrete' domestic work. Because capital, by exploiting labour power, indirectly also appropriates this unpaid reproduction time by way of domestic work, said reproduction time must consequently be understood as part of the exploitation of wage labour. Instead of using the assumptions of rent theory as in the case of Werlhof, Bauböck grasps the exploitation of domestic work through value theory as 'devaluation' ('Wertminderung' in Bauböck, 1988: 17f., my translation). With his attempt to prove that the specific difference between necessary labour time and surplus labour time typical for capitalist exploitation also applies to the sphere of 'unproductive' unpaid care work – not in the form of a surplus but rather as a deficit – Bauböck took the Marxian concept of exploitation even more seriously than Werlhof herself. The assumed devaluation is furthermore an analytical vehicle that can now be utilised to diagnose exploitation in the sphere of 'unproductive' elderly care work taking place within highly state-regulated quasi-markets.

The exploitation of care work in Germany's elder-care quasi-market

The Marxist focus on profits is especially problematic when it comes to the exploitation of care work. Not only because care work is less profitable than the production of goods (see Baumol, 2012), but because it is generally done on so-called 'quasi-markets' which are highly regulated by the state (see Le Grand, 1991). Quasi-markets are different from normal markets such as those Marx primarily had in mind for at least two reasons. Firstly, many providers (like non-profit organisations) do not primarily seek for profit. Secondly price-formation mechanisms are restricted in favour of social budgeting. Thus, prices are determined not by supply and demand, but rather by specific cost pressures induced by the budget principles of public spending or social insurances.

One appropriate example here is the German quasi-market in elderly care. In Germany, the 'mixed economy' (Powell, 2007) of elderly care is composed of private providers, but the state and non-profit organisations are important parts of the care market as well. There is no free price formation because elderly care is financed by the restricted budgets of long-term care insurance, private households, and the welfare state. Furthermore, long-term care insurance only covers a portion of costs while leaving further costs to be covered by private households and social benefits. Especially long-term care insurance creates a specific cost pressure that in turn affects private as well as non-profit service providers on the market. In the end that means that for most small providers it is not profitability but rather 'writing black figures' that is at stake. This is mostly realised via wage dumping, as the practice of reducing wages by the use of unskilled workers, a self-employed workforce, or the illegal utilisation of labour power. Therefore, exploitation within the elderly care market occurs not as profit making but primarily as cost reduction. According to the Marxist concept of capitalist exploitation we therefore do not need to think of a difference in value that creates surplus and thereby profits. On the contrary, we need to think about the exploitative strategy of 'devaluation', i.e. a strategy of systematically reducing the prices of labour power. Hence, when exploitation is understood as a social relation wherein one actor takes advantage of another by appropriating surplus, we can also understand exploitation the other way around: as a social relation where one actor takes advantage of another by reducing the costs of appropriated labour power. That means that we also need to take into account strategies that allow wage-dumping and labour devaluation on a larger scale. Relating to elderly care, the social vulnerability of the underpaid or even unpaid female care workers and the persistent image of elderly care as a 'Jane Doe job' act as key mechanisms for systematically reducing the cost of care.

There are at least two options for exploiting elderly care work: either care work is paid but depreciated via illegal use of labour power, for example the use of illegal migrant workers, or it is unpaid and done by untrained laypersons, volunteers, or relatives. Due to demographic changes and a lack of professional care workers the number of elderly dependents in Germany is predicted to rise to 3.4 million in 2030, requiring 506,000 professional nurses (Prognos, 2012). Under the pressure of increasing demand, a shortage of skilled labour, and cost-saving measures in the care sector, we are now witnessing the increased mobilisation of *lay care work* of the kind traditionally relied upon by Germany's conservative and family-based care regime (Lutz and Palenga-Möllenbeck, 2014: 220). Faced with the cost pressure of long-term care insurance designed only as partial cover, the domestic supply gaps caused by increased female labour market participation have triggered an intense socio-political search since the 1990s for the 'dormant potential' of cheap lay care workers (Haubner, 2017; see also Lessenich, 2008: 108). Thus, to reduce costs in a time of rising demand Germany delegates much of its elderly care work requirements to private households instead of developing public care services. That means we can observe the socio-politically driven and increased involvement of unpaid or poorly funded elderly care done by socially vulnerable groups of the population.

This combination of increasing demand alongside the withdrawal of the neoliberal state from public care underscores the importance of unpaid elderly care. For this reason, elderly care has been increasingly underlined by social policy and nursing science under the heading of 'caring communities' (BMFSFJ, 2012: 115). It is also no coincidence that it is particularly vulnerable population groups who become the focus of social and care policy – female relatives that traditionally bear the burden of domestic care work, female volunteers and retirees navigating old-age poverty, low-skilled and long-term unemployed people, or female migrant workers from Eastern Europe facing racist discrimination and slave-like working conditions. And since elderly care is still regarded in Germany as a 'Jane Doe job' with little regulatory oversight, its private nature means that volunteers, unemployed people hastily retrained as 'additional caregivers', or relatives are assigned tasks that normally require skilled nursing professionals. In order to utilise the informal labour potential of civil society, the state sets up 'cash for care' programmes, strengthens legal support for the elderly with the help of monetised volunteer work, legalises informal domestic work done by Eastern European migrants in the course of the eastward enlargement of the EU, and establishes workfare programmes for the long-term unemployed and low-skilled workers. Hence, by means of active social policy, the exploited cornerstone of a lean welfare state in times of rising demands for elderly care consists of a mostly female 'care reserve army' (Haubner, 2017: 152–156).

Conclusion: social vulnerability and the link between exclusion and exploitation

When it comes to the mechanisms of this exploitative wage-dumping, Marxist-Feminist approaches are very helpful because they systematically expose the *economic* importance of (sexual) discrimination, exclusion, and devaluation. To understand why specific groups of Germany's population are exploited this way, we have to look at the connection between social exclusion, vulnerability, and exploitation. Deriving from sociology of work's research on precarity and informality, the term social vulnerability (Alter Chen, 2013; Castel, 2005) is well-suited to such a theoretical synthesis. It helps to analytically differentiate between processes of exclusion and connect them to the exploitation of socially vulnerable actors. Social vulnerability can be caused by material-economic scarcity, due to the non-possession of assets and means of production, as well as by the exclusion from wage labour or welfare compensations. Those cases result in material vulnerability, forcing the affected persons to make concessions, for instance by accepting informal or precarious jobs.

Additionally, social vulnerability is generated in the cultural-symbolic sphere by practices of discrimination and marginalisation that cause exclusion according to ascriptive attributes. This second axis of cultural vulnerability acknowledges the central influence of socio-cultural factors on the constitution and reproduction of exploitative relations. For cultural vulnerability also forces those affected by sexist or racist discrimination to accept low-paid and informal jobs. Thus, this concept takes account of the insights from feminist research on the exploitation of feminised labour.

When care work is paid less than other work and is mostly done by specific groups of women, the connection between exclusion, discrimination, vulnerability, and exploitation becomes obvious. What the exploited have in common is their specifically female social vulnerability, the result of social exclusion and discrimination. Women are discriminated against when it comes to decent livelihoods: they earn less, suffer from social insecurity, and are still culturally depreciated or naturalised as caring, loving, and devoted. Thus, this form of exploitation works in three steps: exclusion, social vulnerability, and appropriation. Social exclusion therefore produces economic and cultural vulnerability when women are excluded from social security and the labour market, and are discriminated against in terms of sex, race, national origin, etc. This vulnerability can in turn be exploited by the state and capital, especially those segments of the labour market traditionally most affected by deprofessionalisation and underpayment.

Marxist-Feminist theory is useful not only to highlight the underappreciated economic role of exclusionary discrimination and power, but also to show that exploitation does not only occur within free competitive markets, in the context of industrial labour, or through profit-seeking. Marxist-Feminist theory helps to put the labour theory of value back on its reproductive feet. It allows us to broaden the concept of exploitation so that it includes not only the appropriation of surplus value, but also devaluation as an exploitative strategy for systematically lowering the price of mostly female care work. A narrow concept of exploitation that only addresses 'productive labour' while ignoring the economic importance of power and discrimination will inevitably fail to provide a complete analysis of capitalism, which, to quote Federici again, relies upon a 'heterogeneous combination of different types of labour and exploitation'.

References

Alter Chen, M., 2013. 'Informalität, Geschlecht und die globalen Auswirkungen der großen Rezession' in Burchardt, H.J., Peters, S., Weinmann, N. (Eds.), *Arbeit in globaler Perspektive. Facetten informeller Beschäftigung.* Campus, Frankfurt am Main, 149–171.

Barbalet, J.M., 1982. 'Social Closure in Class Analysis: A Critique of Parkin', *Sociology* 16(4): 484–497.

Barrett, M., 1980. *Women's Oppression Today: Problems in Marxist-Feminist Analysis.* Verso, London.

Bauböck, R., 1988. *Hausarbeit und Ausbeutung. Zur feministischen Kritik am Marx'schen Arbeitsbegriff.* Forschungsbericht No. 245. Institut für höhere Studien, Vienna.

Baumol, W.J., 2012. *The Cost Disease: Why Computers Get Cheaper and Health Care Doesn't.* Yale University Press, New Haven, CT.

Beer, U., 1983. 'Marx auf die Füße gestellt? Zum theoretischen Entwurf von Claudia v. Werlhof', *Prokla* 13(50): 22–37.

Berger, J., 1994. 'Ausbeutung' in Berliner Institut für kritische Theorie (Ed.), *Historisch-kritisches Wörterbuch des Marxismus.* Vol. 1. Argument, Hamburg, 736–743.

Berger, J., 2009. *Der diskrete Charme des Marktes. Zur sozialen Problematik der Marktwirtschaft.* VS, Wiesbaden.

Boltanski, L., Chiapello, È., 2003. *Der neue Geist des Kapitalismus.* UVK, Konstanz.

Buchanan, A., 1979. 'Exploitation, Alienation, and Injustice'. *Canadian Journal of Philosophy* 9(1): 121–139.

Bundesministerium für Familie, Senioren, Frauen und Jugend (BMFSFJ), 2012. *Zeit für Familie – Familienzeitpolitik als Chance einer nachhaltigen Familienpolitik.* Achter Familienbericht, Berlin.

Castel, R., 2005. *Die Stärkung des Sozialen. Leben im neuen Wohlfahrtsstaat.* Hamburger Edition, Hamburg.

Crocker, L., 1972. 'Marx' Concept of Exploitation'. *Social Theory and Practice* 2(2): 201–215.

Dalla Costa, M., James, S., 1972. *The Power of Women and the Subversion of the Community.* Falling Wall Press, London.

Daly, M., 2000. *The Gender Division of Welfare: The Impact of the British and German Welfare States.* Cambridge University Press, Cambridge.

Federici, S., 2012. *Aufstand aus der Küche. Reproduktionsarbeit im globalen Kapitalismus und die unvollendete feministische Revolution.* Edition Assemblage, Münster.

Folbre, N., 1982. 'Exploitation Comes Home: A Critique of the Marxian Theory of Family Labour'. *Cambridge Journal of Economics* 6: 317–329.

Gerstenberger, H., 2017. *Markt und Gewalt. Die Funktionsweise des historischen Kapitalismus.* Westfälisches Dampfboot, Münster.

Hartmann, H., 1997. 'The Unhappy Marriage of Marxism and Feminism: Towards a More Progressive Union' in Nicholson, L. (Ed.), *The Second Wave: A Reader in Feminist Theory.* Routledge, New York; London, 97–122.

Haubner, T., 2017. *Die Ausbeutung der sorgenden Gemeinschaft. Laienpflege in Deutschland.* Campus, Frankfurt am Main; New York.

Haug, F., 2015. 'Marxismus-Feminismus' in Haug W.F. et al. (Eds.), *Historisch-kritisches Wörterbuch des Marxismus.* Vol. 8/II. Argument, Hamburg, 1882–1900.

Haug, F., Hauser, K., 1984. 'Geschlechterverhältnisse. Zur internationalen Diskussion um Marxismus-Feminismus' in Projekt Sozialistischer Feminismus (Eds.), *Geschlechterverhältnisse und Frauenpolitik.* Berlin, 10–58.

Hochschild, A., 2001. 'Global Care Chains and Emotional Surplus Value' in Giddens, A., Hutton, W. (Eds.), *On the Edge: Living with Global Capitalism*. Vintage, London, 130–146.

Jürgens, K., 2010. 'Deutschland in der Reproduktionskrise'. *Leviathan* 38(4): 559–587.

Komlosy, A., 2012. 'Arbeit und Werttransfer im Kapitalismus. Vielfalt der Erscheinungsformen und Operationalisierung'. *Sozial. Geschichte Online* 9: 36–62.

Kronauer, M., 2010. *Exklusion. Die Gefährdung des Sozialen im hoch entwickelten Kapitalismus*. 2nd updated and expanded edition. Campus, Frankfurt am Main; New York.

Le Grand, J., 1991. 'Quasi-Markets and Social Policy'. *The Economic Journal* 101(408): 1256–1267.

Lessenich, S., 2008. *Die Neuerfindung des Sozialen. Der Sozialstaat im flexiblen Kapitalismus*. Transcript, Bielefeld.

Lutz, H., Palenga-Möllenbeck, E., 2014. 'Care-Migrantinnen im geteilten Europa – Verbindungen und Widersprüche in einem transnationalen Raum' in Aulenbacher, B., Riegraf, B., Theobald, H. (Eds.), *Sorge: Arbeit, Verhältnisse, Regime*. Soziale Welt Sonderband 20. Nomos, Baden-Baden, 217–231.

Marx, K., 1887. *Capital: A Critique of Political Economy*. Vol. 1. Progress Publishers, Moscow.

Marx, K., 1959. *Capital. A Critique of Political Economy*. Vol. 3. Progress Publishers, Moscow.

Marx, K., Engels, F., 1969 [1848]. *Manifesto of the Communist Party*. Progress Publishers, Moscow.

Marx, K., Engels, F., 2004. *The German Ideology*, Part One with selections from Parts Two and Three, together with Marx, K. 'Introduction to a Critique of Political Economy'. Edited by C.J. Arthur. International Publishers, New York.

McLaughlin, P., 2008. 'The Ethics of Exploitation'. *Studia Philosophica Estonica* 1(3): 5–16.

Mies, M., 2009. 'Hausfrauisierung, Globalisierung, Subsistenzperspektive' in Van der Linden, M., Roth, K.H. (Eds.), *Über Marx hinaus. Arbeitsgeschichte und Arbeitsbegriff in der Konfrontation mit den globalen Arbeitsverhältnissen des 21. Jahrhunderts*. Assoziation A, Hamburg, 257–289.

Molyneux, M., 1979. 'Beyond the Domestic Labour Debate'. *New Left Review* 1(116): 3–27.

Morishima, M., 1973. *Marx' Economics: A Dual Theory of Value and Growth*. Cambridge University Press, London.

Neusüß, Ch., 1985. *Die Kopfgeburten der Arbeiterbewegung oder die Genossin Luxemburg bringt alles durcheinander*. Rasch und Röhring, Hamburg.

Parijs, Ph. v., 1984. 'What (if Anything) Is Intrinsically Wrong with Capitalism?' *Philosophica* 34(2): 85–102.

Parkin, F., 1974. 'Strategies of Social Closure in Class Formation' in Parkin, F. (Ed.), *The Social Analysis of Class Structure*. Tavistock, London: 1–18.

Powell, M., 2007. 'The Mixed Economy of Welfare and the Social Division of Welfare' in Powell, M. (Ed.), *Understanding the Mixed Economy of Welfare*. Bristol: Policy Press, 1–21.

Prognos AG, 2012. *Pflegelandschaft 2030*. Vereinigung der Bayrischen Wirtschaft. www.prognos.com/uploads/tx_atwpubdb/121000_Prognos_vbw_Pflegelandschaft_2030.pdf. Accessed: 7 May 2015.

Roemer, J., 1986. 'New Directions in the Marxian Theory of Exploitation and Class' in Roemer, J. (Ed.), *Analytical Marxism*. Cambridge University Press, Cambridge, 81–113.

Samuelson, P.A., 1971. 'Understanding the Marxian Notion of Exploitation: A Summary of the So-called Transformation Problem between Marxian Values and Competitive Prices'. *Journal of Economic Literature* 9: 399–431.

Sørensen, A.B., 2000. 'Symposium on Class Analysis: Toward a Sounder Basis for Class Analysis'. *American Journal of Sociology* 105(6): 1523–1558.

Steedman, I., 1981. *Marx after Sraffa*. Verso, London.

Vogel, L., 1973. 'The Earthly Family'. *Radical America* 7(4 and 5): 9–50.

Werlhof, C. v., 1981. 'Frauen und Dritte Welt als "Natur" des Kapitals oder: Ökonomie auf die Füße gestellt' in Dauber, H., Simpfendörfer, W. (Eds.), *Eigener Haushalt und bewohnter Erdkreis. Ökologisches und ökumenisches Lernen in der "Einen Welt"*. Peter Hammer, Wuppertal, 187–214.

Werlhof, C. v., Mies, M., Bennholdt-Thomsen, V., 1983. *Frauen, die letzte Kolonie. Zur Hausfrauisierung der Arbeit*. Rowohlt, Reinbek.

Wertheimer, A., 1996. *Exploitation*. Princeton University Press, Princeton, NJ.

Wright, E.O., 1989. *Classes*. Verso, London; New York.

PART II

PRODUCTION

8 | MARX AND SOCIAL REPRODUCTION THEORY

Three different historical strands

Ankica Čakardić

Introduction

This essay aims to contribute to the historical and current discussions on the significance of Marx's understanding of the problem of social reproduction, and to engage with the development of contemporary Marxist-Feminist theory. Concurrently, it illustrates how Marxist critique of political economy is relevant for the study of crucial feminist questions, including: gender oppression, social reproduction, the relationship between productive and reproductive labour, and the relationship between paid and unpaid labour. Lise Vogel contends: 'Marx, Engels, and their immediate followers contributed more to understanding the oppression of women than participants in the modern women's movement usually recognise' (Vogel, 2013: 141). Unlike transhistorical approaches that tend to sever connections between capitalist exploitation and gender oppression, we present different strands of social reproduction theory that analyse specific determinants of gender oppression, and which interact with capitalist modes of production. In the aftermath of the crises of 2008, the empirical effects of global capitalism 'have altered the material conditions in which we live today' and have thus changed 'the organisation of reproduction' (Gimenez, 2018b: 26). In *Marx, Women, and Capitalist Social Reproduction*, Martha Gimenez notes that we have witnessed vast ideological and economic changes in recent decades, and that: 'These changes have affected male and female workers differently' (2018b: 27). In light of these changes, we consider it important to use and develop social reproduction theory (SRT) as a tool for understanding the persistence of gender oppression in capitalism, and for ways of how to fight it.

In an effort to propose a theoretical-historical model that would enable valid analysis of relationships of oppression (primarily understood through categories of gender, race, and sexuality) and exploitation (primarily understood through the category of class), one would indeed use Marx as a point of departure. Although Marx does not systematically analyse the issue of oppression in his works, his explanatory methodological model (primarily in *Capital* and partially in *Grundrisse*) is crucial for analysing the relationship between exploitation and oppression. Marx's critique of the transhistorical assumptions of classical political economy, his definition of the particularities of capitalist societies as 'gigantic collections of commodities',[1] as well as his representation of the whole circulation of capitalist production and reproduction, are crucial elements of SRT (Marx, 1947a: 1). Using Marx's aforementioned epistemological innovations in *Capital* as points of departure, SRT focuses on a particular aspect of the relationship between productive and reproductive labour, which remained, as Tithi Bhattacharya has underlined, 'undeveloped' or 'under-theorized' by Marx (Bhattacharya, 2017b: 12).

Taking this into account, the aims of SRT are to analyse phenomena that are 'hidden' in the production process, to enquire into the mode of process that enables the worker to attend their work, to investigate the conditions of the worker's existence, and to examine the social processes that relate to these conditions. This theory poses the following question to Marxism:

> If workers' labour produces all the wealth in society, who then produces the worker? Put another way: What kind of processes enable the worker to arrive at the doors of her place of work every day so that she can produce the wealth of society? (Bhattacharya, 2017b: 1)

In what follows we aim to illustrate Marx's understanding of the term reproduction within the capitalist mode of production, and ways in which SRT elaborates on these premises.

Marx: reproduction of capitalism as a whole

Marx uses the term 'social reproduction' in his works to signify the meaning of the process of capitalist production as a whole (Bhattacharya, 2017b: 6). As Ben Fine and Alfredo Saad Filho explain, 'Capital, as self-expanding value, is essentially the process of reproducing value and producing new value. The circuit of capital describes this motion' (Fine and Saad Filho, 2010: 46). The problem of the capitalist system as a whole is discussed extensively and meticulously in *Capital*, Marx's all-encompassing scientific project. Volume 1 of *Capital* mainly offers a general analysis of capitalism, and illustrates how social relations 'give rise to economic realities and social developments around production' (Fine and Saad Filho, 2010: 44). The other two volumes extend the main thesis presented in Volume 1. It is essential to stress that in the first three chapters of Volume 1, Marx focuses on commodities and money, leaving 'transformation' – various forms which capital takes – and its reproduction absent from consideration (Marx, 1947a: 1–105). However, once he finishes elaborating on the issues of production and distinction between fixed and variable capital (1947a: 154–165), he thoroughly analyses, in Volume 2, the process of capital circulation, and focuses on the 'periodical nature' of its movement and 'turnover' (see Marx, 1947b: first two chapters). 'The total turnover time' is therefore equal to the sum of production time and circulation time; it is that period of time for which a capitalist must advance invested capital to 'fertilise' it. The general form of the circuit of industrial capital is presented at the very beginning of Volume 2, through its three stages by the formula M—C ... P ... C—M'. Circular flows of individual capitals are interconnected and presuppose one another; the circuit of one capital necessitates that it encounters the products of other capitals on the market. Their mutual co-relation is again confirmed when considering that the reproduction of a particular capital is exclusively realised as a constituent component of the reproduction of social capital as a whole: it cannot be considered in isolation. 'So that a total social capital can be reproduced', argues Michael Heinrich,

> the total product must have a certain *material* proportioning: on the one hand, a certain amount of means of production have to be produced as are required by individual capitals as a whole, and on the other, so many means of subsistence have to be produced as are consumed by workers and capitalists. (Heinrich, 2012: 137)

Marx begins his explanation of the reproduction of the capitalist system as a whole with the analysis of simple reproduction (Fine and Saad Filho, 2010: 52–61). Simple reproduction is understood as meaning that there is no accumulation of capital, and that the entire surplus value is used for the capitalists' subsistence and consumption, hence production does not expand (Marx, 1947b: third chapter). While this state of affairs lasts, no new technical innovations are introduced, the existing pattern of production is repeated, and the economy is reproduced on the pre-existing level of activity. Aiming to illustrate how simple reproduction functions, Marx divided industrial production into two departments, labelled Departments I and II. In this model, Department I produces the means of production, while Department II produces articles for consumption. Certain requirements must be met and a condition of balance must exist to maintain the successful flow of simple reproduction between these two departments: $p_1 = c_1 + c_2$ (product of Department I $\{p_1\}$ must be equal to the sum of the constant capital of Department I $\{c_1\}$ and Department II $\{c_2\}$).[2] Equally, articles of Department II $\{p_2\}$ must be equal to the sum of wages and surplus values of both departments: $p_2 = v_1 + s_1 + v_2 + s_2$. Finally, these two equations of departments of simple reproduction may be combined into a single equation: $c_2 = v_1 + s_1$. If a given capitalist does not consume the whole surplus value, but spends the majority of it on purchasing additional or new means of production, this then becomes a basic presumption for the accumulation of capital. Unlike simple reproduction, in the expanded reproduction model one department assumes the form of subsistence and needs of the capitalist (r), while the other department accumulates (a) and is divided into two parts: one to secure additional production means (ac), and one to secure wages for the newly hired workers in production (av). If social demand for the means of production within simple reproduction is expressed with $c_1 + c_2$, then the equation for extended reproduction is $c_1 + ac_1 + c_2 + ac_2$. In other words, in the case of social demand for commodities for general consumption, this equation is valid: $v_1 + s_1 + v_2 + s_2$. Hence, prerequisites for enabling expanded reproduction may be expressed with the following equation: $c_2 + ac_2 = v_1 + r_1 + av_1$. Particular materials in the process of simple reproduction, like labour, raw materials, and means of production, are also elements of expanded reproduction, in which it is assumed that quantity rather than 'market' is the basic category for its realisation.

Fine and Saad Filho stress that these reproduction schemata have been interpreted in a number of different ways, the most popular being the one which offers a Marxian analysis of *equilibrium*, either static or dynamic (Fine and Saad Filho, 2010: 54). They dismiss both these interpretations, explaining how simple and expanded reproduction are not alternatives; 'rather, the former exists within the latter' (2010: 55). Simply speaking and according to Marx, direct production of capital also represents its process of labour and accumulation of value, and its 'compelling motive is the production of surplus-value' (Marx, 1947b: 304). Marx summarises what crucially determines the relations of circulation of capital and its turnover:

> The process of reproduction of capital comprises this direct process of production as well as the two phases of the circulation process proper, i.e., the entire circuit which, as a periodic process – a process which constantly repeats itself in definite periods – constitutes the turnover of capital. (Marx, 1947b: 304)

In this aggregate circular process, the emphasis is on perpetual renewal and repeated realisation of capital, whether as product, activity, money, or commodity. Here, each form of capital manifests itself as 'an individualized fraction, a fraction endowed with individual life, as it were, of the aggregate social capital, just as every individual capitalist is but an individual element of the capitalist class' (Marx, 1947b: 305). It is crucial to highlight that the movement of social capital is the unified movement of its 'individualized' fragments, the turnovers of individual capitals, and that their necessary movement, observed in their entirety, simultaneously includes movement of capital *and* the movement of general commodities.

Have we completely exhausted the topic of reproduction through our current mode of discussion? What could we mean by implying that Marx's critique of political economy is 'unfinished'? We refer to the notion of labour which is 'in the heart of creating or reproducing society as a whole', and to the notion which, 'ironically, he [Marx] himself failed to develop fully' (Bhattacharya, 2017b: 2). We are relaying Vogel's claim that the reproduction of labour-power in the context of overall social reproduction represents 'a theoretical problem of fundamental significance' for Marxist feminism (Vogel, 2013: 142). 'Socialist theorists', Vogel writes, 'have never sufficiently confronted this problem, yet the rudiments of a usable approach lie buried just below the surface of Marx's analysis of social reproduction in Capital' (2013: 142).

The existence of women's oppression in class societies is a historical phenomenon (Vogel, 2013: 154). Vogel argues that while women have historically had greater responsibility for the ongoing tasks of necessary labour in class societies, 'it is not accurate to say that there is some universal domestic sphere separate from the world of public production' (2013: 152). She goes on to explain that 'the ruling class encourages male supremacy within the exploited classes', and it is 'not the sex-division of labour in itself, that forms the material basis for women's subordination in class-society' (2013: 153). Iris Young argues similarly when she points to the fact that

> [T]he form and character of women's oppression have undergone fundamental historical transformation [and] the existence of pre-capitalist patriarchy need no longer count as evidence that male domination in capitalist society has its foundations in a structure of social relations independent of the system of capitalism itself. (Young, 1981: 58–59)[3]

The range of Marxist-Feminist writings on the history of gender oppression and social reproduction does not form a coherent theoretical or political body of work. In the following, we will try to offer a possible overview of social reproduction theories, three historical and two theoretical strands.

Social reproduction theory: three historical and two theoretical strands

Unlike labour in the productive sphere of society, domestic labour is performed in the reproductive sphere.[4] Reproduction of the working class in capitalism represents three aspects of necessary labour: (a) maintenance of direct producers, (b) maintenance of non-labouring members of the subordinate class (usually implying care-giving to old people, children, and the unemployed) and (c) generational renewal of workers and their lives (birth taken for granted as the biological reproduction of new labour force) (Vogel, 2013: 150; Bhattacharya, 2013). This approach to the issue of reproduction denotes the ontological level of the problem: that which does not hold the significance of labour is *not* labour at all. The mathematics applied here is clear: if this 'non-labour' were to be transferred to the domain of, for instance, the state or to the capitalist who employs the worker, it would require of them to organise a whole range of activities and invest time and money, both of which have traditionally been the burden of the household, in order to meet the needs. The question of an alternative, more egalitarian redistribution of reproductive labour requires fundamental changes in attitudes towards the market and production, but such changes come at a price. As institutionalised structures of family ordinarily become major social sites for the performance of the maintenance as well as of the generational replacement aspects of necessary labour in capitalism, here lies, writes Vogel, 'one source for the historical division of labour according to sex that assigns women and men different roles with respect to necessary and surplus-labour' (Vogel, 2013: 152).

Marxist-Feminist approaches to the issue of reproduction vary, and it is not possible to claim there is one overall theory (see Arruzza, 2013: 79–124). On the one hand, Marxist autonomists gathered around the 'Wages for Housework' campaign offer one approach which uses dual-systems analysis (Dalla Costa and James, 1975; Fortunati, 1981; Federici, 2012). Christine Delphy offers a materialist approach that is structured around the premise that social reproduction is a series of actions performed within the domestic sphere, which are perceived by Delphy (1980) as a particular mode of production. Finally, Lise Vogel (2013) offers a 'unitary theory' approach, according to which social reproduction implies the simultaneous reproduction of labour force and of class society. In the following, we shall attempt to illustrate the continuous lineage of the body of work on SRT during three different time periods,[5] and identify similarities and differences that surfaced during those periods, depending on whether the analysis is structured in dual-systems or unitary theory methodology. We will begin this section by identifying the origins of SRT.

Socialist feminism:[6] early social reproduction theory

Socialist women gathered around the Second International based their universal demands on social-economic foundations, with a full understanding of the interconnection between exploitation and oppression. Unlike bourgeois feminism of that time which, in its lobbying for equal rights, reinforced itself on the basis of the gender oppression of the higher classes, socialist feminists rejected the idea of a struggle based exclusively on identity, and called out on the imminent connection of gender and class. Within the critique of bourgeois feminism from the Marxist perspective, there were four theorists and revolutionaries among others who strongly addressed the issue of class and reproductive labour: Clara Zetkin, Rosa Luxemburg, Nadezhda Konstantinovna Krupskaya, and Alexandra Kollontai. Their conclusions should certainly be interpreted as 'early' SRT and we will attempt to illustrate that.

Clara Zetkin, perfectly aware of the position of working-class women in capitalism, once stressed that 'Women are doubly oppressed, by capitalism and by their dependency in family life' (cited in Riddell, 2014). In her text 'Social-Democracy and Woman Suffrage' she summarises the key issue of reproductive labour and its value, and underlines that it is a mistake to assign reproductive labour to 'private distribution', because that same labour plays a 'general societal part': 'the service rendered by the mother in the home is no private service simply to her husband, but an activity which is of the highest social importance' (Zetkin, 1906). Later in the same text, Zetkin finalises the basic premise of SRT by asserting that reproductive and productive labour should be analysed in equivalent terms: 'All this proves the high social worth of labour which a woman performs in the producing and rearing of children' (Zetkin, 1906).

Rosa Luxemburg investigates the problem of social reproduction in a similar vein. Even though she did not write many texts on the so-called women's question and did not participate directly in the work of women groups, she strongly supported women's labour organisations (Čakardić, 2017). Her outspoken support was most often evident through collaboration with her close friend, Clara Zetkin. However, on occasions when she did explicitly address the so-called 'women's question', she did so by bringing into focus structural issues of reproductive labour. For instance, in her speech from 1912 in which she criticised the capitalist structure of family (referring to Engels), Luxemburg asserts:

> This kind of work is not productive in the sense of the present capitalist economy no matter how enormous an achievement the sacrifices and energy spent, the thousand little efforts add up to. This is but the private affair of the worker, his happiness and blessing, and for this reason non-existent for our present society. As long as capitalism and the wage system rule, only that kind of work is considered productive which produces surplus value, which creates capitalist profit. From this point of view, the music-hall dancer whose legs sweep profit into her employer's pocket is a productive worker, whereas all the toil of the proletarian women and mothers in the four walls of their homes is considered unproductive. This sounds brutal and insane, but corresponds exactly to the brutality and insanity of our present capitalist economy. And seeing this brutal reality clearly and sharply is the proletarian woman's first task. (Luxemburg, 2004: 241)

Nadezhda Krupskaya, a great revolutionary, essayist, and an educationalist, wrote *The Woman Worker* in 1899. It was originally published and circulated in 1901 under the pseudonym 'Sablina', before being banned following the suppression of the 1905 revolution. It was republished in 1925 with a new preface by Krupskaya. Its significance stems from being among the first Marxist works dealing with the situation of women in Russia. In her pamphlet she vividly describes the plight of peasant women in the family, and stresses 'that as a mother, the woman worker has an interest' in 'the joyful happiness of freedom' (Krupskaya, 2017: vi). While examining the condition of woman as a member of the working class, Krupskaya demonstrates how proletarian women suffer not only as workers but also from being women who take care of household and children. At a certain point she writes: 'For the woman worker, family life means being tied into endlessly looking after children. ... With the birth of a child, the peasant woman faces added chores. After all, one cannot both go out to work and care for children' (2017: 12). Analysing the problem of women and bringing up children, Krupskaya clearly draws a distinction between proletarian women and bourgeois women: 'The bourgeois, who is not burdened with having to worry how to feed and bring up children … can provide all manner of comforts, hire all kinds of wet nurses, maids, governesses, servants' (2017: 16). Women, Krupskaya believed, had to be liberated not only from the domination of capitalist exploitation, but also from being confined to the household and its family chores. The road to proletarian women's emancipation lied through winning economic independence and through capitalism being replaced by a socialist system.

Of all socialist women, it was Kollontai who devoted most attention to the analysis of the issue of reproductive labour. In 'Communism and the Family' she asserts that time and energy invested in the performance of household labour are 'lost at the end of the day', in other words, they do not produce value. She calls this type of work 'unproductive':

> The housewife may spend all day cleaning her home, from morning to evening, she may wash and iron the linen daily, make every effort to keep her clothing in good order and prepare whatever dishes she pleases and her modest resources allow, and she will still end the day without having created any values. Despite her industry she would not have made anything that could be considered a commodity … Women's work is becoming less useful to the community as a whole. It is becoming unproductive. (Kollontai, 1977: 255)

If we want to illustrate a continuous theoretical lineage of Marxist feminism that extends over a period from the nineteenth century, via the twentieth century, onto recent theoretical enquiries and into the problem of social reproduction, we would use Zetkin, Luxemburg, Krupskaya, and Kollontai as our points of departure. Although the position of socialist women of the Second International may at times seem functionalist in their nature they easily offer a solid base for a clear theoretical lineage which encompasses in particular ways all three aforementioned historical origins of SRT. The theoretical approach which introduced the question of 'double oppression' (oppression in economic and in domestic spheres), as illustrated by socialist women of the Second International, was taken up and further developed in a more systematic manner during the 1970s by 'autonomist feminists'. Autonomist feminism wanted to take on from socialist women the premise that oppression and exploitation are mutually separated and yet connected phenomena, each of which function according to their own logic. The basis of this theoretical strand is defined by the claim that reproductive labour *is* labour in Marxist terms and that it produces surplus value. Precisely this premise will be of use regarding the recent approaches to a 'unitary' SRT, but this will be discussed in more detail once we finish elaborating on the 1970s.

Autonomist feminism: social reproduction theory of the 1970s

Autonomist feminism is usually associated with the international 'Wages for Housework' campaign. The campaign began in Italy in the 1970s as part of the feminist organisation *Lotta Femminista* ('Feminist struggle'), whose theoretical origins and practice were closely associated with the *Potere Operaio* ('Workerism', also known globally as operaismo) and *Autonomia Operaia* ('Worker autonomy').[7] A focus on the 'working mass', tactical autonomism, and anti-syndicalism, for which was substituted the concept of a worker takeover of surplus value according to the principles of direct action, were all points of departure that had a strong influence on various movements of the period, feminism included. 'Feminist struggle', with its operaist or autonomist tendencies, was formed in the midst of these circumstances.

Leopoldina Fortunati, one of the founders of 'Feminist struggle', observes that operaismo developed a useful epistemological framework and crucial theoretical-practical instruments for future political struggles, but that this Marxist struggle neglected 'women's experience', despite its progressive goals (Fortunati, 2013). Moreover, Fortunati believed that operaismo 're-examined orthodox Marxism' in a powerful way although it 'continued to remain blind towards the reality lived by women' (2013). Operaismo and its discourse included analyses of factory life and the role of the alienated working class within the capitalist mode of production, but it ultimately omitted, as Fortunati stressed, the issue of domestic labour, sexuality, family roles pertaining to capitalism and its reproduction. This is why feminists decided to work on the 'autonomist' feminist organisation rooted in basic operaistic principles. In practice, autonomist feminists were gathered around the Wages for Housework campaign, whereas in theory autonomist feminism emanated from Marx's *Capital*, and a critique of political economy with feminist overtones. In Fortunati's own words,

> On the basis of these political experiences, I decided to dedicate my main effort to analysing women's conditions of life from the perspective of political economy, reconsidered in Marxian terms. Of course, I had to bend the Marxian categories in light of the feminist experience and political tradition. (2013)

Debates pertaining to wages for housework that most often took place in American, Italian, and British leftist feminist circles peaked in the early 1970s. Mariarosa Dalla Costa and Selma James's pamphlet *The Power of Women and the Subversion of the Community* (Dalla Costa and James, 1975), published in 1972, opened up the debate on unpaid domestic labour. By 1975 already, Federici published the article 'Wages Against Housework', which then functioned as a sort of Wages for Housework campaign manifesto (Federici, 2012). In the follow-up, we aim to illustrate the SRT as a variant of autonomist feminism.

Unlike classical economics and its insistence on demand, in his critique of political economy Marx focused not only on labour costs, but on the fact that the capitalist never pays for all realised labour of the worker and thus achieves surplus value. Marx demonstrates that in a case of an eight-hour working day, a worker must essentially be paid half of the amount of the wage in order for the capitalist to be able to appropriate the value created in the following four hours. Using Marx's labour theory of value as a point of departure, autonomist feminism stresses that in Marxist theory another 'mystical' element necessary for the production and reproduction of surplus is missing; the 'hidden' story of unpaid labour:

> We must admit that capital has been very successful in hiding our work. It has created a true masterpiece at the expense of women. By denying housework a wage and transforming it into an act of love, capital has killed many birds with one stone ... To say that we want wages for housework is to expose the fact that housework is already money for capital, that capital has made and makes money out of our cooking, smiling, fucking. (Federici, 2012: 17–19)

Here Silvia Federici analyses reproductive labour as a type of labour with permanent productive potential which is successfully sucked dry and exploited by capital. That argument is made even more explicit by Dalla Costa and James in *The Power of Women and the Subversion of the Community*, in a section titled 'Surplus Value and the Social Factory', where the authors claim that 'housework as work is productive in the Marxian sense, that is, is producing value' (Dalla Costa and James, 1975: 53, footnote 12). According to autonomist feminists, domestic labour has exchange value and hence it always participates in the production of surplus.

In her text 'Wages Against Housework' Federici attempted to clear up the mess caused by inadequate and narrow interpretations of the demand for wages. Although it is difficult to dispute the campaign's focus on the question of money, both in a symbolic and in a material manner, which leads us to believe that 'paying' for housework is the only demand here, Wages for Housework campaign members highlight the importance of the intention behind the campaign, to underline the political role of demand: 'When we struggle for wages we struggle unambiguously and directly against our social role' (Federici, 2012: 19). In addition, Federici's revision of the most critical part of the campaign's title ('for wages' was revised into 'against wages' for housework) is far from accidental. This is her underlining, almost pedagogically, that housework *is* labour, and that the simultaneous gender division of labour successfully secures the foundations for the capitalist mode of production. Autonomist feminists see these foundations of capitalism in the oppression of women in 'patriarchy'. Much like Clara Zetkin's analysis discussed in the previous chapter, autonomist feminism is similarly focused on the phenomenon of the 'double burden' of women.

Autonomist feminism dissolved the Marxian labour theory of value and the concept of the 'working class', focusing instead on the problem of the 'housewife', and her role in the household, capitalism, and leftist organisations. Fortunati suggested an analytical unit within the context of SRT (Fortunati, 1981). Her critique of classical political economy functions through – a term she coined herself – the 'apparent antithesis': production/reproduction. According to the author's premise, it is not possible to examine the capitalist mode of production and its circular nature as a whole if we apply a dual ontology, in which production implies value and reproduction implies non-value. Critique of the principle of naturalisation (which implies that reproductive labour is assumed to arise from natural circumstances rather than relations of production) in this sense also challenges the premise of productive labour which – unlike reproductive labour – creates surplus value. In Fortunati's analysis, the problem of reproductive labour is at least threefold: it is necessary to mathematically establish that reproduction partly creates surplus value, to analyse why reproduction is primarily perceived as a 'natural force of social work', and to elaborate on the distinction between material and non-material categories of reproduction. Fortunati uses these three levels to debate the orthodox Marxian assumptions according to which reproductive labour is a precondition of surplus value production, but at the same time holds no exchange value itself.

Approximately ten years after the Wages for Housework campaign and the ideas brought up by autonomist feminism, Lise Vogel published *Marxism and the Oppression of Women*, a book that deals with the oppression of women, and developed the so-called 'unitary' theory. In a way, the 'unitary', or, so to say, 'third wave' SRT represents the continuation of the debate tackling the issue of reproduction, which is still relevant today (Bhattacharya, 2017b). Unlike the double-systems theory of autonomist feminism, the unitary methodological approach insists on the inseparable nature of the system of oppression and exploitation, claiming with absolute justification that gender and class categories need to be analysed uniformly or 'unitarily'. Finally, let us take a short look at the particularities of the unitary approach to the analysis of gender.

Returning to Marx: unitary social reproduction theory

Unlike the concept of SRT as a dual-systems methodological pattern, 'unitary' theory developed an approach that insists on an integral and uniform understanding of the process of production of commodities and the reproduction of labour-power. Unlike autonomist feminist debates of the 1970s and 1980s, current Marxian theories of social reproduction generally agree that capitalism and patriarchy are analytically inseparable (De'Ath, 2018: 1536). In more rigorous methodological approaches, theoreticians even dismiss the term patriarchy if it leads to a conclusion that women's oppression has its locus in a system other than capitalism. In a very specific approach to the issue of women's domestic labour, Linda Briskin writes:

> 'Patriarchy' is a misleading term because it has no distinct structural reality, and therefore a theory of patriarchy cannot provide us with a satisfactory explanation of women's oppression. Since the family changes with the mode of production, it is more useful to investigate patriarchal *ideas* and to elaborate the way in which their expression and form is mediated by that mode of production. (Briskin, 1980: 147)

The author argues that domestic labour is part of capitalism, but predicated upon a particular set of social relations that are moulded by the dominant relation (Briskin, 1980: 163). She focuses on the relationship between laws governing the capitalist production of value and the historically determined social relations characteristic of capitalism. In developing the argument that domestic labour does not produce value – be it exchange or use value (1980: 154) – and in distinguishing between the abstraction of the theory of value and the historical reality of capitalism, Briskin describes domestic labour as a form of labour that emerges with the rise of capitalism and the development of the capitalist family form.

The methodological key for understanding the oppression of women under capitalism is 'unitarian' when it rejects notions that reproductive work in privatised households is 'productive' of surplus value – capitalistically organised and subject to the law of value (featuring specialisation, technical innovation, and accumulation). Somewhat as an answer to SRT of the 1970s, Lise Vogel discards dual-systems methodology of autonomist feminism in her book,[8] arguing that reproductive labour produces strictly use value but not exchange value. We could summarise Vogel's main thesis by claiming that it is precisely because non-value-producing activities are necessary for creating surplus value that the gender oppression persists. Although debates of the 1970s pertaining to domestic labour gave rise to positions contrary to unitary tradition, positions that increasingly saw domestic labour as 'productive labour' upon which the reproduction of (capitalist) society depended entirely, it would be difficult to analyse the development of unitary theory without taking into consideration clear epistemological contributions of autonomist feminism. Despite their differences, their continual lineage of social reproduction theories within a Marxist-Feminist framework is indisputable.

Unitary tradition, Bhattacharya writes, offered two key fundamental insights (2017b: 2–3). Taking Marx as its point of departure, the first insight offers a premise that human labour is the very foundation of production and reproduction of society as a whole.[9] In direct opposition to a classical-economic understanding of labour, SRT underlines that the 'naturalisation' of performing household labour disables the analysis of the systemic totality of capitalism, in the same vein as capitalist economics is reduced to workers and owners, disregarding the fact, as Susan Ferguson emphasises, that the reproduction of society – even in its everyday chores in households, schools, hospitals, prisons, etc. – 'sustains the drive for accumulation' (quoted in Bhattacharya, 2017b: 2). In other words, if capitalist economics implies that the production of commodities and services requires a 'place', then the preparation of human labour-power for this production is taking place outside the framework of formal economics – that is, in the home (be that in the form of the family, labour-camps, or dormitory facilities). The second insight of SRT deals with the analysis of oppression in a non-functionalistic way: the oppression is interpreted strictly via structural relations within the capitalist mode of production (Bhattacharya, 2017b: 3). It is then interpreted in a more intersectional way, not just as an 'add-on' to basic economic processes. Ever since *Marxism and the Oppression of Women* was published in 1983, and reissued in 2014, the essential analytical approach to women's oppression as determined by Lise Vogel in her book and further developed by current Marxian SRT may be summarised as follows:[10]

> By the early 1980s, the verdict was in, at least among Marxist feminists, who shared a desire to replace the dualism of earlier analyses with what they called a 'unitary' account. To put it another way, instead of conceptualizing social reproduction as having two component aspects (for example, production of commodities and reproduction of labour power) they sought to develop an approach that would enclose both production and reproduction within a unitary framework. (Vogel, 2017: x)

In order to avoid the reductionism of a dual-systems approach, according to which a very complex dynamic of the relation between gender and class is reduced to the question 'what came first – gender or class?', the unitary tradition in SRT insists that we 'try and think through the complexity of capitalist society and its web of relations of exploitation, domination and oppression, avoiding unhelpful simplifications, however reassuring they might be' (Arruzza, 2013: 21). Simply put, the stress is on the unitary logic of capitalism which simultaneously implies both exploitation and oppression, that is, it unifies the 'spheres' of both production and reproduction. In her critique of the dual-systems theory, Young writes how she has 'some trouble conceiving what struggle against patriarchy as distinct from the struggle against capitalism might mean at the practical level' (Young, 1981: 63). She goes on to explain how, for instance, struggles for reproductive rights necessarily involve confronting the structures of the capitalist patriarchal state. 'From a practical level', Young concludes, 'it is simply not possible to separate this most central aspect of struggle against patriarchal structures from the struggle against capitalist structures' (1981: 63).

This is where we return to the first part of the text, to Marx. Let us recall: in his labour theory of value Marx demonstrated the way surplus value is created and what is crucial for the reproduction and accumulation of surplus value. If we agree that Marx developed one of the historically most important analytical breakthroughs with his critique of orthodox political economy and offered a systematic research on particularities of capitalism as opposed to previous systems of production and reproduction, then we are obliged to take a step forward and provide more theoretical space for further development of analysis of the ontology of labour, the unitary tradition in SRT may have analytical potential that would allow us to understand essential links between oppression and the production of surplus value.

According to Marx, our relation to the world is far from being exhausted in what appears to us as reality. This relation is incomplete if it is exclusively based on that which is direct and manifested now. With the premise that perceived reality is but a fragment of complex truth, Marx suggests that perceived 'complete' reality is nothing but a result of a particular and specific historical form. Hence, as Bhattacharya stresses, we need 'science' that is able to adequately tackle the phenomenon beyond boundaries of its superficial incidence or essence (Bhattacharya, 2017b: 15). Not only is the reality always and essentially 'fragmented', but categories that are used to describe it are historical rather than transhistorical. *Capital* is in that sense a critique of an entire mechanism of a category and represents an epistemological revolution contained exactly in the 'critique', or to put it more precisely, in the elaboration of self-understood categories and opinions that lend alleged plausibility to political economics.

In addition to the critique of 'bourgeois' science and the undermining of its theoretical field, Marx also focused his theory on the critique of capitalist social relations. Even though Marx's analysis, roughly speaking, implies that increase in social production power is performed at the expense of the individual worker, Marx's critique did not have any moral dimension. Marx focuses on the 'destructive' potentials of capitalism, deeply inherent to capitalism, rather than on 'unfair patterns'. According to Matthijs Krul, Marx was very keen that his book should be seen not simply as a polemic against capitalism, but as a serious and sober-minded analysis of how it actually works (Krul, 2017).

In relation to SRT, and taking into consideration what has been written so far, it is possible to derive a few key conclusions. The unitary theory tradition of social reproduction avoids, like Marx, descriptive models that serve as 'explanations' of the system of oppression, and aims to build valid analytical mechanisms with the potential to explicate the innate connection between surplus value production and the invisible phenomena, absent from predominant descriptions of reality. These mechanisms are urgently needed because these 'hidden phenomena' (Bhattacharya, 2017b: 15) are not displayed in front of us nor can they be understood immediately. Moreover, reality that assumes its form as, for instance, 'gendered', is not a coincidence, nor a product of a complete and homogeneous form (Bhattacharya, 2017b: 15–16). Intersectionality would contribute to this debate by asserting that reality represents a sum of various 'intersections' (gender, class, race, nation, ethnicity, etc.) resulting in 'threefold', 'fourfold', and so on, oppression instead. Analogous to a dual-systems methodological pattern, the issue of functionalism arises here too, and, as conceptualised by David McNally, the issue of 'multiple mediations of social relations and forms' (McNally, 2017: 104). According to McNally, intersectionality has 'deep theoretical flaws' (2017: 95) visible in the fact that although it can tackle the reality in a descriptive and yet superficial manner, and describe the phenomena of intersections and of overlaps arising in society, it fails, 'like mutually separated routes', to tell us about the 'logic' of their overlapping. Moreover, in instances of the separate 'routes' of different phenomena, each route surely has a logic inherent to it. In Vogel's words, 'I view them [intersections] as primarily descriptive. That is, they provide a conceptual framework for describing and investigating "diversity", but by themselves they do not explain anything' (Vogel, 2018: 281–282). Contrary to the intersectionality or dual-systems methodology, the unitary tradition of SRT attempts to interpret social analysis in a uniform manner, in its totality, and distanced from theoretical premises about the sum of disparate intersections, which allegedly define complex reality.

To finish, we will present a few more insights to conclude the interpretation discussed here, taking Marx as a point of departure for the analysis of relations of oppression and exploitation. This essay is not intended to fill a gap, but to demonstrate the continuing relevance of Marx's concepts of both capitalist social reproduction and social reproduction for contemporary Marxist feminists.[11] Early SRT and autonomist feminism, by elaborating on Marx, presented critical epistemological templates for understanding the issue of oppression. Notwithstanding their methodological shortcomings, SRT of the 1980s has kept the issue of reproduction relevant, this time through unitary theory methodology.[12] Precisely this tradition of SRT represents a chance to supplement Marx's categories of 'reproduction', 'labour', 'value', 'economics', 'working class', and so on, with contemporary meanings, as Marx envisioned with his critique of transhistoricity. This is by no means to say that his categories are useless or obsolete. On the contrary, although these categories were developed in the nineteenth century, they should be historicised, rigorously analysed, and put into a contemporary political-historical context. Marx's late works represent a string of exceptional epistemological breakthroughs, partly due to the political conclusions arising from these works, and partly due to the 'most radical' critique of political economics and society ever presented. This goes beyond the critique of particular corrosive and destructive elements of economics, and tackles Marx's more ambitious, revolutionary, premise that economics itself is a destructive element. Consequently, the unitary tradition of SRT represents an exceptionally useful and valid model for understanding society, as it develops Marx's entire scientific project further into a substantial theory, highlighting the importance of his critique and analysis of those economic processes that form the social reality. It does so by analysing both the phenomena that partially define 'perceived' social reality, and the phenomena that are hidden.

Notes

1 The wording 'social reproduction as a whole' is used here to refer to the theoretical level at which Volume 3 of *Capital* operates.

2 In Marx's equation of total value, 'p' denotes product, 'c' is constant capital (machines, work tools, auxiliary material, raw material), 'v' is variable capital (labour-power which adds new value to the product by simply working, whereas constant capital maintains existing value), 's' is surplus value (unpaid labour which creates surplus-profit), 'r' is surplus value used for subsistence of the capitalist, 'a' is surplus value that accumulates.

3 In a similar tone Young argues: 'Not until well into the nineteenth century did treatises appear arguing that the true vocation of women was motherhood, that women were too frail to engage in heavy work, that women's proper activity was to nurture and create an atmosphere of shelter and comfort for her family' (Young, 1981: 60).

4 The reproduction of labour-power in family households represents only one possible mode of renewing the bearers of labour-power. Vogel points out that labour-camps and dormitory facilities can also be used to maintain workers, and that the workforce can be replenished through immigration or the enslavement of foreign populations, as well as by generational replacement of existing workers (Cf. Vogel, 2013: 144–145).

5 The suggested genealogy does not fully grasp all the theoretical and practical legacies dedicated to issues of social reproduction, housing, and welfare. For instance, the Black Marxist-Feminist tradition is not to be neglected (Katsarova, 2015). Katsarova rightly underlines: 'Marxist and socialist feminists concerned with issues of reproduction and domestic labor for the most part did not acknowledge prior legacies of women of color organizing around issues of social reproduction, in particular housing and welfare. … Drawing genealogies of social reproduction from the perspective of black women's experience, from slavery to the racist politics of the welfare regimes, black feminists demonstrated that the domestic confines of the housewife was the problem of white working- and middle-class women. Some of these ideas were first articulated in Claudia Jones' germinal 1949 essay, "To End the Neglect of the Problems of the Negro Woman", where she coined the idea of a triple oppression of working-class black women' (www.viewpointmag.com/2015/10/31/repression-and-resistance-on-the-terrain-of-social-reproduction-historical-trajectories-contemporary-openings/). Nakano Glenn writes: 'Historically, race and gender have developed as separate topics of inquiry, each with its own literature and concepts. Thus, features of social life considered central in understanding one system have been overlooked in analyses of the other. One domain that has been explored extensively in analyses of gender but ignored in studies of race is social reproduction' (Nakano Glenn, 1992: 1).

6 Although not entirely identical categories, we will interchangeably use the terms 'socialist' and 'Marxist' in this text only.

7 Operaismo was an active current of political thought during the 1960s and 1970s, and was developed by Raniero Panzieri, Mario Tronti, Romano Alquati, and Antonio Negri. See Wright (2002).

8 For a more detailed presentation of the debate between dual-systems and unitary theory as well as a debate on class and patriarchy, see the collection of essays edited by Sargent (1981).

9 It would be highly interesting to further develop here Marx's understanding of human labour as a process in which 'both human and nature participate'. Thus, not only human labour is the foundation of the production and reproduction of society as a whole, but it is labour together with nature (Marx, 1947b: 135; see also Bellamy Foster and Burkett, 2017).

10 One could say that SRT is one of the most vibrant aspects of the development of Marxist theory and thought today. For the latest contributions to SRT see: Gimenez (2018b); De'Ath (2018); Farris (2017); Bhattacharya (2017a); Ferguson (2016); *Viewpoint Magazine* (2015); Arruzza (2014); Gonzalez and Neton (2014); Ferguson and McNally (2013); Ferguson (2008). Also, accounts of trans Marxist feminism and SRT: Lewis (2018); Gleeson (2017a, 2017b); Wilson (2016).

11 For a more detailed analysis of the difference between capitalist social reproduction and social reproduction see Gimenez (2018a).

12 There are also important references to the unitary tradition already in the 1970s: see Vogel (1973); Gerstein (1973); Gardiner et al. (1975); Fee (1976).

Bibliography

Arruzza, Cinzia, 2013. *Dangerous Liaisons: The Marriages and Divorces of Marxism and Feminism*. Merlin Press, Pontypool.

Arruzza, Cinzia, 2014. 'Remarks on Gender'. *Viewpoint Magazine*. www.viewpointmag.com/2014/09/02/remarks-on-gender/?fbclid=IwAR3cr6uKeCNmaTxOzrz5EjTANf6YkS_AWetyfVkdev7phCG_P3TuUwtV17Q. Accessed: 13 December 2018.

Bellamy Foster, John and Burkett, Paul, 2017. *Marx and the Earth: An Anti-Critique*. Haymarket Books, Chicago, IL.

Bhattacharya, Tithi, 2013. 'What Is Social Reproduction Theory?'. *Socialist Worker*. https://socialistworker.org/2013/09/10/what-is-social-reproduction-theory. Accessed: 28 September 2018.

Bhattacharya, Tithi (Ed.), 2017a. *Social Reproduction Theory: Remapping Class, Recentering Oppression*. Pluto Press, London.

Bhattacharya, Tithi, 2017b. 'Introduction. Mapping Social Reproduction Theory' in Bhattacharya, Tithi (Ed.), *Social Reproduction Theory: Remapping Class, Recentering Oppression*. Pluto Press, London, 1–20.

Briskin, Linda, 1980. 'Domestic Labour: A Methodological Discussion' in Fox, Bonnie (Ed.), *Hidden in the Household: Women's Domestic Labour Under Capitalism*. The Women's Press, Toronto, 135–172.

Čakardić, Ankica, 2017. 'From Theory of Accumulation to Social-Reproduction Theory: A Case for Luxemburgian Feminism'. *Historical Materialism* 25(4): 37–64.

Dalla Costa, Mariarosa and James, Selma, 1975 [1972]. *The Power of Women and the Subversion of the Community*. Falling Wall Press, Bristol.

De'Ath, Amy Susan, 2018. 'Gender and Social Reproduction' in Best, Beverly, Bonefeld, Werner, and O'Kane, Chris (Eds.), *The Sage Handbook of Frankfurt School Critical Theory*. Sage, London, 1534–1550.

Delphy, Christine, 1980. 'A Materialist Feminism Is Possible'. *Feminist Review* 4: 79–105.

Farris, Sara, 2017. *In the Name of Women's Rights: The Rise of Femonationalism*. Duke University Press, Durham, NC; London.

Federici, Silvia, 2012 [1975]. 'Wages against Housework' in *Revolution at Point Zero: Housework, Reproduction, and Feminist Struggle*. PM Press; Autonomedia, New York.

Fee, Terry, 1976. 'Domestic Labour: An Analysis of Housework and Its Relation to the Productive Forces'. *Review of Radical Political Economics* 8 (Spring): 1–9.

Ferguson, Sue, 2008. 'Canadian Contributions to Social Reproduction Feminism, Race and Embodied Labor'. *Race, Gender & Class* 15(1–2): 42–57.

Ferguson, Susan, 2016. 'Intersectionality and Social-Reproduction Feminisms'. *Historical Materialism* 24(2): 38–60.

Ferguson, Susan and McNally, David, 2013. 'Capital, Labour-Power, and Gender-Relations: Introduction to the Historical Materialism Edition of Marxism and the Oppression of Women' in Vogel, Lise, *Marxism and the Oppression of Women: Toward a Unitary Theory*, Historical Materialism Book Series. Haymarket Books, Chicago, IL, xvii–xl.

Fine, Ben and Saad Filho, Alfredo, 2010 [2004]. *Marx's 'Capital'*. Pluto Press, London.

Fortunati, Leopoldina, 1981. *L'arcano della riproduzione. Casalinghe, Prostitute, Operai e Capitale*. Marsilio Editori, Venezia.

Fortunati, Leopoldina, 2013. 'Learning to Struggle: My Story between Workerism and Feminism'. *Viewpoint Magazine*. https://viewpointmag.com/2013/09/15/learningto-struggle-my-story-between-workerism-and-feminism/. Accessed: 15 September 2018.

Gardiner, Jean, Himmelweit, Susan, and Mackintosh, Maureen, 1975. 'Women's Domestic Labour'. *Bulletin of the Conference of Socialist Economists* 4 (June): 1–11.

Gerstein, Ira, 1973. 'Domestic Work and Capitalism'. *Radical America* 7 (Fall): 101–130.

Gimenez, Martha E., 2018a. 'From Social Reproduction to Capitalist Social Reproduction' in *Marx, Women, and Capitalist Social Reproduction: Marxist Feminist Essays*. Brill, Leiden, 278–308.

Gimenez, Martha E., 2018b. *Marx, Women, and Capitalist Social Reproduction: Marxist Feminist Essays*. Brill, Leiden.

Gleeson, Jules Joanne, 2017b. 'Transition and Abolition: Notes on Marxism and Trans Politics'. *Viewpoint Magazine*. www.viewpointmag.com/2017/07/19/transition-and-abolition-notes-on-marxism-and-trans-politics/. Accessed: 13 December 2018.

Gleeson, Jules Joanne, 2017a. 'Eight Questions on the Slogan "Abolish the Family", and other modest proposals'. *Hysteria*. www.hystericalfeminisms.com/voices1/2017/7/28/eight-questions-on-the-slogan-abolish-the-family-and-other-modest-proposals. Accessed: 13 December 2018.

Gonzalez, Maya and Neton, Jeanne, 2014. 'The Logic of Gender: On the Separation of Spheres and the Process of Abjection' in Pendakis, Andrew, Diamanti, Jeff, Brown, Nicholas, Robinson, Josh, and Szeman, Imre (Eds.), *Contemporary Marxist Theory: A Reader*. Bloomsbury, London; New York, 149–174.

Heinrich, Michael, 2012 [2004]. *An Introduction to the Three Volumes of Karl Marx's 'Capital'*. Monthly Review Press, New York.

Katsarova, Rada, 2015. 'Repression and Resistance on the Terrain of Social Reproduction: Historical Trajectories, Contemporary Openings'. *Viewpoint Magazine*. www.viewpointmag.com/2015/10/31/repression-and-resistance-on-the-terrain-of-social-reproduction-historical-trajectories-contemporary-openings/. Accessed: 12 December 2018.

Kollontai, Alexandra, 1977 [1920]. 'Communism and the Family' in Holt, Alix (Ed.), *Selected Writings*. Allison and Busby, London.

Krul, Matthijs, 2017. 'Why Read "Capital", 150 Years Later?' *New Socialist: Robus Intellectual Discussion and Intransigent Rabble Rousing*. https://newsocialist.org.uk/why-read-capital/. Accessed: 11 September 2018.

Krupskaya Konstantinovna, Nadezda, 2017 [1901]. *The Woman Worker*. Manifesto Press Cooperative, London.

Lewis, Sophie, 2018. 'Cyborg Uterine Geography: Complicating 'Care' and Social Reproduction'. *Dialogues in Human Geography* 8(3): 300–316.

Luxemburg, Rosa, 1912 [2004]. 'Women's Suffrage and Class Struggle' in Hudis, Peter and Anderson, Kevin B. (Eds.), *The Rosa Luxemburg Reader*. Monthly Review Press, New York, 237–241.

Marx, Karl, 1947a. *Kapital. Kritika političke ekonomije I (Capital, Volume I)*. Kultura, Zagreb.

Marx, Karl, 1947b. *Kapital. Kritika političke ekonomije II (Capital, Volume II)*, Kultura, Zagreb.

McNally, David, 2017. 'Intersections and Dialectics: Critical Reconstructions in Social Reproduction Theory', in Bhattacharya, Tithi (Ed.), *Social Reproduction Theory: Remapping Class, Recentering Oppression*. Pluto Press, London, 94–111.

Nakano Glenn, Evelyn, 1992. 'From Servitude to Service Work: Historical Continuities in the Racial Division of Paid Reproductive Labor'. *Signs* 18(1) (Autumn): 1–43.

Riddell, John, 2014. 'Clara Zetkin in the Lion's Den', *John Riddell: Marxist Essays and Commentary*. https://johnriddell.wordpress.com/2014/01/12/clara-zetkin-in-the-lions-den/. Accessed: 28 September 2018.

Sargent, Lydia, 1981. *Women and Revolution: A Discussion of the Unhappy Marriage of Marxism and Feminism*. Pluto Press, London.

Viewpoint Magazine, Issue 5, 'Social Reproduction'. www.viewpointmag.com/2015/11/02/issue-5-social-reproduction/. Accessed: 13 December 2018.

Vogel, Lise, 1973. 'The Earthly Family'. *Radical America* 7 (Fall): 9–50.

Vogel, Lise, 2013 [1983]. *Marxism and the Oppression of Women: Toward a Unitary Theory*. Historical Materialism Book Series, Haymarket Books, Chicago, IL.

Vogel, Lise, 2017. 'Foreword' in Bhattacharya, Tithi (Ed.), *Social Reproduction Theory: Remapping Class, Recentering Oppression*. Pluto Press, London, x–xii.

Vogel, Lise, 2018. 'Beyond Intersectionality'. *Science & Society* 82(2): 275–287.

Wilson, Colin, 2016. 'Notes on Women, Men, Trans and Intersex: "The Gender Binary Does Not Fit the Facts"', *Revolutionary Socialism in the 21st Century*. www.rs21.org.uk/2016/10/24/notes-on-women-men-trans-and-intersex-the-gender-binary-does-not-fit-the-facts/. Accessed: 13 December 2018.

Wright, Steve, 2002. *Storming Heaven: Class Composition and Struggle in Italian Autonomist Marxism*. Pluto: London.

Young, Iris, 1981. 'Beyond the Unhappy Marriage: A Critique of the Dual Systems Theory', in Sargent, Lydia (Ed.), *Women and Revolution: A Discussion of the Unhappy Marriage of Marxism and Feminism*. Pluto Press, London, 43–70.

Zetkin, Clara [1906]. 'Social Democracy and Woman's Suffrage'. *Marxist Internet Archive*. www.marxists.org/archive/zetkin/1906/xx/womansuffrage.htm. Accessed: 2 March 2018.

9 | THE BEST THING I HAVE DONE IS TO GIVE BIRTH; THE SECOND IS TO STRIKE

Paula Mulinari

Care, emotions, and solidarity in the making of a strike

> Se han llevado a mí vecina en una redada más, y por no tener papeles ay, la quieren deportar.
>
> ¡A la huelga diez! ¡A la huelga cien! ¡A la huelga madre ven tú también! ¡A la huelga cien! ¡A la huelga mil! Yo por ellas, madre, y ellas por mí.
>
> Trabajamos en precario sin contrato y sanidad, el trabajo de la casa no se reparte jamás.
>
> ¡A la huelga diez! ¡A la huelga cien! ¡A la huelga madre ven tú también! ¡A la huelga cien! ¡A la huelga mil! Yo por ellas, madre, y ellas por mí.
>
> Privatizan la enseñanza, no la podemos pagar, pero nunca aparecimos en los temas a estudiar.
>
> ¡A la huelga diez! ¡A la huelga cien! ¡A la huelga madre ven tú también![1]

The song 'La Huelga' (The Strike) was originally written by the Chilean singer and songwriter Roberto Alarcón and popularised in Spain in the 1960s by the singer Chicho Sánchez Ferlosio. More than 50 years had passed when the song was rewritten for the 8 March 2017 global feminist strike.[2] Hundreds of thousands of demonstrators throughout Spain sang the rewritten version of 'La Huelga'.[3] While the original song calls industrial workers to leave their *herramientas* ('Leave your tools, the time has come to fight'), the rewritten version takes as its point of departure both the heterogeneity of the working class and its diverse working conditions – from migrant workers risking deportation to workers with precarious employment, from unpaid reproductive work to paid work. The new song also expands the horizon of social confrontation to the struggles against austerity and ethnonationalistic migration policies. Finally, the rewritten song changes the pronoun from him to her (*ellos por mi* to *ellas por mi*) and invites the mother to join the strike instead of just informing her that the workers are going to strike. While there are differences between the songs' contents, the chorus remains: 'To the strike ten! To the strike one hundred! … To the strike thousands! I for them, mother, and they for me'.

The rewritten song, like the original, focuses on the strike as an act of solidarity, a practice of mutual caring and dependency. Inspired by the song, this chapter explores a strike though the lens of feminist social reproduction theory.

In 2014, 330 railway workers employed at the transnational company Veolia in Skåne,[4] Sweden, went on strike. The strike came as a reaction to the company's layoff of 250 employees (one-third of the total workforce). Veolia declared that many of the workers who would lose their employment would be rehired on part-time or temporary contracts. The Service and Communication Union (SEKO)[5] demanded that a limit to the use of part-time and temporary contracts should be inscribed in the general agreement between labour unions and the company. The negotiations went on for several months, but in the end, they stranded. When the peace agreement ceased on 20 May 2014, SEKO declared that its 330 members at Öresundstågen would go on strike.

In my notes from the first day of the strike, I wrote, 'Where is the strike? What is a strike?' When I arrived at the central station in Malmö, Sweden's third largest city, it was difficult to see or feel that a strike was taking place. In my imagination, I had pictured banners and a multitude of workers, but at first glance, there was nothing that indicated, at least to me, that a strike was taking place. A couple of days into the strike, I interviewed one of the strikers.

Paula Mulinari (PM): How is it to strike?
Interview person (IP) 16: Yes (laughs), there's nothing special about sitting here. It can get a bit slow. Talk to some, go for a walk and play games. So, it can be quite cosy.

The word *cosy* is perhaps not the first term that comes to my mind when thinking of strikes, but she was right, it was rather cosy. People talked and *fikade* [had coffee]; travellers and supporters came with candy and cake. We looked at the new messages and photos posted on the Facebook group Travellers in Support of the Strike (Vi pendlare stödjer SEKOS strejk).[6] I came to the station looking for class conflict and found myself eating cinnamon rolls and discussing everything from temporary employment to gossip and food recipes. Perhaps this was the way through which class conflict was named and given meaning.

This chapter aims to explore a workplace strike though the concept of social reproduction. Through the lens of this concept I will focus on the strike's emotional regime, rather than on its function and impact. I believe that an analysis of the strike through a Marxist-Feminist understanding of social reproductive work not only makes visible aspects of workplace struggles often neglected in mainstream analyses of strikes, but also links workplace struggles to the increasing mobilisation against the commodification of land, care, and life itself. As the rewritten version of 'La Huelga' captures, strikes are struggles beyond the workplace and beyond the people who are on strike. They are acts of solidarity and care that bind people together.

While Swedish scholarship has analysed the role and importance of strikes (Kjellberg, 2011; Cederqvist, 1980) especially within the discipline of history

(Nilsson Mohammadi, 2018; Lindqvist, 2011) and within research on the 'Nordic Model' (Moberg, 2006), there is less research (Linderoth, 2012) on how a strike is carried out in a Swedish context. This article is based on the material gathered from my fieldwork at the Öresundstågen from January to August 2014, with a special focus on the material concerning the time prior and under strike. It is based on interviews, field notes, and other material such as pictures and blog posts.

The first section of the article introduces the feminist inspired concept of social reproduction and argues for its possible contribution to analyses of workplace resistance. The following section explores the emotional script and forms of resistance within the workplace prior to the strike. It discusses how the workers initially identified the company's lack of care and respect (not the layoff itself) as the central problem. The following section analyses the role of social media in challenging the hegemonic language of consent, and thereby creating a workers collectivity. The analyses of the strike explore the importance of care in maintaining the strike and how the workers, though a language of care and solidarity, created strong alliances with other workers and well as travellers. A central topic explored is how the workers transformed the strike from a strike around working time, to a strike for the right to care for one's work, as well as care outside of work. It was a strike that made visible the embeddedness between reproduction and production, and the problems this dichotomy creates. The final section explores the tension between the union leadership and some of the strikers. Finally, the conclusion summarises the chapter's central argument: the fundamental role that issues of care and of the organisation of life itself play in labour struggles.

Struggles of care, caring for struggles

The Marxist-Feminist debate around social reproduction is broad. It explores a variety of issues, among others: how to understand the relationship between capitalism and patriarchy (Hartman, 1979; Walby, 1990), the relationship between paid and unpaid work and the role of domestic labour (Dalla Costa and James, 1975; Federici, 2018). In the last decade there has been a growing interest in exploring the relationship between social reproduction theory and intersectionality (Ferguson, 2016). The tradition, Susan Ferguson, Genevieve LeBaron, Angela Dimitrakaki, and Sara R. Farris argue, still too often tends to narrowly focus on women and the household (Ferguson et al., 2016). Similarly to Ferguson et al., Luxton argues that the concept too often 'still focuses on women's unpaid work in the home' (2006: 32). As Meg Luxton (2006) notes, when the term 'social reproduction' is used narrowly to refer to women's unpaid work in the home, it loses the conceptual clarity required to challenge the invalid separation of reproduction from production (2006: 32). This narrow understanding of the concept, runs the risk of reifying the patriarchal and capitalist ideology that creates boundaries between unpaid home work/paid work, private/public, and reproductive/productive. Michell Murphy develops another argument and stresses that for the concept to be useful feminism needs to let go of the fantasy that the spheres of reproduction can escape capitalism and its colonial legacy. According to Murphy the relations of reproduction are better theorised as already subsumed to capitalism (2015: 303). An important aspect of her critique is that Marxist feminists have tended to neglect the central role that racism has played in the organisations of reproduction (Davis, 1981; McClintock, 1995).

In order for the concept of social reproduction to be useful, Ferguson et al. (2016) argue, it must reject 'the binary legacy of Marxist-Feminism, moving analysis beyond the household, and pushing and exploring the scope of SRF [Social Reproductive Frame] theory in distinct ways' (2016: 32).

In this chapter, I embrace this challenge, by exploring how the concept of social reproduction can be used in analyses of workplace struggles. Through the lens of social reproduction, I argue we can explore three central aspects of workplace resistance and strikes within the current phase of capitalism (Burawoy, 2010).

First, the concept of social reproduction helps us explore an aspect of workplace resistance that is often neglected. In the article 'Feminist Lectures on the Economy and Workers' Organised Production' (2018), feminist scholars Corina Rodriquez, Florencia Partenia, and Patrica Laterra argue that a problem with earlier analyses of cooperatively organised and self-managed workplaces in Argentina is that they have tended to disregard the central role played by women in maintaining the day-to-day infrastructure of the struggles. Work such as taking care of children, cooking, and cleaning has not been read as a central factor in maintaining social struggle. By focusing on the social organisation of care, the authors argue that we can explore aspects of workplace resistance that are seldom recognised. Asking questions about who must take on the emotional labour to maintain workers on strike may be a good place to begin an analysis of workplace resistance that challenges the boundaries between productive and reproductive work. A focus on the social reproduction of a strike provides us with analytical lenses to grasp the aspects of strikes that link them to other spheres and circumstances.[7]

Second, the focus on social reproduction can be used as a tool to explore the bridges between workplace struggles and struggles in other places. According to labour historian Peter Waterman studies of trade unions need to be viewed as part of analyses of social movements (2003). This is important as there is a need to bridge the gap between research on workplace resistance and research on social movements. A feminist perspective challenging the boundaries between public/private, household/workplace can be a good point of departure to explore how different forms of struggles are influenced and embedded into one another.

One shortcoming of current labour research is its tendency to narrow the scope of analyses of workplace resistance to the workplace itself, disregarding how social movements and workplace struggles are interwoven. In contrast, analyses of social movements tend to disregard the workplace and unions as central factors of resistance for social transformations towards an inclusive society.

According to Marxist sociologist Michael Burawoy (2010), the current phase of capitalism is 'characterized by the articulation of the (de)commodification of labor, money and nature, in which the (de)commodification of nature will ultimately take the lead' (Burawoy, 2010: 308).

As will be discussed in this article, workplace struggles are increasingly concerned with issues of care, environmental and social sustainability, and the impossibility of maintaining life under current working conditions. In that sense, they must also be understood as struggles that reach beyond the narrow scope of the workplace. For instance, within Nordic labour research, workplace struggles among the care professions have been read as a critique of new public management and the limitations this new organisation of labour puts on the professionals' possibilities of doing 'care' (Granberg, 2016; Lauri, 2016). While I do not question this, a focus on social struggle through the lens of social reproduction can broaden the analyses to explore how those struggles are intertwined with broader struggles against the commodification of life itself.

Third, a focus on social reproduction places the everyday at the centre (Smith, 2012) in our analyses of workplace struggles. Historian James C. Scott's concept of everyday resistance (Scott, 1985) has been fundamental in challenging and expanding the notion of resistance. The author identifies forms and acts of resistance that are not visible, not mass-organised – quiet, subtle, and informal acts of resistance that occurred in the context of violent colonial oppression, when the cost of visible resistance was too high. While Scott's concept has inspired labour studies in exploration of the meaning of resistance, it has seldom been linked or applied to a feminist understanding of the everyday as the location in which social relationships are created, reproduced, but also challenged, building on the production and protection of life.

Sitting and drinking coffee and eating cinnamon rolls was perhaps the everyday of the Veolia strike, the glue that kept it together and gave it meaning. These actions, through which the production of material things and life itself were no longer separated, came into a dialectic and productive dialogue with each other.

Devastation and resignation, but who cares?

Processes of neoliberal globalisation (Harvey, 2005) have, in a Swedish context, meant increasing levels of precarity, class polarisation, and concentration of wealth (Therborn, 2018). Union density has fallen, but over 70 per cent of all the workers at the railway are still union members. The numbers are higher among engine drivers than among onboard personnel (Kjellberg, 2017). Onboard personnel have higher levels of part-time and temporary employment and lower salaries. The railway workers have, during a period of ten years, had three different employers, all transnational companies that have at different times won the procurement for the railway traffic in Skåne. Veolia, the latest, have increased demands on time (in) flexibility though changes in schedules and employed more workers in temporary and part-time employment. Further they have among other things reduced the number of onboard personnel, increased the amount of work, and placed more demands on control and less on service and security.

One Friday afternoon, Veolia's employees learned – via their work mobiles – that 250 of them would be laid off and the depot in the city of Krisianstad would close. The message sent by the company concluded, 'We hope you have a nice weekend'. On Monday morning, I met up with one of Veolia's employees at the main office of Öresundståg in Malmö Central Station. In the office, workers picked up their technical equipment and took coffee breaks. When I arrived, everyone was talking about the layoff. One employee tried to log into the registration system but failed. Someone said, 'What if they have laid us all off? Then we can all just go home'. The worker I was meeting with read loudly from an email he had received from the company, which said that the company needed increased flexibility; everybody laughed. Suddenly someone asked, 'Where is the cake?' And because everybody continued laughing, I asked about the cake.

IP1: Do you remember? Then [the last time the company laid off people] they invited all the workers for cake that day after the layoff. So now, we all wonder where the cake is.
IP2: They probably made cuts on that too.
(Laughter)
PM: Did they invite all of you for cake?
IP1: Yep.

The lack of information, of answers, and employees' sense of insecurity about what was going to happen are a powerful and continuous presence in my material – from the layoff to the end of the strike. One of the central criticisms of Veolia at an early stage was not so much the unfair working conditions, but rather the company's lack of care for its workers. During those first weeks employees repeated sentences such as 'We are only numbers to them', 'You feel as if you are worthless', and 'They do not care'. They often used the word *aggrievement* – rather than *anger* or *injustice* –when explaining their feelings about the situation. They even expressed their understanding of the corporation's need for flexibility but wished that the layoff could have been done, as one of the workers said, 'with more respect'.

During the days that followed, the layoff was discussed everywhere by everyone. There is no doubt that the lack of information and what was experienced as the lack of rationality in the layoff process served to create resignation and frustration.

IP3: In the beginning, you get upset.
IP4: Yes.
IP3: And now it's more like I've given up.
IP4: Yes, it is like that.
PM: So, there's nothing, you have not seen anything? All you have got is this information [the email]?
IP3: Yes.
IP4: Yes.
PM: That's the information you have received?
IP3: 'You have been informed you will be dismissed'.
PM: That's it?
IP4: Yes.
IP3: That's heartless.

That something is heartless means that an action is cruel, that it lacks the necessary empathy to understand others' suffering. Similarly to the workers of the transnational Volvo corporation (Räthzel et al., 2014) the Veolia workers seem to articulate demands expecting the same commitment and care from the corporation that they put into their work.

The strategy used by Veolia left employees with high levels of uncertainty and confusion as they tried to understand the logic of the layoff strategy. Why so many? Why Krisianstad? Why now?

IP14: I have emailed them a thousand times. Our problem is that we have an employer who never answers. So, I am still waiting for answers to the questions that I have sent to my managers on three occasions over three weeks. Still no answer. I'm not expecting answers either.
PM: But it's a common practice that they do not answer?
IP14: Oh yes. Sure, they have a draft box where you can submit stuff. I've sent four or five suggestions on improvements – but I never received any feedback. 'Thanks for sending your proposal', it replies, but you never get any answer. So, it feels like it's an employer who is nowhere and at the same time everywhere. That is frustrating.

It is important to highlight that lack of information is not the same as lack of rules and orders. Only weeks after the company had informed the workers about their intention to lay off one-third of them, they got a new directive demanding that onboard personnel be more active in controlling passengers. According to the company, the workers allowed too many people to ride on their trains for free.

IP7: Now you need to make sure you blip [the passengers'] cards. Now you need to control how many fees you hand out. It is like this all the time – a hunt; they are hunting people. Managers need to understand that they have laid off people, and perhaps they cannot perform 100 per cent every day, as we have done earlier, because we are workers and have feelings. We are people. Instead, they do the opposite and hunt us.

Veolia is described as an invisible – and, to a certain point, invincible – and heartless company that one day fires one-third of its employees and the next day demands complete enthusiasm and loyalty. Some of the staff went on sick leave after the layoff, and managers responded by implying that this was deliberate.

IP9: That made me very angry. People are on sick leave because they are sick. You can get sick of worrying. It is not strange that people get sick when they do not even know if they have a job to go to tomorrow. It made me angry that they accused us of that. They know how many times we have been at work when we were sick.

In the first weeks after the layoff, partly because no labour union offered spaces where workers could discuss collective forms of struggle or their feelings, individual forms and strategies of resistance evolved. The lack of information from both managers and labour unions led employees to care for one another, identifying which workers were the most vulnerable.

IP8: They say that there are 250 people who are not needed, but you might not take the day off because there is no one who can take your shift.
IP7: That is totally insane.
IP8: You just want to give up. The argument is so crazy and then they call from Human Resources and ask if one can take a shift, but they continue to argue that there are 250 persons too many. Oh well, we have not seen them.
PM: So, they call you and want you to take more shifts?
IP7: Yes, and change free dates and shift to other places.
PM: Did you stop when you got the layoff?
IP7: Yes.
IP8: Yes.

IP7: Yes, we – people like me who have permanent employment – we finished saying yes all the time and accepting extra shifts. The same day that the layoff came, almost 100 per cent of the ones working permanently began to say no.

PM: Did you talk about it before doing it, or it just happened?

IP7: It came up here and there, and we felt so humiliated. We felt so humiliated with so many friends feeling so bad, so we thought they would have to fix it themselves.

The consent between workers and managers – what could be described as the moral economy of the workplace (Sayer, 2004), ideas of what is right, just, and rational in the organisation of work (Mulinari, 2016), was built on the idea that the company cared for the workers even if it was sometimes forced to make tough decisions. According to the unspoken rules of this moral economy, workers expect to be respected for their knowledge and skills. Through the layoff the company has broken these rules by creating a situation in which everybody can be and is easily replaced.

IP9: I only have a temporary contract, and of course I feel afraid that if I, for example, call in sick, they will stop calling me. So, for instance, I went to work even if I was sick, so they would not get suspicious. But I would like to call in sick because all this uncertainty makes me sick. I can't sleep. I can't even relax when I am with the kids because I keep thinking what if I lose the job.

IP10: For me I think it is a little bit easier because as a driver I know I can get another job and they need us. But this affects us all because they [Veolia] want you to permanently feel that you can lose your job whenever they feel like it.

Management through uncertainty and management through absence create a sense of despair and resignation, allowing only a few workers to think about forms of resistance. The absence of a union strategy also influenced the lack of a collective strategy.

Day to day, much of the resistance occurred through caring for one another and giving one anther emotional support.

IP4: We talk and talk, and sometimes it goes all around in my head, because we do not know anything, so everyone is very upset. So, we need to talk and find ways of giving each other energy because otherwise we will all go crazy. But it makes me tired; when I get home, I do not want to talk anymore.

The link between forms of care inside and outside the workplace was a central question. One of the workers, for instance, said that while he did not express his emotions in the workplace, his wife had to take care of him. Another stressed that the uncertainty affected her life at home, as she could not focus on her kids and was more frustrated by them.

IP5: I know that I am frustrated with Veolia, not the kids, but there is no place to express that, so you swallow your frustration and let off the steam on your colleagues and family.

Emotional care between workers and the care of workers outside the workplace were central to maintaining employees' day-to-day work situation. Caring for one another, in a context of extremely insecure work conditions where employees did not know who would be fired and why, created an emotional climate in which workers both completed their everyday tasks and invested an immense amount of time in providing emotional support to one another, particularly to those that where conceptualised as more vulnerable or more at risk of being fired. Doing the emotional work, often located in the field of social reproduction, was a central aspect of the everyday in the workplace after the information around the intended layoff had been received. This was a form of reproductive labour that occurred though workers' solidarity with one another rather than through the labour union.

This solidarity would be expressed in a blog that would transform the everyday script of the workplace at Veolia – from forms of individual resistance and caring, to collective resistance and a clear-cut script of labour conflict.

The blog: creating new horizons of struggle

On 9 March, a couple of weeks after the layoff, I was back at the train station and immediately sensed a change in the atmosphere; resignation seemed to have been replaced by engaged gossip and laughter about a possible wildcat strike. These transformations in the workplace's emotional regime were the consequence of a blog named Öresundstågsbloggen. It presented itself in this way.

> The Blog Is for Us All
>
> Posted on 7 March 2014
> This blog is for everyone who works at Veolia, regardless of union membership. The only ones it is *not* for are managers and those who run their errands. Comments from them will be deleted immediately. They already have other channels to express their opinions.
> In times like this, it is dangerous to criticise the company. Lack of loyalty is a very common accusation and a reason given for firing people, often because people write about the company on Facebook. So, don't do that. Write here instead.
> As I, who have made this blog, would be immediately fired, I will not write my name. As I said, I will not be loyal.
> Let's do this.

By addressing all workers in this way, the blogger(s) created a platform not defined by membership in a specific labour union, but rather intended for all those suffering as a result of the company's policies. One engine driver wrote:

> During the last weeks I have felt sad, listless, bitter and weak. After finding the blog an enormous feeling of community, anger, fighting spirit and stubbornness has built up. (Posted on 10 March 2014, signed: Driver)

The blog created a space for discussion that was less framed by labour unions' discourses on negotiations and agreements. In this way, the blog gave room to other voices and social networks that took as their point of departure the solidarity between all workers.

The blog also created a platform through which people could express feelings about Veolia and its managers that before had only been expressed in closed spaces between workers who trusted one another. In this way, the blog changed the emotional script on the trains. Where before there had been resignation, now there was hope and workers collectively.

> Veolia and county traffic companies have understood it completely wrong.
>
> Never forget that we are the core of our business.
>
> When the offices are empty – the train continues to roll.
>
> When the train lacks personnel – the trains will stand still.
>
> It's not us who depend on Veolia – it's Veolia that depends on us!
>
> It's not us who depend on the railroad – the railroad is dependent on us!
>
> Our competence and willingness to take responsibility are priceless!
>
> In the end, it is we who have the trump card, the question is only: Does Veolia really want us to play our cards? It will be expensive for them.

On the blog, current and former workers employed by Veolia, as well as employees from other companies, engaged in conversation. The blog, with its focus on the everyday life of workers and their working conditions, created a space in which the relationship between paid and unpaid work became visible.

> Schedules that go against the clock, schedules that jump hysterically between morning, night and everything in between, schedules that make you sleep bad, so you can barely stay awake day 3 or 4 at work. And just because my example was about two weeks here, it does not mean that the schedule will look the same for the next few weeks. When workers with children cannot even plan when to leave and get their children in good time from kindergarten, how the hell should we be able to plan and work on normal part-time jobs? Come on! (Loranga 25 March 2014, 13:51)

Several of the debates on the blog were concerned with the impossibility of doing a job they liked, the care work of every day. One blogger, who signed off as 'Defeated and Tired', wrote:

> I principally love my job. Being a driver of the road means that you can see nature's changes all year round. To experience a sunrise or sunset in the summer is magical and to be part of people's everyday life, people's meetings and goodbyes are a lovely feeling. But Veolia has managed to kill the passion I once had.

The passion for one's work, and the care for colleagues and travellers was a central theme in the blog. A passion that was destroyed by the company's demands that resulted in workers having to do care work both at work and at home. The blog made the connection between paid and unpaid work visible, as well as issues of inequality. The workers at Veolia were not only fighting for their right to permanent contracts, but also for the right to be able to do care work outside the workplace.

In the blog it seemed that care for workers came from other workers, and there was no hope that the company would care for workers. Now, where there had been disappointment, there was anger; where there had been an understanding of Veolia's need for flexibility, there was a stronger emphasis on the total irrationality of the company's decisions. Employees were no longer willing to wait until the parties reached an agreement; they wanted action, here and now. The blog initiated a lively debate, which was followed by the local organisation of the infrastructure for a wildcat strike.[8]

The organisation of the wildcat strike was a fact, and several of the depots had lists with the names of people who wanted to join the strike. Even union management at the local level later argued that the blog affected the decision to strike because it created pressure from the inside. One of the local union leaders I interviewed emphasised that the blog 'did not determine why we went on strike, but it created a pressure that was difficult to disregard'. The blog created a space that the traditional labour union culture had not yet explored. The blog and the increasing risk of a strike gained enormous media coverage, and the blog was often referred to as a factor pushing the union to strike. For instance, union information (from the leadership) was published on the blog during the strike, even though the blog had been highly critical of the union's actions (prior to the strike).

As the general agreement had not expired, SEKO could not go on strike; however, the union leaders' focus on negotiations created a vacuum at the workplace, which was partially filled by the blog – even if many employees were simply giving up and resigning from Veolia. The blog's focus on care and solidarity for one another as workers challenged the hegemonic idea of consensus as well as the earlier dominant idea that the company should care for the workers. Instead, the focus turned to the importance of collective care and struggle, something that would become central in the everyday of the strike.

The strike is here: bring on the cinnamon rolls

On the night of 3 June, at 3 o'clock in the morning, the strike broke out. SEKO's federal chairman, Janne Rudén, said:

> We cannot accept the dumping of our labor conditions in the railway industry. At one point you are full-time employees; then you will be forced to resign and instead will be offered an insecure hourly appointment in the same company. With the model Veolia launched, you must wait by the phone while you search for other jobs to manage your existence. Therefore, there will be a strike. (SEKO, 2014)

The organisation of the strike at the local level was done primarily by people who did not hold leadership positions in the union; many had not even been active in the union. Most of the workers had never gone on strike before, and while there was big support for the strike among them, many were unsure about what to do while on strike. In my interviews with people about the strike, words like *fun, cosy, stressful,* and *boring* were common. These words expressed the everyday activities during the strike; people filed petitions, walked around, and talked to one another.

I spent most days sitting in the central station in Malmö drinking coffee, eating cake, and talking. The workers went on rounds, collecting names and talking to travellers, but many also sat and followed the Facebook group Travellers in Support of the Strike, and the blog (however, now to a lesser extend). The everyday reality of the strike was, in many ways, not very dramatic, and some of the workers I interviewed were a little disappointed by this. However, many workers also expressed the feeling that what they were doing was important. One of the workers organised a petition so that people could express their support of the Veolia workers and the criticism of the company. This made it easier for workers to talk to travellers and explain the purpose of the strike. In her words:

> IP6: But people understand. Everybody knows someone who has a temporary job – a son or a daughter, a friend – so people understand that we need to do this, and that of course we would like to work, because I love my job. But it feels like we are standing up for one another, and it is not only important for us; it is for all workers because we are all at risk of getting temporary jobs.

The focus on time rather than salaries meant that the juncture between the sphere of work and the outside sphere became a central topic of discussion during the strike.

IP6: We are going back to the eighteenth and early nineteenth centuries, when workers only got work when it suited the employer. We have colleagues today who sit by the phone 24/7, so they can answer as soon as possible to be the first in line when the company needs to call in people. You cannot live life like this.

The strike was so much more than what the labour union organised. While the union primarily organised strike guards, workers found other ways to make the strike visible and alive. Some even came to strike when they were not on strike duty (which they only were when they should have been at work).

IP17: I used to go to the Central Station even though it was not my turn – because it was fun, but also because it felt so important, that we could influence such an important issue. And all the support we had, so much support, so many people that cared.

If the practice of the strike was one of solidarity, the language was one of care – care for other workers, but also care for travellers. This broke the boundary between the personal and the public, as did drawings and colourful posts by children and family members of the striking workers. The support of people outside the workplace was also central to the feeling of the strike, a feeling that people cared.

IP12: It's so wonderful that I never thought in my wildest imagination that we had that backing.
IP13: It's as if you're on the Hyllie buses going to Kastrup, people – even if it is hard for them – say 'Just keep the fight going', even after two weeks.
PM: It's a long time.
IP12: Yes.
IP13: They still lift their fists and say, 'Fight back'.
IP12: I did not think that we'd have them on our side this long. But constantly there is more and more support. I never thought that people cared.
PM: Why do you think you have received so much support?
IP12: People have understood what we are striking about. Veolia and their lies. Everyone knows someone who works for hours, and everyone knows that you cannot always do that.

Much of the daily activity of the strike occurred around a set of tables; here people talked, ate, chatted, and checked the news.

IP11: We wanted people to see us, and if they wanted to support us, to be able to show it. So, we made it possible for people to draw a hand or write a note and put it up on the platform.

PM: How did you get the idea?

IP11: It was one of my colleagues who said to me, [excitedly] 'You know when you were a little boy in the kindergarten and you wrote your hand. Then you had to put your hand and paint a little about what you would be when you grow up'. So, it was, well, from there that the idea came.

People passing by posted different messages of support, and children traced their hands. The strikers used a variety of methods to visualise and colour the strike and to enact the space of the strike.

In Hässleholm, signs were set up, in Kristiansand, posters were painted and put on a bridge. In Lund, the platforms were painted; in Malmö, banners where set up in the Central Hall, along with a figure that people could take pictures of.

After a couple of days, I felt that the strike was more alive. Politicians came and provided their support (from the Social Democratic and the Left parties); the strikers brought homemade cakes; travellers came and cheered. The link between the workers' demands for better working hours and the travellers' (and others') impressive support for the strike showed the need for a more active exploration of the local embeddedness of different forms of struggle.

The workers did not receive any information about the negotiations between the labour union and the company on a day-to-day basis during the strike. The strikers got most of their information through email or social media (for instance, the blog and Facebook). However, there were a few meetings organised by the union, including a demonstration at the beginning of the strike and a meeting in a small, warm room at the Central Station at the end of the strike, where one of the labour representatives from Stockholm spoke. According to my field notes from that event:

> It is warm. One of the main negotiators from Stockholm has come to update the workers. First, the chairman of Malmö talks, and then the guy from Stockholm. He emphasises that they will not surrender and that the workers are doing an impressive job. Everyone applauds and yells. Especially when the guy reads about all the sympathy strikes that had been declared – all 12 LO federations had declared different types of solidarity strikes that would totally stop all trains not only in Skåne but in all the country – the roof seems to blow off.

In the little hall, it felt like anything was possible. It was a feeling that many brought with them, with tenderness for the solidarity of others and pride in having responsibility for the collective struggle. Several people, including me, cried. There was a sense of the impossible being possible, of really being able to challenge a company that at the beginning of the strike had appeared to be invincible.

On 18 June, before any other federation engaged in solidarity strikes and before the strike reached the traffic in Stockholm, the labour union ended the strike. The union leaders described the strike as a victory. Fewer than 250 employees were laid off, and the company signed an agreement that limited the amount of temporary workers that Veolia could employ.

I met two workers who had been active in the strike at the home of one of them two months after the strike. Both were disappointed, especially concerning the labour union. While the union spoke about a victory, both workers I interviewed spoke about a defeat:

IP15: I mean, some had to go, and then no thanks, no meeting to discuss if we can learn anything from the strike. We worked a lot; we did it because it was important, and I never regretted it, but it felt like they did not understand that we made the strike possible, that we were the strike.

The first meeting since the end of the strike took place on the 1 September. During the discussion, several workers expressed their frustration over the lack of information from the labour unions when leaders decided to end the strike. One of the workers present was laid off, and she said that while she was active in the strike, she did not understand what she got out of it. Others responded that it was not a strike for individuals, but for the collective. The union leaders' focus on negotiations made them less present in the day-to-day activities of the strike. For the strikers, wearing the yellow vest with the words, strike guard, every day, created bonds of care and alliances with fellow workers, travellers and even the notion of belonging to a collective of (precarious) workers. The lack of acknowledgment and articulations of these somewhat different worlds created a great deal of frustration, but mostly confusion. As one of the workers asked at the meeting, 'But what do we do now, is it only over?' The feeling of care, solidarity and strength that the strike had created was a force that many of the workers felt was needed to be taken care of, as one of the workers I interviewed expressed it 'We cannot go back'. In my notes I have written 'are the union leaders afraid of the power the feelings the strike might unleash?' The strike had not only raised questions beyond the ones being negotiated, but in many ways questioned the logics of exploitation and made visible the strength there is in solidarity and practices of care. In that sense it challenged the fundament of the Swedish model, based on the idea of mutual dependency and consent between workers and employers,

Many, even those who were laid off, thought it was imperative to strike. Although there was criticism of the organisation of the strike and how it all ended, there was never a critique of the strike as a form of resistance. As one of the women I interviewed expressed it: 'The best thing I have done is to give birth, the second is to strike'.

Final reflections

The Veolia strike focused on time and the impossibility of being able to work and care, both in the workplace and outside it, given the company's demands. It made the embeddedness of the spheres of paid and unpaid work visible, which shaped the ways in which the strike was framed – as a struggle for the right to be able to both work and live in a more human way, and as a struggle for the right to be able to care for one's work, as well as caring for people within and outside work.

An analysis of a strike through a reproductive lens has given me the possibility to see three central aspects of workplace resistance. First, it enabled me to understand the role of care and solidarity in labour struggles. During the strike this often invisible form of labour struggle was to a large extent made by workers that had no prior experience of organised labour conflicts. The concept helped me see the centrality of everyday forms of care within a working environment with high levels of uncertainty, and how workplace resistance, individually and collectively, is shaped by this. Second, the concept could be used to explore how the workers through a language of care and solidarity, focusing on the impossibility of maintaining a human life under the pressure of a company demanding flexibility, managed to create a strong sense of collectively beyond the workplace, identifying people as workers, parents, friends, partners, and kin who were caring for others, hence broadening the scope of who the strike concerned. Here the blog played a central role, by challenging the hegemonic language of consent and mutual reasonability between workers, unions, and managers, and stressing the importance of a collectivity of workers. The alliances between workers and other actors, the focus on social reproduction, in and outside work, the challenge of austerity politics and its logics, I argue, locate the strike within the more general social struggles against austerity politics and the commodification of care and life. There is a need to further explore how struggles in and outside workplaces mutually shape each other. Finally, it helped me to explore how practices of resistance are also practices of care, and for the right to care, both at the workplace as well as outside it.

The strike produced a creative and caring environment of struggle – a place where new horizons of hope were articulated, central questions were asked (Do we really need managers? Can we make our own schedule so it fits our life?), and workers who had been on the margins of the union were suddenly at the centre of the struggle. These workers gave the strike spirit, making its presence visible and creating an alliance with all the other workers affected. Care and solidarity – but also anger and a strong feeling of injustice – were articulated and given a space during the strike. Forcing workers to prioritise profit and marginalise reproductive work is a central practice within capitalist patriarchy. The strike – through its language of care and solidarity, and by making visible the social reproductive aspect of workers' struggles – challenged not only Veolia, but also the male-dominated labour unions, with their focus on negotiations rather than the care and the needs of their members.

In the book *El patriarcado del salario. Criticas feministas al Marxismo* (2018), Silva Federici, a central feminist political and theoretical figure in debates on social reproduction and the relationship between paid and unpaid work, argues that the synthesis between Marxism and feminism is important not only to understand the history of capitalism (and its dependency on the subordination of women and the Global South), but also to read the present. According to the author, the question of social reproduction is at the core of today's social struggles. The current phase of capitalism operates through the politics of neoliberalism with, on the one hand, its constant attacks on the public and on non-profitable forms of reproduction, the privatisation of collective infrastructures (as for instance railways), and the commodification of land and water, and on the other, its austerity politics. We see attacks on labour rights as well as reproductive rights. All those attacks, place the question of social reproduction at the core of social struggles.

However, Federici, as many other social reproduction theorists, as Murphy argues, tends to describe the reproductive work, or the so-called feminist commons, as a place outside the circuit of capitalism. Murphy, on the contrary, stressed that a re-theorisation of the concept of reproduction,

> involves letting go of the fantasy that woman, sex and reproduction might provide a special escape from capitalism. Instead, the relationships of reproduction are better theorized as already subsumed by capitalism and thereby provoking the political task of looking towards ways of 'becoming with many' that can proliferate possibilities towards other forms of life. (Murphy, 2015: 301–302)

The strike shows, I argue, how care and reproductive work and the protection of others' lives are a central aspect of workplace struggles, but also that workplace struggles are bearers of visions of other forms of organising work, everyday life, and how we care for each other. Workplaces are always subsumed by capitalism, but even there, there are practices, emotions, forms of struggle, that resist the individualisation, subordination, and exploitation. During the strike new horizons of hope and collectivity were shaped. The question is therefore perhaps not to locate the sphere most delinked from capitalism as there is none, but to explore the practices in all spheres that try to find ways of challenging the current order, and the ways in which those spheres are embedded into each other.

One of the strengths of Marxism-Feminism is its ability to explore the links between different spaces such as private and public, reproduction and production, which have been described as separated, to maintain and naturalise power relations. I have taken my point of departure as the workplace, rather than the home or the sphere of unpaid work, to see how care and reproductive work is made at the workplace, but also to argue for the need to explore workplace struggles in conjunction with and embedded within larger social struggles against the commodification of life.

To strike, as the song says, and as the workers interviewed stressed, is an act of solidarity – I for them and they for me. *A la Huelga*.

Notes

1 They have taken my neighbour away into another deportation round, and because she does not have papers they want to deport her. To the strike ten! To the strike hundred. To the strike mother, you come along as well. To the strike hundred. To the strike thousand. I for them mother, and they for me. We work precariously without contracts and health protection; domestic work is never divided. To the strike ten ... They privatised education and we cannot afford it, but we never appear in the subjects that are studied. To the strike ten ... (author's translation).

2 www.theguardian.com/world/2017/mar/08/international-womens-day-political-global-strike.

3 https://tn.com.ar/internacional/el-emocionante-himno-que-entonaron-las-espanolas-en-el-8m_855702.

4 Skåne, in the southernmost region in Sweden, has one of the country's highest population rates and a high degree of commuting.

5 There were two unions active among railworkers, The Union of Civil Servants (ST), affiliated to The Confederation of Professional Employees, and SEKO affiliated to LO , The Swedish Trade Union Federation.

6 www.facebook.com/stodsekostrejken.

7 This question is for instance also explored in the film *Salt of the Earth* (1954), directed by Herbert J. Biverman and written by Michael Wilson. The film, the actors as well as the producers where all blacklisted in the US. The movie is based on a miner's strike in 1951, against the Empire Zinc Company and explores issues that focus on women as central political actors. It shows how workplace struggles are embedded in struggles in what is often conceptualised as the private sphere (or the location of reproductive work). In other words, a wonderful film about a strike.

8 A strike not sanctioned by the union. In Sweden unions are not allowed to strike as long as the peace agreement is active.

References

Burawoy, M., 2010. 'From Polanyi to Pollyanna: The False Optimism of Global Labor Studies'. *Global Labour Journal* 1(2): 301–313.

Cederqvist, J., 1980. *Arbetare i strejk: studier rörande arbetarnas politiska mobilisering under industrialismens genombrott: Stockholm 1850–1909* (Workers on Strike: the Political Mobilization of the Working Class in Stockholm 1850–1909). Diss., Stockholm University.

Dalla Costa, M., James, S., 1975. *The Power of Women and the Subversion of the Community*. Falling Wall, Bristol.

Davis, A.Y., 1981. *Women, Race and Class*. Vintage, New York.

Federici, S., 2018. *El patriarcado del salario. Criticas feministas al marxismo*. Traficantes de suenos, Madrid.

Ferguson, S., 2016. 'Intersectionality and Social-Reproduction Feminisms: Toward an Integrative Ontology'. *Historical Materialism: Research in Critical Marxist Theory* 24(2): 38–60. doi:10.1163/15692 06X-12341471.

Ferguson, S., LeBaron, G., Dimitrakaki, A., Farris, S., 2016. 'Introduction to a Special Issue on Social Reproduction'. *Historical Materialism: Research in Critical Marxist Theory* 24(2): 25–37. doi:10.1163/15692 06X-12341469.

Granberg, M., 2016. *Care in Revolt: Labor Conflict, Gender, Neoliberalism*. Diss. Mittuniversitetet, Sundsvall, Sweden.

Hartmann, H., 1979. 'The Unhappy Marriage of Marxism and Feminism: Towards a More Progressive Union'. *Capital & Class* 3(2): 1–22.

Harvey, D., 2005. *A Brief History of Neoliberalism*. Oxford University Press, Oxford.

Kjellberg, A., 2011. 'Storkonflikten 1980 och andra stora arbetskonflikter i Sverige'. *Arbetarhistoria: meddelande från arbetarrörelsens arkiv och bibliotek* 138–139(2–3): 33–53.

Kjellberg, A., 2017. *Fackliga organisationer och medlemmar i dagens Sverige*. 3rd edition. Arkiv, Lund.

Lauri, M., 2016. *Narratives of Governing: Rationalization, Responsibility and Resistance in Social Work*. Diss. Umeå universitet, Umeå.

Linderoth, K., 2012. 'Svenska Kommunalarbetareförbundets strejk 2003 – debatter och erfarenheter'. https://proxy.mau.se/login?url=https://search.ebscohost.com/login.aspx?direct=true&db=edsswe&...

Lindqvist, C., 2011. *Kvinnlig majoritet, manlig makt: kvinnors villkor och strategier i fyra svenska fackförbund under perioder av strejk, uppror och ekonomisk kris 1900–1925*. Ekonomisk-historiska institutionen, Stockholms universitet, Stockholm.

Luxton, M., 2006. 'Feminist Political Economy in Canada and the Politics of Social Reproduction' in Luxton, M., Bezanson, K. (Eds.), *Social Reproduction: Feminist Political Economy Challenges Neoliberalism*. McGill-Queen's University Press, Montreal.

McClintock, A., 1995. *Imperial Leather: Race, Gender, and Sexuality in the Colonial Contest*. Routledge, New York.

Moberg, E., 2006. *Lockout, strejk och blockad: en strategisk analys av konfliktvapnen på den svenska arbetsmarknaden*. Ratio, Stockholm.

Mulinari, P., 2016. 'Weapons of the Poor: Tipping and Resistance in Precarious Times'. *Economic and Industrial Democracy* 3(33): s441–461.

Murphy, M., 2015. 'Reproduction' in Mojab, S. (Ed.), *Marxism and Feminism*. Zed Books, London, 287–304.

Nilsson Mohammadi, R., 2018. *Den stora gruvstrejken i Malmfälten: en muntlig historia*. Diss. Stockholms universitet, Stockholm.

Räthzel, N., Mulinari, D., Tollefsen, A., 2014. *Transnational Corporations from the Standpoint of Workers*. Palgrave Macmillan, Basingstoke.

Rodríguez, E., Corina Partenio, F., Laterra, P., 2018. 'Lecturas feministas de la economía y la autogestión'. *Autogestion para economia*. http://autogestionrevista.com.ar/index.php/2018/06/23/lecturas-feministas-de-la-economia-y-la-autogestion/.

Sayer, A., 2004. *Moral Economy*. Department of Sociology, Lancaster University, Lancaster.

Scott, J., 1985. *Weapons of the Weak: Everyday Forms of Peasant Resistance*. Yale University Press, New Haven, CT.

SEKO (2014). www.seko.se/press-och-aktuellt/nyheter/2014/seko-varslar-om-strejk-pa-jarnvagen/.

Smith, D.E., 2012. *The Everyday World as Problematic: A Feminist Sociology*. Northeastern University Press, Boston, MA.

Therborn, G., 2018. *Kapitalet, överheten och alla vi andra: klassamhället i Sverige – det rådande och det kommande*. Arkiv förlag, Lund.

Walby, S., 1990. *Theorizing Patriarchy*. Basil Blackwell, Oxford.

Waterman, P., 2003. 'Adventures of Emancipatory Labour Strategy as the New Global Movement Challenges International Unionism'. www.labournet.de/diskussion/gewerkschaft/smu/smuadvent.html.

10 | WOMEN IN SMALL-SCALE FISHING IN SOUTH AFRICA

An ecofeminist engagement with the 'blue economy'

Natasha Solari and Khayaat Fakier

Introduction

A Marxist-Feminist engagement with the discourse and practice of 'development' necessarily involves a focus on state, capital, and social interaction with nature. Globally, contemporary notions of development wrapped up and tied together in economic policies and growth plans centred on 'green' economies and 'blue' economies, require us to consider our relationship in and to nature. Our attention focuses on a wave of industrialisation and marketisation (Cock, 2014; Salleh, 2012) which is on the surge in the form of the commodification of the environment (water, land, and air) as economies attempt to stretch the limits environmental degradation imposes on accumulation.

For the Global South, nature-economy approaches to 'development' have special implications, as concerns with 'economic necessity' (Salleh, 2012: 141) entrench inequality between North and South, exacerbate climate impact in the South (Räthzel et al., 2018), and tie labour movements in the Global South, as much as those in the North, into positions opposing de-growth arguments and movements as the immediacy of underdevelopment stares its people in the face (Stevis et al., 2018).

The metabolic rift, employed by Marx to describe the exploitation of nature in the pursuit of accumulation, widens when a 'market' logic is imposed on development approaches focused on repairing and restoring our natural environment. Thus, Goodman and Salleh (2013: 411) suggest with regard to the confluence of 'markets' and ecological sensibilities that 'ecologism appears to become a rationale for extending market activity'. The discourse of a 'green economy' which has the twin goals of economic growth and environmental protection has animated South African society. More recently, South Africa is moving ahead with plans for a 'blue economy', a tributary of the 'green' economy, which we suggest is another 'empty signifier' (Cock, 2014: 219) opening up the space for the state and capital to enclose nature in intensified processes of accumulation. Indeed, as Goodman and Salleh (2013: 411) argue about the green economy, 'the transnational capitalist class is using the global ecological crisis to revive its failing financial system'.

This chapter focuses on the lived experiences of women working in, with and opposing the imposition of blue economy policies in small-scale fishing (SSF) in South Africa. Small-scale fisherwomen are in a particular relationship to the fishing industry; meta-industrial workers[1] on the margins of the large-scale industrial fishing sector, but also marginalised by men inside the SSF sector. Women have been inextricably linked to nature, and women's roles and activities within the small-scale fishing industry have been reshaped and remade, in much the same way as nature has been reshaped and remade. Yet, both women and nature are assumed to be controllable, productive, and passive and therefore not heard when state and capital embark on 'new' paths of development.

A Marxist ecofeminist framework offers an analysis of the exploitation of women in the SSF, while also bringing to the fore the ways in which women resist and attempt to capture some of the potential of policy frameworks. As such, the chapter seeks to politicise women's engagement with eco-developmental discourse and practice, rather than to romanticise and 'naturalise' our connection with nature.

In the next section we present the theoretical framing and how it pertains to working-class women in SSF in South Africa, and ecofeminism broadly. This is followed by an analysis of the 'blue economy', a rushed approach to economic development which prioritises economic growth over feminist ecological concerns. In the following section, we discuss our methodological design and introduce two fishing communities in the Western Cape province in South Africa where our research was conducted. We then discuss the findings obtained from women who fish, work and reside in Kleinmond and Steenberg Cove. Finally, we conclude the study by arguing that the ways in which women contest and work with developmental approaches directly contradicts assumptions about women's passivity in nature.

Theoretical positions

For Marx, nature under conditions of capitalism 'has become an object of utility, and has ceased to be recognised as a power in itself' (Eagleton, 2011: 231). Material production allows society to standardise, facilitate, and control the relationship between humanity and nature itself. As a metabolic exchange between humanity and nature occurs, nature according to Marx is an eternal condition, while the various manners in which humanity works on nature are constantly changing. In assessing the practice of the 'blue economy', what we see is rather an emergence of a 'blue capitalism', which captures nature as opposed to sustaining it.

Theoretical and political position: Marxist ecofeminism and the 'blue economy' in South Africa

Ecofeminists adopt varied styles of argument, most consider environmental and social crises an inexorable outcome, the damage wrought by patriarchal capitalism on society (Salleh, 2001). At its most basic, Marxist ecofeminism claims that the locus of environmental and social crises can be attributed to the accumulation motive of capital. They argue that women and nature are dominated and exploited, as the material and discursive institutions of patriarchal capitalism necessitate this for surplus extraction. Materialist ecofeminists have sought to shift the analysis of naturalising differences, to rather analysing the material structures that fashion the relationships between women, men, and nature (Sydee and Beder, 2001: 284). For them, the central contradiction within capitalism is between reproduction and production (or the production of life vs the production of the means of life as referred to by Haug and Räthzel et al. elsewhere in this book). Economically acknowledged and valued labour performed by men is distinguished from the invisible domestic labours performed by women, and especially those in the South. Therefore, women's labour is assumed to remain in nature, while men's labour is removed from nature (Sydee and Beder, 2001). Implicit in the term ecofeminism is the struggle to access women's rights to natural resources as a human right, while asserting an ecological position from which such a struggle arises. This connects the exploitation and domination of women with that of the environment and argues that there is a connection between women and nature which is given meaning by their shared history of oppression (Salman and Iqbal, 2007).

Ecofeminism is animated by a demand for a feminism that is driven by women's grassroots organising, which emphasises women's connection to nature and everyday practices (MacGregor, 2006). This conception holds the potential to ignite global politics and unite social movements in both the South and the North around the environment in relation to the subsistence needs shared by all people regardless of culture, class, race, ideology, or economic position. Thus, ecofeminist writings have progressively shifted away from theory and moved towards a more 'activist' nature, which MacGregor (2006: 19) highlights as 'lived experience'. Ecofeminism can thus be established as an activist stance and theory by recognising the strength of women participation in grassroots activism (Sydee and Beder, 2001).

In attempting to answer the question about the relationship between women and nature, theories premised on maternalism have been embedded in certain ideologies and granted predominately white middle-class women entry into the realm of politics of ecology (MacGregor, 2006). Thus, excluding a large population of women, particularly from the Global South, this enforces the idea that black women are passive caretakers of nature, without consideration of their lives as political subjects. Our chapter explores this assumption about women as special caretakers of nature, and considers their engagements also as political agents, and what the consequences are for women to bear such an immense responsibility.

Feminist engagements with nature are characterised by theoretical tensions and debate. While this chapter cannot cover the full extent of these debates, it is important to signal that the discourse and practice of 'development' as embedded in the development approach of the green economy (on which the articulation of blue economy policies draws) have animated theoretical positions on race, capital, and colonialism in relation to ecofeminism (Harcourt and Nelson, 2015). An ecofeminist engagement with how the conservation of nature is drawn into a capitalist frame of 'economies' (green or blue), they argue, should be attentive to longstanding feminist engagements with the very notion of development. For women in the South, 'development' (Kabeer, 1994; Rai, 2002, 2008) often implies a neglect of feminist concerns or a misappropriation of women's position in nature in favour of capital–state alliances

In opposition to the concepts of 'classism' and 'racism' within hegemonic Northern ecofeminism (Gaard, 2011: 31), in Latin America, Indigenous feminism is understood as a central contribution to the struggle against the vestiges of colonialism, and for the protection of nature (Feminismos de Abya Yala, https://francescagargallo.wordpress.com/ensayos/librosdefg/feminismos-desde-abya-yala/). The Indigenous ecofeminist tradition draws on feminist writing, poetry, storytelling, art, and sculpture, in contrast to only academic writing, to illustrate women's resistance to environmental degradation and their protection of and relationship to nature. While we do not aim to dissolve the tensions and contradictions in the ecofeminist genealogy, our position draws on its influences to develop a race-, class-, and nature-sensitive understanding of the working lives and ecological sensibility of SSF women.

In the contemporary context of South African society, which remains dominated by white-owned capital, and state regulations complicit in neoliberal capitalism, we forward a Marxist ecofeminist position that politicises women and does not romanticise their capacity. Such a politics requires both Marxism for its critique of state–capital alliances embedded in neoliberal capitalism and the class inequalities on which it is based and entrenched, and ecofeminism for its commitment to the abolition of gender-, race-, and class-based inequality in women's relation to and in nature (Fakier and Cock, 2018). Thus, our view of ecofeminism is intent on analysing the cost and consequences imposed on women who engage in environmental activism, as well as to question who has control over natural resources. It is with this lens through which we analyse the 'blue economy'.

The blue economy: a hurried approach to the development of ocean resources

Gunter Pauli (2010) is seen as the innovator of the term the 'blue economy', a business model grounded in a systemic approach which aims at scientific innovations in marine and coastal environments for the benefit of the environment, to create economic revenue and provide social benefits. However, this concept gained most of its traction from the United Nations

Conference on Sustainable Development (also known as Rio +20) which had as one of its broad aims to refine institutional frameworks to ensure 'sustainable development', by means of the 'green economy' approach (UN, 2014).

At the instigation of island and coastal countries (some of them from the South), the blue economy was used to insert marine economies into frameworks developed for the green economy. Thus, in 2015, the United Nations assigned one specific Sustainable Development Goal (SDG 14) to focus on the conservation and sustainable use of the seas, oceans, and marine resources in pursuit of sustainable development (Bhattacharya, 2017). In 2016, the UN hosted the first World Ocean conference to support SDG 14, and a commitment to reduce or eradicate harmful fisheries subsidies was made.

Its proponents suggest that adopting a blue economy approach, in line with the Sustainable Development Goals of the current 2030 Agenda, could enhance economic growth while protecting the marine environment and its resources. However, misguided policies, institutional and regulatory frameworks, and inefficiently planned and unregulated coastal development challenge the implementation of this approach (Waruhlu, 2019). Thus, ongoing trends of degradation and exploitation of marine and coastal ecosystems have been prevalent, and the gap between the Global South and Global North countries on areas of maritime commerce have expanded.

Nevertheless, the potential of the 'blue economy' as a site for economic growth has surged into common policy usage around the globe. The 'blue economy' involves all aquatic and marine spaces, including the seas, oceans, coasts, lakes, rivers, and underground water and attempts to integrate into a single developmental approach a vast range of commercial sectors, such as transport, energy, underwater mining, aquaculture, tourism, and fisheries (UNECA, 2016). As 'an integrated, participatory and holistic approach' (UNECA, 2016: 6), it promotes the idea that the productivity of healthy ocean and freshwater ecosystems is a pathway for maritime-based and aquatic economies, which potentially could ensure that areas where coastal communities are situated can benefit from the resources. Thus, it attempts to highlight that the oceans are not merely repositories for the extraction of resources and the dumping of waste products.

However, in 2015 the World Wildlife Foundation (WWF) pointed out two divergent stances on the blue economy (WWF, 2015). For some, the blue economy means the use of the sea and its resources for sustainable economic development. For others, it simply refers to any economic activity or means in the maritime sector, whether sustainable or not. Thus, they suggest that principles bridging this gap should seek to ensure that the economic development of the ocean contributes to true prosperity, today and into the future. In Africa, it is suggested that the blue economy could shift the global economy in favour of the continent and holds the promise of a new economic and geopolitical order, especially for countries with vast access and connections to oceans, lakes, seas, and rivers (Bhattacharya, 2017).

Mahawa Kaba Wheeler (2018) argues that even if 'the blue economy has quite rightly been described as the New Frontier of the African Renaissance', it needs to become truly inclusive, allowing all people to reap the dividends from marine environments and resources (Wheeler, 2018: 1). However, he continues, the marine industry in Africa is dominated by men, therefore an evident issue is the lack of representation and inclusion of women in the development frameworks of the blue economy.

Against this background, Operation Phakisa, announced in 2014, by then-president Jacob Zuma, is intended to unlock the economic potential of South Africa's oceans and its coastlines. The 'growth potential' of the plan is seen to be able to contribute up to R177 billion to the Gross Domestic Profit (GDP), coupled with the possibility of providing between 800,000 and one million job opportunities. Initially, oversight of the oceans was shared by all government departments, which created competition between them rather than holistic planning.

As such the implementation of Operation Phakisa has altered this, placing the Environmental Affairs Department as the lead actor (Kings, 2016). The central focus of Operation Phakisa is on four priority sectors, namely offshore oil and gas exploration, marine protection services and governance, marine transport and manufacturing, and aquaculture.

One of the major flaws of Operation Phakisa is hinted at in its nomenclature. Phakisa means 'hurry up' in Sesotho, one of South Africa's 11 official languages, and appears to impart an urgency in opening up access to ocean resources, and in ecological concerns. However, the focus on 'economic necessity' takes precedence, with the ecology taking second place, and the historical involvement of small-scale fishers, outside the circuit of state–capital linkages, a distant third. One of the implications of a hurried approach is, as our earlier research has illustrated, the neglect of communities' needs and engagements with the environment (Fakier, 2018) and the imposition of top-down conservation policies which are resisted by members from disenfranchised communities.

At a global forum, held in Johannesburg in November 2018 by the Trust for Community Outreach and Education (TCOE), Operation Phakisa and the overall framework of the blue economy was likened to the exploitative and environmentally destructive operations of extractive mining (http://tcoe.org.za/2019/01/13/tsf-and-the-blue-economy/). The testimonies of fisher folk from South Africa, Madagascar, Papua New Guinea, India, and the Philippines converged around a statement that 'the Blue Economy needs to be exposed as a process of primitive accumulation through the dispossession of small scale fishers and coastal communities of their territories and maritime resources' (http://tcoe.org.za/2019/01/13/tsf-and-the-blue-economy/). This assembly was unanimous in its rejection of the 'blue economy' as a vehicle for equity and environmental justice, and instead referred to it at as 'blue imperialism' and 'ocean grabbing'.

However, women in fishing communities, as in other South African communities, are not passive recipients of state–capital exertions and show their resistance 'sometimes in survivalist, defensive and ameliorative ways, but also in challenging neoliberal capitalism and promoting alternatives' to environmentally destructive capitalism (Fakier and Cock, 2018: 52). Thus this chapter sets out to explore whether and how women account for and resist the discourse and practice of neoliberal capitalism embedded in development approaches such as the 'blue economy' and its activation through Operation Phakisa.

Research methods in context: Steenberg Cove, Kleinmond, and research selection

This chapter focuses on two research sites: Steenberg Cove and Kleinmond. These are both small-scale fishing communities that rely on fishing as a means of subsistence and as a way of life, where fishing is imbued with cultural and historical significance. The fisherwomen that reside in these communities are also involved in women's cooperatives, through which they market and sell homemade and fish products harvested from the ocean. Through a local network, we had access to very knowledgeable key informants that enabled entrance to the respective communities and the fishers, particularly women, who are currently involved (directly or indirectly) in the small-scale fishing industry and fighting in the heart of the current fishing rights struggle, operating under conditions of a 'blue economy'.

Preliminary scouting of the sites was done via three means, initially through an ecology expert at the University of Cape Town, who provided us with the contact details of Hermin,[2] who is a key research participant who introduced us to various other fisherwomen, and allowed us to observe and be part of her working day. We then ventured to the small town of Mamre, where we were invited into her home, which boasted an exquisite garden, a true testament to her philosophy of 'living from the earth'. We conducted an informal interview to establish how we would proceed in going to the first fishing community of Steenberg Cove. The second means was through a face-to-face introduction at a small-scale fisheries workshop in May 2017. Here we met our another important participant, Sarah, who revealed significant information on the workings of the small-scale fisheries sector. The final means was through an online connection at the local Kleinmond WWF offices, who was able to initially be the contact point between other fisherwomen women in the Kleinmond area and ourselves.

Steenberg Cove

St Helena Bay is a coastal town on the west coast of South Africa. This town is defined by a sharp contrast between the beautiful natural coastal surroundings and the industrial factories which overshadow the shoreline (Shultz, 2015). St Helena Bay boasts one of the largest fishing zones along the coast, abundant in various pelagic fish, such as snoek. However, despite this large fishing zone, only the industrial and commercial sector reaps benefit from the sea, whereas small-scale fishers are heavily regulated, and unable to indulge in the ocean's offerings, as their forefathers once did. Similar to most South African towns, St Helena Bay is segregated spatially in terms of race and class. On the western side lies the 'Golden Mile', and the wealthy white neighbourhoods of Shelly Point, Britannia Bay, and Duiker Eiland. In contrast, to the east, predominately low-income 'coloured' fishing communities reside, such as the neighbourhoods of Laingville, Stompneusbaai, and Steenberg's Cove, the latter being one of the research sites in this study.

Steenberg Cove is the oldest neighbourhood in St Helena Bay and is characterised by informal housing situated near the beach, with lines of hand-caught fish hanging from the doors, and children running and playing on the dirt roads keeping themselves entertained. If you find yourself walking along the beach you will see fisherwomen and young children harvesting periwinkles and mussels from the rocks. Evidently, despite the relaxing and laid-back atmosphere of this quaint coastal neighbourhood, there are myriad boards towering everywhere advertising real estate and development projects. The long-term fisher residents refer to the intensification of commercialisation of property by city dwellers, which threatens to evict fishers from their place of residence. This is evident with a case that occurred in 2010, where developers were trying to acquire and displace the fishers residing on the land to develop a waterfront. The residents of Steenberg Cove were able to get legal aid and argue that this would disrespect and disrupt the cultural and social importance of the historical graves next to their homes, as most residents have buried their family members there. While the nature and instances of marketisation manifest clearly in St Helena Bay and specifically in Steenberg Cove, they nevertheless indicate patterns that become apparent in other fishing communities around the Western Cape, such as Kleinmond.[3]

Kleinmond

Kleinmond is a small coastal town located in the Overberg region of the Western Cape, on the opposite coast to St Helena Bay. It is situated between the jagged Palmiet mountain range and the cold Atlantic Ocean. The towns name can be translated as 'small mouth', due to its location at the mouth of the Bot River lagoon. Kleinmond has a rich history of stories around shipwrecks, cattle thieves, and slavery, which has been overtaken by its current character as a retirement and holiday destination as opposed to a fishing town characterised by historical anecdotes. The community of fishers who currently reside in the township on the slopes of the Kogelberg mountains explain that their families initially established themselves at Jongensklip during the mid-1900s as a fishing community. In 1948, when the first Village Management Board was established, under conditions of apartheid, fishers who stayed at or near the present-day Kleinmond harbour were forcibly removed (WWF, 2015) and situated higher up on the mountain slopes away from easy access to the ocean. More fishers were displaced away from the ocean when the harbour was declared an industrial area in 1954. One of our participants' family had a house where the harbour parking lot stands today; they have since recreated a home in the informal settlement on the mountain slopes.

At the bottom right-hand side of the Kleinmond harbour is a minuscule World Wildlife Fund (WWF) office, whose ocean mission statement is 'aimed at creating healthy oceans that support abundant biodiversity, sustainable livelihoods and a thriving economy'. This is vastly different to Steenberg Cove, which has no such resource available to members of their fishing community. However, what became evidently clear during interviews with the fisherwomen of Kleinmond, is that not all fisherwomen were aware of this resource, nor was it always used in the best interest of the fishing community.

Methodology employed

The notion of the blue economy, and understandings and experiences of policy and regulations within subsistence fishing communities are multifaceted. We are interested in how women SSFs understood their daily lives in this context. As such, in order to obtain an in-depth, hermeneutic understanding and analysis of these notions, a qualitative research method that followed an interpretivist epistemology was employed. This approach is embedded in the way in which people make sense of their lived realities and experiences, and how they attach meanings to it. The multidimensional nature of this research demands the use of a range of data sources. The research data was obtained through policy analysis, library-based research, and fieldwork, which constituted participant observations, informal conversations, interviews, and focus group discussions around the topics of small-scale fisheries, the blue economy, and women's place in it. The data extracted was then related to the broader notions of the blue economy, ocean grabbing, and framed theoretically within a Marxist ecofeminist tradition.

Discussion and analysis of findings in Steenberg Cove and Kleinmond

Women in nature: constructions of illegality in the blue economy

When asked about the status of fishers in the blue economy, Rodwin, a thirty-four-year-old third generation fisherman states:

[They are] just a bunch of illegal people, fishing illegally, catching more than they should and selling their catch illegally.[4]

These perceptions of fishers highlight their roots in how black people were excluded from all meaningful forms of social life. Similar to other sectors in South Africa's economy, the fishing industry still suffers from a quota system, favouring commercial and industrialised fishing. At the end of apartheid, the sector was an industrialised white-owned sector which had systematically implemented its management system and influence over the government to control access to fishing (Isaacs, 2013). Thus, on the margins of the ocean economy is a class of fishers comprising subsistence and artisanal fishers forced to fish informally or through recreational permits, selling their produce in an informal fish market (Isaacs, 2013). The post-apartheid government implemented a system of 12 individual transferable quota allocations which pits fishers against each other and which provides little real access to ocean resources for small-scale fishers as a group. These are regulated through 'interim relief permits', implying that this would eventually lead to permanent access to fish for small-scale fishers in need of income relief. However, this system has neglected a large group of fishers and has been in operation for over ten years with no end in sight. This further indicates how the inaccessibility to ever-evading rights in a post-apartheid environment has resulted in fishers becoming further entrenched in conditions of poverty. The exclusion of small-scale fishers by industrial and technologically driven fishing exploitation is a global phenomena. What is particular about our chapter is that such exploitation builds on South African regimes of inequality inherited from apartheid.

The notion of legality and access to fish and other ocean produce is often couched in the language of conservation and its opposing term, poaching. South African newspapers report on the poaching of Cape lobster and abalone on a weekly basis. These highly prized delicacies are endangered, and harvested and distributed through 'smuggling rings' to local and international consumers. Thus, the women interviewed reported how their presence on beaches elicits scrutiny from the middle class – beachgoers or beachfront property owners – who have no hesitation to call on the police to report 'suspicious behaviour'. These perceptions are also racialised. As Hermin says, 'Ja ... any disturbance of their [white middle-class property owners'] view, blocking from their property ... any hotnot[5] walking past, upsets them'. Referring to another instance when fishers, in possession of fishing licences, were accused of poaching, Hermin remarked, 'die boere[6] don't want us here'.

Fisherwomen have divergent views on poaching and conservation. During an interview with Reena, a car with young people from her community pulled up to the harbour and she recognised them as being involved in crayfish and abalone poaching and remarked 'Shoes and fancy cars are all these young people are interested in'. She went on to say that the youth need to be educated about the 'traditional' values of fishing communities which are based on preserving ocean stock and which flout 'modern' patterns of overconsumption of luxury goods as well as scarce resources. Hermin, on the other hand, denies the legitimacy of the term poaching with regard to the fisherwomen and says, 'I don't call it poaching anymore. It's an assertive action[7] ... it's putting bread on the table'.

Expressing understandings of their connection to ocean environments, the women from Kleinmond talk about how one of their roles on fishing boats is to ensure that the lobster caught comply with minimum size regulations. In talking about lobster, they refer to it as '*onse kreef* [our lobster]' indicating their authority over lobster stocks and responsibility to conserve such stock for future generations. They also noted the diminished number of lobsters around the zone where they usually fish and pointed out more protected locations further into the sea where they were monitoring pods of lobsters. Their deep knowledge of the sea thus guides them to the locations frequented by lobster of 'legal' size. In this regard one woman commented that 'If all you do is to throw your nets on the sand [in shallow water] there would be no lobster'. Implied in this comment is a connection between a long-developed understanding of the feeding and nesting patterns of ocean stock, and how women respond to the pressure to push beyond the boundaries of safe waters to wrest a living from the ocean.

The next section, which focuses on women's work in SSF, is thus separated into two spheres, even while we show how they bleed into each other. The one sphere is the SSF sector and the other is that of the household and community.

Marginalisation of women's work within the SSF sector

Hermin, when asked about what women do in the SSF sector, states, 'we have been more at sea than at church'. This quote expresses a dual sentiment, firstly referring to how involved, intertwined, and passionate fisherwomen are about the ocean, possibly to the exclusion of formal religious practice. Secondly, a more idiomatic sentiment underlies the statement, i.e. 'to be lost at sea', which indicates the capriciousness of the small-scale fishing industry, particularly with the undervalued and underpaid work women conduct. These forms of work do not follow a conventional pattern, but rather one that is porous and adaptable. The women constantly consider where their work is located in relation to their households. The pressure to be close to their homes limits the movement of some of the women and provides a means through which domestic responsibility bleeds into labour into SSF. Thus, they reported that their fishing-related work is primarily based on shore: in market areas, or in vicinities closer to their household. This results in the women spending a few hours a day working in the SSF and then coming back to household duties. Contrastingly, men are out at sea all day and are unwilling, unable, and/or too tired to assist with household responsibilities.

Upon closer inspection of the SSF locally and globally, there is recognition that while certain fishing activities and roles are more frequently assumed by men, others are dominated by women (Harper et al., 2013: 56). Women are involved with various activities and roles within the fisheries value chain, from capturing, processing, selling, marketing, and all the way down to political and rights activism, yet many of these roles and activities are still persistently overlooked and rarely acknowledged. However, women's important role in fishing globally has gained significant recognition, particularly within the domain of academia, yet within broader society, governmental, non-governmental organisations (NGOs), and international agencies, recognition is not as widely practised.

Fisherwomen's [underpaid] activities

'We make our living from the sea', says single mother, Welma. 'It is our bread and butter', echoes Minkie, capturing their dependence on the ocean to secure their livelihoods. Interview data reveal that the fisherwomen are predominately engaged with indirect fishing activities which comprise pre- and post-harvest activities that encompass the preparation of bait, mending of nets, cleaning and filleting of fish, various fish processes (smoking and salting), and selling and trading of fish and fish products. Most of the fisherwomen from both Steenberg's Cove and Kleinmond are also involved in small-scale harvesting, which is predominantly the collection of invertebrates from the shore also known as inshore[8] gleaning of marine species.

'The ocean is my life ... when the ocean smiles, then we fetch [glean from the rocks]'. These words, expressed by Welma,[9] indicate the intimate, personal connection to the sea, yet volatility of gleaning inshore produce.

On a typical day of gleaning, the women will get up early in the morning to assess the tide patterns and should it be low enough they will make their way to the rocky shore on the beach – accompanied by children and grandchildren. There they use a kitchen knife to pry alikreukel and mussels off the rocks, filling up previously used plastic bags. Once these bags are full, they take them back home where they prepare a portion for the evening's meal for the family by cooking it with vegetables into a curry, and then processing the rest to sell as cooked, smoked, or pickled products and bottled into jars. These jars, depending on the size of the jar or the type of seafood, are sold for between $1.50 and $6.00.

In addition, the women make and embroider household items, which are sold to their neighbours, and at open-air markets in the surrounding areas. Once the fishermen arrive in the harbour with their catch of fish (usually snoek, hottentot, and kreef) the women engage in post-harvest activities. They get a small fee or small portion of catch to clean the catch and to find customers. When they have a customer, the women fillet the fish to customers' specifications for a small fee (between $2 and $4) depending on the size of the fish. The meagre prices offered to these women for quite an arduous task is diminutive.

The money fisherwomen receive for their work is too meagre to make a substantial living, despite the amount of time and effort they exert. Fisherwomen cannot always glean marine species or create hand-made products because of changing weather conditions, being excluded from permits, and having care responsibilities. Importantly, when the fisherwomen engage in pre- and post-harvest activities, they are only able to do this work during a specified season that spans a period of three months. Within this period there are only certain days in which pre- and post-harvest activities can take place due to previously mentioned policy regulations and climate patterns. As such, the vulnerability of this sector requires the women to assume additional (under) paid work over and above the roles and activities in which they are already engaged. In the general context of South Africa and similar to other parts of the world (Masifundise, 2015), it is rare that women are solely involved in the direct task of fishing out at sea.

Much of fisherwomen's work is seen as complimentary to men's fishing and framed within a household livelihood strategy context. Women's work is seen as 'support' for their husbands or households. There are not many women involved in direct fishing in South Africa, and the fisherwomen of Steenberg Cove attribute this to patriarchal and superstitious ideas surrounding women on boats. The older generation of fishermen (from Steenberg Cove) are still steadfast in not allowing women on their boats as they believe 'women out at sea are not good people ... red [menstrual blood] indicates bad luck and no fish'. Fisherwomen are also assumed to lack the physical strength to engage in various fishing activities. However, Minkie[10] points to another reason why she cannot fully participate in fishing: 'I am so in love with the ocean, [especially] when it is flat ... I so badly want to swim, I am so upset that I can't. Before [I reach] sixty [years], my sister, I will learn how to swim'. However, she has a plan for when she needs to go out as the caretaker of a fishing licence, 'I think the caretakers of the West coast must go to the sea, we really must ... except with life jackets'.

Women in Kleinmond, however, are involved in direct fishing and indicate that the lack of sanitation on boats is at first an obstacle for women to join a fishing trip. However, they also suggest that current conceptions and delineations of the terms 'fishers' and 'fishing' are too narrow since they do not take into consideration all the roles women assume in addition to catching 'fish', including their activities that are done inshore (such as the gleaning of shellfish). As such, all the women engaged in inshore gleaning are doing so on a limited recreational permit, or without a permit. Interestingly, most of the women also referred to themselves as 'women who fish' and not necessarily as a 'fisher' or 'fisherwomen'.

Even though most of the women interviewed are predominantly occupied with pre- and post-harvest activities, three fisherwomen from Kleinmond work on small boats catching lobster. One woman describes what they do at sea,

> We go out on the boat [and we watch] what the men do with our crayfish … [We] make sure that everything runs smoothly on the boat. Yes, we sell it to the [fish] factories in Cape Town. So, for us this is a living. For example, even if I get off the boat and I have just had two days' work, it helps to sell it to the factory as the cash comes directly to me, so I can put it on the table at home. [Otherwise] [t]here is not much for you to spend money on, to enrich yourself, you understand?[11]

The fisherwomen from Kleinmond seem to assume a much more direct involvement and authoritative stance over the fishing activities based on their description of ensuring that everything runs smoothly during a trip out to catch lobster. These women are exhibiting more influence within small-scale fishing, by using their intimate knowledge of ocean stock in the hands-on roles that they assume in helping with the catch, as well as the crucial post-harvest role they play in ensuring the fish get sold to a company that can better compensate them than the general public. As such, they demand respect by pushing the confines as to how women can participate within the small-scale fisheries sector.

However, the fisherwomen who work on these boats do so on an infrequent basis; most of the time they are involved with post-harvest activities. They say that physical strength is needed for labour involved in catching fish. This is particularly so when fishing for snoek, as once it has been caught fishers immediately snap the snoek's necks to prevent them from thrashing around and spoiling the flesh.[12]

Rowina owns her own boat and has been involved in the small-scale fisheries sector for over 30 years. She sees herself as an owner-producer and distinguishes herself from other women and fishermen by asserting:

> I am a fisherwomen! Yes! I have my own boat and go out to sea myself. I go to sea, to catch my lobster, because I enjoy it. This is my labour. I enjoy going out to sea. Yes! I enjoy it. This is what I do.

Rowina was taught to fish by her father from whom she inherited the boat. Her crew is mostly fishermen – whom she says 'respect' her – and a few fisherwomen who occasionally work on the boat when lobster is being caught.

> [Women] help with the crayfish because [the men] cannot do everything. [They pull out a big catch of crayfish], then those crayfish need to get measured and if they are undersized then they must be thrown back. They pull 15 nets after each other. Can you imagine 15? To pull a net, [and] to measure is too much for them, it is too much work, yes.[13]

The above quotes indicate how Rowina and the small number of fisherwomen she hires are directly involved in catching lobster. Rowina's labour ranges from managing and maintaining the crew, helping to pull the nets, measuring the lobster, and throwing undersized ones back into the sea. The latter two activities are ones for which women are seen to be especially suited. Rowina is currently also the caretaker of the interim relief permit for the community of Kleinmond, and thus controls who is allowed to fish as well as their fishing weight allocations.

This illustration of fisherwomen directly involved in fishing activities is an example of outlier cases specific to women in Kleinmond, and this is not the case in Steenberg Cove. The respect offered to these women can be attributed to the fact that Rowina is the caretaker of the permit, and thus also controls who can apply to be on the permit list for the upcoming seasons. The women working with her are not happy with being handed the residual tasks that fishermen cannot manage, and expresses how it impacts on their income. If they do not fish at sea, they do not get income for that. As a result they need to engage in more time-consuming gleaning or production of other goods which are not paid as much as for fish.

Fisherwomen's unpaid work

Often an unaccounted dimension of work, the reproductive[14] labour of women in SSF includes important work to replenish and maintain fishing communities and to transfer knowledge of nature to others. This is particularly evident in sustaining fishing communities and families, as well as ensuring that there are future generations to continue to fight for and uphold the traditions of the SSF sector. These forms of labour are unpaid and not acknowledged as important to the sustainability of SSF.

Reproductive work occurs alongside productive work. It starts with the care of children, particularly younger ones in the households who need to be tended to in the morning (from as early as 04:00 am) before the women can set out to accomplish their paid work for the day. Older children are drawn into some of these tasks, such as preparing breakfast, before they leave for school and when they return home. Pre-school children accompany the women when they glean periwinkles and mussels in what is seen as 'tradition' in these communities. Many of the women remarked that this is what happened when they were growing up.

When Reena[15] says, 'All of us in this community removed periwinkles from the rocks when we were children', she also refers to how children at a young age connect to their environment. From a young age the children are easily navigating their way over sharp boulders and deep gullies, develop a good command of knives to pry the sea creatures off the rocks, and are steeped in knowledge, love, and respect for the ocean. Welma remarks on how much her son loves this life: 'He loves the sea very much. He is on the beach every day'.

Fisherwomen teach their children the traditions of fishing communities, which they believe is based in respect for nature and an appreciation for the sustenance nature provides. Thus, their children are not only taught how to glean, prepare, and process ocean food, but also how to use all the parts of the fish and are cautioned against wasteful behaviours. The participants indicated that they were all raised being taught how to live from the sea and land sustainably. This is evident by the organic nature in which they say the older fisher generations raised them to eat freshly caught fish, plant and harvest vegetables from their home gardens, and collect fresh eggs from their chickens.

Women incur a significant amount of additional social reproductive responsibilities, such as taking care of their own and the children of others. These activities are often disregarded and undervalued in sustaining a fisher household and its members, particularly within governmental regulations as well as with the previous generation of fishermen, which still strongly embrace patriarchal behaviours within the small-scale fishing sector. Arguably, women form the beating heart of the community, and these contributions by women are what affords the SSF sector a vitality to endure amid changing social, economic, environmental, and political conditions. Their activism and how it involves guiding the younger generation, among other activities, will be discussed next.

The power, activism, and feminism of fisherwomen: engaging with the promises of 'blue economic justice'

Women fishers are especially vulnerable to climate change impacts, which is due to their significant exposure to climate variation, as well as their relatively low adaptive capacity, particularly with their low-impact technology that they use to harvest marine resources. Fishers also struggle with migration patterns of fish, which coupled with fighting against other marine species for the 'catch', makes it an arduous task. Particular marine species, such as the pyjama shark, 'blou haai' (blue shark), seals and 'pers' (hagfish), make it very difficult to catch kreef.

There has been a strong indication of fisherwomen at the forefront of conserving the ocean, which bears out in this research. However, what often is seen as an empowering role for women also becomes an extra burden for women, who assume the role of teaching the youth and adults about conservation and living sustainably from the ocean.

Notably, fishermen from the Steenberg area are minimally involved in the cases of conservation of the ocean environment, unless they are heavily involved in local organisations for fishing rights. However, in Kleinmond, there does seem to be more engagement with fishermen, who are involved with WWF (World Wildlife Foundation) projects, which offer incentives for fishers taking responsibility for managing fish stocks and fishing behaviour.

There is also the contestation (for both men and women) surrounding the unfair allocation of permits and regulations, which leads fishers to question their integrity and deviate from these in order to secure fish, which, they declare, is one of their basic human rights. The struggles that women take up are those surrounding poverty in their communities, fisheries regulation, policy development, and the privatisation of the ocean and its resources. The fisherwomen indicated that the main limitations to women's fishing activities and roles pertain to poor access or lack of sufficient social services, climate change, and lack of proper representation, and respect and acknowledgement of women within the small-scale fisheries sector.

> We cannot make the same mistakes as our parents and grandparents, and [we must] fight for what is right if we do not have knowledge … [I]f we are going to fail [in this] then the next generation will also fail, and we will end up with no small-scale fisheries in 30 to 40 years.[16]

These words capture the despair many of the women experience of losing even what little access they have to the ocean. It is a fear for the impact of overfishing on the ocean, and for the demise of a way of living for their children which pushes them to guide younger generations and to fight for fishing rights. In both of these communities, the majority of the community work involving youth, and policy and regulation workshops are conducted by women. As such, despite the wide range of activities and roles that women assume within the small-scale fishing industry and households, women still actively engage with the political sphere in representing the fishers for their rights to fair regulations and permits, as well as being involved with the wider fishing communities, particularly concerning the youth.

Their fear of losing their space in fishing communities forms part of their memory of forced removals under the Group Areas Act of apartheid South Africa. Their parents and grandparents could not resist the apartheid state violence when they were forcibly removed from their homes. This was the case of Hermin's grandparents who were pushed out of Greenpoint (since apartheid a white-owned wealthy neighbourhood) and forced to move to Manenberg, far removed from fishing sites on the Cape Flats. This is also the case with Sarah from Kleinmond, whose husband's family was forcibly evicted from their home, which is now the current harbour.

A big issue raised by the women was their recognition and representation by the government and various small-scale fisheries officials. Rowina reported that there are many women representing fishing communities at government meetings and workshops with the Department of Agriculture, Forestry and Fisheries (DAFF). Thus, there is a presence of women within the political sector of small-scale fisheries discussion. Yet most of the time at these meetings or workshops, their deep-seated knowledge about the sector is disregarded and unacknowledged by officials. All women participants interviewed indicated at some point they have applied for permits; however, most of them were denied. However, as previously indicated, Rowina is, and Sarah was, caretaker of the interim relief permit. Without these interim relief permits, women fishers would have even less access to knowledge of small-scale fishing affairs, as no contact from the government is made to inform communities. Women's cooperatives are also significantly under-acknowledged and also void of proper financial start-up capital structures, as well as resources on how to progress with such an economic venture in cooperative ways.

'Women also have to fight!', says Hermin. Women engage in public protest through demonstrations at DAFF offices. There they are usually at the forefront, singing struggle songs and bearing signs proclaiming their anger and frustration with being excluded from the fishing sector. The bandanas they wear are brightly coloured and indicate their various positions in this struggle. Hermin explains: 'we call ourselves, the ninja fishers warriors, and we wear bandanas to make a statement ... the colours are powerful and people stop and listen then'. She further depicts what some of the colours mean: 'to wear the black bandana is to commiserate with the ones that have passed (died) for their struggle, and for the negotiations we can have white and turquoise for peace, purity, calmness, and the ocean, to show we are open to communication'.

Hermin, however, feels the time for peaceful protest is over. She said in an interview, 'This is our season of assertive action, we are hurting the child that the government is favouring'. The 'child' favoured by government is commercial fishing companies, who are contrasted to small-scale fishing communities, whom Hermin correctly states were the first fishers in South Africa. Despite the centuries-old existence of fishing communities, they were excluded from government support, and especially so since the 1970s when the apartheid government accorded politicians in cahoots with commercial fishing enterprises fishing quotas, while SSFs has to operate 'illegally'. In the post-apartheid era, fishers operate under 'interim relief permits', a system which promises to accord rights and quotas to SSFs, yet they are constantly under surveillance from the middle-class and police inspectors. As Fakier (2018) argues, it is often the poor and women who become targets for environmental policy, and as a result their activities in nature are subjected to constant scrutiny and censure. In contrast, the overfishing and contraventions of over-generous fishing quotas by fishing companies are covered up. This ocean grabbing contradicts even formal policies, and more so the conservation of the ocean environment, thus compelling the women to 'rebel' against formal procedures.

Alongside ongoing negotiations, Hermin insists that fisherwomen should be more aggressive and leave the wearing of white and turquoise for peaceful expression, and instead don black clothing to mourn fishers who have died with no rights and to express a more assertive struggle. The 'MAN-made poverty' which the fishers experience, she says, should be fought by attacking commercial enterprises directly by cutting their fishing ropes. Marching in protest to the DAFF, she suggests, does little for their struggle and further depletes their limited resources as it does little to counteract the capture of the state by capital.

Rodwin, son of Hermin, illustrates the reproduction of environmental knowledge and politics between mother and child that many of the women aim for. He and Hermin are members of Coastal Links, a mass movement actively attempting to secure the rights of fishers and protection of the environment. Thus, he is equally sceptical of the potential of Operation Phakisa and identifies how the notion of 'blue economic justice' was stolen from activist language and transformed into its opposite. In 2011 at COP 17 in Durban, protesting fishers used the term 'blue economic justice' in their posters. Shortly after this, Operation Phakisa was announced and promised 'blue economic justice' with, according to Rodwin, little delivery on justice. 'We were talking about this a long time ago ... What is being done under operation Phakisa is not what the small-scale fishers envisioned with blue economic justice'.

Rodwin suggests that racial exclusion still operates in attempts to transform fishing policy. Thus, bodies such as the fisheries transformation council are both removed from the material conditions and demands of fishing communities and are being swayed by big fishing companies to protect capital's interests. No benefit accrues to SSFs in the post-apartheid era, he suggests when he says, '[The] same people [are] preforming the same atrocities they did under periods of racism in our country ... and now [we] are in a democracy which makes it worse for us as small-scale fishers'.

In contrast to Hermin and her son, Mary expresses her activism through formal involvement with the state as a community representative in DAFF consultations. She was for a long period overseeing permit regulations in Kleinmond and monitors the catch of local fishers, gathering data about the catch and bycatch in order to avert allegations of poaching. The interim relief permit she used to oversee is one for the entire community and therefore she argued that complying with regulations is a communal and collective responsibility. She points out, however, that communities in other parts of South Africa are less amenable to working with the state and would much rather control their engagement with the ocean themselves.

Mary recognises state failure in the late release of permits (that is one month after the start of a three month season), the allocation of quotas for fish they do not have the resources to catch (e.g. for tuna which require bigger boats than they can afford), and the ignorance of state officials about the kinds of fish available in their area (and therefore being issued with permits to catch fish which do not inhabit this stretch of the ocean). However, her hopes for the community are still vested in accessing the resources promised by Operation Phakisa. She intends to approach the DAFF to replicate a fish farming venture in her community, as was funded by Operation Phakisa close to coastlines in other parts of the country. Mary's commitment to connect the youth in her community with their natural environment through fish farming ventures suffers from a fundamental oversight. That is, how harmful fish farming is to the environment and SSF way of living. Fish farming, mariculture, or aquaculture as it is also known, displaces catch fishing, depletes fishing stock to feed the carnivorous fish being farmed, employs intensive rather than extensive labour, and industrialises fishing for profit even further (Ertör and Ortega-Cerdà, 2017). Thus, should the quick-fix Operation Phakisa arrive on the shores of Kleinmond, it would intensify the inequality between those fishers excluded from its approach and capital, and cause conflict between those in the community with high expectations for Operation Phakisa and those committed to conserving the environment.

Conclusion: ecofeminism as politics

State and capital continue their alliance in the post-apartheid fishing sector. The women who fish in Steenberg Cove and Kleinmond are exploited and marginalised not only by capital and the state, but also by the men in SSF communities. Theirs is a triple burden of production in fishing and related areas, equally productive work in households and their communities, and context-specific activism (Afshar and Barrientos, 1999). Shoved onto the margins of the SSF sector by blue capitalism, they draw on their long-held knowledge of the natural environment – human and oceanic – to resist constructions of illegality and exertions of power by the state, capital, and men in SSF.

Our data show that women in SSF are engaged both in the production of life and the production of the means of life. Their marginalisation in the fishing sector is coloured by constructions of illegality which is in stark contradiction with their everyday, ecologically sensitive practice drawn from long-held knowledge about the ocean. Thus they are still subjected to race-, class-, and gender-based exclusion. Women activists like Hermin forcefully, or assertively as she terms it, contest these constructions. Others, such as Mary, respond to these allegations by distancing themselves from the 'poaching' by others and attempting to access the promise of frameworks such as Operation Phakisa, which has the actual potential to eradicate the way of living of small-scale fishers.

In contrast to some understandings that women's connection to nature is a reflection or outcome of their passivity and acquiescence to the forces of production, some of the women activists engage in assertive action to wrest back power and control over their material existence. In this process, the interlinkage of state with capital is identified as the root of ocean grabbing, and the developmental potential of the 'blue economy' and Operation Phakisa is contested.

This chapter also addresses the notion of 'sustainability', banded about loosely in development approaches, and suggests that when women–nature relations are ignored, important opportunities to reverse human exploitation of nature are lost. The inability and unwillingness of the South African state to reverse the exclusion and exploitation of apartheid capitalism means that women have to wrest their right to lead lives in and of nature from the control of post-apartheid state–capital collusion. The particular position that women are forced into in the SSF sector in South Africa is a reiteration of the notion that humans are separate from, and 'superior' to, the natural environment. We show that the exploitation and domination of women intensifies the domination and exploitation of nature in capitalism.

Marxist-Feminist analysis has shown how women's unpaid work reproduces the working-class acts as a subsidy for capital as it separates production of life from the production of the means of life (Fakier and Cock, 2018). Fraser (2014) argues further, that it is not only such women's work (also known as social production) which makes up the backbone of capital, but also that the domains of ecology and politics operate in the shadows and subsidise capitalism. In a neoliberal time, when state power is slipping ever more out of the reach of ecologically devastated communities, collective and communal politics become an important force in a struggle resisting capital's attacks on human–nature connection. Such a struggle fundamentally involves women, not because of essentialist linkings of women to nature but arising out of their deep-seated knowledge and respect for and in nature. The challenge for Marxist ecofeminists, both in South Africa and across the globe, is to recognise such struggles, support them, and connect them to struggles in other parts of the world, in order to develop transnational solidarity to protect and conserve our future.

Notes

1 A hitherto unrecognised class whose labours and value orientation in relation to 'nature' leave them at the margins of the tele-pharmo-nuclear complex. Strictly speaking, meta-industrial categories such as women domestic workers, subsistence farmers, and Indigenous Peoples, are both inside and outside dominant hegemonic capitalism. They are inside in as much as they are essential 'resources' but as political 'subjects' they are largely outside (Salleh, 2000).

2 All names used in the chapter are pseudonyms, unless referring to public figures.

3 See Ferreira and Visser (2007) for a description of how coastal development in South Africa is starting to mirror that in the North, where the notion of urban entrepreneurialism has led to an increase in the building of 'waterfronts'.

4 Rodwin, Male, 34, interview: 2 November 2017.

5 Afrikaans derogatory term referring to the Khoi roots of 'coloured' South Africans.

6 The terms 'die boere' or 'die boers' literally translates to 'the farmers'. However, colloquially it refers to Afrikaans-speaking white people.

7 In an interview with Hermin (Female, 60, interview: 2 November 2017) she uses the term 'assertive' on many occasions to emphasise the activism required in SSF.

8 Any harvesting that takes place in the ocean up to 30 meters deep requires minimal

fishing gear and is less invasive than offshore or deep-sea fishing.

9 Female, 45, interview: 30 November 2017.

10 Female, 48, interview: 28 November 2017.

11 Rowina, Female, 55, interview: 30 November 2017.

12 *Pap snoek* is a local term that refers to the mushy and inedible texture of the snoek flesh when it has thrashed around repeatedly after capture. This term has also developed a colloquial meaning. Someone referred to as a *pap snoek* is a person deemed weak and useless.

13 Rowina, Female, 55, interview: 30 November 2017.

14 Social reproduction refers to a set of practices that ensures the daily maintenance and long-term generational survival of humans (Bakker and Gill, 2003).

15 Female, 46, interview: 30 November 2018.

16 Rodwin, Male, 34, interview: 30 November 2017.

References

Afshar, H., Barrientos, S. (Eds.), 1999. *Women, Globalization and Fragmentation in the Developing World*. Women's Studies at York Series. Palgrave Macmillan, London.

Bakker, I., Gill, S., 2003. 'Ontology, Method, and Hypotheses' in Bakker, I., Gill, S. (Eds.), *Power, Production and Social Reproduction*. Palgrave Macmillan, Basingstoke, 17–41.

Bhattacharya, S., 2017. 'Issues Relating to the Blue Economy'. *CUTS International*. www.cuts-citee.org/pdf/Viewpoint_Paper_Blue_Economy.pdf. Accessed: 17 January 2019.

Cock, J., 2014. 'The Green Economy: A Wolf in Sheep's Clothing or an Alternative Development Path in South Africa?' in Fakier, K., Ehmke, E. (Eds.), *Socio-Economic Insecurity in Emerging Economies: Building New Spaces*. Routledge Earthscan, London, 219–231.

Eagleton, T., 2011. *Why Marx Was Right*. Yale University Press, New Haven, CT.

Ertör, I., Ortega-Cerdà, M., 2017. 'Unpacking the objectives and assumptions underpinning European aquaculture'. *Environmental Politics* 26(5): 893–914.

Fakier, K., 2018. 'Women and Renewable Energy in a South African Community: Exploring Energy Poverty and Environmental Racism'. *Journal of International Women's Studies* 19(5): 165–176.

Fakier, K., Cock, J., 2018. 'Eco-feminist Organizing in South Africa: Reflections on the Feminist Table'. *Capitalism Nature Socialism* 29(1): 40–57.

Ferreira, S., Visser, G., 2007. 'Creating an African Riviera: Revisiting the Impact of the Victoria and Alfred Waterfront Development in Cape Town'. *Urban Forum* 18(3): 227–246.

Fraser, N., 2014. 'Behind Marx's Hidden Abode: For an Expanded Conception of Capitalism'. *New Left Review* 86: 55–72.

Gaard, G., 2011. 'Ecofeminism Revisited: Rejecting Essentialism and Re-placing Species in a Material Feminist Environmentalism'. *Feminist Formations* 23(2): 26–53.

Goodman, J., Salleh, A., 2013. 'The "Green Economy": Class Hegemony and Counter-hegemony'. *Globalizations* 10(3): 411–424.

Harcourt, W., Nelson, I., 2015. *Practising Feminist Political Ecologies: Moving beyond the 'Green Economy'*. Zed Books, London.

Harper, S., Zeller, D., Hauzer, M., Pauly, D., Sumaila, U.R., 2013. 'Women and Fisheries: Contribution to Food Security and Local Economies'. *Marine Policy* 39: 56–63.

Isaacs, M., 2013. 'Small-scale Fisheries Governance and Understanding the Snoek (Thyrsites atun) Supply Chain in the Ocean View Fishing Community, Western Cape, South Africa'. *Ecology and Society* 18(4): art. 17.

Kabeer, N., 1994. *Reversed Realities: Gender Hierarchies in Development Thought*. Verso, London.

Kings, S., 2016. 'Government's Ambitious Plan to Build an Ocean Economy'. *Mail and Guardian*, 19 February. https://mg.co.

za/article/2016-02-18-governments-ambitious-plan-to-build-an-ocean-economy. Accessed: 6 June 2017.

MacGregor, S., 2006. *Beyond Mothering Earth: Ecological Citizenship and the Politics of Care*. UBC Press, Vancouver.

Masifundise, 2015. 'Women's Role in Fishing Industry Not to Be Underestimated'. *The Hook*, 18 March. http://masifundise.org/womens-role-in-fishing-industry-not-to-be-underestimated/. Accessed: 17 May 2017.

Pauli, G.A., 2010. *The Blue Economy: 10 Years, 100 Innovations, 100 Million Jobs*. Paradigm Publications, Taos, NM.

Rai, S.M., 2002. *Gender and the Political Economy of Development: From Nationalism to Globalization*. Polity Press, Malden, MA.

Rai, S.M., 2008. *The Gender Politics of Development: Essays in Hope and Despair*. Zed Books, New Delhi; London.

Räthzel, N., Cock, J., Uzzell, D., 2018. 'Beyond the Nature–Labour Divide: Trade Union Responses to Climate Change in South Africa'. *Globalizations* 15(4): 504–519.

Salleh, A., 2000. 'The Meta-Industrial Class and Why We Need It'. *Democracy and Nature* 6(1): 27–36.

Salleh, A., 2001. *Ecofeminism as Politics, Nature, Marx, and the Postmodern*. Zed Books, London; New York.

Salleh, A., 2012. 'Green Economy or Green Utopia: The Salience of Reproductive Labor post-Rio+ 20'. *Journal of World-Systems Research* 18(2): 141–145.

Salman, A., Iqbal, N., 2007. 'Ecofeminist Movements: From the North to the South [with Comments]'. *The Pakistan Development Review* 46(4): 853–864.

Shultz, O.J., 2015. 'Defiance and Obedience: Regulatory Compliance among Artisanal Fishers in St Helena Bay'. *Marine Policy* 60(C): 331–337.

Stevis, D., Uzzell, D., Räthzel, N., 2018. 'The Labour–Nature Relationship: Varieties of Labour Environmentalism'. *Globalizations* 15(4): 439–453.

Sydee, J., Beder, S., 2001. 'Ecofeminism and Globalisation: A Critical Appraisal'. *Democracy and Nature* 7(2): 281–302.

United Nations (UN), 2014. 'Blue Economy Concept Paper'. *Sustainable Development Knowledge Platform*. https://sustainabledevelopment.un.org/content/documents/2978BEconcept.pdf. Accessed: 15 January 2019.

United Nations Economic Commission for Africa (UNECA), 2016. *Africa's Blue Economy: A Policy Handbook*. ECA Printing and Publishing Unit, Addis Ababa. www.uneca.org/publications/africas-blue-economy-policy-handbook. Accessed: 3 March 2017.

Waruhlu, R., 2019. 'Blue Economy Can Be a Life Line for Africa'. *Inter Press Service (IPS) News Agency*. www.ipsnews.net/2019/01/blue-economy-can-lifeline-africa/. Accessed: 17 January 2019.

Wheeler, M.K., 2018. 'Women Must Be at the Heart of Africa's Blue Economy'. *Inter Press Service (IPS) News Agency*. www.ipsnews.net/blueeconomy2018/2018/11/21/women-must-heart-africas-blue-economy/. Accessed: 17 January 2019.

World Wildlife Foundation (WWF), 2015. 'A Delicate Balance: Protecting Oceans, Fishing and People'. *Africa Geographic*. https://africageographic.com/blog/a-delicate-balance-protecting-oceans-fishing-and-people/. Accessed: 19 December 2018.

World Wildlife Foundation (WWF), 2015. *Principles for a Sustainable Blue Economy*. http://wwf.panda.org/homepage.cfm?249111/What-a-blue-economy-really-is. Accessed: 2 February 2017.

Zuma, J., 2014. Address by President Zuma at the *Operation Phakisa: Unlocking the Economic Potential of the Ocean Economy Open Day*. International Convention Centre (ICC), Durban. www.gov.za/speeches/view.ph. Accessed: 18 December 2018.

11 | THE 'CRISIS OF CARE' AND THE NEOLIBERAL RESTRUCTURING OF THE PUBLIC SECTOR

A feminist Polanyian analysis

Rebecca Selberg

Introduction

In her introduction to social reproduction theory (SRT), Tithi Bhattacharya (2017: 2) explains the basic premise of Marxist-Feminist analyses of work as that of a total social organisation (cf. Glucksmann, 1995). Rather than viewing productive labour for the market as the only existing and legitimate form of work, which is the reigning perspective under capitalist rule, SRT and Marxist-Feminist analyses view 'the relation between labor dispensed to produce commodities and labor dispensed to produce people as part of the systemic totality of capitalism' (Bhattacharya, 2017: 2). Our understanding of capitalism is incomplete, Bhattacharya insists, if we do not explore the ways in which the system is reproduced through 'daily and generational reproductive labor that occurs in households, schools, hospitals, prisons, and so on' – labour that 'sustains the drive for accumulation' (Ferguson, 2015 quoted by Bhattacharya, 2017: 2). SRT views the production of goods and services, the reproduction of life and the reproduction of the system as parts of an integrated process, and while Marxist theory has placed class struggle mainly at the point of production, Marxist feminism considers 'the myriad of social relations extending between workplaces, homes, schools, hospitals' as 'a wider social whole' coproduced by human labour in 'contradictory yet constitutive ways' (Bhattacharya, 2017: 3).

This article starts out from an SRT perspective, but acknowledges that while work takes place both within and outside production, with both types of work part of the same socio-economic process (Bezanson and Luxton, 2006: 37), labour processes and labour as a category are produced under distinct conditions and social relations under commodity and service production on the one hand, and spheres of reproduction on the other. Feminist scholars have illustrated this through detailed studies of labour processes in reproductive work, highlighting, for example, care work as 'a process or practice that has a strong emotional dimension and is based on human connection in relationship' (Duffy, 2005: 68); the specific class, gender, and ethnic divisions of tasks within reproductive work (Glenn, 1992; Roberts, 1997); the pressures that come from manoeuvring complex subjugation in spheres of intimacy (Anderson, 2000; Lutz, 2002; Gavanas, 2013); and the misrecognition and systemic undervaluation of reproductive labour (England et al., 2002).

Despite the significant attention paid to labour as practice and relation in the reproductive sphere, the public sector, which is of strategic interest to feminists and anti-capitalists, is somewhat under-emphasised in the field of Marxist feminism (although see Mohandesi and Teitelman, 2017), despite its central role in organising daily and generational reproductive labour. Granted, the role and the size of the public sector differ across nation states, but in many countries of the world it does play a significant role in providing state services necessary for the extended workforce to uphold a sustainable standard of living.

From a global perspective, public sector governance is a vast and complex web of arrangements mixing private contractors, NGOs, and public organisations and officials to provide public services and make and enforce regulations (Bertelli, 2012). No wonder key transnational political and economic institutions have realised that the public sector plays a strategic role for them, too; the World Bank regularly launches public sector performance projects geared towards 'improving' governance and stimulating and shaping public sector reform. Oran (2017), in her discussion on pensions and social reproduction, reminds us that Marx noted in the *Critique of the Gotha Program* that the social reproduction of the working class is paid through the total social product. What is allocated for the working class's needs depends on the necessities of the class as a whole, and it is the class struggle in the political sphere that will determine 'how much of the total social product will be devoted to social reproduction' (Oran, 2017: 159). This helps explain the continued interest on behalf of the capitalist class in the size, role, and management of the public sector; it also explains why issues such as pensions, social insurance schemes, and the accessibility and quality of services related to care are placed squarely at the centre of political conflicts around the world.

Taking Swedish public sector healthcare as its main example, this chapter enters into a dialogue with SRT and more specifically the notion of an inherent crisis tendency of reproduction within the capitalist system. By linking Nancy Fraser's concept of a 'crisis of care' to Michael Burawoy's discussion on the new wave of marketisation in Polanyian terms, this chapter aims to explore the public sector as a conduit between spheres of production and spheres of reproduction – an arena in which resources necessary for the reproduction of labour power are amassed, distributed, and produced and in which compliance – a central element of social reproduction under capitalism (Brenner and Laslett, 1991) – is organised. The public sector is where the state provides for and represses people and the market all at once, and it's an arena in which labour is performed for wage but outside capitalist profit. It connects the market with polity through occupational groups and professions who face society and people rather than the market. The article engages with the question of the radical potential in the standpoint of care workers, by taking up Therborn's assertion that there are three main challengers to late stage capitalism, the three 'P's: the precariat, the proletariat, and the professions.

Middle-class professionals in humanist occupations today play a central role in radical political mobilisation, according to Therborn (2018: 80). He is not the first to note this. Achinstein and Ogawa (2006: 32) identify a shift in how resistance among teachers is conceptualised in research, away from viewing it as an expression of a psychological deficit among 'resistors' or an attempt to solidify control over institutional practices, towards a view of resistance as politically necessary in the 'current instructional climate'. In countries across the world, public sector unions have been increasingly involved in broad political conflicts and mobilisations as they respond to austerity politics. In Romania, healthcare trade unions have adopted a more militant stance since the latest economic crisis (Adăscăliței and Muntean 2018), and in Chile, conflicts have centred on education, with teachers and students involved in street protests.

Taking the Swedish retrenchment, privatisation, and neoliberalisation of the public sector following the economic crisis of the 1990s as an example, Therborn argues that welfare professions such as physicians, nurses, social workers, and teachers have been the main targets of the finance and 'welfare' capital. The sustained attacks on their professional discretion, their wages, and working conditions have radicalised them and turned them into a core oppositional force against neoliberal management regimes and austerity politics (Therborn, 2018: 148). The risks involved in a total confrontation with the knowledge professions are too great for both state and capital, according to Therborn, and measures have been introduced to break up occupational unity instead. In Sweden, such measures have included implementing new hierarchies and career opportunities for a limited number of workers, such as promoting a few teachers at each school to 'career teachers' earning higher salaries than coworkers. Likewise, the nursing profession is increasingly differentiated between a proletariat stuck in intense, repetitive, fractured, and misrecognised high-touch care work and an upper tier immersed in management, research, and/or administrative positions (Selberg, 2012). In other countries, measures have been more explicitly violent, such as union busting specifically targeting public sector unions in the US (Bottari, 2018), or severely crippling the right to strike and mobilise on behalf of political parties or positions in the UK (*The Guardian*, 2015).

For Polanyi, the market wave was noticeable and resisted by farmers. In late capitalism the same processes can be analysed by focusing on public sector employees, and especially those in occupations responsible for daily and generational reproductive labour. The assaults on the public sector that followed the oil crisis of the 1990s and the ensuing phase of financialised capitalism created, across the Western world, a new state-driven strategy that 'allowed the ruling class to disarticulate and discipline the working-class, reunite themselves into a coherent ruling bloc, and restore profitability' (Mohandesi and Teitelman, 2017: 63).

The article begins with a discussion on the development of the Swedish public sector, in order to trace the contours of the relation between the productive and reproductive sphere; between state and market. The analysis centres on the contribution of Fraser, Burawoy, and Polanyi to an understanding of public sector care work and its role in neoliberalism.

Production and reproduction: invented and re-imagined

What is the genesis of the public sector in capitalist welfare states? The expansion of waged labour 'thoroughly transformed the composition of the proletarian households, as well as the relationship between production and social reproduction' (Mohandesi and Teitelman, 2017: 42). Even as, as historians have proved, the separation was not complete, households grew increasingly dependent on the wage, giving greater social power to men (2017: 42). The role of the household and women's domestic labour were reduced by a culture and ideology that emphasised the male wage-earner (and rendered invisible women wage-earners). The domestic tasks of wives and mothers, according to Mohandesi and Teitelman (2017: 43), became invisible work, while at the same time dependence on the wage 'not only integrated men and women into capitalist relations, but worked to formalize a rigid and hierarchical gendered division of labor within working-class households'.

The misrecognition of care work can thus be thought of as a key aspect of the ideological dominance of the so-called productive arena and of patriarchal power. This power relation is based on the separation of production and reproduction dating back to the onset of capitalist methods of production (Bradley, 1989: 33). As labour was removed from the household, the market and the private home became nodes in two seemingly separate systems; productive labour was linked exclusively to production of goods for sale on the private market, whereas domestic labour was linked to production of use value for immediate consumption – and its value was effectively concealed (Liljeström and Dahlström, 1981: 32). Reproduction, in this context, can be defined as the creation and maintenance of social bonds – generationally (birthing, raising children, caring for the sick and the elderly) as well as horizontally (sustaining ties among friends, family, neighbourhood, community). These activities are simultaneously affective and material (Fraser, 2016b: 30). Care is, in this sense, labour (paid or unpaid) that accommodates reproduction, and which contains a constitutive element of aiding or providing for someone who is unable to fully maintain herself (Yeates, 2005: 228).

For Nancy Fraser (2016a, 2016b), the different stages of capitalist development come with a distinctive character of the relationship between production and reproduction. Under the epoch of early industrialisation, liberal competitive capitalism combined industrial exploitation in the European core with colonial expropriation in the periphery, and left workers (including women and children, who were drawn into industrial production) to 'reproduce themselves "autonomously", outside the circuits of monetized value, as the states looked on from the sidelines' (Fraser, 2016a: 104). The 'murderous rates of exploitation' (Harvey, 2015: 182) caused a crisis of social reproduction, which ensuing campaigns for protective legislations proved inadequate to counter (Fraser, 2016b: 32). In Sweden, liberals at the turn of the century argued that social reforms were needed if one were to assume 'the working population's solidary sustenance of the consisting state order' (Gustafsson, 2000: 127). Social reproduction was then recast as the women's domain within the realm of the family, creating a new imaginary of domesticity through two separate spheres: the public and the private (Scott and Tilly, 1975; Game and Pringle, 1984). Though few actually had the means to live up to this emerging model of family life, the separation between these two spheres became a central cultural ideal (Åmark, 2005: 56f).

Largely due to the struggles of the labour movement, the liberal regime was replaced during the twentieth century by a state-managed capitalist society in which the markets were re-embedded. Fraser (2016a: 104) describes this phase as based on large-scale industrial production and domestic consumerism in the core, supported by ongoing colonial and postcolonial expropriation in the periphery, and an 'internalized social reproduction through state and corporate provision of social welfare'. The household was to be maintained through the family wage model, wherein male industrial workers earned enough to support a family, and women focused on caring for it. Again, few could actually organise family life fully according to this ideal, which nonetheless had a broad impact on culture, law, and policy throughout the West.

Early twentieth-century Sweden was a country where social reproduction was a central site of working-class struggle; food and housing were, as in many other countries, key points of contestation (Mohandesi and Teitelman, 2017: 45). Swedish sociologist and politician Alva Myrdal's efforts to tackle the reproductive crisis is one example of how the cultural transition and political situation was seized upon by policy makers. In 1932, Myrdal offered a diagnosis of the reproductive crisis of liberal capitalism and a prognosis of the transition to state-managed capitalism. Two main processes have demolished the conditions for stable family relations, she argued. First, industrialisation, which stripped the household of its productive capacity and made women take up work outside the home. Second, the reduced size of the family unit, which demanded an increased reliance on institutions such as schools. Taken together, these processes called for an increased rationalisation of the households, including improved forms of housing. Myrdal argued that women should work outside the home (and this is the general historical tendency, she argued; only moral-sectarians would disagree, Myrdal, 1932: 603), but realised that this called for political solutions to secure the stability of social reproduction. 'The new motto on all fronts in society is organization, cooperation, and rationalization', she stated – a neat adage for the period of social engineering that would characterise the expansive phase of the twentieth-century Swedish welfare state regime.

Myrdal's discussion hints at the specific form of state-managed capitalism developed in the Nordic countries, usually conceptualised as a social democratic welfare regime (Esping-Andersen, 1990), a universalistic model (Korpi and Palme, 1998), or simply 'the capitalist welfare state' (Bergh, 2009), characterised by de-commodification (including the diminished impact of market forces on distribution), a comprehensive range of publicly provided benefits and services with broad coverage of the population (Sainsbury, 1996: 31f), and corporatist models of labour market negotiations (Bergh, 2009). The expansion of the public sector thus served both to secure growth and stability of the market, and to assist those who were affected by the 'unyielding market system' (Liljeström and Dahlström, 1981: 211). It cemented a horizontal and vertical gender segregation of the Swedish labour market. The low wages it paid women workers drew them from unpaid reproductive work in the domestic sphere (where they often depended on the wage labour of men) into under-valued reproductive work in the public sphere (where they to this day still depend, to a degree, on wages of others in the household). While the expansion of the public sector created a female proletariat, it also served to reinforce the division of labour between 'Swedish' women and migrant women workers, who toiled in factories instead, or as ancillary service workers in the backrooms of the public sector (Knocke, 1986; cf. Roberts, 1997). It was the result of a compromise between labour and capital that would save many workers from poverty and reduce risk for vast segments of the population, as well as reorganise the composition of the working class, reinforce internal divisions, and foreclose experiments in self-reproduction (Mohandesi and Teitelman, 2017: 56). It was, as Mohandesi and Teitelman put it, an exchange wherein the state began to subsidise many of the costs of social reproduction while working-class households became largely dependent on capitalist relations.

In Sweden, the expansion of the public sector started with the increased responsibilities placed on municipalities and counties, which grew both in volume and in political authority. According to Hasselbladh et al. (2008: 50), the debate surrounding the public sector in the 1960s and 1970s focused primarily on how much, how fast, and where it should expand. Between 1960 and 1985, the entire Swedish national job growth was generated by increased levels of hiring in the public sector, primarily among women (Ringqvist, 1996; Sundin and Rapp, 2006); by the mid-1970s, during the so-called 'golden years' of Swedish economic growth (Bergh, 2009), the public sector accounted for more than 50 per cent of the GNP. The 1980s was characterised by an exceptionally low unemployment rate, which by 1989 had dropped to a mere 1.5 per cent (Eliason, 2011: 4). For women, the public sector was the primary place of employment.

The expansion of the public sector was not free of tensions, however. As was the case in other countries where social programmes expanded, political activists disagreed sharply over long-term strategic goals. Mohandesi and Teitelman discuss the US New Deal, but their description captures processes at play in Sweden too:

> Some groups wished to widen, democratize, and ultimately improve social relief from the government, even if the capitalist foundations of federal welfare remained intact. Others hoped to use these various federal programs to build power and deploy the welfare state against other forms of oppression, for example domestic abuse. Still others argued that the compromise, however beneficial to workers in the short run, functioned to manage or recuperate class struggle, unite competing capitalists, and keep profits flowing smoothly, ultimately strengthening the capitalist mode of production. (Mohandesi and Teitelman, 2017: 58)

There was much debate across the Nordic countries on the rational procedures of the public sector and the quality of the services provided. Activists, public intellectuals, and scholars argued that the professionalisation of care entailed an increased emphasis on rationality and instrumentality at the expense of 'expressiveness' or flexibility, to the detriment of patients/clients. The left theorised the public sector in terms of a repressive apparatus that served ideals of national purity and capitalist ideology (cf. Sjöström, 1977). The 1970s further witnessed a growing critique of the 'Gesellschaft' welfare state. According to Hasselbladh et al. (2008: 50), these debates were a mix of nostalgia, radical ideals of democracy, and criticism of the large-scale operations in the services provided. Part of this critique, Hasselbladh et al. argue, was a broader tendency in the West to question expert rule, bureaucracy, alienation, and the medical-industrial complex. In Sweden, there was also a growing critique of the overlap between public officials and politicians; the political and administrative spheres were increasingly conflated through the introduction of long-term budgets and sector-by-sector production plans in municipalities and counties, as well as programme budgeting in the state sector (Hasselbladh et al., 2008: 51; Sundström, 2016: 150). The expanding welfare state thus created a tighter overlap between previously separate domains and logics of action wherein technocrats operated in environments where 'rational planning techniques' and ideological-political considerations intertwined; 'the twilight zone wherein politics and economics mix institutionally', as Czarniawska (1985: 83) described it.

The strong position of the professions was another major area of critique (Henriksson et al., 2006). As Brante (2014) has noted, the Swedish welfare state and the professions 'took off' together. From the late nineteenth century onwards, medical doctors were, just like university professors and schoolteachers, incorporated into mostly public organisations (Brante, 1992), but they nonetheless retained their autonomous position and complete control over knowledge production and labour processes. As pointed out by Gustafsson (2000), the professions and semi-professions were moulded as part of the Swedish *ämbetsmannastat*, the specific bureaucratic model that emerged during the late eighteenth century and both integrated public servants into the state apparatus and secured their independence (Andersson, 2001). In terms of nurses, it is long since established that the occupation came to be characterised by a gendered notion of care as a calling (Bessant, 1992), but its ideals of compliance and organisational precision (Selberg, 2012) can also be linked to an influence from the Swedish church and the military – i.e. the Swedish state apparatus (Kvarnström and Waldemarsson, 1996, cited in Gustafsson, 2000: 35). This fact, that the professions remained autonomous and immensely powerful within the public sector, was by the 1970s considered a democratic as well as an organisational problem (Ahrne, 1985). Activist groups staged spectacular protests, produced influential journals dedicated to democratising the public sector, and launched civil society solutions to support and organise patients, clients, and inmates (Meeuwisse, 1997).

By the 1980s, the disapproval of Swedish bureaucracy, technocracy, and expert rule had reached a critical point, and in 1982 the Social Democrats launched a reform programme to 'renew' the welfare sector (Pierre, 1993: 391). According to Pierre, 'the gap between high taxes and insufficient public services' challenged the legitimacy of the public sector. The sheer size of it, and the already high level of taxation, also made it politically difficult to justify further expansion. It was the lack of quality, the rigidity, the hierarchical and centralised character of the organisation, the red tape, the confluence of polity and bureaucracy, the autonomous position of the professions and their concurrent hard institutional embeddedness which circumcised agency, the democratic deficit, as well as a broader political turn to the right that made way for restructuring (Pierre, 1993; Hood, 1991; see also Forsell, 1999). By 1990, 50 per cent of respondents in the yearly electoral poll wanted to reduce the size of the public sector (Pierre, 1993: 394).

... to restructuring and neoliberal transformations

In 1985, the revised Public Administration Act came into force, giving clients a stronger position than before. According to Pierre's (1993: 397) summary, a key goal of the politics of public administration in Sweden in the 1980s was to

> transform the national bureaucracy from a traditional Weberian bureaucracy to a more open, client-oriented, and responsive public administration. Put differently, in order to regain some legitimacy for the public sector and the public bureaucracy, the state tried to soften the boundary between the state and civil society.

Mohandesi and Teitelman (2017: 59) argue that in the US, even the most revolutionary activists of the 1960s and the 1970s incorporated the welfare state's precepts into their movements, even as they tried to subvert them. The same can be said of Sweden. It was not that activists challenged the idea behind an embedded capitalism – rather, they called for a more humanist version of the public services, with more space for civil society and (state-supported) self-care. What happened was, instead, a broad reform programme aiming to introduce an entirely new mode of government 'predicated on the establishment of regulated zones of freedom and self-governing actors' that were supposed to 'adapt and improve themselves according to norms of conduct and the central role of expert languages' (Hasselbladh and Bejerot, 2007: 176). By the end of the decade, several state agencies were involved in reforming the public sector, aiming to increase efficiency in municipalities, cut costs in county budgets, and decentralise the healthcare system. The public sector was no longer going to be 'hampered by stagnant, inflexible structures, practices and traditions'; instead, public administration and the public sector should 'henceforth be characterized by *continuous change and improvement*' (Hasselbladh et al., 2008: 54, italics in original). According to Pierre (1993: 398), public bureaucrats found themselves in a dilemma. Maintaining the organisational objectives that they were once developed to warrant (public policy implemented through vertically integrated hierarchies) would further jeopardise the overall legitimacy of the public sector, while emphasising efficiency instead would imply entering into a game they were not designed for. In the long run, this option might also erode legitimacy of public institutions. Hence, Pierre notes, privatisation emerged as a powerful option.

During the 1980s and 1990s the transformation of the welfare state intersected with the 'international management revolution' that called for radical changes in the public sector with the aim of reducing costs, implementing pseudo-market mechanisms, and improving services (Montin, 2012: 2). Boltanski and Chiapello (2005: 97) describe the new management techniques as a response to the critique outlined above, and trace their roots to the 'denunciations of hierarchy and aspirations to autonomy that were insistently expressed at the end of the 1960s and in the 1970s'. The new management thus partly hailed from the left, and emphasised spontaneity, rhizomorphous capacity, multitasking, conviviality, openness and novelty, creativity, informality, and receptiveness (Boltanski and Chiapello, 2005: 97). However, these themes were not combined with the core critique of the left – of capitalism and of exploitation:

> The critique of the division of labor, of hierarchy and supervision – that is to say, of the way industrial capitalism alienates freedom – is thus detached from the critique of market alienation, of oppression by impersonal market forces, which invariably accompanied it in the oppositional writings of the 1970s. (Boltanski and Chiapello, 2005: 97)

Instead, the critique was appropriated by the growing efforts to establish a neoliberal agenda in which the public sector in itself was seen as an impediment to development and growth (Hugemark, 1994). The ensuing changes within public sector organisations, which took place in most Western countries during the 1990s, are commonly referred to as New Public Management (NPM). Some of the inspiration came from Japanese lean production methods such as the '*kanban* system', which originated in the Toyota corporation (Boltanski and Chiapello, 2005: 73). NPM involves not only changing management techniques and accounting models, but also implies 'a more fundamental shift in norms and beliefs concerning the public sector and its relation to the private sector' (Blomgren, 1999: xi), wherein public sector organisations model their governance on private companies.

As I have illustrated elsewhere (Selberg, 2013), NPM has produced complex challenges for care professionals. Austerity ideology has resulted in severe work intensifications, increasingly unpredictable labour processes, and progressively fraught and risky work structures. However, it is important to note that the justification for implementing many of these changes was not just to reduce the size of the public sector, but to improve the quality of service. The nursing profession in particular was able to seize this opportunity to expand their field; as Erlöv and Petersson (1992: 185) noted, one would have to 'look back to the days of Nightingale to find a corresponding attention directed at the care work performed by nurses', as was the case at the end of the 1970s. Despite calls for a focus on versions of what some feminist sociologists called caring rationalities (Waerness, 1984), the nursing profession opted for managerial influence and professionalisation. They entered into a Faustian pact with NPM, in which they gained authority in a system that would also undermine the very labour processes that they secured as their jurisdiction (Selberg, 2012; Blomgren, 2003). According to Boltanski and Chiapello (2005: 81), it is precisely this move 'from control to self-control, and the externalization of control costs formerly met by organizations on to wage-earners and customers' that may be regarded as 'the most significant features of evolution of management in the last thirty years'. A vital part of modern forms of governance, according to Hasselbladh and Bejerot (2007: 179), is the systematic organisation of rationalised agency. Neoliberal governance constructed agency as a governmental technology, and expanded, incorporated, and organised individual and collective subjectivity as an integrated part of practices of power:

> In contrast to previous regimes that either set out to free the citizen from government intervention (market-oriented liberalism) or cushion the vulnerable citizen by means of social security systems and public services (welfarism), the new regime attempts to constitute various actors in zones of regulated freedom. The individual actors are expected to make their own

choices (consumers to choose their own doctors or electricity suppliers), while collective actors (expert groups, corporations, agencies) are positioned (by a range of measures from legal demands to 'invitations') to partake in a game of semi-regulated freedom, whereby the role of the state is often restricted to the provision of facilities and rules and, if necessary, the creation of accountable actors. (Hasselbladh and Bejerot, 2007: 181)

Here, the new landscape of rationalised action becomes 'a way of securing calculability, accountability and equality', with the aim to embed the mobilised agency in formal systems, structures, and role positions wherein professional jurisdiction is dispersed.

The public sector workers under financialised capitalism

It is in this landscape that welfare professions are now beginning to mobilise against neoliberal management regimes and austerity politics. Today, social reproduction is once again the main site of class conflict in Sweden, and the service ability, quality, and inner workings of the public sector has become a subject for major conflicts, intense scrutiny, and protest. After years of public sector retrenchment, there is now a new type of crisis: that of protesting care workers. The exit of nurses has continued to the point where employers and the nursing union have been debating whether mass resignations constitute an illegal industrial action (Granberg, 2016), and news stories of entire nursing staff resigning in protest have become increasingly common. Hospitals in all areas of Sweden have been at the centre of protest, from demonstrations and rallies to occupations and so-called 'die-ins' (where protesters lie down pretending to be dead in front of a hospital's entrance). In viewing the reasons given for such radical protests, it is evident that healthcare staff continually cite a sense of responsibility for patients. As research has illustrated, care workers mobilise around collective notions of both worker and patient advocacy (Selberg, 2012; Mulinari, 2016). They both strike and avoid strikes depending on how they gauge the effects for patients (Selberg, 2012). Therborn (2018: 149) illustrates that humanist professions such as physicians and nurses strongly oppose austerity measures in the public sector, and they are among the core participants and members of social democratic and left parties in Sweden and of May Day demonstrations; they formulate publicly the critique against market mechanisms and the overlap between private and public. 'Everyday I see it, how bad it works. How could you destroy an organization that was fully operational … today it's in shambles, a catastrophe', a midwife is quoted as saying in Therborn's book.

How can we explain the acute crisis of care and the political strife in the current mode of state-organised social reproduction? Gustafsson (2000: 105ff.) argues that the social problems caused by liberal industrial capitalism were met with two types of reform politics in Sweden: 'external', in the form of labour market and industrial policy, and 'internal', in the form of workplace regulations. This process of institutionalisation limited the political aspects of the state-as-employer. Instead, welfare services were thought of as a social cost, as reproduction, and as redistribution. 'Internal' reform politics were thought of as ancillary, and accumulation within commodity and service production in the private market placed front and centre. In this context, Gustafsson contends, it was seen as 'natural and necessary' to import managerial models from private, for-profit commodity production. As the critique against the public sector grew in the 1970s and 1980s, new management models were implemented – yet again, for-profit commodity production was the place of extraction.

The implementation of industrial management techniques in the public sector speaks to a core feature of state governance under capitalism. Throughout the twentieth century and well into the new millennium, a main political conflict between left and right has centred on the relationship between the state and the market and the role of the public sector in providing social services and securing reproduction. However, this conflict has, according to Gustafsson, essentially played out within the logical confines of industrial capitalism; it is the 'institutional structures and approaches' of industrial capitalism that has characterised the visions and conceptualisations of both perspectives. The underlying capitalist logic of the welfare state was never explicitly challenged. This means that neither the political left nor the right has been able to organise, or been interested in organising, the public sector in ways that part with logics of production. While the system of yesteryear was deemed insufficient because of the supremacy of economic and bureaucratic rationality and instrumentality, the current organisational form under neoliberal rule is experienced as increasingly irrational and widely unacceptable – but for much of the same reasons. The move from 'overly-rational' and instrumental to irrational and dysfunctional reflects the same rationality under a new phase of intensified marketisation – hyper-rationality may be a more fitting concept. What is central here is that on the floor and in face-to-face interactions between staff and client, both managerial regimes – the instrumental, Fordist one and the decentred, neoliberal one – appear at odds with notions of acceptable conditions for providing care. The main difference is that the public sector has been the target of a more pure capitalist assault, in that the organisations now are managed explicitly like private corporations, complete with an abundance of management consultants, in-house markets and competition, and pursuit of quasi- and actual profits. What is more, the general retrenchment of public services that has been going on since the 1990s constitutes a serious attack on social reproduction in a wider sense, since the compromise between labour and capital means people are dependent on a combination of wages and state-provided services, benefits, and insurances. The increasingly aggressive invasion of capital in welfare provisions, the public sector, and its professions, alongside its tendency to expand the precariat, creates new forms of social conflicts, according to Therborn (2018: 150). The major social conflict of our time, Therborn argues, is that between 'labor, creation, care, knowledge and professionalism' and 'profitability, in which all workers are exchangeable'. The major shift brought about by financialised capitalism is that in the context of embedded capitalism's class compromise, certain areas were in some ways exempt from capitalist exploitation, especially in teaching, healthcare, and bureaucracy. This is no longer the case, and this is what propels radical mobilisation.

Conceptualising the crisis of care

When outlined like this, Nancy Fraser's (2016a: 100) argument that there is an inherent crisis tendency in reproduction under capitalism is sustained empirically:

> My claim is that every form of capitalist society harbors a deep-seated social-reproductive 'crisis tendency' or contradiction: on the one hand, social reproduction is a condition of possibility for sustained capital accumulation; on the other, capitalism's orientation to unlimited accumulation tends to destabilize the very processes of social reproduction on which it relies. This social-reproductive contradiction of capitalism lies at the root of the so-called crisis of care. Although inherent in capitalism as such, it assumes a different and distinctive guise in every historically specific form of capitalist society – in the liberal, competitive capitalism of the 19th century; in the state-managed capitalism of the postwar era; and in the financialized neoliberal capitalism of our time.

The present strains on care are not accidental, Fraser (2016a: 100) contends, but have 'deep systemic roots in the structure of our societal order'. The broader turn to Marxist understandings of internal contradictions of capital after the 2008 financial meltdown have brought the notion of a built-in tendency to self-destabilisation to the fore of critical analyses (Harvey, 2015). However, as Fraser points out (2016a: 101), Marx's point about the tendency of falling rates of profit limits our understanding of the full range of crisis tendency. Capitalism's economic subsystem depends on social reproductive activities, according to Fraser – just as it depends on polity for certain aspects of organisation and nature as a source of productive inputs (Fraser, 2014a). In a sense, capitalism 'free rides' on activities that form its human subjects, sustain them as embodied natural beings, and constitute them as social beings (Fraser, 2016a: 101). All the work that goes into these processes, including giving birth, raising children, caring for the old and the sick, maintaining households, building communities – all of this is 'an indispensable background condition for the possibility of economic production in a capitalist society' (Fraser, 2016a: 102). As many feminists have pointed out, though, these activities have often been thought of as 'outside of' economic relations (Folbre, 1995), part of 'the private sphere' (Federici, 2012: 97), and have even when commodified been poorly remunerated and recognised – an assertion which is at the heart of Waerness's argument. Fraser conceptualises this as 'separation-cum-dependence-cum-disavowal', and places it at the centre of destabilising processes of accumulation.

The 'social contradiction' inherent in the capitalist society grounds a crisis tendency, but it is located not 'inside' the capitalist economy. Rather, this contradiction is realised at the perimeter that 'simultaneously separates and connects production and reproduction' (Fraser, 2016a: 103). Fraser's argument here is that crisis hits when capital's drive to expanded accumulation 'becomes unmoored from its social bases and turns against them', in which case 'the logic of economic production overrides that of social reproduction, destabilizing the very processes on which capital depends', which essentially are about merging the social capacities needed to sustain accumulation over the long term.

Drawing on Gustafsson's analysis, we can see that the crisis tendency is less muted than Fraser suggests. While it is true that the state-capitalist settlement that resulted from a class compromise and produced social democratic models of welfare capitalism served to stabilise social reproduction (for some and for a while) (Fraser, 2016a: 110), it is also true that these models incorporated and built on organisational forms of capitalist production. They were already an aspect of the 'functional imbrication' of marketised and non-marketised spheres (Fraser, 2014b: 59), and if we hark back to feminists' and other activists' critique in the 1970s of the dominance of scientific/bureaucratic rationality over a so-called caring rationality, we see that economic production was overriding the very practices of social reproduction from the incipience of public welfare provision. This point may seem both counter-intuitive and trivial at once, depending on perspective. On the one hand, care in the post-war period was not marketised but made public; thus, it was described as de-commodified and essentially withdrawn from market logics (Esping-Andersen, 1990). Today, one can detect nostalgia among critics of austerity politics for the 'people's home model' of post-war Sweden (Andersson, 2009). This was the period in which the working class mobilised and opted for 'family, country and lifeworld against factory, system and machine' (Fraser, 2016a: 110), in contrast to liberal-era protective legislations that brought denigration rather than political incorporation. The arrangements of the welfare state did ease material pressures on family life and represented a democratic advance for majority-ethnicity workers in the capitalist core (Fraser, 2016a: 110). On the other hand, these same arrangements were premised upon the incorporation into non- or de-commodified spheres of action the logics of capitalist industrial production and, in the case of Sweden, the repressive logics of the state apparatus. It was mainly women and marginalised people who would absolve the contradictions of providing acceptable care under instrumental regimes. The model was not sustainable, and it 'dissolved in the course of a protracted crisis' involving tensions in the political sphere, civil society, and the financial domain (Fraser, 2016a: 112). Today's model seems no more sustainable.

Thinking with Polanyi, Fraser, and Burawoy: the potentials of the care crisis

The crisis of care is, according to Fraser (2014a), part of a severe and multidimensional crisis of economy and finance, of ecology, and of social reproduction. In order to understand this complex crisis, we need a conceptual framework, and Fraser suggests turning to Polanyi's *The Great Transformation* (1944). The basic argument of this classical book is that the nineteenth-century market liberalism produced major financial and political crises because it, according to Fraser (2014a: 543) 'disintegrated communities, destroyed livelihoods and despoiled nature':

> Its roots lay less in intra-economic contradictions than in a momentous shift in the place of economy vis-à-vis society. Overturning the heretofore universal relation, in which markets were embedded in social institutions and subject to moral and ethical norms and to political regulation, proponents of the 'self-regulating market' sought to build a world in which society, morals, ethics and politics were subordinated to, even modeled on, markets.

Polanyi's analysis centres on the process of marketisation in which the leading forces of production (labour, money, and nature) become subject to market exchange; they become 'fictitious commodities'. The commodification destroys their use value, and leads to a destruction of entire communities. This spawns a counter-movement to protect society, what Polanyi calls the 'double-movement' – a conflict between proponents of the free markets on the one hand, and forces to embed the market, on the other. Waves of marketisation are, according to Burawoy (2014: 4), 'marked by successive articulations of the commodification of labor, money and nature with corresponding counter-movements off different scales and defending particular rights'. This means that marketisation will differentially affect countries according to their history and placement in the world economy. Counter-movements will also take different shapes. In Europe, Burawoy notes, the counter-movement following the First World War saw a rise to fascism, Stalinism, and the Scandinavian social democratic welfare states.

The notion of fictitious commodities has been subject to much scholarly debate, but the identification of nature, labour, and money as central nodes of conflict and crisis is highly pertinent today, Fraser argues, as 'efforts to create a "market society", composed of commodities all the way down, necessarily trigger crisis' (Fraser, 2014a: 546). In light of transnational mobilisation to protect land and nature on the one hand, and growing protests spurred by discontent with care arrangements on the other, this argument seems valid. The care crises seen across the globe today raise claims that are 'tantamount to the demand for a massive reorganization of the relation between production and reproduction', and these struggles over social reproduction are, according to Fraser (2016a: 116) 'as central to the present conjuncture as are class struggles over economic production'. These claims for reorganisation are based in experiences not of exploitation, but of commodification, and specifically on the 'experience of the market as distinct from experience of production' (Burawoy, 2010: 306). Do they constitute a counter-movement? Fraser (2016a: 116) argues that struggles at capitalism's constitutive institutional divisions – such as where production meets reproduction – have redrawn the institutional map of society. It was, according to this view, the mobilisation for protection that propelled the shift from liberal capitalism to state-managed capitalism. As the history of the Swedish public sector illustrates, the cycle is more complex than what Polanyi described, though. Rather than a simple trajectory of 'market devastation followed by counter-movement and regulated de-commodification' (Burawoy, 2010: 307), the history of reproductive labour under capitalism is one of complex interlockings of logics of capital and counter-movements to sustain alternative rationalities. This is the way that the history of the entire capitalist system should be seen, according to Burawoy (2010: 307) – as a succession of great transformations and complex intertwining of marketisation and counter-movements.

The role and the character of the state are central here. Leaning on Burawoy's critique, one could argue that the class struggle and the ensuing class compromise that characterised the social democratic welfare state organised the working class and modes of reproduction *within* the framework of capitalism. The state recognised and enforced the material interests of workers not just through trade unions and parties, but also by implementing in the public sector the same operational means functional in private commodity production. Thus, the state could contain the 'ravages of the market' and reproduce its core practices simultaneously. But even under organised capitalism, wherein the state protected both capital and workers, there was mobilisation against commodification, represented by among other things the notion of 'rationality'.

By zeroing in on the concept of rationality, Nordic feminists at the end of the 1970s and others were able to launch a fundamental critique of the workings of public healthcare while defending the idea of care as a public responsibility. However, the critique of instrumentalism became detached from the critique of the supremacy of economic rationality as the public sector was transformed. This coincided with the new round of marketisation that began to assert itself by the end of the 1970s (Burawoy, 2010: 44). The language of new management promised flexibility – exactly what many activists and feminists (such as Norwegian sociologist Kari Waerness in an influential paper from 1984) asked for. But the 'discrediting of bureaucracy and its project of eliminating everything that is not "rational"' (Boltanski and Chiapello, 2005: 98) did not facilitate a 'more human modus operandi' – it facilitated, instead, a deepened commodification that penetrated even more deeply into the relationships that constitute care work. The notion of a public sector 'in shambles', invaded by a new capitalist logic, should be viewed as more than a description of the costs and effects of everyday actualisations of contradictions and shortsightedness – rather it holds a potential for inciting struggles that may transform the present regime. It should be understood and treated as a critique of commodification, as an expression of experiences of conflict between social reproduction and rationalities of the market. This is a conflict that operates on two levels: first, it is a conflict over how much of the total social product should be allocated to social reproduction. This is a conflict between labour and capital and centres on issues such as working time and the reach and breadth of pensions, insurance schemes, and other state-provided services. It is also a conflict over the operational aspects of how daily and generational social reproduction is organised. Here, the underlying capitalist logic needs to be explicitly challenged; subversion of the welfare state needs to move beyond incorporating its precepts. The struggle for social reproduction under the current crisis of care should create a more utopic understanding of care at the centre. For care workers, the concept of care is closely linked to the concept of ethics, which is why when the Swedish Medical Society rejects 'corporate newspeak', they do so by reminding their members to remain mindful of 'professional ethics' and to 'ask [themselves] whether the system within which [they] work allows for those ethical principles' to govern. The tension between ethics of care and logics of production is being and should be emphasised whenever class conflict revolves around social reproduction, and any critique that is based on a privileging of rationalities of care instead of rationalities of production may serve to conceptualise alternative modes of securing and expanding social reproduction.

It is during crises, Harvey (2015: ix) notes, that 'the instabilities of capitalism are confronted, reshaped and re-engineered to create a new version of what capitalism is about'. The current crisis of care might produce changes in how we think about, understand, and envision public institutions. It may also, as Fraser (2016b: 117) suggests, reinvent the reproduction-production division. In such a situation, it is imperative to understand the material and ideological conditions and effects of previous transformations – indeed, to acknowledge the historicity of them – and to circle back to calls for care that this time around explicitly reject the domination of logics of capital.

This chapter started out with a discussion on social reproduction theory, noting that SRT takes an integrative perspective on production and reproduction. I have illustrated in this text that the public sector is of strategic interest to feminists and anti-capitalists; in it, conflicts over competing goals, values, and spheres of life are made explicit. The assaults on the public sector allowed the ruling class to discipline the working class and the professions in new ways, but it has also opened up for counter-movements challenging the dominance of the market and bringing forward calls for a primacy of care rather than capital. It is, I argue, social reproduction that will be the main site for social conflict now and in the future, and as Marxist feminists we need to create visions for its conditions, operations, limitations, and enclosures.

References

Achinstein, B., Ogawa, R., 2006. '(In) Fidelity: What the Resistance of New Teachers Reveals about Professional Principles and Prescriptive Educational Policies'. *Harvard Educational Review*, 76(1): 30–63.

Adăscăliței, D., Muntean, A., 2018. 'Trade Union Strategies in the Age of Austerity: The Romanian Public Sector in Comparative Perspective'. *European Journal of Industrial Relations* 5(2): 113–128.

Ahrne, G., 1985. *Den irriterade medborgaren – en undersökning om erfarenheter och upplevelser av byråkrati*. Sociologiska institutionen, Stockholm.

Åmark, K., 2005. *Hundra år av välfärdspolitik: välfärdsstatens framväxt i Norge och Sverige*. Boréa, Umeå.

Anderson, B., 2000. *Doing the Dirty Work? Global Politics of Domestic Labour*. Palgrave Macmillan, London.

Andersson, C., 2001. *Ämbetsmannaetos och demokrati*. Stockholm: SCORE centrum för forskning om offentlig sektor Stockholm.

Andersson, J., 2009. 'Nordic Nostalgia and Nordic Light: The Swedish Model as Utopia 1930–2007'. *Scandinavian Journal of History* 34(3): 229–245.

Bergh, A., 2009. *Den kapitalistiska välfärdsstaten*. Norsteds akademiska förlag, Stockholm.

Bertelli, M.A., 2012. *The Political Economy of Public Sector Governance*. Cambridge University Press, Cambridge.

Bessant, J., 1992. '"Good Women and Good Nurses": Conflicting Identities in the Victorian Nurses Strikes, 1985–86'. *Labour History* 63: 155–173.

Bezanson, K., Luxton, M. (Eds.), 2006. *Social Reproduction: Feminist Political Economy Challenges Neo-liberalism*. McGill-Queen's Press, Montreal.

Bhattacharya, T., 2017. 'Introduction: Mapping Social Reproduction Theory' in Bhattacharya, T. (Ed.), *Social Reproduction Theory: Remapping Class, Recentering Oppression*. Pluto Press, London, 1–20.

Blomgren, M., 1999. *Pengarna eller livet? Sjukvårdande professioner och yrkesgrupper I motet med en ny ekonomistyrning*. Department of Business Studies, Uppsala.

Blomgren, M., 2003. 'Ordering a Profession: Swedish Nurses Encounter New Public Management Reforms'. *Financial Accountability and Management* 19(1): 45–71.

Boltanski, L., Chiapello, E., 2005. *The New Spirit of Capitalism*. Verso, London.

Bottari, M., 2018. 'Behind Janus: Documents Reveal Decade-Long Plot to Kill Public Sector Unions'. *Portside*, 25 February 2018. https://portside.org/2018-02-25/behind-janus-documents-reveal-decade-long-plot-kill-public-sector-unions. Accessed: 17 December 2018.

Bradley, H., 1989. *Men's Work, Women's Work: A Sociological History of the Sexual Division of Labour in Employment*. University of Minnesota Press, Minneapolis, MN.

Brante, T., 1992. 'Expert Society: The Origins and Development of Professions in Sweden'. *Studies of Higher Education and Research* 2, 1–18.

Brante, T., 2014. *Den professionella logiken. Hur vetenskap och praktik förenas i det moderna kunskapssamhället*. Liber, Stockholm.

Brenner, J., Laslett, B., 1991. 'Gender, Social Reproduction, and Women's Self-Organization: Considering the US Welfare State'. *Gender & Society* 5(3): 311–333.

Burawoy, M., 2010. 'Marxism after Polanyi' in Williams, M., Satgar, V. (Eds.), *Marxisms in the 21st Century*. Wats University Press, Johannesburg, 34–52.

Burawoy, M., 2014. 'From Polanyi to Pollyanna: The False Optimism of Global Labor Studies'. *Global Labour Journal* 1(2): 301–313.

Czarniawska, B., 1985. 'The Ugly Sister: On Relationships between the Private and the Public Sectors in Sweden'. *Scandinavian Journal of Management Studies* 2(2): 83–103.

Duffy, M., 2005. 'Reproducing Labor Inequalities: Challenges for Feminists Conceptualizing Care at the Intersections of Gender, Race, and Class'. *Gender & Society* 19(1): 66–82.

Eliason, M., 2011. 'Undersköterskor och sjukvårdsbiträden i kristider'. IFAU report 2011: 3. IFAU, Uppsala.

England, P., Budig, M., Folbre, N., 2002. 'Wages of Virtue: The Relative Pay of Care Work'. *Social Problems* 49(4): 455–473.

Erlöv, I., Petersson, K., 1992. *Från kall till personlighet. Sjuksköterskans utbildning och arbete under ett sekel*. Pedagogiska institutionen, Lund.

Esping-Andersen, G., 1990. *The Three Worlds of Welfare Capitalism*. Polity, Cambridge.

Federici, S., 2012. *Revolution at Point Zero: Housework, Reproduction, and Feminist Struggle*. PM Press, Oakland, CA.

Folbre, N., 1995. '"Holding Hands at Midnight": The Paradox of Caring Labor'. *Feminist Economics* 1(1): 73–92.

Forsell, A., 1999. 'Offentlig reformation i marknadsreformernas spår'. *Kommunal ekonomi och politik* 3(3): 7–23.

Fraser, N., 2014a. 'Can Society Be Commodities All the Way Down? Post-Polanyian Reflections on Capitalist Crisis'. *Economy & Society* 43(3): 541–558.

Fraser, N., 2014b. 'Behind Marx's Hidden Abode: For an Expanded Conception of Capitalism'. *New Left Review* 86: 55–71.

Fraser, N., 2016a. 'Contradictions of Capital and Care'. *New Left Review* 100: 99–117.

Fraser, N., 2016b. 'Capitalism's Crisis of Care'. *Dissent* 63: 30–37.

Game, A., Pringle, R., 1984. *Gender at Work*. Pluto, London.

Gavanas, A., 2013. 'Migrant Domestic Workers, Social Network Strategies and Informal Markets for Domestic Services in Sweden'. *Women's Studies International Forum* 36: 54–64.

Glenn, E.N., 1992. 'From Servitude to Service Work: Historical Continuities in the Racial Division of Paid Reproductive Labor'. *Signs: Journal of Women in Culture and Society* 18(1): 1–43.

Glucksmann, M., 1995. 'Why "Work"? Gender and the "Total Social Organisation of Labour"'. *Gender, Work & Organization* 2(2): 63–75.

Granberg, M., 2016. *Care in Revolt: Labor Conflict, Gender, Neoliberalism*. Mid University Sweden, Sundsvall.

The Guardian, 2015. 'Biggest Crackdown on Trade Unions for 30 Years Launched by Conservatives'. 15 June 2015. www.theguardian.com/politics/2015/jul/15/trade-unions-conservative-offensive-decades-strikes-labour. Accessed 17 December 2018.

Gustafsson, R.Å., 2000. *Välfärdstjänstearbetet: Dragkampen mellan offentligt och privat i ett historie-sociologiskt perspektiv*. Daidalos, Gothenburg.

Harvey, D., 2015. *Seventeen Contradictions and the End of Capitalism*. Profile Books, London.

Hasselbladh, H., Bejerot, E., 2007. 'Webs of Knowledge and Circuits of Communication: Constructing Rationalized Agency in Swedish Health Care'. *Organization* 14(2): 175–200.

Hasselbladh, H., Bejerot, E., Gustafsson, R.Å., 2008. *Bortom New Public Management: Institutionell transformation i svensk sjukvård*. Academia Adacta, Lund.

Henriksson, L., Wrede, S., Burau, V., 2006. 'Understanding Professional Projects in Welfare Service Work: Revival of Old Professionalism?' *Gender, Work & Organization* 13(2): 174–192.

Hood, C., 1991. 'A Public Management for All Seasons?' *Public Administration* 69(1): 3–19.

Hugemark, A., 1994. *Den fängslande marknaden: Ekonomiska experter om välfärdsstaten*. Arkiv, Lund.

Knocke, W., 1986. *Invandrade kvinnor i lönearbete och fack: en studie om kvinnor från fyra länder inom Kommunal- och Fabriksarbtareförbundets avtalsområde*. Arbetslivscentrum, Stockholm.

Korpi, W., Palme, J., 1998. 'The Paradox of Redistribution and Strategies of Equality: Welfare State Institutions, Inequality, and Poverty in the Western Countries'. *American Sociological Review* 63(5): 661–687.

Kvarnström, L., Waldemarsson, Y., 1996. 'Jakten på de statsanställda – gemensamma utgångspunkter' in Kvarnström, L, Waldemarsson, Y., Åmark, K. (Eds.), *I statens tjänst: Statlig arbetsgivarpolitik och fackliga strategier 1870–1930*. Arkiv, Lund.

Liljeström, R., Dahlström, E., 1981. *Arbetarkvinnor i hem- och samhällsliv*. Tiden, Stockholm.

Lutz, H., 2002. 'At Your Service Madam! The Globalization of Domestic Service'. *Feminist Review* 70(1): 89–104.

Meeuwisse, A., 1997. *Vänskap och organisering: en studie av Fountain House-rörelsen*. Arkiv, Lund.

Mohandesi, S., Teitelman, E., 2017. 'Without Reserves' in Bhattacharya, T. (Ed.), *Social Reproduction Theory: Remapping Class, Recentering Oppression*. Pluto Press, London, 37–67.

Montin, S., 2012. *Politik och förvaltning i förändring: en forskningsbaserad översikt*. SKL Rapportserie, Stockholm.

Mulinari, P., 2016. 'Det tar tid att fånga samtiden' in Sandberg, Å. (Ed.), *På jakt efter framtidens arbete*, Tankesmedjan Tiden, Stockholm, 83–90.

Myrdal, A., 1932. 'Kollektiv bostadsform'. www.markeliushuset.se/Markeliushuset/Litteratur_files/Myrdal%201932.pdf. Accessed 18 May 2017.

Oran, S.S., 2017. 'Pensions and Social Reproduction' in Bhattacharya, T. (Ed.), *Social Reproduction Theory: Remapping Class, Recentering Oppression*. Pluto Press, London, 148–170.

Pierre, J., 1993. 'Legitimacy, Institutional Change, and the Politics of Public Administration in Sweden'. *International Political Science Review* 14(4): 387–401.

Polanyi, K., 1944. *The Great Transformation*. Farrar & Rinehart, New York.

Ringqvist, M., 1996. *Om den offentliga sektorn: vad den ger och vad den tar*. Fritze/Statskontoret/SCB, Stockholm.

Roberts, D.E., 1997. 'Spiritual and Menial Housework'. *Yale Journal of Law & Feminism* 9(1), 51–80.

Sainsbury, D., 1996. *Gender Equality and Welfare States*. Cambridge University Press, Cambridge.

Scott, J., Tilly, L., 1975. 'Women's Work and the Family'. *Comparative Studies in Society & History* 17: 44–45.

Selberg, R., 2012. *Femininity at Work: Gender, Labour and Changing Relations of Power in a Swedish Hospital*. Arkiv, Lund.

Selberg, R., 2013. 'Nursing in Times of Neoliberal Change: An Ethnographic Study of Nurses' Experiences of Work Intensification'. *Nordic Journal of Working Life Studies* 3(2): 9–36.

Sjöström, K., 1977. *Socialpolitik eller socialism?* Arbetarkultur, Stockholm.

Sundin, E., Rapp, G., 2006. *Städerskorna som försvann – individen i den offentliga sektorn*. Arbetslivsinstitutet, Stockholm.

Sundström, G., 2016. 'Strategisk styrning bortom NPM'. *Statsvetenskaplig tidskrift* 118(1): 145–171.

Therborn, G., 2018. *Kapitalet, överheten och alla vi andra: Klassamhället i Sverige – det rådande och det kommande*. Arkiv, Lund.

Waerness, K., 1984. 'The Rationality of Caring'. *Economic & Industrial Democracy* 5: 185–211.

Yeates, N., 2005. 'A Global Political Economy of Care'. *Social Policy & Society* 4(2): 227–234.

12 | GENDER REGIMES AND WOMEN'S LABOUR

Volvo factories in Sweden, Mexico, and South Africa[1]

Nora Räthzel, Diana Mulinari, and Aina Tollefsen

Introduction

Much needed research has been conducted in so-called export processing zones (EPZ) (Benería et al., 2016; Benería and Roldán, 1987; Ong, 2006; Salzinger, 2003) across the countries of the Global South, where surplus profits are made on the basis of super-exploitation and violence, practices generally condemned across the political spectrum. In contrast, our research on the working lives of workers at the Swedish transnational corporation Volvo is an attempt to understand the 'normality' of globalising capitalism.

Therefore, our aim was to ask whether a form of capital accumulation that does not rely on overexploitation, obvious forms of violent control, and repression of the labour force but instead is known as paying fair wages and engaging in gender equality, would stick to these principles in countries of the Global South, where corporate agreements like in Sweden never existed or have been erased in the wake of post-Fordist global transformations. We therefore chose the Swedish company, Volvo, which has been perceived in Sweden and internationally as a good employer, paying good wages and being one of the first companies to replace the assembly line by teamwork, which allows workers greater flexibility and control over the workplace (Berggren, 1994).

We wanted to analyse the experience of workers as *Volvo workers* and to grasp how these experiences are structured through the company's transnational profile and through the national and social-political histories, within which workers made sense of their experiences. This led us further to the question about the role gender plays as a symbol, an identity, and a social relation in the construction of Volvo workers within different societal contexts. In this text we develop one dimension of that question, namely, whether women's experiences as industrial workers in an industry dominated by men show similarities and/or differences across different countries of the Global North and South. We investigated the Volvo plants in Umeå (Sweden), Tultitlán, Estado de Mexico, Durban (South Africa), and Bengaluru (India).[2]

In the last decades, feminist scholars have explored the complex web articulating gender as a social relation, an identity, and a category appropriated by neoliberal ideologies and practices in the context of increasing female employment. As the International Labour Organization (ILO) argues, this has been one of the major changes in the structure of the labour force globally. However, the increased integration of women into paid employment has taken place in the context of an increasing precarisation of work, or, as Standing expressed it, a feminisation of work (Standing, 1989). He used this term to describe the increased entry of women into the workforce but under conditions which reflected the character of women's work, namely being part-time (time flexible) and low-paid. This, he argued went hand in hand with a general 'flexibilisation' of work for men and women alike. Feminist scholars have noted that in spite of the fact that women have predominantly been employed in precarious jobs, they have developed new identities as women working in paid employment (Darkwah, 2007; Eraydin and Erendil, 1999). It is against the background and in difference to this research that we are discussing the experiences of industrial women workers in the Global South and the Global North. We differ from this research in that the women who talked to us were not in 'feminised' jobs, but employed as industrial workers in 'men's jobs' and under conditions that pertained to the 'old' model of employment, having permanent[3] full-time jobs. As we will explain below, this was part of our goal to investigate the 'normality' of capitalist relations of production.

This chapter has four sections: First, we discuss the theoretical insights that have informed our analysis, second, we give an account of our methods, third, we present an analysis of our data, followed by, fourth, a discussion of our contribution to Marxist-Feminist analyses of women workers.

Theoretical reflections

Capitalist normality

We derive the concept of 'normality' from Marx's analysis of capitalism. In the introduction to *Capital* he explains his method comparing it to that of a physicist: 'The physicist either observes physical phenomena where they occur in their most typical form and most free from disturbing influence, or, wherever possible, he makes experiments under conditions that assure the occurrence of the phenomenon in its normality' (Marx, 1887/1998: 22). Marx specifies this concept throughout his work, the first time when he analyses the transformation of money into capital: 'The conversion of money into capital has to be explained on the basis of the laws that regulate the exchange of commodities, in such a way that the starting-point is the exchange of equivalents' (Marx, 1887/1998: 239). The reason why it was so important for Marx to analyse capitalism under the assumption that it works according to its own laws and regulations (even if that is never the case), is that only then could a critical analysis understand how capitalism works as a system. Analysing cases that are deviations from what is seen as the laws of the capitalist mode of production (equal exchange, a fair wage, free market forces, etc.) can lead to the assumption that putting the system back into functioning 'normally' will solve the problem. However, if it is under the 'normal' functioning of the system that exploitation occurs, then the system itself is the problem, not its malfunctioning. For instance, if 'feminisation' of employment is seen as the fundamental problem, the solution could be seen in creating stable, long-term, full-time employments. Analysing capitalism where it is meant to function normally can broaden our perspective of its inherent contradictions.

We are certainly not the only ones aiming to understand women's position in society within a Marxist-Feminist theoretical framework. Feminist scholars have analysed class, gender, and race relations globally within the capitalist mode of production (Enloe, 2004; Gibson-Graham, 2006; Federici, 2014), including the ways in which patriarchal formations situate women differently across multiple axes of domination and exploitation (Ferguson, 2016; Grabham et al., 2009; Hennessy, 2000).

The Swedish transnational Volvo corporation can be seen as the embodiment of the Fordism Gramsci analysed (Gramsci, 1971). However, as we show in our book (Räthzel et al., 2014), Volvo is rapidly transforming itself into a post-Fordist neoliberal corporation based on lean production methods and takt-time. In this sense our research contributes to studies that have addressed the connections between the global hegemony of financial capital, transformations of gendered divisions of labour as an effect of neoliberal economic adjustments, and the ideologies of neoliberalism that legitimise these processes (Glenn, 1992; Mohanty, 2003, 1997).

Gender regimes

When we analyse the structures of gender relations in the different factories as gender regimes, we relate to Connell's development of the concept, which she explained in her analysis of the state: 'women and men tend to occupy particular positions within the state, and work in ways structured by gender relations within institutions, which can be analyzed by taking a structural inventory' (Connell, 1990: 508). The positions women and men occupy in an institution are dependent on, though not just a reflection of the wider gender order in a society. A gender regime is co-constructed by all members of an institution, not only the management. Female and male workers bring the socially constructed images of men and women into the workplace where they negotiate their positions within the given relations of power in society and at work. We therefore ask, what kind of gender regimes develop within the different Volvo plants we investigated given the specific socio-historical contexts in which they are situated and the management strategies which take advantage of and shape these regimes?

The significance of place

Given that we are investigating factories in different countries belonging to one transnational corporation Doreen Massey's insight that the 'local' and the 'global' cannot be seen as dichotomies is specifically important for our analysis (Massey, 2005). In fact, the intersections of different levels and scales (the local, the national, the global) were impossible to ignore when speaking with workers. They explained their positions as a combination of belonging to a transnational corporation and how that influenced their position among friends and relatives, what the presence of the corporation meant for their country and the place they lived in. They felt connected in different and sometimes ambivalent ways to other Volvo workers across the globe. They definitely experienced a 'global sense of place' (Massey, 1994). Thus, we need to question fixed notions of identities linked to spatial entities, such as national stereotypes or 'national work cultures', while at the same time recognising that local places also demand adjustments from global corporations. We aim to analyse the ways in which national, local, and globalising work cultures intersect in specific times and places. Our main focus is women's subjectivities, the ways in which women workers live unequal working relations formed through different gender regimes at different places.

Gender regimes – place – and women's subjectivities

Angela McRobbie (2009) has argued that neoliberal ideologies have appropriated the discourse of women's liberation and equality by bending it into a discourse of individualistic 'entrepreneurship' (= free enterprise, meaning that anybody is free and able to set up their own business). They suggest that women, particularly young women, are the ideal entrepreneurs. While the women in our study were ordinary employees, the ways in which they identified with their work could be understood as fitting into such a neoliberal appropriation. However, we want to develop an understanding of gender subjectivity that identifies both the structural forces and forms of creating and regulating gender regimes *and* the human ability to transgress, challenge, and even transform them. The feminist political philosopher Lois McNay (2000) contends that a reconceptualisation of the role of agency is needed within feminist theory. It would have to avoid both deterministic and voluntaristic conceptions. The author recognises the contribution of recent work on gender and subjectivisation that connects language, body, and power. She also asserts the need to understand actions and social transformation at the mundane, everyday level. It is on this level that our research is situated. As we will show, concepts such as embodied experience and recognition are fundamental for the ways in which women define themselves and their position within the workforce. We follow McNay's argumentation that an intersectional analysis aiming to understand gender subjectivity and women's agency needs to engage in a broader reading of gender relations beyond the narrow focus on sexuality and femininity. Women industrial workers challenge simultaneously notions of what a woman is and what an industrial worker is. What kind of female subjectivities evolve, when women transgress the traditional forms of gendered divisions of labour? How and in which ways does their 'being there' on the male-dominated shopfloor shape the relations between workers in general?

On method

Workers' narratives of their experience in a transnational corporation help us to understand global processes. However, experiences are filtered through the narrator's worldviews, and through the ways in which they are co-constructed by the interviewee and the interviewer. We as authors do an additional filtering by deciding which elements of the story are going to be told and how. Such ambiguities can partly be addressed by using the tradition of institutional ethnography as feminist sociologist Dorothy Smith (2002) suggests it: (a) taking as a point of departure Volvo workers' experiences of work, (b) identifying some of the institutional processes that are shaping that experience, and (c) investigating those processes in order to describe analytically how they operate as the contexts of the experiences recorded. This approach is similar to sociologist Michael Burawoy's 'extended case method', which he describes as follows: 'The extended case method applies reflexive science to ethnography in order to extract the general from the unique, to move from the "micro" to the "macro" and to connect the past in anticipation of the future, all by building on pre-existing theory' (Burawoy, 1998: 5). In other words, we do not aspire to generalise our findings in a quantitative sense, claiming that a majority of women in transnational corporations feel and think the way our interviewees did, but rather to find, on the basis of our examples, some general structures that characterise the ways in which gender regimes can be established in transnational corporations, which deal with a fundamental contradiction: to motivate workers to do a job well for its own sake by simultaneously denying them the essential sine qua non for such motivation, namely to control the conditions of their work and decide about its purpose.

We interviewed 97 members of the Volvo Corporation, of which 90 were workers on the shop floor and 7 managers. In Mexico the management chose our interviewees according to criteria we gave them: gender, age, position at the workplace, length of stay in the factory. In Umeå, since the management did not want us in the factory, we interviewed workers chosen by the trade union according to the same criteria. In South Africa, we were allowed to choose the workers ourselves. In all countries, except Mexico, we were allowed to record the interviews, which were then transcribed and analysed with the help of the Max QDA system for qualitative analysis.

Almost all our interviews were conducted individually (one-on-one) but the fact that we were all simultaneously present at the respective sites during the field work created a productive environment where we could exchange and discuss our interpretations and theoretical approaches and conclusions.

While reading the interviews and our notes from Mexico, we coded statements that related to our main research question, namely the way in which work shaped peoples social relations inside and outside work and their identities as workers of a transnational corporation. This required paying attention to the ways in which people constructed themselves and were constructed as workers by managements. This included their descriptions of their working conditions in terms of salaries, horizontal and vertical forms of cooperation, gender specific relationships at the workplace and outside, family contexts, including spatial movements from home to work but also in terms of possible migration processes. For this article we selected the most vivid statements related to the ways in which gender relations were lived and created horizontally between male and female workers as well as vertically through the practices and policies of the respective managements. In our monograph and in other articles we have analysed other forms of working relations in the four countries under investigation (Mulinari et al., 2011; Mulinari and Räthzel, 2009; Räthzel et al., 2014, 2008).

As a qualitative study the number of workers is not meant to be representative, but to enable us to listen to workers from a range of different social and work specific positions in each country. We were struck by the similarity of workers' experiences and their ways of articulating these experiences while we talked to them across different economic, social, and political contexts.

Three factories, three gender regimes

A woman's day

> I wake up at 4.30, put the heating on, make breakfast and the children's lunch. I phone the kids while I am on the bus so that they get up to go to school. In the afternoon when I come back from work it is their homework that I have to supervise, go through what they do not understand at school … My day comes to an end at 23.30. I go to bed at 0.30. I sleep between three-and-a-half and four hours each night. (Olga, Tultitlán)

> That is the biggest problem. I have to wake up very early. There is no problem with the older one, she manages alone. But the little one: I have to prepare for myself and dress him while I prepare their lunch packages. Then he must come into my room because I have to lock my room. That is the thing. He has to wait more than an hour dressed liked that. We must be at work before seven. One gets tired. I get tired after tea, after two. For example, next week we are going to have overtime and we were talking about this. It is difficult to work from seven to seven. But we will try. (Lesedi, Durban)

> When we come back from work at 16.30, we go through the hall and leave our working bags and then we go out through the garden door and begin to talk. And then when we have done the things we feel are more important, then I go in and fix food. (Maya, Umeå)

Olga, Lesedi, and Maya share similar positions. They are female industrial workers in male-dominated work places. They are coded as women within factory regimes located in societal contexts where gendered divisions of labour prevail. Each of them has two workplaces: the factory and the home. However, their ways of talking about their working day illuminate not only differences of the three workplace regimes but also of the gender regimes in the three factories.

Olga and Lesedi experience working days that include the tiresome process of transportation, a two-hour journey between their working place and their homes. Olga's introduction of the phone as a fundamental tool to bridge her dual role of mother and worker demonstrates the tension between private and working life. Lesedi's attempt to comply even with more unfavourable working hours shows the existential need for work in a country with increasing unemployment rates, where one wage has to feed a family, even an extended family as we later learn. Olga's working conditions are ameliorated by the bus that the Mexican plant provides, while Lesedi has to use expensive private collective taxis. The absence of a company bus reinforces race and class hierarchies in a segregated city. One of the female workers we spoke to in Durban travelled 108 km a day to get to the plant. Class hierarchies overruled race hierarchies when it came to housing, since the members of management, whether defined as white, black, or Indian, lived close to the factory. Their class privilege and the material resources that come with it enabled them to overcome the racialised geographical separation between workplace and home, which was a feature of apartheid town planning. But the problems of the home–work journey also illuminated gendered ways of imagining a solution. For almost all the young black men in the plant buying a car was their first priority to solve the transportation problem, while the women wanted to buy a house closer by. Olga and Lesedi refer to their roles as mothers, highlighting what in our material appears as a source of conflict between Volvo and its female employees.

Maya's story is different. Her description of her day begins with her and her husband coming back from work together and relaxing in their garden. Most workers we spoke to in Umeå own houses closer to the factory, many of them with large gardens. The Swedish welfare state provides public child care allowing Maya, who has raised two children during her 20 years at the company, to combine family and work. In the Swedish Volvo factory households have two, not only one wage earner. Spouses and often several family members work at the Volvo plant, creating a specific relationship between the gender regime outside and inside the factory. Within the factory, a discourse of equality prevails (we will see later that it does not represent the actual practices). But despite gender equality policies in Sweden, Maya, like most of the women in Sweden, is the one principally responsible for household tasks. The tensions between work and family become visible in the 'we' through which Maya refers to the homecoming with her partner and the 'I' that enters into her story and marks the making of the meal as a woman's job.

Two commonalities bridge the North–South divide: Women in all three factories continue to be responsible for reproductive work and, as we will show in the next sections, women were seen as 'out of place' in their condition of industrial workers.

Mexico: neoliberal economies – gender transformation

The shift from a national development strategy based on import-substitution to a neoliberal model oriented towards an export-driven strategy during the 1980s in Mexico led to a profound economic and social restructuring in the country, including changing gender and working conditions (Gutierrez Arriola, 2006). In the following decades women's waged labour increased in the Maquiladoras, in the privatised national industry as well as in care and service work (Benería, 1992; Cortés, 2000; de la Rocha, 2015). Multiple incomes of household members have become a decisive buffer against the economic crisis (Rocha and Latapí, 2009). However, only 17 per cent of the female labour force is located within the industrial sector (Arciniega, 2012; https://vanguardia.com.mx/articulo/solo-17-de-las-mujeres-trabajan-en-la-industria-en-mexico).

The centrality of women's paid employment for the survival of households and communities (de la Rocha, 2015; Scott, 2008) was a central theme in the stories of the Mexican women workers. We spoke with eight women, three of whom had husbands who had emigrated to the North searching for work.

> My husband has been in the US for one year. He has been working in different places, he was going to come back in December but this will not be possible ... He got a one-year contract now. One must be patient. The situation is very hard everywhere. The economic situation is not stable in Mexico. You have to do it for your children. You have to sacrifice yourself for your children. Jobs in the US are not as stable as they are here. He was forced to go to a factory where the salary is very low and he sends every penny he is paid, but we have not seen any benefits. (Gaby)

Gaby characterises the gendered experience of migration from the point of view of those (women) left behind. She is introducing the notion of 'sacrifice', a notion that women often used in Mexico and South Africa explaining that they endured unfair working conditions for the sake of the needs and the future of their children. We will see, however, that women's identification with the reproductive sphere is double edged (Lagarde, 2011). It can lead them to accept higher levels of exploitation but it can also lead to gendered forms of awareness when their work conflicts with their role as mothers (Solis de Alba, 1990).

For most women, *ama de casa* (homemaker, literally soul of the house) is an identity of the past when working-class men could earn a salary high enough to feed a family. This became clear in the way women talked about their work. More often than the men we spoke with, they emphasised their pride in being able to work in the production process and to handle this work even better than their male counterparts:

> He said that this is perfect. He was surprised. And I learned that I can do any task they give us. I have heard comments about people doing pieces that then couldn't be used. (Olivia)

> The satisfaction of doing a job that was done by two people before, and now I am doing this all alone, I am managing alone. This gives me the satisfaction that yes, I can do this. As women we really accomplish what we start with. We are more agile. Like in the house. The women come home, get going with the household stuff and think of tomorrow. We have a rhythm. And the man doesn't. (Elena)

What became visible in these different stories of women at work (inside and outside the factory) is that paid labour was for them not just a way of earning money but a way of developing a new confidence and a new identity – an identity of women who 'can do it', can do the work that is defined to be a man's job. Simultaneously, the 'household stuff' became something that one does quickly, efficiently, but without investing much emotional identification in it. The changing gender order in society at large meant that women were able to see themselves differently. They were able to develop independence through the experience that they were competent and they enjoyed learning new things. However, given the conditions under which they worked, this new confidence had a high price: a working day that stretched from dusk to dawn. The gender regime at work which defined the shopfloor as a space where women did not belong and for which they were not qualified meant that women had to constantly struggle for recognition:

> They [the male colleagues at work] believe we want to conquer, and how can you want to conquer, when the only thing you want to do is to go home and sleep. You want to do a decent job, that's all. But they will be losing this idea, because you show them what you are worth. (Inez)

But we also saw signs of the gender regime changing: there was a generation gap between the male workers regarding women's paid employment (Husson et al., 1995; Gutmann, 2006). While most men in their thirties talked about their wives' employments as something normal, those over 50 expressed their respect for their wives by defining them as 'good administrators' of the men's income. They thought that if women were 'good administrators' and if men and women disciplined their desires (no beer, no luxuries) there was no need for (married) women to become Volvo workers.

South Africa – black women in industrial employment: women's care and workers' pride

Iris Berger's (1992) work on women industrial workers in South Africa identifies not only the connection between race and gender in specific industries but also the central role that women as workers have played within unions and in the struggle against apartheid. However, as Tshoaedi (2012) argues, in the post-apartheid area women have been marginalised by trade union policies, diminishing their role in workplace politics. In addition, the demands put on some of the black women industrial workers by family and work exhausted them. While they called themselves survivors and fighters, in the context of an absent (neoliberal) state (Mosoetsa, 2005; Darkwah, 2007) these demands made their lives difficult:

> I have a job that is much better now. The little ones cannot work. Sometimes I am the only one supporting my family. It is my duty. They raised me until I was twenty-two. I am doing my best. My mama is not working and my father is sick. So I have to take care of them. They are my family ... I am the oldest at home. And my brothers. I have to give them a future. Then it could be the time to have my chance. I treat the little one as my son ... I take him as my child. He is my first son. As a mother your first son is your first priority. So he [her fiancé] understands. He said that it was too late to marry in 2007 and then I said, we must wait until I have done everything for my parents and my brothers. (Cebile)

Cebile describes a tension between her desires and her duties. She is torn between her wish to care for her family and her desire to create a family of her own. She tries to solve the tension by declaring her little brother as her son. She accepts, though with sadness concerning the perspectives to form a family of her own, her role as the breadwinner as an 'obligation'. In a society where the unemployment rate of black women is 34.2 per cent in South Africa, while the general unemployment rate is 27. 7 per cent. The highest unemployment rate, 40.0 per cent exists for black women between 15 and 34 years (www.statssa.gov.za/?p=11375, accessed December 2018). Cebile's position as breadwinner is an exception and thus maybe there is also an element of pride in her ability to play that role for her family.

As for Cebile, for our other interviewees the concept of household was flexible. Some workers grew up with their aunts or grandparents, and they cared not only for the immediate members of a household like siblings and parents but also for relatives living elsewhere. In a country with only scant elements of a welfare state, where the unemployed have no welfare support, family members, especially the younger ones, who are able to get employment, are the only resource they can rely on in order to survive. The discourse of a moral economy with rights and obligations provides the ideological legitimation for people's actions. Reciprocity is one of its concepts that we found in all South African narratives: parents have sacrificed their lives and resources to bring them up, now it is their, children's turn, to do their 'duty', as Cebile puts it. A duty they fulfil but often at the expense of their own future. According to feminist scholar Obioma Nnaemeka, collaboration, negotiation and compromise are key features of African gendered life (Nnaemeka, 1998; Tshoaedi, 2012). In the context of economic restructuring, and new (insecure) labour regimes, the exchange patterns that regulate household economies become fractured, putting special stress on those family members who were able to channel resources to different members of the household/family unit, prioritising others rather than themselves (Gibson and Rosenkrantz Lindegaard, 2003; Bezuidenhout and Fakier, 2006).

Our interviews conveyed a picture of the previous generation being worn out, sick, and/or unable to get employment. Therefore, the burden of survival rested on the young people who had been lucky to get this job. They appeared to be safe now and able to care for their families at last. However, neither were their jobs secure nor did they pay enough for them to pay their dues back to their families. When we came back two years later and learned that the majority of the workers we had interviewed had been fired as a result of a strike for higher wages, we wondered what had become of them and their parents, siblings, nieces, and nephews.

And yet, while many women workers (but also many of the male young workers) ached under the burden of having to take care of family members while doing a demanding job, their subjectivities cannot be reduced to this aspect of their life. The description of women as being crushed under the 'double burden' of waged employment and household responsibilities did not hold for the Mexican women in our sample and it did not hold for the South African women at Durban's Volvo plant either:

> I have a good hand with the trucks. When I am with my friends and a Volvo truck passes by I can say, look, my hands are there and then they say: ladies cannot do such a thing … You know how guys are, when I told my friends that I was applying for Volvo, they said, no you cannot do that. It is for guys. Why are you saying such a thing, you cannot do a man's job? Maybe. But I try. And then there was a party and I took the photo so I am the one that is constructing the thing. We are ladies and we can do men's jobs. (Emana)

Emana, a young Zulu woman describes how cultural products and specific technologies are gendered. Her statement, 'you know how guys are' builds a bridge between the young South African worker and the middle-aged interviewer from Sweden/South America. It assumes, rightly, that in spite of coming from different class and national backgrounds, both women have something in common: knowing about unequal gender relations and how gender differences are performed. To understand men's resistance to her working aspirations as natural, that is as just 'the way they are' is a strategy Emana uses to challenge men's authority. Men are seen as claiming truths not because of knowledge or skills but because of who they are. Emana continues her ways of resistance by confronting prejudice with facts: her photo near a truck. The gender regime in the Durban Volvo factory was nevertheless more hostile to women wanting to transcend the position assigned to them than the Volvo factory in Mexico (where buses were constructed). While in the latter women did work on the line, even if many of their male colleagues resented it, in Durban only a few women were granted their wish to do so:

> No you are a woman they said … Do not tell me that, that I cannot do it, because I can. And here at the plant, they say you cannot do it because it is very heavy. In the line I tell the guys, let me try and if I fail I call you. Wait and see. I do it again. I do it stronger. I can do it.

We were told by almost all the male workers in Durban that working on the line was 'too heavy' for women. An argument that aimed to convey the special care men were taking of women. There was an open contradiction between men's claim that women did only minor jobs on the line and women's description of their work that they did the same things that men did. In Mexico as well as in Durban women workers were challenging the gender regimes that prevented them from entering workplaces and work practices coded as male. Women were more successful in Mexico, partly due to management strategies, who used women's enthusiasm for their newly conquered positions to set them against their male colleagues.

Sweden – gender equality as gender segregation

Sweden is often described as a pioneer of gender equality. The welfare state has developed policies aiming to combine family and paid employment. However, despite these policies and women's long presence in paid employment the glass ceiling has not been broken and women are overrepresented in specific areas like care work and the public sector. Additionally, in spite of important changes, they continue to bear the main responsibility for household work (Lundqvist, 2011; Martinsson et al., 2016).

The flight from care work

If in Mexico women were forced to explain their presence in industry by asserting that they really needed a job and were better qualified for it than men, in Sweden women often feel the need to explain why they are not in care work. This seems to be the result of a national context where femininity (and especially working-class femininity) is historically linked to work in the care sector. Our interviews in Volvo's Umeå plant show how women workers understand their employment at Volvo[4] against the traditional employment patterns for Swedish working-class women within the public health-care system (Selberg, 2012). Carina recounts:

> I was trained as a welder before I worked in health care because there were no jobs as a welder in the countryside. And when I had been working down here as a personal assistant in care during almost one year I felt that, no, if I do not get into emergency care then I do something else. And then there was a friend who said, 'but you are a welder. They need welders at Volvo. Apply. You are a girl. You will get the job'. So I applied and got the job.

Gender as a system of social organisation can be read on different levels here. Carina becomes a welder, a profession coded as male (Askegård, 2002), but her first job is as a personal assistant in the public health system, an employment coded as female and available for people without further qualifications. It is thus not surprising that Carina wants to leave this job, but it is surprising that her first strategy is to move to a more challenging position within the health-care system instead of using her original qualifications. Volvo's recruitment policies allow her to move out of a 'women's job' into a 'men's job' precisely because she is a woman. Volvo has an interest in employing a female welder in order to fulfil the Swedish requirements of gender equality.

Maria has also moved from care into industrial production. Before she came to Volvo she worked as a child minder:

> It was rough. You have to recognise that. But it was a wonderful time. First because you can have children around you, they speak to you as a person, you are important to them: my dagmamma, my mum ... The children were with me until they grew out of my care. It was good. But then I felt now I have done my share. I have accompanied these children so many years and ours were growing up as well. I felt, I had done my share.

The repetition of the words, *jag har gjort mitt* (I have done my share) is worth further reflection. On the one hand Maria identifies with the way the gender regime defines care jobs, namely through the personal relationships that make the caregiver important for the caretakers. On the other hand, it seems as if she considers care work a duty that can be given up once a 'fair share' has been done. However, at first Maria does not change her path dramatically. Deciding to get an education as an auxiliary nurse she remains within the domain of care work. In the wake of neoliberal restructuring of the health-care system, the number of auxiliary nurses employed in Swedish hospitals has decreased considerably. This is a job that has historically been an important opportunity for working-class women (Selberg, 2012). After two years of training, Maria is not able to get a full-time job, which is what she needs.

Her husband has been working at Volvo many years and therefore she tries her luck there:

> I was a little desperate, so I phoned Volvo ... I told them who I was and asked if they had any use for a 35-year-old woman ... 'Yes, you should apply. Production will increase and we will need people in the future'. I left my papers on Monday and was employed by Friday. That's how it was and I do not regret the decision. I don't regret anything ... Things turn out differently than what one has thought.

Maria still seems to feel uneasy about leaving the care sector, needing to convince the interviewer – and possibly herself – that there is nothing to regret and finally assigning the course of events to a *'force majeure'* that acts differently than the actor might have done. While job conditions and the much higher salary at Volvo are important reasons for her satisfaction with the job, she also likes painting and working with robots. A good deal of her description of working at Volvo is devoted to describing gendered social relations. There is solidarity among women, but there are also conflicts with male colleagues, against which Maria defends herself, for instance against being called nicknames: 'I pushed him against the wall and said: "I call you by your full name and I want you to call me by my full name" ... I think one has to mark ... a kind of boundary'.

In spite of these experiences, when asked what her expectations were when she started to work at Volvo she answers, 'I thought this is how I will stay now, this is it. And I have good colleagues, a good work and one is satisfied with that'.

We note the differences in Maria's descriptions of her job as a child minder at home and her work at Volvo. While being a child minder (which included minding her own children) was seen as a passing phase in her life, as a duty that was required from her until she had done her fair share, working at Volvo is perceived as definite from the beginning. Her satisfaction may be a sign of resignation for not having been able to remain in the care sector. But it can also be seen as a result of the way in which the sectors of care and production are perceived in society at large: care work is not only marked by low salaries and low security, it is also not considered 'real work'. Rearing children, caring for the elderly, domestic chores are perceived as something that women do. In contrast, industrial work (and work in the digital economy) is considered the source of society's wealth. It is a man's job and thus, a real job.

Conclusions

The contradictions of women's pride as producers

A fundamental challenge in our research has been to acknowledge both the exploitative working conditions offered to the women workers we met and women workers' satisfaction, pride, and even pleasure with their work. Women also connected in their narratives what they did at the workplace with what they did at home. They either described how they used the capabilities and routines from home at work to the benefit of their working achievements or by describing their work at home as being a 'man's job' already. In both cases they presented themselves as bridging the gap between alienated, paid employment and homework. By experiencing their capabilities at work through their capacities as female homeworkers and vice versa they made their work place their home place just as their home was their work place and not, as for the majority of male workers, the place of rest and recreation. Through these narratives a 'producer's pride' (Räthzel et al., 2014) emerges as a central and unexpected feature from our empirical material. However, under the given conditions of a gender regime that positions women at the margins of the industrial work place and a societal gender order, in which women remain the main carers at home, the producer's pride is not only a double- but a triple-edged sword.

To start with its positive dimension, working in a 'men's job' allows women to develop a new subjectivity as capable, qualified workers who 'can do it'. This allows them independence in a material sense, as wage earners. Though as we have seen, especially in the case of South Africa, this independence works also in the opposite direction, placing a heavy burden on women (and young men) to care for extended families. Perhaps more importantly even, this new subjectivity allows women to become less dependent on male acknowledgement, because, as one woman in Mexico put it so aptly: 'I know that I can do any task I am given'.

It was precisely their self-confidence as industrial workers that Volvo was able to exploit to set the women in competition against their male colleagues. When a woman was proud that she could do a job on her own that was previously done by two men, this meant a man was losing his job or was moved to a less interesting position. The transnational corporation's policy of gender equality worked to create a divide between male and female workers.

This strategy functioned not only because women workers could develop their capabilities and were proud of their achievements but because male workers did not include women in their class organisation, they did not help them to balance their identification with the content of their work (which was a central feature for the male workers as well) with a resistance against capitalist exploitation. Instead they fell into the trap the transnational corporation prepared for them and regarded women as competitors. By marginalising women and questioning their capabilities they drove women to see managers who gave them challenging work tasks and believed in them as their allies.

Three plants, three gender regimes

In all three plants women were simultaneously positioned as homemakers and as workers, while their integration into the plant was regulated by three different gender regimes. While gender was a central feature, women's lives were also shaped by other social relations and identities. Race and age were central frames in South Africa, as black women struggled to be carers by earning a wage and being responsible for household work. In Mexico changing gender relations and rising unemployment created the conditions for women (many of them married) to enter the labour market, which they lived as a broadening of their experiences as well as an additional burden. Our interviewees' sense of duty but also their sense of deprivation speaking through their narratives exemplify the contradictions between what cultural norms prescribe: share and take responsibility for others; and what neoliberal consumer society demands: individuality, self-development, the nuclear family.

In Sweden women were included into the factory as family members but at the same time relegated to certain areas of work that were regarded as less 'heavy', more in line with what was seen as female capabilities and limitations. However, working in the factory serves as a flight from care work inside and outside the household, which nevertheless remains an important source of women's identity, as something they can only leave when they have done their share of the care duty. Women often entered the industrial workforce because the care sector did not need them anymore or did not provide sufficient income. As opposed to their colleagues in the Global South, however, Volvo workers in Sweden still have the privilege to be paid a living wage, even if their working conditions have deteriorated.

Beyond the work–life balance and doing gender: the neoliberal appropriation of a producer's pride and the satisfaction of caring for others

The way in which capitalist forms of production have been successful in colonising women's (and men's) desire to do something useful and to take care of others is perhaps the most tragic dimension of capitalism's and especially neoliberalism's success story. Not only has capital been successful in appropriating these human needs through a carrot-and-stick strategy of providing women workers with the possibility to develop capabilities, while threatening them with unemployment if they do not subordinate themselves to the company's wishes, it has also been able to separate producer's pride and the carer's satisfaction from each other, thereby transforming their constructive power into destructive practices: the desire to do a job well for its own sake, cut off from the ability to care for others and to work in solidarity becomes an individualistic desire for success at the expense of others, thus turning it also into a self-destructive practice. Similarly, the desire to care for others, cut off from the possibility of creating useful means for life, turns into a self-sacrificing practice that makes others dependent on that care.

Gender regimes need to be understood not only in their historical and spatial context but also in the context of the everyday practices of production within which and through which they are constructed. It is not just a question of 'doing gender, race, or class' (Fenstermaker and West, 2002). It is through these categories that people are forced to and also subordinate themselves to pursue fractured lives, half-lives. In allowing them to develop only parts of their possibilities, they deny them in reality the development of any of them. Researchers propagating the 'end of work' (Rifkin, 1995) or arguing that one has to give up the idea that work is liberating (Barchiesi, 2012) do not take into account that even under the exploitative and alienated conditions of capitalist forms of production workers can experience the ability to do a job well not only as liberating but as a broadening of their human capabilities.

Scholars have explored how globalisation processes are gendered, identified the impact of neoliberal forms of primitive accumulation in communities and households, and in the creation of a cheap and 'flexible' global female workforce (Nagar et al., 2002; Salzinger, 2003). However, they have failed to consider how these transformations create spaces for emerging forms of female agency and self-confidence leading to contradictory subjectivities at the crossroads of the category of women (identified with the production of life) and the category of workers (identified with the production of the means of life).

Women in paid employment, who enjoy being productive, even under the exploitative governance of a capitalist company, are torn between the ability and enjoyment to develop a new self-confidence and the need, under the given merciless neoliberal regimes, to take responsibility for their families, which requires 'sacrifice'. The endlessly discussed work–life balance, also known under the concept of women's double or triple burden (Nilsen et al., 2017; Lewis, 2009) are but abstract and even euphemistic concepts covering up the deep split that goes right through the hearts and minds of women workers. As their stories of enjoyment and suffering show, two half-lives do not add up to a whole life that satisfies human needs.

A similar problem applies when women are seen as the drivers of the commons, and of an alternative, caring economy due to their role as care givers at home and in the care sector. As Federici rightly writes (Federici, 2010), the privatisation and atomisation of the reproduction of life within the capitalist mode of production has left cooperation to the sector of the production of the means of life. It is precisely this separation that makes it debatable why women should be the one force able to regain the commons. Since each sector lacks what the other has and entails what the other does not, caring for others becomes also a burden, where it is practised in isolation and without resources or under exploitative working conditions. It can therefore be as equally wrought with aggression, competition, and (self-)exploitation as work in the production sector. In turn, working in production can create the satisfaction of producing something useful as well as relations of solidarity and support. In other words, the sector of social reproduction and the sector of production cannot be separated into dichotomic areas, where one is 'good' and the other is 'bad'. They need to be seen as communicating systems each influencing the practices of the other, since they both exist within a broader context of capitalist relations of production and reproduction. It is therefore decisive to overcome the compartmentalisation of social reproduction and production. Both sectors are connected by being shaped through the varieties of the capitalist mode of production existing across the globe. Both sectors are productive and reproductive as well. Caring is a production, it creates new life and re-produces existing life. Equally, producing the means of life relies on the reproduction of resources and machines. It is clearer then, to speak of the production of life and the production of the means of life as opposed to situating production on one and reproduction on the other side (Haug, 2011).

What do our analyses tell us about the 'normality of capitalism'? The different faces of Volvo in Sweden, Mexico, and South Africa have shown us that a normality, something like capitalism 'with a human face', paying liveable wages, allowing decent working hours and security for children, only exists as long as workers have enough power (Silver, 2003) to force companies into such a 'normality'. In the countries of the South we investigated we were told that Volvo, and Swedish companies in general, were the worst employers. One and the same company was forced to act as a relatively fair employer in the Global North and was able to act as an over-exploitive employer in the Global South, thus reviving the colonial pattern of paternalism towards citizens and exploitation of its subordinated others.

The only way this could be overcome would be by workers of the Global South and the Global North working together to achieve a 'level playing field' globally. However, and this is the catch: such a North–South as well as a South–South cooperation between workers and their trade union representatives would need to overcome the marginalisation of industrial women workers at the workplace and within the unions themselves.

Acknowledgements

We are grateful to our co-editor Khayaat Fakier for her supportive and succinct comments to a previous version of this text.

Notes

1 This article is a revised extraction of some of the results published in our book: *Transnational Corporations from the Standpoint of Workers* (Räthzel et al., 2014).

2 The plants in India are not discussed in this article since the only way gender relations worked in those factories was through the exclusion of women from the sites of production.

3 Permanent did not mean that they couldn't be fired but it meant their contracts were not limited to a certain time from the outset.

4 For different descriptions of the plant and its workers see Ohlsson (2008) and Wallace (2004).

References

Arciniega, R.S., 2012. 'Participación de Mujeres en el Mercado Laboral del Estado de México'. *Journal of Latin American Geography* 11: 121–141. https://doi.org/10.1353/lag.2012.0022.

Askegård, J. (Ed.), 2002. *Kvinnor tar plats: arbetsmarknad och industriarbete på 1900-talet*. Arbetarrörelsens arkiv och bibliotek, Stockholm.

Barchiesi, F., 2012. 'Liberation of, through, or from Work? Postcolonial Africa and the Problem with "Job Creation" in the Global Crisis'. *Interface: A Journal for and about Social Movements* 4: 230–253.

Benería, L., 1992. 'Accounting for Women's Work: The Progress of Two Decades'. *World Development* 20: 1547–1560. https://doi.org/10.1016/0305-750X(92)90013-L.

Benería, L., Berik, G., Floro, M., 2016. *Gender, Development, and Globalization: Economics as if All People Mattered*. Routledge, New York; London.

Benería, L., Roldán, M., 1987. *The Crossroads of Class and Gender: Industrial Homework, Subcontracting, and Household Dynamics in Mexico City*. Women in Culture and Society. University of Chicago Press, Chicago, IL.

Berger, I., 1992. *Threads of Solidarity: Women in South African Industry, 1900–1980*. Indiana University Press; James Currey, Bloomington, IN; London.

Berggren, C., 1994. *Volvo Experience: Alternatives to Lean Production in the Swedish Auto Industry*. Repr. (with a new introduction) edition. Macmillan, Basingstoke.

Bezuidenhout, A., Fakier, K., 2006. 'Maria's Burden: Contract Cleaning and the Crisis of Social Reproduction in Post-apartheid South Africa'. *Antipode* 38: 462–485. https://doi.org/10.1111/j.0066-4812.2006.00590.x.

Burawoy, M., 1998. 'The Extended Case Method'. *Sociological Theory* 16: 4–33. https://doi.org/10.1111/0735-2751.00040.

Connell, R., 1990. 'The State, Gender, and Sexual Politics: Theory and Appraisal'. *Theory and Society* 19: 507–544.

Cortés, F., 2000. *La evolución de la Desigualdad del Ingreso Familiar durante la decada de los Ochenta*. Cent. Estud. Sociol, Mexico.

Darkwah, A., 2007. 'Making Hay While the Sun Shines: Ghanaian Female Traders and Their Insertion in the Global Economy' in Gunewardena, N., Kingsolver, A.E. (Eds.), *The Gender of Globalization: Women Navigating Cultural and Economic Marginalities*. School for Advanced Research Advanced Seminar Series. School for Advanced Research Press, Santa Fe, NM, 61–84.

de la Rocha, M.G., 2015. 'From the Resources of Poverty to the Poverty of Resources: The Erosion of a Survival Model' in Chant, S., Beetham, G. (Eds.), *Gender, Poverty, and Development*. Critical Concepts in Development Studies. Routledge, London, 72–100.

Enloe, C.H., 2004. *The Curious Feminist: Searching for Women in a New Age of Empire*. University of California Press, Berkeley, CA.

Eraydin, A., Erendil, A., 1999. 'The Role of Female Labour in Industrial Restructuring: New Production Processes and Labour Market Relations in the Istanbul Clothing Industry'. *Gender Place and Culture* 6, 259–272. https://doi.org/10.1080/09663699925024.

Federici, S.B., 2010. 'Feminism and the Politics of the Commons' in Hughes, C. (Ed.), *Uses of a Whirlwind: Movement, Movements, and Contemporary Radical Currents in the United States*. AK Press, Edinburgh, 283–294.

Federici, S.B., 2014. *Caliban and the Witch*, 2nd, revised edition. Autonomedia, New York.

Fenstermaker, S., West, C. (Eds.), 2002. *Doing Gender, Doing Difference: Inequality, Power, and Institutional Change*. Routledge, New York.

Ferguson, S., 2016. 'Intersectionality and Social-Reproduction Feminisms: Toward an Integrative Ontology'. *Historical Materialism* 24: 38–60. https://doi.org/10.1163/1569206X-12341471.

Gibson, D., Rosenkrantz Lindegaard, M., 2003. 'South African Boys with Plans for the Future: Why a Focus on Dominant Discourses Tells Us Only Part of the

Story' in Schefer, T., Ratele, K., Strebel, N., Shabala, N., Nuikema, R. (Eds.), *From Boys to Men: Social Constructions of Masculinity in Contemporary Society*. University of Cape Town, Cape Town.

Gibson-Graham, J.K., 2006. *The End of Capitalism (as We Knew It): A Feminist Critique of Political Economy*. University of Minnesota Press, Minneapolis, MN.

Glenn, E.N., 1992. 'From Servitude to Service Work: Historical Continuities in the Racial Division of Paid Reproductive Labor'. *Signs: Journal of Women in Culture and Society* 18: 1–43. https://doi.org/10.1086/494777.

Grabham, E., Cooper, D., Krishnadas, J., Herman, D. (Eds.), 2009. *Intersectionality and Beyond: Law, Power and the Politics of Location*. Routledge-Cavendish, Abingdon.

Gramsci, A., 1971. *Prison Notebooks*. International Publishers, New York.

Gutierrez Arriola, A., 2006. *La empresa transnacional en la reestructuración del capital, la producción y el trabajo*. Casa Juan Pablos, Mexico.

Gutmann, M., 2006. *The Meanings of Macho: Being a Man in Mexico City*. Tenth anniversary edition. University of California Press, Berkeley, CA.

Haug, F., 2011. 'Towards a Theory of Gender Relations'. *Socialism and Democracy* 16: 33–46.

Hennessy, R., 2000. *Profit and Pleasure: Sexual Identities in Late Capitalism*. Routledge, New York.

Husson, M., Hirata, H., Roldán, M., 1995. 'Reestructuraciones productivas y cambios en la división sexual del trabajo y del empleo: Argentina, Brasil y México'. *Sociología del Trabajo* 24: 75–98.

Lagarde, M., 2011. *Los cautiverios de las mujeres: madresposas, monjas, putas, presas y locas*, Colección La cosecha de nuestras madres. Horas y Horas, Madrid.

Lewis, J., 2009. *Work–Family Balance, Gender and Policy*. Edward Elgar, Northampton, MA.

Lundqvist, Å., 2011. *Family Policy Paradoxes: Gender Equality and Labour Market Regulation in Sweden, 1930–2010*. Bristol University Press, Bristol.

Martinsson, L., Griffin, G., Giritli Nygren, K. (Eds.), 2016. *Challenging the Myth of Gender Equality in Sweden*. Policy Press, Bristol.

Marx, K., 1998. *Capital: A Critique of Political Economy*, 1887 ed. ElecBook, London.

Massey, D., 1994. *Space, Place and Gender*. Polity Press, Cambridge.

Massey, D.B., 2005. *For Space*. Sage, London; Thousand Oaks, CA.

McNay, L., 2000. *Gender and Agency: Reconfiguring the Subject in Feminist and Social Theory*. Polity Press; Blackwell Publishers, Cambridge; Malden, MA.

McRobbie, A., 2009. *The Aftermath of Feminism: Gender, Culture and Social Change*. Sage, Los Angeles, CA; London.

Mohanty, C.T., 1997. 'Women Workers and Capitalist Scripts: Ideologies of Domination, Common Interests and the Politics of Solidarity' in Alexander, M.J., Mohanty, C.T. (Eds.), *Feminist Genealogies, Colonial Legacies, Democratic Futures*. Routledge, New York, 3–29.

Mohanty, C.T., 2003. *Feminism without Borders: Decolonizing Theory, Practicing Solidarity*. Duke University Press, Durham, NC; London.

Mosoetsa, S., 2005. *Micro-level Responses to Macro-economic Changes: Urban Livelihoods and Intra-household Dynamics in South Africa*. PhD thesis, Faculty of Humanities, University of Witwatersrand, Johannesburg.

Mulinari, D., Räthzel, N., 2009. 'The Promise of the "Nordic" and Its Reality in the South: The Experiences of Mexican Workers as Members of the "Volvo Family"' in *Complying with Colonialism*. Ashgate, Farnham; Burlington, VT, 67–84.

Mulinari, D., Rathzel, N., Tollefsen, A., 2011. 'Everyday Working Lives in a Transnational Corporation in Mexico: The Contradictory Cooptation of Trade Unionists'. *Economic and Industrial Democracy* 32: 379–399. https://doi.org/10.1177/0143831X10377811.

Nagar, R., Lawson, V., McDowell, L., Hanson, S., 2002. 'Locating Globalization: Feminist (Re)readings of the Subjects and Spaces of Globalization'. *Economic Geography* 78: 257–284.

Nilsen, W., Skipstein, A., Østby, K.A., Mykletun, A., 2017. 'Examination of the Double Burden Hypothesis: A Systematic Review of Work–Family Conflict and Sickness Absence'. *European Journal of Public Health* 27: 465–471. https://doi.org/10.1093/eurpub/ckx054.

Nnaemeka, O., 1998. 'This Women's Studies Business: Beyond Politics and History (Thoughts on the First WAAD Conference)' in Nnaemeka, O. (Ed.), *Sisterhood, Feminisms and Power*. Africa World Press, Trenton, NJ, 351–386.

Ohlsson, B., 2008. *Vi som stannade paa Volvo: en etnologisk studie om äldre bilindustriarbetares arbetsliv och framtidsplaner*. Arkipelag, [Gothenburg].

Ong, A., 2006. *Neoliberalism as Exception: Mutations in Citizenship and Sovereignty*. Duke University Press, Durham, NC.

Räthzel, N., Mulinari, D., Tollefsen Altamirano, 2014. *Transnational Corporations from the Standpoint of Workers*. Palgrave Macmillan, Basingstoke.

Räthzel, N., Mulinari, D., Tollefsen, A., Molina, I., Mählck, P., 2008. 'Unvollendete Transformationen: Widerstreitende Zugehörigkeiten, aufbrechende Geschlechterverhältnisse, Stadt-Land-Beziehungen. Arbeitsalltag in einem europäischen transnationalen Unternehmen in Mexiko'. *Forum Kritische Psychologie* 52: 29–51.

Rifkin, J., 1995. *The End of Work: The Decline of the Global Labor Force and the Dawn of the Post-Market Era*. G.P. Putnam's Sons, New York.

Rocha, M.G., Latapí, A.E., 2009. 'Choices or Constraints? Informality, Labour Market and Poverty in Mexico'. *IDS Bulletin* 39: 37–47. https://doi.org/10.1111/j.1759-5436.2008.tb00443.x.

Salzinger, L., 2003. *Genders in Production: Making Workers in Mexico's Global Factories*. University of California Press, Berkeley, CA.

Scott, J.W., 2008. 'Reflections on Women and Gender in Twentieth-Century Mexico Introduction'. *Gender and History* 20: 149–151. https://doi.org/10.1111/j.1468-0424.2007.00511.x.

Selberg, R., 2012. *Femininity at Work: Gender, Labour, and Changing Relations of Power in a Swedish Hospital*. Arkiv förlag, Lund.

Silver, B., 2003. *Workers' Movements and Globalization since 1870: Forces of Labour*. Cambridge University Press, Cambridge.

Smith, D., 2002. 'Institutional Ethnography' in May, T. (Ed.), *Qualitative Research in Action: An International Guide to Issues in Practice*. Sage, London, 150–161.

Solis de Alba, A.A., 1990. 'Las trabajadoras y el movimiento obrero en México, 1982–1988'. *Revista Iztapalapa* 19: 125–142.

Standing, G., 1989. 'Global Feminization through Flexible Labor'. *World Development* 17: 1077–1095. https://doi.org/10.1016/0305-750X(89)90170-8.

Tshoaedi, M., 2012. 'Women in the Forefront of Workplace Struggles in South Africa: From Invisibility to Mobilization'. *Labour Capital and Society* 45: 58–83.

Wallace, T., 2004. 'Innovation and Hybridization: Managing the Introduction of Lean Production into Volvo do Brazil'. *International Journal of Operations and Production Management* 24: 801–819. https://doi.org/10.1108/01443570410548239.

PART III

RELIGIONS AND POLITICS

13 | RELIGIOUS RESISTANCE

A flower on the chain or a tunnel towards liberation?

Gabriele Dietrich

In the context of the Marxist-Feminist debate on religion, it is relevant to go back to the Marxist critique of religion and debates of women's movements in South Asia on religion, fundamentalism, and communalism (Dietrich, 1986). This paper tries to develop the question whether women's agency in 'genuine religious reform' from a feminist perspective can contribute to open up democratic spaces and safeguard secularism, political participation, and curtailing of violence. This itself could yield important contributions to the dismantling of patriarchy and caste and thus strengthen the class struggle for transformation of a capitalist system, which races towards its own destruction by devastating the material base of society through climate change and a nuclear arms race. In this situation, life on Earth itself is now in jeopardy.

Limitation and potential of the Marxist critique of religion

It is definitely a limitation that the Marxist critique of religion is mainly developed in two writings: these are 'On the Jewish Question' and 'Contribution to the Critique of Hegel's Philosophy of Law' (Marx, 1975a, 1975b). Unfortunately, the critique of religion has no role at all in the analysis of patriarchy (Marx and Engels, 2011). This has to do with the fact that 'The origin of the family, private property and the State' is mostly concerned with property relations and different modes of production, while the control over the mind in different modes of production does not come into the picture in this context.

Marx's response to Bruno Bauer's *The Jewish Question* (1843) is of relevance in today's context, because Bauer makes a strong plea for a secular state. However, he thinks that this should be achieved by the abolition of religion. This obviously is a theoretical shortcut to a complicated and painful problem.

Marx points out: 'It is possible therefore, for the *State* to have emancipated itself from religion even if the *overwhelming majority* is still religious. And the overwhelming majority does not cease to be religious through being religious in *private*' (Marx, 1975a: 152). Thus, the state becomes an intermediary for political emancipation. Marx compares this to the abolition of private property as a criterion for political participation in many states of North America. This does not mean that private property ceases to exist or that it has become irrelevant.

Religion, thus confined to the private sphere,

> has become the spirit of *Civil Society*, of the sphere of egoism of *bellum omnium contra omnes*. It is no longer the essence of *community, but the essence of difference* it has become the expression of man's *separation* from the *community*, from himself and from other men – as it was *originally*. It is only the abstract avowal of specific perversity, *private whimsy*, and arbitrariness ... This emancipation therefore neither abolished the real religiousness of man, nor strived to do so. (Marx, 1975a: 155)

The right to practise religion and adhere to religious faith is recognised as a human right and a right of the citizen. Religion becomes a marker of identity in civil society. This is similar to the right to private property becoming a marker for social difference. Implicitly, this is a strong critique of the identity politics which took over during the 1990s under post-modernism. The 'difference' tends to have power implications which need to be understood.

When comparing feudal society with capitalism, Marx says: 'Hence man was not freed from religion, he received religious freedom. He was not free from property, he received freedom to own property. He was not freed from the egoism of business, he received freedom to engage in business' (Marx, 1975a: 67). This kind of transition to modernity can today be seen in the 'development' of global capitalism in India, while at the same time, we observe tendencies to create a religious state in the shape of a Hindu Nation, while tension is going on with the 'Islamic Nation' of Pakistan and Hindu nationalist forces of the Rashtriya Swayamsewa Sangh (RSS) are fomenting conflict as Gau Rakshaks (protectors of Mother Cow) are feeding into the Islamophobia against ISIS and the tendencies to build up an Islamic state in West Asia, which may be totally unconnected to the local situation.

It is significant that Marxists internationally and in India have not been fully clear regarding the rising fascism in India under a regime which aims at establishing a 'Hindu Nation'. Perry Andersen in his book *The Indian Ideology* completely underestimates the destructive potential of Hindutva (Anderson, 2013; Dietrich, 2014).

The protest potential within religion

It is of relevance that in his 'Contribution to the Critique of Hegel's Philosophy of Law', Marx acknowledges the protest potential within religion, though he qualifies it also as illusory.

Right at the start of the essay Marx states: 'For Germany the *criticism of religion* is in the main complete and criticism of religion is the premise of all criticism' (Marx, 1975b: 174). He states:

Man makes religion, religion does not make man. Religion is an *inverted world consciousness*, because state and society produce religion, an inverted world consciousness because they (state and society) are an inverted world. Religion is the general theory of the world, its encyclopaedic compendium, its logic in a popular form, its spiritualistic *point d'honneur*, its enthusiasm, its moral sanction, its solemn complement, its universal source of consolation and justification. It is the *fantastic realization* of the human essence because the *human essence* has no true reality. The struggle against religion is therefore indirectly a fight against *the world* of which religion is the spiritual *aroma*.

Religious distress is at the same time the *expression* of real distress and also the *protest* against real distress. Religion is the sigh of the oppressed creature, the heart of a heartless world, just as it is the spirit of spiritless condition. It is the *opium* of the people. (Marx, 1975b: 175)

Abolishing the illusory happiness of the people is to demand the *real* happiness. Criticism tears the imaginary flower from the chain not so that people will wear the unadorned chain but that they will shake off the chain and pluck the living flower. Of course, in today's world we are compelled to ask: Where have all the flowers gone? Marx states:

The *task of history*, therefore once the *world beyond the truth* has disappeared, is to establish that *truth of this world* ... Thus, the criticism of heaven turns into the criticism of the earth, the *criticism of religion into the criticism of law* and the criticism of theology into the criticism of politics. (1975b: 176)

To summarise: the important points identified in the Marxist critique of religion are the *need for a secular state* and the *protest potential within religion*. In India, secularism is a very crucial concept within the Indian Constitution, in contrast to Pakistan, which is officially a Muslim state. The present attempts by the Bharatiya Janata Party (BJP), the RSS, and the central government to transform India into a 'Hindu Nation' has very deep impact on ideological and religious pluralism and is highly destructive of the democratic fabric. Saffron is the preferred colour of Hindutva. The historical reference of this process is clearly Hitler's National Socialism (Basu et al., 1993).

In this kind of a pluralistic situation, the right to freedom of religion, including the right of freedom *from* religion needs to be defended (i.e. the right to be an agnostic or an atheist must be safeguarded). At the same time, the right to religious conversion must also be upheld. (Several states in India, which are ruled by the religious right, have stringent anti-conversion laws in place.) At the same time so-called re-conversion into the Hindu fold is depicted as 'home coming' (*Ghar Vapasi*). This happens through a violently imposed ritual.

Civil Society as a space of contestation for democratic rights

Before going into examples of intervention in religious cultural spaces, it is necessary to briefly discuss some aspects of civil society in India. It is well known that society in India is strongly permeated by caste. The caste system has played a major role in creating political participation (castes often become 'vote banks'), and the system has been robust in adjusting to the requirements of modernity (Rudolph and Rudolph, 1987).

It has been pointed out by Dr Ambedkar, that caste is not so much a religious phenomenon, but a social agreement which is based on social arrangements of marriage within a particular marriage cycle. It is based on intimidation as well as on coercion (Ambedkar, 1979). The mechanisms for enforcing caste are handed down by the family system and by rules of purity and pollution. There is also a local jurisdiction of caste *panchayats*.[1] Caste is defined territorially and by kinship. Marriage circles operate also by rules of diet and occupation. Caste has also been described as an energy-capturing system, i.e. a system which gives access to material as well as cultural goods. The Indian Constitution safeguards equality and non-discrimination on the ground of gender, caste, class, race, occupation, language. Corrective access for marginalised sectors has been safeguarded in the form of reservations.[2]

The debates on civil society have been very important in India. After the Emergency from 1975 to 1977 under Indira Gandhi, Rajni Kothari came out with his book *The State Against Democracy* (1987), and Neera Chandoke, a feminist political scientist, has restated the need for a vibrant civil society in her book *State and Civil Society* (Chandoke, 1995). She draws on Hegelian, Marxian, and Gramscian traditions. The following two pages are a summary of her argument. Hegel ascribed a high value to civil society as a sphere where the individual could legitimately pursue his self-interest, a potential of subjective freedom which was partly anticipated in Roman Law, Christianity, and the Enlightenment. He saw civil society as progressive, enlightening, and emancipatory. It is supposed to allow realisation of individual potential. This is different from the ascriptive values of traditional societies. Hegel located civil society between the family and the state.

Hegel saw civil society as the seat of ethical life, but this ethical life is also formed by the family and the state. Hegel pondered how the modern rootless individual could be provided guidance by an ethical community. The problem is to avoid egoism and fragmentation. Hegel felt that the interaction of individuals could create community in taking up labour as a social act. It leads to social interdependence. Hegel thought that the conflict between the individual and interactive community can be regulated by the state. So, the question arises whether civil society provides organisation or suppression of individual needs and aspirations.

Marx, in contrast to Hegel, focused on the *Incivility of Civil Society*. He saw civil society as the place where selfish interests encounter each other and appropriation of surplus labour takes place. This historical stage must be transcended. He did not see the state as holding civil society together, but on the contrary, he saw the state as being held together by civil society. He also sees the state to be oppressive, especially through the bureaucracy. He writes in 'The Jewish Question' that only where man has recognised and organised his *'forces propres*' (own powers) as social forces and consequently no longer separates social power from himself in the shape of political power, only then will human emancipation be completed.

Marx conceptualises man as producer, who enjoys his creativity and satisfies human needs by his production. Such autonomous, reflexive work forces the individual to recognise his species being. But in bourgeois society, the worker is reduced to labour power. But specialisation and mechanisation lead to repetitive routine work. This hems in the personality. For Hegel the unincorporated poor constitute a problem, for Marx it is rather the existence of a social order which excludes the poor from membership which is the problem. If the existence of the poor is *customarily accepted* in civil society, then this is a devastating criticism of its standards of universality, rationality, and humanity.

Marx thinks that only the proletariat which is outside civil society can assess the conditions for the revolution and can have the *conscience* required for revolutionary activity. The proletariat is 'the other' of the members of civil society. When Marx moves to Paris, he overcomes this romanticised notion and analyses the situation from the point of view of political economy. As the production process is based on appropriation of labour, the working class can abolish itself as a class and transform the production process. In this view, the proletariat is not *outside* civil society. The class is indispensable for transformation through political action.

While Hegel dismissed the working class as a social actor, Marx conceptualised the working class as the universal actor capable of displacing the existing system of oppression and replacing it with a human system. Marx had lived through a period of intense working-class struggles in England and France.

In contrast to this, Gramsci (1891–1937) wrote in a situation where capitalism had succeeded to streamline production through Fordism and the everyday lives of the workers could be controlled. The First World War had constructed power systems in Europe. In Italy, fascism had demolished the working class and was threatening to annihilate all gains and forms of political struggle. Gramsci had to grapple with the lessons learnt from the Russian Revolution and the rise of fascism in Italy which defeated the working class. Economic crisis had not led to political crisis. Gramsci had to search for ideological interventions in the cultural and ideological fields. The existing positivist socialist tradition had to be rethought.

Gramsci distinguishes between the coercive forces of the state, the prison system, the judicial system, the armed forces, and the police. 'Civil Society is the location where the state operates to enforce invisible intangible and subtle forms of power, through educational, cultural and religious systems and other institutions' (Chandoke, 1995: 149). Gramsci focuses on the systems which produce consent, controlling mind and psyche. Civil society is the site where the fundamental classes of society, namely the capitalists and proletarians, express their experiences in these practices.

In Gramsci's view the Russian Revolution was possible because there was no civil society to produce consent. The totalitarian power of the Tsarist state could be dislodged by the proletariat. The sophisticated bourgeois state can be opaque, because civil society can act as a protective filter for the state.

The protest potential lived out; conversion as a tunnel for liberation

This section briefly goes into two spectacular conversions: Pandita Ramabai and Dr Ambedkar. While Dr Ambedkar's conversion continues to inspire Dalit mass conversions, Pandita Ramabai's remained a solitary feminist protest. Feminists have taken up the conversion of Dr Ambedkar in order to relate themselves more deeply to Dalit movements and to dismantle the oppressive system of the laws of Manu, laid down in the ancient lawbook of the *Manu Smriti* (Rege, 2013). The fact that Pandita Ramabai's heroic struggle against Brahminical patriarchy in Maharastra has been extensively documented by Uma Chakravarti (1998) has made her enormous contribution highly visible. It has, however, not contributed to encourage feminist faith in 'genuine religious reform', of which there is indeed not very broad evidence. Feminists are today involved in opening up secular spaces in their own faith communities of origin and to build links across widening religious rifts.

Pandita Ramabai

Pandita Ramabai (23 April 1858–5 April 1922) was born into a Brahmana Chitpavan family (Chakravarti, 1998). Her father Anand Shastri Dongre was a non-conformist personality. He was born and trained as a Sanskrit scholar in the last days of the Peshwa. When the British took over Poona and the Peshwai territories, Anand Shastri returned to his home in Malherambi (Mangalore). He tried to teach Sanskrit to his first wife, but met with resistance. He had been widowed and while travelling, he met a Brahman in search of grooms for his two daughters. Anand Shastri, a widower of 44, was married to the older girl, nine-year-old Lakshmi Bai. Once again, he tried to teach Sanskrit to his wife. She picked it up well, but Anand Shastri was ostracised for his heresy. Ramabai remembered her father as an ardent reformer of women's position. The young second wife acquired a deep knowledge of Sanskrit and Puranic teaching and later passed this knowledge on to her daughter Ramabai.

Anand Shastri Dongre invented a life style of collective pilgrimage for his family. (The 'normal way' was pilgrimage first and then house holders' life in a ritually controlled setting. But Anand Shastri's family lived in collective household pilgrimage, free from the system of oppressive practices.) She remained unmarried far beyond the acceptable age for Brahman girls. Her father exhorted her to live an honourable life and serve god all her life. Not long after, Ramabai's mother Lakshmibai died of starvation before the food for which Ramabai had begged could reach her. Srinivas and Ramabai went on a pilgrimage of 4,000 miles. They went up to Kashmir and from there to Calcutta in 1878.

Calcutta was a haven for the intellectual elite, including pundits and reformers. They had been working for 50 years by this time, talking of figures like Gargi and Maitreyi, and Ramabai was greeted as a new version of these. She was encouraged by Keshab Chandra Sen to study the Vedas and gave lectures on women as well. By reading the *Dharmashastras*, Ramabai was led to question the fundamental propositions of Brahmanic Hinduism. She discovered contradictory statements on almost everything. She also found that the *Dharmashastras*, *Puranas*, modern poets, and popular preachers all agreed that low-caste people and women could not achieve *moksha* (salvation) on their own.

Ramabai, overwhelmed by the misogynism of the *shastras*, now discovered the stranglehold of Brahmanical patriarchy. Now in the grip of Brahmanical society, she lost all meaning of religious faith. In the midst of all this, she also lost her brother Srinivas to a sudden illness. She was now all alone, without economic support and homeless. She therefore decided to marry a close friend of her brother. Her husband, Bipin Behari Medhavi, was a Shudra and they decided for inter-caste marriage, which was strictly forbidden by the *shastras*. There were enough 'modernist' Brahmana suitors from Maharastra available but Ramabai did not bother to look at such 'fitting' proposals. She married under the Civil Marriages Act as neither of them believed in Hinduism any longer. Unfortunately, her husband died after two years and she was left with a baby girl to support. There was a lot of speculation why Ramabai had not been married during puberty. Rumours came up that she had been dedicated to Krishna as a child. Some thought she was a child widow. Her exceptional childhood was in some ways acceptable, but her inter-caste marriage had been a sacrilege. Her learning could not compensate for this any longer. Now widowhood had made her a 'dangerous' figure. She refused to withdraw into domesticity. She turned the tables on orthodox society and decided to serve the most oppressed section: upper-caste widows. Ramabai decided to return to western India. She went ahead with founding an institution to support upper-caste widows. Her quest was of a very different nature than that of the male reformers. Ramabai's position was experienced as highly threatening and she was often shouted down by aggressive men.

She pleaded before the Hunter Education Commission for women's education to create women teachers and doctors. As a widow, she was much more vulnerable than any of these men. She was also treated with scorn by Brahmin women. The Arya Mahila Sabha took utmost offence at her critique of Brahmanical patriarchy. Thus, Ramabai had no 'community'. She was extremely vulnerable. She had a need for religious fulfilment and also pursued a social agenda. Ramabai, being a public personality, was approached by missionaries. She had read St. Luke's Gospel in Bengali while in Calcutta. In Poona, a missionary, Miss Hurford, taught her English and introduced her to the Bible in Marathi.

Ramabai started to take care of child widows and discovered that she had to expand her own skills to meet the challenge. She decided to go to England and pursue medical education. She found a contact to the Church of England Mission in Pune and left for England in 1883. To raise money, she wrote a book on the 'morals' of women: *Stri Dharma Niti*. This book is along the lines of the Brahmana reformers and contrasts greatly with her book *The High Caste Hindu Woman*, which is a much more devastating indictment of Brahmanical patriarchy. She was one of the earliest women to write and lecture for a livelihood in the nineteenth century.

Even in December 1882, Ramabai still maintained she had no intention to convert to Christianity. She was attracted by the life of Jesus and the inter-religious worship expressed in the story of the Samaritan woman in John 4. Even after conversion, she never held on to a denomination or adhered to any dogmas. She made it clear that she did not believe in the Trinity.

When she founded her institution for upper-caste widows, she did not want the women to become Christians, as it would forfeit the purpose of integrating them in society. She wrote her book *The High Caste Hindu Woman* as a scathing attack on upper-caste misogynism but also stayed in dialogue with the reformers and her original background. She travelled widely in the US and raised funds for her institution. She taught the women crafts and acquired land for agriculture to be self-sufficient. She took her daughter Manoramabai on her travels. She also learnt Greek and Hebrew to translate the bible into Marathi. She was approached by fundamentalist missionaries and some inmates of her institution took to speaking in tongues. She herself never did this, but she also did not discourage it, because the women who were widows were searching for ways to express themselves. Her institution has been assimilated by evangelical Christians. Pandita Ramabai's revolutionary contribution to women's liberation has been acknowledged by Indian feminists. Uma Chakravarti's monograph on the life and time of Pandita Ramabai acknowledges her great acumen. It is, however, strange that Ramabai has hardly been owned by feminist theologians or by Dalit organisations, though she married a Shudra and challenged the caste system courageously (Adhar, 1979; Hedlund et al., 2011).

Dr Ambedkar's conversion to Buddhism

The other spectacular conversion, which has been of more public impact, was Dr Ambedkar's conversion to Buddhism. He hailed from the Mahar caste of untouchables in Maharastra. Dr Ambedkar started announcing at a massive conference of Depressed Classes at Yeola near Nasik on 1 October 1935: 'I will not die a Hindu'. Partly this was due to the failure of temple entry movement. He made his announcement in front of 10,000 people. He contemplated different options, like Sikhism, Islam, and Christianity, and finally opted for Buddhism, having identified it as the original faith of the Dalits. His main attraction to Buddhism was that he felt it was a faith which incorporated freedom, equality, and fraternity (Zelliot, 2013).

It is not possible to do justice to Dr Ambedkar's life in a brief paper like this. He was one of the most influential personalities in modern Indian history; the Indian Constitution could not have come into being without him. His output as a writer has been phenomenal, as can be gathered from the publication of his collected works over many years. At the same time, his contribution to the abolition of untouchability and to emancipation of the most oppressed sections has been path breaking, though this is still an unfinished task. He was not only a pioneer of education, but also a very inspiring organiser of the working class. He unleashed the famous struggle for access to water in Chowdar Tank in Mahad during the 1920s and led this struggle in 1927, topping it off with the burning of *Manu Smriti*, the law book of Manu, on 25 December of that year. The court case on the matter was decided in favour of Dr Ambedkar only in 1937. Dalit women's organisations even today celebrate 25 December as their women's day (Zelliot, 2013; Rege, 2013).

While the role of Dr Ambedkar in the abolition of untouchability and in shaping the Indian Constitution and realisation of democracy has been tremendous, his importance has not been understood internationally, because the freedom struggle was dominated by Gandhi, and post-independence democracy was represented by Jawaharlal Nehru and the Congress Party. Ambedkar, born in 1891, lived in a period which witnessed the uprising of the community against untouchability and discrimination. The traditional role of Mahars, the largest untouchable caste of Maharastra, was that of village servants like watchmen, sweepers, caretakers. Under British rule new opportunities arose like the building of roads and bridges, railroad lines, work in mills and ammunition factories, and even recruitment into the armies of the British. Ambedkar grew up among educated ex-army men. He also benefitted from the Hindu reform movement against untouchability, which opened up new possibilities. As he was very bright, he gained access to scholarships for his higher studies. He was also inspired by the anti-caste movement led by Jotiba Phule (1827–1890), a Mali (gardener caste), who had risen up, together with his wife Savitri Phule, to claim equal rights to the use of water and education. Ambedkar grew up in an atmosphere of awakening emancipation and was able to give a sense of purpose to the Mahars, while at the same time also building links with the anti-Brahmin movement in Madras and the reform movement of the Ezhavas led by Sri Narayana Guru in Travancore.

The first phase of Ambedkar's involvement among the Mahars was from 1919 to 1935, a period when the Mahars formed a large-scale organisation, started various newspapers in different parts of Maharastra, opened hostels and held Satyagraha for water use and temple entry. Simultaneously, Mahar representatives appeared before all the governmental reform bodies, like the Southborough Committee on Franchise, the Simon Commission, the Round Table Conference, and the Franchise Commission of 1932. By 1935, a new phase was reached, because it became clear that the attempts at 'Sanskritisation' (i.e. seeking acknowledgement within the religious value system) had come to an end. This coincided with Ambedkar's announcement that he was going to leave Hinduism. Although the implementation of the announcement came after over 20 years, the scathing critique of religious denigration made a great impact.

With his kind of methodology, Dr Ambedkar was in sharp conflict with Gandhi, because he had ruled out any form of reconciliation with the caste system. Gandhi, for much of his life, did not object to the caste system as such in the form of *varna* (the fourfold division of Brahmin, Kshatria, Vaishya, and Shudra), because he felt it was based on a 'given' division of labour which safeguarded 'bread labour' and prevented competition. He objected to untouchability and insisted on everybody cleaning the toilets in his ashram. However, only at the end of his life did he support inter-caste marriages. He wanted upper-caste Hindus to repent and redeem untouchability by 'change of heart' and social support through organisations like the Harijan Sarva Sewa Sangh.[3] Dr Ambedkar abhorred the very term 'Harijan' (people of god), which he experienced as patronising and totally misleading. In the early 1930s, there was a rift between Ambedkar and Gandhi regarding the demand for separate electorates for Dalits, which resembled separate electorates for Muslims. It implied that the community voted for its own candidates. The conflict was about the question of whether Hinduism could abolish untouchability from within. Ambedkar held that it was impossible and that the only way for Dalits was to convert to another religion. The question was mostly to which religion to convert. Christianity was ruled out as the religion of the colonisers and as a religion which had practised caste discrimination itself from ancient days in Kerala. Islam became problematic because of the growing communal divide between Hindus and Muslims, which finally led to partition. Sikhism had the advantage of being an indigenous faith, but it was not free from caste and was seen as a sub-section of Hinduism by many. The struggle for the separate electorates was disrupted by Gandhi in 1932 by a fast unto death. This twisted Dr Ambedkar's arm beyond endurance. Ambedkar gave up his demand for separate electorates in the Pune Pact in September 1932, which was actually a supreme act of sacrifice on his part to save the life of his antagonist and thus the life of innumerable Dalits. This no doubt strengthened his resolve that quitting Hinduism for good was the only way out for the Mahars and for Dalits in general. Ambedkar felt that different Dalit communities had to find their own way to take this step, as creating unity among Dalit castes appeared to be a losing battle.

Gandhi campaigned and also fasted to achieve a change of heart among Hindus to abolish untouchability, which led to the foundation of the Harijan Sewa Sangh. This promoted reforms for untouchables and some inclusion of untouchables in provincial cabinets became possible. But equal rights in religious matters and full participation in social and economic life were not achieved.

It took over 20 years from the original announcement of conversion to the implementation, shortly before Ambedkar died. This had to do with the fact that Ambedkar felt in 1936 that he wanted to form a political party to strengthen the political movement of the Mahars. The Mahars had been politically active since 1890. The situation attained a new quality in 1935, when the Scheduled Castes, as they were now called, were to be represented according to their percentage of the population, in seats especially reserved for them. The Independent Labour Party was announced on 15 August 1936 in the *Times of India* only two months after the Mahar conference on conversion had been held. Ambedkar assured the Mahars that hard-won political privileges would not be given up after conversion (Zelliot, 2013: 176). Ambedkar had worked on the question of political representation of the untouchables in all the commissions and committees that considered the reforms since 1917. He was confident in 1937 that a separate political organisation, independent of the Congress Party, would succeed. He made three different political attempts. The Independent Labour Party was focused on workers' rights; it had a clear class perspective. In 1942, the Scheduled Castes Federation was founded, to draw together the different castes in unity, before the British would withdraw. The third attempt was the Republican Party, which was meant to create a Scheduled Castes movement to form an alliance between all the oppressed and underprivileged sections. This political work, aimed at uniting the working class, took up much of his time, while his battle with Congress politics also went on. After independence, his work as law minister took up his time and the monumental work of drafting the Constitution required his energies. He resigned over his inability to reform the Hindu Code Bill, for which he could not get the support of Sardar Patel and Jawaharlal Nehru. It was this defeat which firmed up his resolve to convert to Buddhism only weeks before his death. In his resignation speech he said:

> To leave inequality between class and class, between sex and sex, which is the soul of the Hindu society, and to go on passing legislation relating to economic problems is to make a farce out of our Constitution and to build a palace on a dung heap. (Omvedt, 2004: 134)

The ideological conflict between Ambedkar and Gandhi comes out in very clear relief in Ambedkar's speech, 'Annihilation of Caste', a speech he never delivered, because the Jat-pat-Todak Mandal of Lahore, an anti-caste organisation which had invited him in 1936 to preside over a Congress of theirs, cancelled the event in view of Dr Ambedkar's radical position. Ambedkar immediately published his speech and circulated it widely. It had a vast impact. A carefully annotated critical edition of this text was published in 2014 by S. Anand of Navayana, with an extensive introduction titled 'The Doctor and the Saint' by Arundhati Roy (Anand, 2014). This republication was a very decisive intervention at a point when Hindutva was taking over Indian political life in earnest, though the election in 2014 was won by the BJP with only 31 per cent of the vote.

The republication of Dr Ambedkar's speech 78 years after it was written helped a new generation to catch up with the turmoil of the freedom struggle and to come to terms with the new onslaught of Hindutva. The publication found acclaim with historians and social scientists, but met with criticism from several quarters. The spirited essay by Arundhati Roy, which helped her to live down the adulatory, uncritical veneration of Gandhi which was part of her upbringing, hurt many Gandhian sentiments. Of course, she also did not spare Ambedkar either and points out that Ambedkar's views on Adivasis are not really better than Gandhi's views on the South African indigenous population or on 'Harijans' for that matter. This raised eyebrows among some Dalit organisations, who were sensitive to a critique of their leader.

Arundhati Roy pinpoints the drawbacks of Ambedkar's modernity. Her critique is rooted in her experience of the Adivasi struggle in the Narmada Valley against the Sardar Sarovar Dam (Roy, 1999) and solidarity with the struggles upstream in Madhya Pradesh. Not only that, she has also taken it upon herself to explore the Adivasis' struggles in Chhattisgarh and on the Andhra border (Roy, 2010). This touches upon her anti-capitalist convictions which she summarises in her introductory essay:

> Today, Adivasis are the barricade against the pitiless march of modern capitalism. Their very existence poses the most radical question about modernity and progress – the idea that Ambedkar embraced as one of the ways out of the caste system. Unfortunately, by viewing the Adivasi community through the lens of Western liberalism, Ambedkar's writing which is otherwise so relevant in today's context, suddenly becomes dated. (Roy, 2014: 46)

Interestingly, Roy explicitly acknowledges Pandita Ramabai's conversion as a feminist step and points out that even as a Christian she continued to be unorthodox (Roy, 2014: 75).

The critical contribution of this publication lies in exposing sharply the misleading representation of *varna*, which gives the impression of there being 'four major castes', based on a 'division of labour', which Gandhi conflated into his theory of 'bread labour'. Ambedkar was very clear from the outset that what must be dealt with is *jathi*, the innumerable units of caste into which people are born and which are hierarchical and bound up with purity and pollution. He exposed the fallacy of the colonial theories on caste with great clarity in his early paper on 'Castes in India: Their Mechanism, Genesis and Development'. He pointed out that the caste system as it evolved was a combination of exclusion, coercion, as well as intimidation. Mahatma Gandhi gave the impression that untouchability could be dealt with separately, without abolishing the caste system. Dr Ambedkar was clear that this was not possible.

While conversion has not been taken up in the republication of 'Annihilation of Caste', the issue of using conversion to Buddhism as a way out of untouchability has again and again surfaced in contemporary relevance. While the controversy on caste and untouchability between Gandhi and Ambedkar shows the contradiction in all its irreconcilable sharpness, the search for the Buddhist past took place in the Tamil country as well and led to a significant conversion movement even before Dr Ambedkar's efforts. The Tamil Buddhist Movement led by Pandit Iyothee Thassar is less widely known (Aloysius, 2015) because it was rooted in the Tamil language and therefore did not achieve prominence at the national level to the extent Dr Ambedkar's re-discovery of Buddhism became a catalyst. It is important to acknowledge this history, because there is often an underlying assumption that Dr Ambedkar with his Western education projected the values of the French Revolution onto Buddhism (Ambedkar, 1957). This is re-enforced by Dr Ambedkar's re-interpretation of Buddhism in a fashion which purges it completely of religious content and denies re-incarnation and the idea of a soul (Ambedkar, 1990). Ambedkar connected untouchability with the survival of Buddhism and beef eating in the communities who withstood the Brahmin counter-reformation which promoted vegetarianism to out-do Buddhist non-violence. All these aspects have regained significance in the public debate under rising Hindutva since the BJP came to power at the centre in 2014. In the meantime, critical historians have pointed out that beef eating was extremely widespread in Vedic times (Puniyani, 2017).

However, Gau Rakshaks (cow protectors) are ruling the roost and mob violence against Muslims and Dalits in the name of the holy cow have been rampant. Not only that, pressure has been applied on academic institutions.

The academic world was shaken by the suicide in Hyderabad of a gifted science student at doctoral level, Rohit Vemula. He and his Dalit colleagues had been facing harassment in a hostile social and academic milieu worsened by partisan political interference from right-wing establishment forces. Vemula was driven to suicide, but his suicide exposed the caste politics and ignited widespread protest. Political forces from the right tried to construct a case which denied his Dalit origin and upbringing. His mother Renuka

Vemula proved her case and together with her surviving son Raja Chaithanya later converted to Buddhism at the Diksha Bhoomi in Nagpur. Rohit was an Ambedkarite and a Marxist. This brings us back to the question of an alliance of progressive forces in the present constellation (Shankar, 2016b).

New Alliances in times of rising 'Hindutva' nationalism

The rise of Hindutva, especially since the elections of 2014, has brought about a situation which makes it unavoidable to strike new and unusual alliances. This is not easy. For example, in the light of the rising 'cow politics', alliances between Muslims and Dalits have come into being, which were earlier not easily forged. The murder of Mohamed Akhlaq in Uttar Pradesh for having 'unidentified meat' in his fridge, which on examination was found to be mutton, set a precedent not easily forgotten. The severe mob violence against four Dalits in Una (Gujarat), who were skinning a cow which had been killed by a tiger, showed how precarious Dalit working conditions really were. This later led to an alliance between Dalits and Muslims from 4 October 2016 where a campaign 'Chalo Udupi' (Go to Udupi) from Bangalore to Udupi (a Hindutva stronghold in south Karnataka) connected the Una violence against Dalits with Muslim demands for cultural and livelihood rights under the slogan 'Food: Our Choice, Land: Our Right'.

There is reluctance on the Marxist (CPI-M) side to identify Hindutva with fascism. This has to do not only with the fact that left parties have been divided since 1964 (war with China) and more so since the formation of the armed struggle which started in Naxalbari in the late 1960s, but also with the fact that the communist parties have not taken on board the analysis of caste at sufficient depth, as the leadership has remained generally upper caste. Their position on Hindutva has remained hazy. This difficulty to come to grips with religious nationalism and with caste is also found in the international debate. It so happened that I was writing a review of Perry Anderson's book *The Indian Ideology* (2013) during the election campaign in 2014 and was astonished how a renowned Marxist writer had missed out on the relevance of Ambedkar and the immense danger to Indian democracy under Hindutva (Dietrich, 2014). There is also a lack of understanding in the Western world about how important the concept of the secular state is in the Indian context. This secularism is very much rooted in the radical position of Dr Ambedkar. Mahatma Gandhi came around to a secular position when interfering fearlessly to quell communal riots during the partition in Noakali. It is consistent in this historical context that Gandhi was murdered by Nathuram Godse, who had his political formation in the RSS (Setalvad, 2015). It is important that the background to Gandhi's assassination has been documented thoroughly by Teesta Setalvad, who together with Javed Anand had published *Communalism Combat* and who is the most tenacious supporter of Zakia Jaffri, the widow of Ehsan Jaffri who has stood up in the horrendous case over the massive violence in Gulmarg society against the implication of the Gujarat government in the massive anti-Muslim carnage of March 2002 following the Godhra train incident of mass arson (Setalvad, 2017). The documentation on Gandhi's assassination is of utmost importance, lest the conflict between Dr Ambedkar and Gandhi be misunderstood with Gandhi portrayed as a protagonist of Hindu Rashtra. He paid with his life for his fearless solidarity during the violence of partition. Today, there are attempts to revive and celebrate the 'patriotism' of the murderers.

It is against this backdrop that the debate on rising fascism in India is of utmost importance. Ram Puniyani has edited important contributions to the debate which has been going on since the destruction of the Babri Masjid on 6 December 1992 and has published them in the present context (Puniyani, 2017). The political assessment is not only a question of electoral alliances, but the more disturbing factor is the saffronisation of popular culture, be it out of opportunism or out of a frustrated upsurge of unmet aspirations.

However, there have been popular uprisings which have tried to express an alternative culture. For example, a campaign against the lynching mentality, called 'Not in My Name', took off and received good response in over 20 cities in late June and early July 2017. There have been extensive debates at different universities, most of all Jawaharlal Nehru University in Delhi, regarding nationalism and who is an enemy of the nation (Azad et al., 2016). Writers have returned national awards in protest against the destruction of free speech. One of the promising aspects of the present situation seems to be that apart from the constraints of political alliances; there is also a certain confluence of lived lives, which forms an undercurrent of new possibilities. These lived lives show traces of a confluence of feminism, Marxism, freedom of religion, secularism, freedom from caste, communalism, and violence, which help us to uphold courage in future struggles.

It so happens that in May 2013, feminist friends got together to publish the writings of Mythili Sivaraman, a committed woman activist of the CPI-M, who had been in the forefront of discussing feminist issues in the party when this was not yet accepted (Sivaraman, 2013). V. Gita and K. Kalpana put it all together and organised the release. Mythili raised caste issues even in the 1980s when the party had a class reductionist line. She energetically took up the horrendous violence of landlords in east Thanjavur in December 1968 which led to the burning alive of 44 Dalits, mostly women and children. Uma Chakravarti was present at the book release, giving the keynote. She also showed to a smaller group the video film on Mythili's life which she made while Mythili was losing her memory due to Alzheimer's. Uma Chakravarti, a Marxist teaching as a historian in Delhi University, has done very thorough work on Buddhism as well as on the origins of caste and patriarchy. Her work on Pandita Ramabai has to be seen against this background. While she is an agnostic herself, she has made the Ramabai's conversion visible as a pioneering feminist act. Uma Chakravarti has also worked as a human rights activist. She has also been interviewing women activists who are imprisoned as ultra-left or Naxalites. This reveals much broader alliance building than in the left parties. People's struggles preserve more rigour than party lines and different connections can come together to solve survival questions.

In 2014, a striking novel by poet and journalist Meena Kandasamy hit the bookshops under the innocuous title *The Gypsy Goddess* (Kandasamy, 2014). This novel is a most riveting narrative of the December 1968 massacre in Keezhvenmani, which Mythili Shivaraman had brought to public notice earlier. Although Kandasamy makes all the disclaimers of a fiction writer, her capacity to conjure up the drama between bonded labourers and landlords and the fervent determination of the people to uphold the red flag and pursue the revolution is extremely captivating. The people's struggle completely surpassed the sterile statements of party leaders in the present situation.

The events in Venmani in the late 1960s have also brought Krishnammal Jagannathan and S. Jaganathan to the villages, where the need for land distribution was very urgent. While the Gandhian background of Vinobha Bhave's Gramdan Movement was certainly alien to the villages, it needs to be put on record that people of the region have indeed been able to benefit from land struggles and have acquired much more self-reliance, including housing, than could have been expected at the outset (Dietrich, 2005). This shows that there are different layers of ideological backgrounds and approaches in aiming at self-reliance and overcoming landlessness and untouchability and the violence of 'normal' life.

Where do we go from here?

The question of freedom *of* religion and *from* religion has much wider ramifications than could be made visible by only comparing the conversions of Ramabai and Dr Ambedkar. Towards the end of his life, when Dr Ambedkar was convinced that Buddhism was the only option for the untouchables, he envisaged a massive exodus from untouchability in the name of Buddhism. He was convinced that Buddhism was aiming at a socialist transformation of society, which would outlast Marxism, because it would be democratic and non-violent (Ambedkar, 1956). While it is true that socialism in Eastern Europe has been unable to survive experimentation with democracy and China has not even tried, one also does not feel too confident about Buddhist countries which have morphed into dictatorships.

Ambedkar resigned as law minister in 1950 over his inability to pass through the Hindu Code Bill, which tried to give women decisive property rights. After that, he pursued the aim of mass conversion for untouchables with great determination. He explained his radically secular re-interpretation of Buddhism in his book *The Buddha and His Dhamma* (Ambedkar, 1957).

Ramabai and Ambedkar have in common that their motivation for conversion was effective social transformation, overcoming patriarchy and caste. They also were similar in rejecting doctrine and ritual in their new religious context. The rise of religious totalitarianism, be it in the form of Hindutva or Islamic State, shows that the question of religion under global capitalism is far from being resolved or 'outdated'. One of the crucial questions is how to uphold a secular democratic state in times of rising fundamentalism and totalitarianism. Ironically, this question has even arisen in the United States under Donald Trump and the Republicans. There are two major dangers which need to be overcome: nuclear weapons proliferation and climate change. The governments in the Subcontinent and in the US are in total denial of these threats to the survival of the planet. The conversion towards life for all requires a synergy between all religious and secular forces based on compassion, empathy, and solidarity. For this, we have to convert ourselves from the 'Great Derangement' (Ghosh, 2016) to the courage to see and act.

It is obvious that religious regimes, especially when they are possessing nuclear technology and nuclear arms, are a great threat to survival on Earth. The South Asian region, where Hindu nukes are lined up against Muslim nukes, is one of the most jeopardised and jeopardising areas on Earth. While the first nuclear device was tested in May 1974 under Indira Gandhi, the Pokhran explosion of 11 May 1998 under the National Democratic Alliance (NDA) regime led by Atal Bihari Vajpayee, chose the code name 'The Buddha is smiling' for this achievement, a labelling which stirred up great indignation among Dalits, who rightly understood this naming as an attack on Dr Ambedkar and the Indian Constitution.

Religious nationalism not only attacks freedom of religion and the rights of minorities, it also goes against rationalists. The shocking murder of Gauri Lankesh, the fearless editor of *Lankesh Patrike*, in Bangalore on 5 September 2017 was a signal that her courageous resistance against religious chauvinism was unbearable (Menon, 2017). She was gunned down by as yet unidentified gunmen in front of her house on her return from her office (Shankar, 2016a). Police investigations have concluded only that the weapon used seems to have been the same as the one used in the murders of Dr Narendra Dabolkar, Govind Pansere, and Dr M.M. Kalburgi, who were gunned down in Maharastra and Karnataka in recent years for propagating rationalism.

Gauri Lankesh was very popular as a journalist, writing in Kannada, the vernacular of her state, protesting the rise of Hindutva fearlessly. Within a few days of her murder, a massive protest procession and meeting were organised in Bangalore with about 20,000 participants. Interestingly, the meeting was not only attended by political activists from all over the country, it also received strong support from religious heads of Mutts of the Lingayats, a politically influential caste, which stands for the reform movement of Basavanna who stood up against the caste system. His contemporary Akka

Mahadevi (twelfth century), who is famous for her hymns to the 'Lord of White Jasmine' (Shiva) and who is said to have roamed 'dressed in the tresses of her hair', has today lent her name to the Women's University in Bijapur in the north of Karnataka. There were about six heads of Mutts attending the protest meeting, all dressed in saffron, who, one after the other, spoke in glowing tones about Gauri and also said 'we are not Hindus'. Their demand is that the Basavannas reform movement and the tradition of the Lingayats must be recognised as a separate religion. This demand has in the meantime been granted by the state government, which is formed by the Congress Party.

While Gauri Lankesh was clearly a rationalist, she was also very active in the defence of religious pluralism. She was continuously engaged in the battle to protect Sri Guru Dattatreya Bababudan Swamy Dargah, at Chikkamagaluru, a symbol of syncretistic culture venerated by both Hindus and Muslims, which is under attack from Hindutva forces, who want to convert the site into a Hindu temple. This struggle has flared up again and again over many years (Sayeed, 2018). The kind of Islam found in this *dargah* is obviously a highly non-exclusive variety which needs to be supported in the present situation, where the tendency to project Muslims as terrorists fighting for Islamic State is very prevalent. Instead of supporting this history of tolerance, there is an attempt by Hindutva forces to revive the campaign for a temple construction in Ayodhya, where the Babri Masjid was demolished on 6 December 1992 to make way for a temple on the site of the 'birth place' of Lord Ram.

There are different opinions regarding the declaration of Lingayats as a religious minority. Lingayats are a caste in Karnataka which upholds the history of Basavanna, who was born in 1131 to a Brahmin couple in Vijayapura (Bijapur). He was a religious reformer who wrote *Vachanas* (poetry) in Kannada and abandoned the *Vedas* and religious ritual. He addressed his followers as Sharavas (citizens of a welfare state). Part of the community has also formed the Veerashaiva reform movement, which follows Vedic ritual. Many Lingayats have been pro BJP. There are about 1,000 Mutts of the Lingayats in Karnataka, some of them very progressive regarding the abolition of untouchability.

In the present situation, the move to declare the Lingayats an independent religious minority has many political ramifications. The Lingayats have originally favoured the BJP, but at present, Karnataka has a Congress government and the fact that this government has given the Lingayats a religious minority status has been welcomed by the majority of the community. This is a case of a whole influential community opting out of the Hindu majority religion collectively, much to the consternation of the BJP, RSS, and other Hindutva forces, who try to depict this move as a political trick of the Congress Party. On the other hand, several people in popular movements have serious hopes that the situation in Karnataka may encourage people to move away from the rising fascism of the BJP. The struggles of peasants' movements have drawn attention to the deepening agricultural crisis, while Dalits have been protesting the watering down of the Scheduled Caste and Scheduled Tribe (Prevention of Atrocities) Act.

One of the most disturbing things during the BJP regime has been the systematic hatred mobilised against religious minorities in mob violence. Heart-rending gang rape cases have aroused public revulsion. Opting out of Hindutva has become an attractive option. Protection of the Constitution of Dr Ambedkar has become a task of utmost urgency.

Notes

1 Caste *panchayats* are caste-based decision-making bodies that wield a lot of power.

2 This regulates access to study places, job opportunities, etc.

3 Harijan social service society.

References

Adhar, S.M., 1979. *Pandita Ramabai*. CISRS, Bangalore.

Aloysius, G., 2015. *Lothee Thassar and Tamil Buddhist Movement: Religion as Emancipatory Identity*. Critical Quest, New Delhi.

Ambedkar, B.R., 1956. *Buddha and Karl Marx*. Speech to the 4th Conference of World Fellowship of Buddhists, Kathmandu.

Ambedkar, B.R., 1957. *The Buddha and His Dhamma*. Siddharth College Publication, Bombay.

Ambedkar, B.R., 1979. 'Castes in India' in *Writings and Speeches*. Vol. 1. Education Department, Government of Maharashtra, Bombay, 5–22.

Ambedkar, B.R., 1990. 'Who Were the Untouchables and Why They Became Untouchables' in *Writings and Speeches*. Vol. 7. Education Department, Government of Maharashtra, Bombay, 233–379.

Anand, S. (Ed.), 2014. *Annihilation of Caste: The Annotated Critical Edition*. Navayana, New Delhi.

Anderson, P., 2013. *The Indian Ideology*. Verso, London; New York.

Azad, R., Nair, J., Singh, M., Roy, M.S., 2016. *What the Nation Really Needs to Know: The JNU Nationalism Lectures*. Harper and Collins, New Delhi.

Basu, T., Datta, P., Sarkar, S., Sarkar, T., Sen, S., 1993. *Kaki Shorts and Saffron Flags: A Critique of the Hindu Right*. Orient Blackswan, New Delhi.

Chakravarti, U., 1998. *Pandita Ramabai: A Life and a Time*. Kali for Women, New Delhi.

Chandoke, N., 1995. *State and Civil Society: Explorations in Political Theory*. Sage, New Delhi.

Dietrich, G., 1986. 'Women's Movement and Religion'. *Economic and Political Weekly* 21(4), 25 January.

Dietrich, G., 2005. 'Is the Women's Movement on the Move?' in Ray, B. (Ed.), *Women of India: Colonial and Post-Colonial Periods*. History of Science, Philosophy and Culture in Indian Civilization, Vol. 9, Part 3. Sage, New Delhi, 585–604.

Dietrich, G., 2014. *Indian Journal of Secularism* 18(2) (July–September): 87–110.

Ghosh, A., 2016. *The Great Derangement: Climate Change and the Unthinkable*. Penguin India, Gurgaon.

Hedlund, R., Kim, S.C.H., Johnson, R.B. (Eds.), 2011. *The Life and Legacy of Pandita Ramabai*. MIIS/CMS/ISPCK, New Delhi.

Kandasamy, M., 2014. *The Gypsy Goddess*. Fourth Estate, New Delhi.

Kothari, R., 1987. *State against Democracy: In Search of Humane Governance*. Ajanta Publications, New Delhi.

Marx, K., 1975a. 'On the Jewish Question', in Marx, K., Engels, F., *Collected Works*. Vol. 3. Progress Publishers, Moscow, 146–175.

Marx, K., 1975b. 'Contribution to the Critique of Hegel's Philosophy of Law', in Marx, K., Engels, F., *Collected Works*. Vol. 3. Progress Publishers, Moscow, 175–187.

Marx, K., Engels, F., 2011. 'The Origin of the Family, Private Property and the State' in *Selected Works*, Vol. 3, People Publishing House, New Delhi, 204–334.

Menon, P., 2017. 'A Dissenter Silenced'. *Frontline*, 30 September.

Omvedt, G., 2004. *Ambedkar: Towards an Enlightened India*. Penguin Books, New Delhi.

Puniyani, R., 2017. *Fascism in India: Debating RSS-BJP Politics*. Media House, New Delhi.

Rege, S., 2013. *Against the Madness of Manu: B.R. Ambedkar's Writings on Brahmanical Patriarchy*. Navayana, New Delhi.

Roy, A., 1999. *The Greater Common Good*. India Book Distributors, Bombay.

Roy, A., 2010. 'Walking with the Comrades'. *Outlook*, 20 March.

Roy, A., 2014. 'The Doctor and the Saint' in Anand, S. (Ed.), *B.R. Ambedkar: Annihilation of Caste. The Annotated Critical Edition*. Navayana, New Delhi, 16–179.

Rudolph, I.L., Rudolph, S.H., 1987. *In Pursuit of Lakshmi: The Political Economy of the Indian State*. University of Chicago Press, Chicago, IL.

Sayeed, V.A., 2018. 'A Battle Front in the South'. *Frontline*, 2 March, 106–112.

Setalvad, T., 2015. *Beyond Doubt: A Dossier on Gandhi's Assassination*. Tulika Books, New Delhi.

Setalvad, T., 2017. *Foot Soldier of the Constitution: A Memoir*. Left Word, New Delhi.

Shankar, K., 2016a. 'The Death of a Dalit Scholar'. *Frontline* 33(3): 4–12.

Shankar, K., 2016b. 'Who Was Rohit Vemula?'. *Frontline* 33(3): 13–16.

Sivaraman, M., 2013. *Haunted by Fire: Essays on Caste, Class, Exploitation and Emancipation*. Left Word, New Delhi.

Zelliot, E., 2013. *Ambedkar's World: The Making of Babasaheb and the Dalit Movement*. Navayana, New Delhi.

14 | A MARXIST-FEMINIST PERSPECTIVE

From former Yugoslavia to turbo-fascism to neoliberal postmodern fascist Europe

Marina Gržinić

The aim of this text is to situate feminist analysis inside the changes brought by neoliberal global capitalism, since only with the transformation of the current capitalism, is it possible to think about a radical change. The time frame I want to challenge with this text encompasses the social, political, economic, and cultural changes that were brought to life specifically by two events: the fall of the Berlin Wall in 1989 and the attacks on the World Trade Center in New York on 11 September 2001.

Today the outcome of globalisation is on the one side a growing uncertainty and marginalisation, ranging from uncertainty regarding living conditions to the (im)possibility of securing stable employment (forced precarisation), and on the other rising fascism with 'naturalised' processes of misery and subjugation, while life is being constantly subjugated to capital exploitation. Today we can detect elements of the escalation of fascism in neoliberal capitalist Europe. We see the rise of different far-right groups in the West and former East, with clear fascist tendencies and programmes, on the one hand, and the refugees in Europe, abandoned, banned, and excluded, on the other.

Therefore the main aim of this chapter is to present an analysis of how fascism in its new forms coincides with 'older' racial, gender, and class categories. Finally I want to map racism, sexism, and exploitation in relation to new forms of fascism.

In the 1960s–1970s, life was seen as an autonomous source for capital accumulation. This was the time of the Fordist mode of production and what was going on outside the factory was seen as an 'autonomous' source of not only consuming but 'creative' producing. This period was not only marked by student riots (education was separated from the Fordist production), but also by different subcultures and different forms of life, from hippy to punk, that produced different forms of 'autonomous' counter-movements in the social sphere. In the 1980s and 1990s life changed into a canvas for cultural industry, and was completely taken over by spectacle and mass culture, a process already announced by Adorno and the Frankfurt school. This period was characterised by separation (high culture and mass culture, etc.) and the bridging of this separation through nomadic processes, mobility, multiculturalism, and of course, migration. Postmodernism teaches us how new media technology facilitated and mediated this passage for capital.

Lastly, today we have a complete hybridisation of life and capital and a total subsumption of life to capital. Specifically it works through an entanglement that hides the global post-Fordist division of labour, which can best be described as an international division of labour between the First, Second, and Third Worlds. This division is effective yet hidden under the veil of globalisation.

Feminist analysis in the time of necrocapitalism

This section elaborates on the hybridisation of life and capitalism that involves no 'autonomy' as in the 1960s/70s, and no 'opposition' as in the 1980s or 1990s, but a total capturing, exploitation, and expropriation of life by the force of capital.

Basically, the last decades have revealed that neoliberal global capitalism, historically, in order to progress, not only did away with the Berlin Wall (1989), but intensified a rupture in the modes of proper established governmentality. As conceptualised by Michel Foucault (2010) in the mid-1970s, biopolitics designates the entry of phenomena peculiar to the life of human species into the order of knowledge and power, or simply, into the sphere of political techniques.

I reformulate *biopolitics* (*bios* means life in Latin) as '*make live and let die*' (in the 1970s a 'let die' attitude was ascribed to all the worlds outside the capitalist Occidental First World).[1]

But with neoliberal global capitalism this biopolitical managing of life changes radically into a dystopian project of necropolitics that now administers death and not life. Coined just 15 years ago by Achille Mbembe (2003), necropolitics today seems already historical, but unfortunately this is not the case. Today necropolitics works at full power. 'Necropolitics' clearly shows the implementation of a military corpus after the 9/11 attacks in 2001, which presents itself not as an administration of life but a governing over death.

I define *necropolitics* (*necro* means death in Latin) as '*let live and make die*'.

Obviously, to *make live* (biopolitics) was the 1970s welfare-state slogan for the liberal capitalist First World, while today the slogan is just to *let live* (necropolitics). To make live and to let live are clearly two radically different modes of life (Gržinić and Tatlić, 2014). Subsequently this also means to just *let* live even the so-called 'real' in blood and soil nation-state citizens of the capitalist neoliberal First World.

Necropolitics confronts us with the horrors of the human condition: death and killing, and with the new relation between life and death and capital accumulation. The shift from biopolitics to necropolitics involves the shift from biocapitalism to necrocapitalism as well as from biopower to necropower.

After the deaths of a massive number of refugees near the coast of Lampedusa in 2013, Italian Prime Minister Enrico Letta said: 'The hundreds who lost their lives at Lampedusa yesterday are Italian citizens as of today'.[2] The state burial that the victims received was less expensive than sending the bodies back to their point of departure. But what about those who survived? According to the law that was in force at the time, not only did they not receive citizenship, they faced fines and detention for illegally trying to cross a state border of a foreign country. The case of Lampedusa made me rethink what was not reflected publicly, that these dead people got, unfortunately, what they needed: the opportunity to live a life of their own in the EU, though this was given to them only after they died on EU soil. In 2013 I named this citizenship *'necropolitical citizenship'* – that is, citizenship given to those who are left to die (refugees, asylums seekers, and primarily non-registered migrants). Therefore, our EU citizenship is no longer an 'old' form of a 'natural' citizenship (it never was!), but just a biopolitical citizenship. The most important element of this shift is that it is not just a structuralist division or poststructuralist differentiation, but it is established along the colonial/racial divide.

In claiming this necropolitical and biopolitical citizenship we have to elaborate this state of affairs along several other passages: from liberalism to neoliberalism, from multiculturalist capitalism to global capitalism, from the administration of life towards the administration of death, and from a change in the capitalist First World of imperial nation-states to militarised war-state powers. Furthermore, historical colonialism changed into a contemporary colonial matrix of power presenting moreover a change in, or the reappearance, of two forms of power: governmentality and sovereignty.

All these hyper-violent passages, these cuts, have brought with them at least two different ways of constituting the social bond: on the one side a post-socialist, ex-Second World (former Eastern European states) transforming into *turbo-fascist societies*, while on the other side the old colonial imperialist Occidental states, which were once nation-states, becoming not only war-states but retaining a *postmodern fascist social structure* (of pure individualisation, fragmentation, and flesh mobilisation with the persistent rejection of the 'Other').

I propose a further thesis: a genealogy of governmentality and sovereignty after the Second World War.

In Foucault governmentality and sovereignty are separated, in Giorgio Agamben they are conflated, and in Achille Mbembe they are projected onto each other and simultaneously duplicated. Furthermore, sovereignty is foundational, vertical, militarised, while governmentality is de-foundational, apparently horizontal, dispersed, and if necessary can be confiscated, instantaneously seized by sovereignty. It can be suspended: social transfers blocked, public access to knowledge and space immediately revoked.

Who should live and who must die is as well the most concise description by Achille Mbembe of necropolitics that he develops in his seminal text published in 2003.

Moreover, today the notion of the 'subject' in the capitalist First World is reserved only for the citizens (fully acknowledged) of this capitalist neoliberal First World. Therefore the 'old' political 'subjects' are seen as a form of archaic subjectivity and delegated to the so-called Third Worlds' capitalisms.

Turbo-fascism and postmodern fascism

This section will dive further into the two forms of contemporary fascism.

Turbo-fascism

Coming from the former Yugoslavia – being a citizen of Slovenia – and being formed in a setting of Marxist theory and ideology, with Marxism being the main ideology of all social, political, and economic sciences, I want to take this point centrally and connect it with a feminist analysis that was developed at the end of the 1990s regarding the militarisation and Balkanisation of the former Yugoslavia, as well, but not least, its fascism.

The war was initiated by the Communist Party leaders in power and supported by the military apparatus of the former Yugoslavia. The war resulted in a massive annihilation of people, an ethnic cleansing, becoming an emblematic case of contemporary genocide after the Second World War in the heart of Europe. The Srebrenica genocide in July 1995 refers to killings during the 'Balkan war' in Bosnia and Herzegovina when more than 8,000 Bosnians (Bosnian Muslims), mainly men and boys, were slaughtered in and around the town of Srebrenica by units of the Army of the 'Republika Srpska' ('Serb Republic') under the command of General Ratko Mladić, supported by Slobodan Milošević and by the mass media and public opinion in Serbia. After the war the ethnic cleansing continued through a myriad of processes of racialisation, dispossession, exploitation, and deregulation.

At the end of the 1990s, and within such context, the Serbian theoretician and feminist scholar Žarana Papić (2002) described the processes of the period 1980–1990 in Serbia as *Turbo-Fascism*. She stated 'I am freely labelling this as *Turbo-Fascism*'. The text 'Europe after 1989: Ethnic Wars, the Fascisation of Social Life and Body Politics in Serbia' (2000), in which she developed her thesis, was also Papić's penultimate text. She passed away in her mid-fifties in 2002. The text, in which she draws lines of co-relations between power, transition, capitalism, labour, class, and gender, was written in 2000, the year Milošević was sent to the Hague Tribunal. This was a year before the first pride parade in Belgrade, when the LGBT community protested peacefully against being constantly and persistently oppressed, and was attacked by hundreds of right-wing cleric-orthodox-ultra-nationalist Serbians, while the police, supported by the political elite in power, did nothing whatsoever to offer them any protection.

In her text, after naming the reality in the former Yugoslavia, specifically in Serbia, 'turbo-fascism', Papić clarifies:

> It is, of course known that Fascism is a historical term; that the history of Nazi Germany is not the same as that of Milošević's Serbia. However, in postmodernist and feminist theory we speak of 'shifting concepts' when a new epoch inherits with some additions concepts belonging to an earlier one, like, for instance the feminist notion of *shifting patriarchy*. In my view, we should not fear the use of 'big terms' if they *accurately* describe certain political realities. (Papić, 2002: 192)

The main characteristics of turbo-fascism in post-socialist transitional states from 2000 on developed steadily in what can be called a neoliberal capitalist right-wing reality of the once Eastern European territory. Therefore, paraphrasing Papić, it would be possible to describe turbo-fascism in the post-socialist former Eastern European countries in the time of neoliberalism in the present tense. Papić's designation of turbo-fascism referred to Serbia but today it can be straightforwardly extended to the whole former Eastern European territory, emphasising that turbo-fascism has its own concentration camps, its own systematic representation of violence against Others, its own cult of the family and cult of the leader, an explicitly patriarchal structure, a culture of indifference towards the exclusion of the 'Other', and a closure of society upon itself and upon its own past; it has a taboo on empathy and a taboo on multiculturalism; it has a powerful media acting as proponents of genocide; it has a nationalist ideology; it has an epic mentality of *listening* to the word and *obeying* authority. The prefix 'turbo' refers to the specific mixture of politics, culture, 'mental powers', and the pauperisation of life: the mixture of rural and urban, pre-modern and postmodern, pop culture and heroines, real and virtual, mystical and 'normal', etc. In this term, despite its naive or innocent appearances, there is still fascism in its proper sense. Like all fascisms, turbo-fascism includes and celebrates a pejorative renaming, alienation, and finally removal of the Other(s). Turbo-fascism in fact demands and basically relies on this *culture of the normality* of fascism that had been structurally constituted well before all the killing in the wars started.

I have therefore modified what Papić wrote in 2000, and which was published in 2002, in order to expose the actuality of her analysis today. Papić (2002) described a process that has at its core a specific process of class racialisation, which refers to the assigning of racial connotations to the activities of those termed subhumans due to their ethnic, class, and gender differences.

Postmodern fascism

This turbo-fascist reality in the former space of Yugoslavia can be connected with another process that the Spanish theoretician Santiago López Petit

(2009) identifies firstly, as a change from nation-state to war-state in the time of global neoliberal capitalism, and secondly, as a specific way of structuring the social in the Occident that he names postmodern fascism. Postmodern fascism designates a society of hyper-individualisation that disconnects politics and society and that presents itself as an 'imaginary' horizontal society. But this myth is necessary for the Occident, in order to constantly cover that centralisation and militarisation are in the hands of those that govern war, accumulation, and rampant financialisation.

The war-states are today those sovereign nation-states from the past (the so-called First World European states and the USA) that in the meantime transformed themselves into war-states. At the same time the post-socialist countries or neoliberal turbo-fascist countries remained 'just' nation-states (Slovenia, Hungary, Romania, etc.) without real sovereignty, though having an (EU) mandate, to control and systematically push nationalism, insisting on heterosexual relations, hegemony of the majoritarian nation group, and violent marginalisation of minorities, etc. but inside their state borders. In this context nationalism plays an important role and is an atavistic format of ideology.

While turbo-fascism is reserved for those regions emerging from the war situations of recent history (war in the Balkans, massive deregulation of the social, direct, and brutal clearing of history from any counter-hegemonic historical events), postmodern fascism presents a process of implosion, a *pastoral mechanism* of fragmentation, with almost invisible processes of ferocious privatisation, all done under a formal system of judicial regulation and administration.

Postmodern fascism functions with the sterilisation of the 'Other' and constant evacuation of the conflict. Sterilisation of the 'Other' means that all those seen as the 'Other' are simply muted, cleared from the public realm, and fiercely controlled. The war-state is central to the capitalist First World and works to maintain both the illusion of society and the illusion of the biopolitical mode of life (from the politics of taking care of the life of the population towards systematically controlling it). To do this it uses specific measures that I name necropower measures: abandonment, ban, exclusion. This is evident these days in Austria, Sweden, Italy, Germany, etc., in relation to refugees. This means that from its biopolitical regime the contemporary neoliberal state persistently transforms into a necropolitical regime.

In this change from nation-state to war-state we have as well the so-called 'missing' link that is the racial-state. Thus this passage from nation-state to war-state goes through a racial-state that has at its core racism, brutal processes of racialisation, and class racialisation.

The colonial/racial divide

In this section, in order to understand these changes that are touching each of us, as subjects and individuals, we examine two distinct territories: on the one side governmentalities and on the other the procedures, tactics, and logics of division. We therefore see that 'life' as a dispositive is already being captured through processes of hierarchy and division, and by being re-framed discursively and visually, organisationally and institutionally, politically and socially, aesthetically and technologically.

If we take that biopolitics and necropolitics are two forms of governmentality that apply to neoliberal global capitalism modes, procedures, tactics, logics, laws, and institutional regulations, then all these fenced and foreclosed spaces in Europe are connected through a very perverse situation. As Eric Fessing and Marie Adam (in Sanyal, 2017) have observed, there is first a process of ghettoisation that is nothing other than a form of securitarian governmentality. Its objective is the containment, deterrence, and displacement of asylum seekers, but not yet their outright expulsion – something we can see in the Western European context. Why? Because complete expulsion would make clear that the Occidental protection of human rights is only a myth – in reality all the procedures to protect refugees today are tightly connected with '*deading life*' (Stanescu, 2013), that is the way that leads towards death, but is not death yet.

In addition, a vocabulary of violence is formed in order to deal with systems of surveillance and seclusion that works with abbreviations: FRONTEX – European border enforcement agency; EUROSUR – European Border Surveillance System, etc.

Kirstine Nordentoft Mose and Vera Wriedt (2015) argue that the militarisation of border spaces is achieved through (a) a horizontal extension of border control, through agreements with countries of origin and transit countries, and (b) a vertical intensification of surveillance via drones or unmanned aerial vehicles (UAVs). So, what is it we get here? It is important to state that the border between the Fortress of Europe and Africa functions as a colonial border that is presently enhanced through a hyper-militarised technology transforming it in a three-dimensional, fully racialised space of control. These procedures of militarisation are the major ways of regulating the lives of the refugees, that is, a political life under violent destruction where the erasure of fingerprints transforms their proper flesh into political flesh.

It is in/at the border where past colonialism and the present neoliberal coloniality meet. Women from continents like Latin America, Africa, and Asia, and from former Eastern European countries come into the EU to fill the *gaps*, as stated by Luzenir Caixeta (2013), in reproduction and service work – the so-called world chain of care work, which is gendered female and racialised. Therefore, feminisms in plural are developing new political concepts and strategies for action that radically call into question what has previously been regarded as generally true: namely that the political subjects of feminism are women, but especially women according to a certain notion: white, heterosexual, submissive, and from the middle class.

The result of these processes is that in its most basic sense, Europe – precisely the European Union – is today constituted, as exposed by Angela Mitropoulos (2009: 5), by 'the problem of the legal form of value, of its imposition and perseverance', as well as by the problem of 'origin and lineage'. In other words, as stated by Melinda Cooper and Angela Mitropoulos, there would be in

> the violent positing of the frontier as the space of exploration, cultivation and the extraction of wealth – in the scarcities that are obliged as precondition and condition of a market in labour, in the criminalisation and recapture of fugitive and wayward (re)production ... – a periodic recourse to the naturalizing magic of genealogy to settle matters of orderly progression and authenticity. (2009: 264)

It is at the frontier, at the EU Schengen border, 'where (un)legitimate labour (that is nothing more or less than the very distinction between wage labour and slavery) and (un)authorized reproduction are decided' (2009: 263).

The European Union functions precisely in such a way today by transforming mostly migrant labour into pure servitude (and not only in Spain, Italy, France, Austria). In Slovenia, migrant workers coming from the former republics of a common state known as Yugoslavia are today working in conditions of slavery; excluded from the law, they become 'non-existent', lacking the most basic rights. Or even more precisely, what occurs at the Schengen border (that is, the frontier between the European Union and the rest of Europe) can be paralleled with another border, the Tijuana border (32 km from downtown San Diego, the busiest point of entrance into the USA from Mexico), which affects employment, social security, the deportation of illegal workers, or relations of increasing criminality and paralysed social and political space.

Here it is possible to state that the relation between labour and capital is a relation of exploitation and dispossession in connection with, as formulated by Encarnación Gutiérrez Rodríguez, feminisation, migration, and coloniality (2011).

Araba Evelyn Johnston-Arthur (Johnston-Arthur and Kazeem, 2007) describes the situation in Austria as twofold. On the one side, we have migrants who were invited into the country by the government in the 1960s to help the post-war reconstruction of the country, and on the other, we have a new, vast group of refugees, fugitives, asylum seekers, and deported persons (as in August 2010, when France – supposedly 'legally', as their action was based on EU laws – deported hundreds of Roma back to Romania and Bulgaria) who find themselves caught in the ever-changing immigration laws established and reinforced daily by the EU and implemented (inter)nationally.

Therefore, on the one hand, we have the 'former West', the once capitalist First World that is the Christian-capitalist patriarchal regime of power, with its processes of financialisation and liberalisation that go hand in hand with the inclusion in its capitalist (global neoliberal) matrix of power of all those once perceived as 'Others', the non-heterosexual identities (though there is still a big discrimination of transsexual and intersexual people). On the other, and at the same place and time, we have necropolitics, a brutal logic of violence, persecutions, discrimination, and racialisations in the former Eastern European space (ex-Yugoslavia, Russia, and other post-Soviet countries, etc.). To be precise it is not about the new 'enlightened logic' of the 'former West' against the 'former East', but it is a new process of discrimination that takes into its borders the 'Other' to produce new 'Others' in the West: the migrants, refugees, *sans-papiers*, people and women of colour coming from other parts of the world and religious backgrounds. Therefore, the necropolitical horizon of dispossession and exploitation, part of the technosexual matrix of global capitalism today, teaches us that neither gender nor sex are natural conditions of our lives.

But for those of us who come from the former Eastern European context into the European Union without borders – as it is 'daily' presented – we, the former, 'taste' the conditions of racialisation 'without a race' daily as well. This portrayal of structural racism of and in Europe is further developed by Philomena Essed (2012), who argues in her lecture 'Racism in Europe: Humiliation and Homogenization':

> The European unification has been foremost a project of whiteness. Notions of tolerance, multiculturalism and anti-racism, somewhat popular in the 1980s, have all but disappeared from political agendas. The turn of the century has been witness to the emergence of what I call entitlement racism: the idea that majority populations have the right to offend and to humiliate the 'Other'. Expressions of this form of racism vary according to racial, ethnic and religious group attributions and can range from assimilative paternalism to extreme cultural humiliation.

Essed specifically concentrates on 'Dutch racism' (2012). She states that,

> The Netherlands has passed through history as a tolerant country. That tolerance is mainly the legacy of the religious reform during the sixteenth century. It was the time when the repressive Catholicism was confronted and other Christian religions found their place in most parts of The Netherlands. 'Tolerance' is understood as almost equivalent to 'not racist'. However, can a tolerant country be racist? Or is it blindness that prevents a collectivity to perceive its own form of racism? Talking about Dutch racism, in The Netherlands, is something that only the brave do. (2012: lecture text, no pagination)

Sexual difference

In this section I want to show how biopower and necropower are exercised totally and fully on the body of the individual and not only on the body of society.

Žarana Papić (2002) defined as the basis of turbo-fascism a systematic representation of violence against the 'Others', the Muslim women that were raped in thousands in the 1990s at the time of the Balkan War in the former Yugoslavia, presented therefore in addition to the hyper-violent engagement with sexual difference in necrocapitalism. In the 1990s, during the Bosnian War, femicide towards Muslim women in Bosnia took the form of a hyper-violence that assumed a gender-targeted form of military violence through the use of rape. While men from all ethnic groups committed rape, the great majority of rapes were perpetrated by Bosnian Serb forces of the Army of the 'Republika Srpska' ('Serb Republic') and Serb paramilitary units, who used genocidal rape as an instrument of terror, as part of their programme of ethnic cleansing. Estimates of the number of women and girls raped as a new form of militarised necropolitical violence vary, ranging 'from 12,000 to 50,000, the vast majority of whom were Bosniaks raped by Bosnian Serbs. UNHCR experts have claimed 12,000 rapes. The European Union estimates a total of 20,000, while the Bosnian Interior Ministry claims 50,000. The UN Commission of Experts identified 1,600 cases of sexual violence'.[3]

We see a direct relation between gendered violence and hyper-violence that discloses itself through necro-gendering of spaces and of subjectivities that are part of the deep processes of de-subjectivation. It is also important to note that in the past femicide was confined to domestic settings and connected to poverty and class racialisations.[4] In the time of necrocapitalism we see a process of externalisation that engages different contexts not only patriarchal and heteronormative, but hyper-militarised violence as well.

When we talk of the relation between sexual difference and the neoliberal necropolitical regime we cannot bypass the level of the 'peaceful', so to speak – that is, the public and civic spaces of the neoliberal Occident. Gabriele Dietze (2009) shows in her compelling analysis how necropolitics organise the relation between gender and ban in the ('former') West. Ban is always a prohibition; it functions as a gatekeeper that safeguards different state and civic power structures that limits the rights of others to live their lives. Dietze shows this in the case of the control of headscarf-wearing and in relation to the white Occidental regime of gender (I call this violent 'genderisation'). As Dietze exposes today, the oppression of headscarf-wearing women has become the benchmark of the so-called 'community of values' (*Wertegemeinschaft*) based on the repudiation of 'Oriental mores' or – to put it differently – as a means to construct a superior Occidental identity (as Dietze elaborates, to construct Occidentalism in the sense of Occidental self-affirmation).

Refugees and necrocapitalism

In this section I expand on this process of production of the 'Other' and connect it to the 'crisis of the refugees in Europe'. Simply put, the increasing immiseration of the working class in Europe today is not a result of the failure of the globalised economic model but of its success. It is a process that was conducted from the 1980s on. The unemployment, insecurity, and poverty resulted in a transformation of the whole spectrum of how life was not only divided but also became the direct target of the sovereign power. This led to radical change in relations towards refugees, in particular making them superfluous, obsolete, as a category of life and work (Gržinić, 2018).

Giorgio Agamben in the 1990s, after the fall of the Berlin Wall, in his *Homo Sacer: Sovereign Power and Bare Life* (1998), suggested the division of life into three categories: *Zoe*, *Bios*, and *Bare Life*. Agamben conceived of the banished life in the figure of *Homo Sacer*. This precise figure will signal in the 1990s the return of sovereignty (that will be subsequently elaborated by Achille Mbembe) as a form of life that allows the sovereign to decide over the life and death of the population through an act of ultimate and deliberate violence. In Agamben the biopolitical 'make live and let die' is conflated with the not yet named necropolitical 'let live and make die'. This is why Agamben's notion of abandonment of specifically envisioned groups of people will shift after 2017 into a ban. Though this shift is not sudden it is developing hand in hand with the transformation of neoliberal global capitalism into necrocapitalism.

Bios designates a life with a form but without, I would insist, politics. We can see this form of life easily change into a hyper-populist mob during the events in Chemnitz (Germany) in 2018. This mob protects a 'proper' way of white, Christian, Occidental life that is always reserved for the citizens of the capitalist First World.

Chemnitz, in the east German state of Saxony, was on 26 August 2018, after a festival celebrating the city's founding, the site of a crime. In the early morning of that day a fight broke out resulting in the death of a German-Cuban man and serious injuries to two other people. Two Kurdish immigrants, one Iraqi, and one Syrian, were named as suspects. The incident re-ignited the tensions surrounding immigration to Germany, which had been ongoing since 2015, and the European migrant crisis. In response, mass protests against immigration were ignited by far-right nationalist groups. The protests spawned riots and were followed by counter-demonstrations.

Zoe (a life as a bundle that is not differentiated) and *Bare Life* constitute the *Homo Sacer* that presents a life that can be killed without punishment and cannot be sacrificed. This is what we see applied to the refugees in that strip of territory in Libya that was transformed into a huge 'island' where the refugees are in the last instance abandoned (let die) to such an extent that they are in fact in a situation to be killed. We see clearly here that abandonment changes into a ban.

Abandonment is already present during Foucault's time, when he defines the biopolitical, but it is not registered by him. Abandonment was for a long time a status of economic migrants; they were needed to rebuild the Occident, post-Nazi Western Europe, after the Second World War. This labour was cheap and needed but the migrants were prevented from entering any public discourse in the Occidental (Western) public space. Integration of migrants is also a form of abandonment, as it is imposed *tout court* without a historical envisioning of differences. Namely, we see in the last years a shift in migrant integration policy; one of the most problematic is called mainstreaming migrant integration policy. It is adopted in some EU countries, for example in France, and consists in increasingly neighbourhood-oriented migrant integration approaches rather than developing, envisioning, or adopting measures oriented towards the foreign-born, or according to religion or cultural specificities.

Therefore, these three categories – Bios, Zoe, and Bare Life – that were conflated in the past, are used in the time of neoliberal necrocapitalism selectively, and in the hands of new sovereign figures (Trump, Orban, etc.), hyper-violently and murderously. Bios and Zoe are attached to biopower, and Bare Life to necropower. Bare Life produces a 'necro-subject' that is not at all a subject but 'excrement' that has to be disposed of, and therefore can be easily banned. It is important to state that abandonment, ban, seclusion, segregation, etc. are today necrocapitalist mechanisms of death. They are as well notions, rhetorical figures, and semiotic and semantic 'utensils' that denote death, social death, isolation, and maximum deprivation.

Refugees, in order to arrange their status, are passing more and more through humiliating, long-lasting and hyper-violent procedures. Therefore, when we engage with abandonment and ban we see that refugees are perceived as superfluous. The outcome of a ban is also the above-described paradoxical form of citizenship that is necrocitizenship. This changes the refugee into an object to be disposed of. However, in the Occident, which capitalised for decades on the protection of human rights – which is still done through a whole set of carefully selected systems of media, law, and security regimes – it is an outcome of different paranoias, as for example the idea of contagion.

As stated, prior to the refugee we had another figure of abandonment in capitalism: the migrant, who, apprehended as a *Zoe*, is connected to a certain 'animality'.

Her way of life as a Turkish, Yugoslav, etc. migrant consisted in being a fundamental labour power after the Second World War. In the segregated Western Europe she was left out of the social structures of Western society. Such abandonment resulted as well in a spatial removal from society, transforming the surrounding in which migrants lived in the West during the 1970s into ghettos.

However, from the point of view of the present moment of neoliberal necrocapitalism, such a 'merciful' situation (to be just abandoned and let live) is not valid any more for the refugees. This is when abandonment changes into ban, segregation, and seclusion. This is done through the bureaucratic system of necro-governmentality, as the refugee, the 'Other', is arbitrarily accepted or just transformed into *Homo Sacer*; her life, as a refugee, can be 'saved' by an irrational administrative decision, or she can be 'killed', which means expulsed, deported, or imprisoned.

A good example is the decision based on 'Too gay? Not gay enough?' that was the reason why the Federal Office for Immigration and Asylum in Vienna denied in 2018 asylum to a refugee: his appearance was not gay enough! It sounds like a bad joke, but it isn't. This is a brutal and violent situation that shows that necropolitics works with a special logic of implementation of laws and regulations; it is a logic of (murderous) arbitrariness.

Achille Mbembe talks in relation to such arbitrariness of a contingency that opens as well the dimension of responsibility inside the Western morality based on Christianity. Moreover, the whole topic of arbitrariness relates to an administrative, bureaucratic apparatus, akin to the analysis of the Nazi system in the past, where the Nazi administration in its genocidal pedantry and 'liberty' decided who will stay alive and who must die immediately. And those who decided on the life and the death did it without any culpability or remorse. Furthermore, the whole situation of the refugees, like the imprisonment of thousands, and children dying of hunger in Yemen in 2018 (400,000 malnourished children waiting to die), is presented as a natural catastrophe. It is said that society has to decide on its own; wealthy stars of show business give a few bucks here and there; middle-class Western subjects send donations. Eastern Europeans are the worst, they help only their fellow nationals; the refugees are not 'their/our' business. Angela Merkel 'instructed' the east of Europe in 2015 how to show Christian mercy regarding the refugees. However, the West and the East are both hyper-irresponsible communities, their difference towards irresponsibility is just historical, until they met in Chemnitz (known from 1953 to 1990 as Karl-Marx-Stadt, in the past part of East Germany).

The necropolitical duplicates and triplicates itself as necrocitizenship, necro-subject, necro-body, necro-space, necro-aesthetics, necro-labour, etc. For all these figures and conditions, it is important to see that death and not life organises their terrain. Necropolitics actively participate in citizenship, border organisation, and in forms of governmentality of humanity and the production of 'subhumans'.

Becoming human

Finally, in this section I elaborate on various racial, gender, and class technologies that are implemented to produce subjectivity by 'normalising' and hybridising the life of the individual with the technologies of control and with mechanisms of power, and then to exercise control over the individual by strictly imposing a technology of reproduction, moral codes, social norms, data quantification etc. We see that after the fall of the Berlin Wall the agenda of protection of human rights by the Occident steadily and continuously started to fail and we witness a violent process of unstoppable dehumanisation. Humanity is today relegated to the status of being a citizen (though many are symbolically, socially, politically economically, second- and third-grade citizens in the EU) while refugees are the non-citizens.

'Becoming human' is a specific process of racialisation that works hand in hand with class racialisation. Racialisation transforms societies into racialised societies through stigmatisation and labelling based on the constructed category of race. It functions in Europe through the manufacturing of the former Eastern Europeans, of former 'non-subjects', so to speak, into gendered, European, white, middle-class subjects. It is about *us* acquiring our capitalist's conservative, chauvinistic, patriarchal, mostly petit-bourgeois lineage with which to safeguard the heterosexual family and the racialised nation's 'substance'. The European Union aims to manufacture former 'barbarian communist' Eastern Europeans into 'humanised' and 'civilised' Europeans. Of course, this process is provided with its 'ghastly underside: the story of the racialized subject's *dehumanization*' (Carr, 1998: 120).

Brian Carr elaborated in 1998 this relation of the production of 'humans' by posing a question: what is left at the threshold of the process of manufacturing the humans? His answer is punctual – race! Europe has to critically review its colonial and racial past and present. I will say that in this case it is important to differentiate between a 'naive, benevolent' support of women's practices in Eastern Europe, on one side, and the feminist and theoretical imperialism that can be unmistakably recognised throughout recent decades, on the other. As was exposed by Maria Lugones (2007), Chandra Talpade Mohanty (1984) and Fatima El-Tayeb (2015) for example, at the centre of such imperialism lies a colonial politics of representation, expressions of cultural tolerance, and attempts to identify with the 'Other' (wo/man). But this imperialism works hand in hand with the worship of capitalism as freedom, the celebration of a privatised selfhood, and a gender politics that become a measure of biopolitical governmentality.

It is important to understand that after the fall of the Berlin Wall, this 'Other' was celebrated precisely by privileging identity politics and culture as divided from the social and political, not to mention the colonial and neoliberal. How can we rethink all these cases not only as cultural identity 'failures' of dumb and conservative post-communist national bodies, but as phenomena of a much bigger discrimination and deregulation of capital? In these former Eastern European countries, neoliberal turbo-capitalism pushed forward the raw processes of capitalism's racialisation. What is the result? A massive pauperisation, millions without jobs on the street; in a word, a new division of labour not only in Europe, but also on a new established line of geopolitical dispossession. Capital has a myriad of names – cognitive, immaterial, and financial – but we can connect all of them with racialisation. What we have as the promise of liberation by capital, therefore, is a paradoxical and cynical measure whereby liberation is presented as an infinity of fragmentations, but not of just any kind. There is a process of capitalism's racialisation at work here. One of the functions of 'the colonial matrix of power', a term coined in the 1990s in Latin America that frames historical colonialism's actualisation by means of new forms of coloniality, is, according to Nelson Maldonado-Torres, a control of labour that works hand in hand with racial formations and racial knowledge production (2007: 243).

On the other side, this is hidden also by global capitalism's demand not to talk about racism, a demand made by saying that there is no racism in contemporary global societies. A case par excellence is France, being a 'colonial republic'. Can you see the absurdity of this coinage with which the French republic describes its past colonial implementations of fraternity, freedom, and equality in Africa and elsewhere? One possible proposal will be to expand our analysis on the discussion of identity politics and its processes of culturalisation by including processes of global capitalism's racialisations. Racialisation is not just a process of producing tropes, which means it is not only about a fast process of capital's narrativisation of racialisation, not only about immanent levels of dispossessions, so to speak; racialisation is a process inherent to capital itself. This means that a process of racialisation is actually at the core of the organisation of contemporary global capitalist society: it supported the process of identity politics, which is not simply a multicultural process, not simply a cultural differentiation in society, but a process of steady racialisations within the racial scale of contemporary society.

I stated that 'the human' and 'race' reside in an asymmetric, ghastly position. The humanisation of former Eastern Europeans is done at the expense of racialised 'non-subjects' whose access to the representational status of the 'human subject' is fundamentally halted. Or more, following Carr, and as I tried to present earlier, 'the gendered white bourgeois subject is "made", of course, with racialised/colonised subjects being ... "unmade"' (1998: 120).

What we witness today in Europe is actually what was announced by Partha Chatterjee already in 1993, and reworked in the essay by Brian Carr, written in 1998. There exists a limit in the Foucauldian understanding of the modern regime of power, a limit on which the contemporary biopolitical resides today. Actually, when biopolitics was elaborated in the 1970s, it was a mode of governmentality only for the capitalist First World, and its apparatuses. In that time migrants were invisible; the 'Other' did not exist – it was there but made invisible and mute. Therefore, in Europe we have two modern regimes of power working at once! Researchers such as Foucault, Deleuze, Derrida,

Agamben, Mitropoulos, Essed, Lugones, etc., in their analysis departed from the generalisable modern regime of power to focus in the current times of crisis throughout the global world on modes of control, austerity, and debt.

This regime of control, austerity, and debt functions by demanding integration, and even more by the 'distribution' of debts (!), fear, and fantasies. The 'Other' functions through exclusion, marginalisation, de-symbolisation, and disfiguration.[5] We have, therefore, two regimes of discrimination, racialisation, and exploitation that are *almost* the same, though the latter is not white! (Carr, 1998: 146). These regimes' entanglement is visible in the myriad of class racialisations. 'Race thus stands at the vanishing point where sexual difference and the human resolve into the ungendered figure of dehumanized racial "flesh"' (Carr, 1998: 125). Similarly, I can say that there exist two regimes of ban in neoliberal global capitalism, one is the ban as described by Gabriele Dietze's (2009) analysis that of course differs from the ban that fully prohibits the entrance of refugees into the Fortress of Europe. First, it is important to state that both bans are based on a legal implementation of the ban by the neoliberal capitalist state; both bans are not just an exchange of opinions, of racialised and discriminatory statements in public; they are legally repressively instituted, though the line of difference between them is passing via death. In the first case the ban in the Occident prohibits but doesn't (yet?) kill, whereas the ban of refugees coming to Europe is, as we can see in 2018, frightening and leads to the death of refugees. Florian Westphal, managing director of the aid organisation Doctors Without Borders, contended in an interview with the telling title 'Europe's Apathy toward Humanitarian Rescue Outrages NGOs', that in the Libyan refugee camps:

> thousands of refugees are being held in dreadful conditions. Some of the camps are totally overcrowded. Often there is not enough clean water, and the hygienic conditions are catastrophic. We also come across people who have been tortured and abused, who have been victims of sexual violence and forced labor.[6]

I conclude by stating that because of what was said up until now we can think of this flesh in political terms as a political flesh, and therefore presents a possibility through violent de-subjectivation to regain a new political subjectivity.

Coda

In this chapter I analysed life and humans (constitution, locality of forms of humans and life), the question of labour/gender/race/class and processes connected to neoliberal capitalist racialisation and class racialisation, as well as migration, refugees, and regimes of control, regulations in relation to feminism, and decoloniality. More to the point, I put forward an analysis of how fascism in its new forms coincide with 'older' race, gender, and class categories. I try to map racism, sexism, and exploitation in relation to new forms of fascism.

By analysing these processes, I want to shed light on the systems of seclusion, degradation, and exploitation that will help us in the future, maybe, to conceive of ways to resist.

Notes

1 The eighth James Bond film proclaimed the Occidental biopolitical title: *Live and Let Die* (1973).

2 See: 'Italy to Hold State Funeral for Lampedusa Victims, Eritrea Objects'. 9 October 2013. www.tesfanews.net/italy-to-hold-state-funeral-for-lampedusa-victims-eritrea-objects/ (accessed 16 November 2018), and 'Lampedusa Victims Include a Mother and Baby Attached by the Umbilical Cord'. 10 October 2013. www.theguardian.com/world/2013/oct/10/lampedusa-victims-mother-baby-umbilical-cord (accessed 16 November 2018).

3 Source: https://en.wikipedia.org/wiki/Rape_during_the_Bosnian_War.

4 See 'Femicide in Brazil Is Directly Linked to Race and Class, According to Researchers'. www.brasildefato.com.br/2017/11/08/femicide-in-brazil-is-directly-linked-to-race-and-class-according-to-researchers/ (accessed 16 November 2018).

5 All terms are used by Brian Carr in citing numerous scholars, among others Hortense Spillers.

6 Source: www.dw.com/en/europes-apathy-toward-humanitarian-rescue-outrages-ngos/a-46642711.

References

Agamben, G., 1998. *Homo Sacer: Sovereign Power and Bare Life.* Translated by Daniel Heller-Roazen. Stanford University Press, Palo Alto, CA.

Caixeta, L., 2013. 'Minoritized Women Effect a Transformation in Feminism'. Translated by Aileen Derieg. In The Editorial Group for Writing Insurgent Genealogies (Eds.), *Utopia of Alliances, Conditions of Impossibilities and the Vocabulary of Decoloniality.* Löcker, Vienna, 145–148.

Carr, B., 1998. 'At the Thresholds of the "Human": Race, Psychoanalysis, and the Replication of Imperial Memory'. *Cultural Critique* 39 (Spring): 119–150.

Chatterjee, P., 1993. *The Nation and Its Fragments: Colonial and Postcolonial Histories.* Princeton University Press, Princeton, NJ.

Cooper, M., Mitropoulos, A., 2009. 'The Household Frontier'. *Ephemera* 9(4): 363–368.

Dietze, G., 2009. 'Occidentalism: European Identity and Sexual Politics'. Revised English translation of Dietze, G., 2009. 'Okzidentalismuskritik. Grenzen und Möglichkeiten einer Forschungsperspektivierung'. In Dietze, G., Brunner, C., Wenzel, E. (Eds.), *Kritik des Okzidentalismus. Transdisziplinäre Beiträge zu (Neo) Orientalismus und Geschlecht.* Transcript, Bielefeld.

El-Tayeb, F., 2015. 'Creolizing Europe'. *Manifesta Journal* 17: 9–12.

Essed, P., 2012. 'Racism in Europe: Humiliation and Homogenization'. Lecture at Macquarie University Art Gallery, Sydney, Australia.

Foucault, M., 2010. *The Birth of Biopolitics: Lectures at the Collège de France, 1978–1979.* Translated by Graham Burchell. Picador, New York.

Gržinić, M., 2017. 'Queer, Politics, Racism and Resistance' in Blagojević, J., Stošić, M., Fridman, O. (Eds.), *#political (Collectanea).* Faculty of Media and Communications, Belgrade, 299–318.

Gržinić, M. (Ed.), 2018. *Border Thinking: Disassembling Histories of Racialized Violence.* Publication Series of the Academy of Fine Arts Vienna, Vol. 21. Sternberg Press, Berlin.

Gržinić, M., Tatlić, Š., 2014. *Necropolitics, Racialization, and Global Capitalism: Historicization of Biopolitics and Forensics of Politics, Art, and Life.* Lexington Books, Lanham, MD.

Gutiérrez Rodríguez, E., 2011. 'Politics of Affects'. *Transversal Conviviality.* http://eipcp.net/transversal/0811/gutierrezrodriguez/en. Accessed: 16 November 2018.

Johnston-Arthur, A.-E., Kazeem, B., 2007. 'Cafe dekolonial. "Sag zur mehlspeis'leise servus ..."' (Decolonial Café: 'Say Silently Good Bye to the pastry ...']. *Reartikulacija* 1. Ljubljana. http://grzinic-smid.si/wp-content/uploads/2013/02/Rear2007tikulacija1SLO.pdf. Accessed: 16 November 2018.

López Petit, S., 2009. *La movilización global. Breve tratado para atacar la realidad* (Global Mobilization: Brief Treatise for Attacking Reality). Traficantes de Sueños, Barcelona.

Lugones, M., 2007. 'Heterosexualism and the Colonial/Modern Gender System'. *Hypatia* 22(1): 186–209.

Maldonado-Torres, N., 2007. 'On the Coloniality of Being'. *Cultural Studies* 21(2): 240–270.

Mbembe, A., 2003. 'Necropolitics'. *Public Culture* 15(1): 11–40.

Mitropoulos, A., 2009. 'Legal, Tender'. *Reartikulacija* 7. Ljubljana. http://grzinic-smid.si/wp-content/uploads/2013/02/Rear2009tikulacija7.pdf. Accessed 16 November 2018.

Mohanty, C.T., 1984. 'Under Western Eyes: Feminist Scholarship and Colonial Discourses'. *boundary 2* 12/13(3): 333–358.

Nordentoft Mose, K., Wriedt, V., 2015. 'Mapping the Construction of EU Borderspaces as Necropolitical Zones of Exception'. *Birkbeck Law Review* 3(2): 278–304.

Papić, Ž., 2002. 'Europe after 1989: Ethnic Wars, the Fascisation of Social Life and Body Politics in Serbia'. *Filozofski vestnik*, special number 'The Body'. Edited by M. Gržinić Mauhler. Institute of Philosophy ZRC SAZU, Ljubljana, 191–205.

Sanyal, D., 2017. 'Calais's "Jungle" Refugees, Biopolitics, and the Arts of Resistance'. *Representations* 139(1): 1–33.

Stanescu, J., 2013. 'Beyond Biopolitics: Animal Studies, Factory Farms, and the Advent of Deading Life'. *PhaenEx* 8(2): 135–160.

15 | FEMINISM, ANTISEMITISM, AND THE QUESTION OF PALESTINE/ISRAEL

Nira Yuval-Davis

Introduction: why is the question of contemporary antisemitism and its relationship to the Palestine/Israel conflict a feminist issue?

Some might wonder why I chose to write about antisemitism and the question of Palestine/Israel for a volume on Marxist/socialist feminism. I would argue, however, that the topic is not just highly 'trendy' but also important for a feminist agenda.

First, because, in my many years of experience and participation in feminist activism, very rarely have I seen the level of emotional involvement and upset among feminists as regarding that topic. Indeed, I remember the fights as well as tears in meetings on that subject, after Israel invaded Lebanon in 1982, between Jewish feminists and feminists of colour (who adopted the Palestinian issue as representing an on-going colonial project) in London. I actually haven't seen or heard of similar scenes throughout the years since till last year when similar scenes took place between transgender activists and 'women born as women' activists. When some of us pondered on that similarity, we came out with the conclusion that in both cases there have been competing claims on victimhood as constructing subjectivities in what some have been calling identity politics 'Oppression Olympics' (Hancock, 2011). How socialist feminists should relate to such issues is an important feminist question to which I shall return at the conclusion of the paper.

Another reason that this issue is of concern for socialist feminists is because there have been incidents, including one in a world renowned European Gender Studies Institute, in which grants for the Global Southern Lecture series have been withdrawn because the feminists invited support the BDS (Boycott, Divestment and Sanctions) against Israel as a means of political pressure against the Israeli occupation. The claim was that such support is antisemitic and what has been most alarming is that there have been divisions among the Centre's feminist staff as to the validity of such a claim. Moreover, one of the most important contemporary socialist feminists, Angela Davis has recently had her prestigious human rights award from Birmingham (the US city where she grew up) withdrawn due to her support of Palestinian rights, which was perceived as antisemitic. The Women's March in the USA has also been seriously and bitterly disrupted around accusations of antisemitism directed against a Palestinian and a Black woman who were among the main organisers of the march.

Thus, I feel that a clarification of some of the issues involved is required and that as an anti-Zionist Diasporic Israeli Jew, whose family was mostly murdered by the Nazis and their local helpers in Lithuania during the Second World War and who professionally has been working on issues of racism and nationalism for many years, my situated gaze can offer some light on the issue beyond stereotypical dichotomies.

Last but not least, the issue is of concern for socialist feminists because for us, women's liberation is just one facet of human liberation which is our common goal, and the issues of both antisemitism and Zionism need to be addressed within such a normative frame of reference, especially as so much of the recent debate about antisemitism has focused on antisemitism and the Left.

Racism and antisemitism

I cannot go into detail here regarding the genealogy of the term 'antisemitism' (Casillo, 1988). However, I have always considered (and of course I'm far from being the only one) the term 'antisemitism' vague and inaccurate – for example, are all Semites (including Arabs) included as the objects of antisemitic ideologies and practices, or do we actually mean, as it is mostly the case these days, racism against Jews only – and I'll return to this issue towards the end of the chapter. In this chapter I do stick with the notion of antisemitism, as the on-going controversy in the UK, Europe, and more globally, uses that term. However, in my other writings I usually use the term anti-Jewish racisms (e.g. Yuval-Davis, 2013, 2015). It is important to remember that antisemitism is a particular form of racism.

Racism, or, rather, the process of racialisation, is a discourse and practice which constructs immutable boundaries between collectivities that are used to naturalise fixed hierarchical power relations between them (Yuval-Davis and Anthias, 1992; Back and Solomos, 2013; Rattansi, 2007; Goldberg, 2009).

As Barth ([1969] 1998) and others following him have argued, it is the existence of ethnic (and racial) boundaries, rather than any specific 'essence' around which these boundaries are constructed that is crucial in processes of ethnicisation and racialisation. Any physical or social signifier, from the colour of the skin to the shape of the elbow to accent or mode of dress, can be used to construct the boundaries which differentiate between 'us' and 'them'. Different technologies – from the flagging of derogatory stereotypes to the use of actual violence – can be used to maintain and reproduce these boundaries for the purpose of either partial or total exclusion of the racialised from access to different kinds of social, economic, and political capital, and/or for the purpose of their subjugation and exploitation. The ultimate logic of racialised exclusion is genocide and of racialised exploitation slavery.

'Classical antisemitism' focused on discrimination against, denial of, or assault upon the rights of Jews to live as equal members of whatever society they inhabited. However, most of the contemporary controversies around antisemitism have been a result of the spread of the notion of 'new antisemitism' (Klug, 2003). The 'new antisemitism' involves the discrimination against, denial of, or assault upon the right of the Jewish people to live as an equal member of the family of nations, with Israel as the targeted "collective Jew among the nations'" (Lerman, 2013). Thus, the 'new antisemitism' concept largely conflates the notion of racism against Jews with any critique of Zionism, the Israeli occupation, or the Israeli state in generic terms.

While the notion of 'new antisemitism' spread during the first decade of the twenty-first century, it was not a new phenomenon. I have written an article in the British feminist paper *Spare Rib* (Yuval-Davis, 1984) which warned against the long-term dangers of such a conflation. However, in recent years the legitimacy of this notion has spread from the USA to the EU and elsewhere and received a particular legitimation when the International Holocaust Remembrance Alliance (IHRA) adopted in 2016 a definition of antisemitism which incorporated the 'new antisemitism' into its definition. Since then this definition has been adopted by many national and international bodies. According to the IHRI:

> antisemitism is a certain perception of Jews which may be expressed as hatred towards Jews. Rhetorical and physical manifestations of antisemitism are directed toward Jewish or non-Jewish individuals and/or their property, towards Jewish community institutions and religious facilities.

The composers of this definition emphasise that the detection of antisemitism should be contextual and thus they supply a long list of illustrative examples of what might be interpreted as antisemitic in particular contexts. However, the illustrative examples include and thus equate the use of traditional antisemitic stereotypes as the Jewish conspiracy to rule the world or blood libel, to claims that the state of Israel is a racist endeavour or comparing any Israeli policies to those of the Nazis, no matter the context or the basis of these claims.

The most recent controversy on the subject in the UK has been the partial adoption of this definition by the Labour Party, attempting to exclude some of the examples of antisemitism which conflated it with critique of Israel. However, at the last Labour Party conference, this struggle has been lost (at least for now) and the whole definition has been adopted.

Part of the reason that the conflict around Labour's adoption of the definition has been so controversial and so emotional is not only because of its internal inconsistencies or because it has become a tool of the right, in and out of the Labour Party. It is also because, like among Jewish feminists in 1982, constructions of subjectivities of British Jews all too often are embedded in what Jamie Hakim (2015) has called 'popular Zionism', which constructs the support of Israel as a central plank of their self-identities as Jews. So, while the definition talks about antisemitism as perceptions of people about

Jews, in actuality, it has become not less about perceptions of Jews about antisemitism – an important theoretical and political issue that needs examining and to which I shall return to towards the end of the paper.

Antisemitism and the Left

Because of the conflation of antisemitism and critiques of Israel, together with the growing global recognition, especially among the Left, concerning the nature of Zionism, the post-1967 Occupation and the Israeli state, there has been a certain bifurcation concerning attitudes to antisemitism, especially in the Left. On the one hand there are those who reject the notion that there is any real antisemitism in any section of the Left. Indeed, claims of antisemitism in the Labour Party started after it had, for the first time, a Jewish leader. Interestingly, that Jewish leader, Ed Miliband, had been the first leader of the Labour Party who 'dared' to criticise Israel and its occupation of the Palestinians. Once Jeremy Corbyn, with a long record of support for Palestinian rights, came to that leadership position, the accusations became a flood, aided and directed by those, inside and outside the Labour Party, who looked for an excuse to get rid of Corbyn by any means available. They were aided by the oiled Israeli propaganda machine (Al Jazeera, 2018).

However, it would be wrong to completely dismiss accusations of antisemitism within the Left, as the racialised constructions of Jews have a long and culturally embedded history in Europe. Because of the traditional confines of the occupations of Jews as a people-class (Léon, 1972) in Medieval Europe and in Eastern Europe till the late nineteenth century, Jews have tended to work in the pre-capitalist financial sector and then became part of the emerging capitalist class. For this reason, in addition to religious Christian demonisation, they often became the scapegoats in between the ruling classes and the peasantry. As a result, they were also constructed in parts of Marxist literature as embodiments of capitalism. Not everyone was as careful as Marx, in his writing on the 'Jewish Question' (1844), to separate Jews as individuals from the imaginary of Jews. Indeed, The German socialist leader, August Bebel, has called antisemitism – which around that time turned from a Christian-based demonology into a radical-populist trend, 'the socialism of fools' (Wistrich, 1977). Nevertheless, antisemitism, like other forms of racialisations, has survived among socialists as among other sections of society – although, because of the overall normative principles of the Left, I would argue that it survived to a lesser extent or in a more indirect unconscious way. An example of the latter is that Mear One, the artist of a famous poster for which Corbyn has been so criticised for his 2012 Facebook support (*The Guardian*, 2018), has argued that the people he based his description of capitalists on were mostly not even Jews. However, whoever they were, they were drawn in the antisemitic tradition of the Nazi *Sturmer* cartoons without the artist (or Corbyn) even being aware of this.

On the other hand, there are those on the Left, especially Jews and non-Jews from Germany or other countries, in which support for the Nazi genocide of the Jews during the Second World War has taken place, who feel that any critique of Zionism and Israel, as the legitimate embodiment and representation of the Jews as a collectivity, is indeed antisemitic. They perceive that such a critique delegitimises the Jewish right for national self-determination and a homeland as a safe haven and their own subjective identities as Jews.

This raises the thorny questions, to which I briefly relate below, of first, to what extent should we accept that Zionism and Israel are the legitimate representatives of all Jews? Secondly, how should we deal with conflicting rights, in this case of those Jews who are hurt by critiques of Israel and Zionism and the Palestinians who continue to live under colonial occupation.

Thirdly, of course, there is the question, which I raised earlier, to what extent the situated gazes and perceptions of those Jews should be the determining factor in assuming antisemitism. This links to wider issues of identity politics.

Is Israel the legitimate representative of and a safe haven to world Jewry?

At least till 1967, and definitely till 1948, only a minority of world Jewry supported the Zionist movement. The Zionist movement was also not the only manifestation of collective Jewish identity. Even if we put aside for the moment religious organisations, Zionism was not the only Jewish national liberation movement – notably there has been the Jewish Bund (Tobias, 1972), which fought to liberate the Jews in Eastern Europe as a national collectivity, but not by creating a separate Jewish state, let alone as a settler colony. Instead, they envisioned Jews as part of a socialist federation in Eastern Europe.

Unlike the Bund, the Jewish nation the Zionist movement has claimed to represent has not been the Yiddish speaking Jews of Eastern Europe but all those who saw themselves ethnically and/or religiously as Jews.

It is important to mention that until the 1967 war, let alone 1948 – the year the Israeli state was established, Zionism was a minority trend among world Jewry. However, even then, both among Jews and among non-Jews, Zionism was perceived primarily as a movement of national liberation and there has been massive support of Israel as the only democracy in the Middle East, a small but brave state that stood against and defeated the mighty armies of all the Arab states in 1948 and provided refuge for all the Jews persecuted anywhere in the world who could claim the right to 'return' to the Jewish homeland (after 2000 years) and claim immediate full citizenship. The opposition to Zionism among diasporic Jews, especially the non-socialist among them, has often been a fear that such support would construct them as disloyal to their country of citizenry. Indeed, one interpretation could state that only antisemites and Zionists argue that Jews do not belong to the societies in which they live. After 1967, the combination of the overwhelming support of Israel by Western states as well as the legitimation and normalisation of multiple identities in multicultural societies have removed this fear from most Jews' agenda.

There has been a fierce debate in the literature regarding to what extent the Jewish people constitute a nation or not (Sand, 2010). I do not think that this is a valid argument against Zionism, as virtually all nationalist movements have been constructed on a mythical original golden age and there are very few nations, if any, which are ethnically homogenous. Nor do I see as crucial the argument, which I agree with, that the construction of the Jewish nation has been inherently racist, since European Jews have used Middle Eastern and other Southern Jews as a racialised labour force to further the 'populate or perish' demand of the Zionist movement as a settler colonial project (Shohat, 1988). In most nations, ethnic stratification is part of the nation's social and political constitution.

However, there has been another argument which many diasporic anti-Zionists have held to, against the notion of Israel as the safe haven of the Jews from all over the world – a notion that has gained Israel most of its legitimation in the post-Nazi Holocaust world. The argument has been that if the role of Zionism has been to protect them against another potential holocaust and national extinction, gathering all the Jews from all over the world to one territory lessens, rather than heightens, the chance of Jewish survival. The fact that my parents survived the Holocaust, unlike the rest of their families was not because of the magic of migrating to the 'Jewish homeland'. It was because the British defeated the Germans in North Africa before they were able to occupy Palestine and murder the Jews there as they'd done in all the other territories they conquered. Moreover, given the reality of Israel as a permanent war society, the physical danger to Jews, since the end of the Second World War, has been higher in Israel than anywhere else in the world. And all this without mentioning the crucial role in keeping Israel safer that Diasporic Zionist Jews have fulfilled since the establishment of the state with their financial and political support of the state of Israel.

While for many years the Palestinians' situated gaze on Israel was virtually invisible, gradually the realities of the post-1967 occupation have made the Palestinian cause the focus of anti-colonial struggles, fulfilling a somewhat similar symbolic role as apartheid South Africa fulfilled beforehand. Gradually, also, more and more Jews have distanced themselves from Israel as their collective representation and organisations like Independent Jewish Voice, Jews for Justice for Palestinians, and others have emerged. While most of the critique has been in relation to the post-1967 reality, others in the Left have pointed out the continuity between post-1967 and the original Zionist settler project, a continuity of confiscation of Palestinian lands and establishing a society which presented itself as 'the only democracy in the Middle East' but in actuality has legally and informally discriminated against the Palestinians under its governance, including those who are Israeli citizens. There is no space here to get into an analysis of Zionism and Israel as an on-going settler colonial society (see, e.g., Abdo and Yuval-Davis, 1995; Kimmerling, 2002; Masalha, 2000; Pappe, 2007), but to equate its critique with racism against Jews is more than problematic. The conflation of antisemitism and the critique of Zionism and Israel is especially dangerous to Jews in the longer term. If a critique of occupation, discrimination, oppression, and the killing of children is antisemitism then one might think antisemitism is not such a bad thing.

The conflicting claims of rights over Palestine/Israel

A basic humanitarian argument, which I support, is that a just solution to the Palestinian/Israeli conflict should not be by a simple zero-sum game. This would be the case if the return of the Palestinian refugees would mean the transformation of the Israeli Jews into refugees, just as there was no justification to transform the Palestinians into refugees in order to settle Jewish immigrants to Palestine after the Second World War Holocaust and before that the pogroms against Jews in Eastern Europe.

Of course, there is one major difference – the Palestinians are not those who caused the Jewish misery while the Zionist Jewish settlers have caused the Palestinian misery. And yet, a transformative justice cannot just go back and 'undo' history.

Many believe that the right solution, then, is to divide Palestine/Israel into two states, Jewish and Palestinian, in the spirit of the solution first offered by the UN in 1947 and quite the different one mentioned at the Oslo agreement of 1993. However, such a solution treats the Israeli/Palestinian conflict basically as a border conflict between two national collectivities for which the main issue is where the border should pass. However, because Zionism has been a settler colonial project, such a separation is impossible except by causing new major population transfers with extreme human misery as Palestinians, who constitute about a quarter of Israel's present citizenship, are settled throughout the country. In addition, since 1967, there have been many Jewish settlements in the West Bank, many of them home to racialised and poor Israeli Jews who moved there because of the heavily subsidised housing terms.

The solution will have to come via the dismantling of Israel as a Zionist state which, as the recent Israeli nationality law just made explicit, is a state for the Jews only. Dismantling the Zionist Israeli state is not an antisemitic genocidal annihilation of the Jews, just as the dismantling of the South African apartheid state was not genocidal to White South Africans, let alone the dismantling of the UK in a case of Scottish independence would be a genocide of the British. There is an immanent difference between the regime of the state and its citizenry.

Of course, to transform Palestine/Israel into a state in which all its citizens, and even more so all the people governed by it, would become equal citizens, is a transformative project which would be neither simple nor costless. Unlike in South Africa, there has not been in Israel a major political movement which developed such a political project, although many of us have been attempting to work on this throughout the years.

Whether or not this is a realistic political project is not the focus of this article. What concerns us here is that criticising the Israeli state, the occupation atrocities or even the inherent Zionist settler colonial character of the Israeli state is not inherently antisemitic.

Antisemitism, identity politics, and socialist feminism

The American Jewish author, Nobel Laureate, and Holocaust survivor Eli Weisel wrote once (2001) that 'Jerusalem is in my heart' and therefore he has a right to claim it.

He has put his sense of identity and belonging to a country in which he has not lived before the claims of the Palestinians who are continuing to live under Israeli occupation and control. His claim is just an extreme expression of the claim of 'popular Zionists' that they feel offended and hurt if somebody criticises Israel and Zionism and therefore this should be considered as antisemitism. These sentiments were very prevalent in the recent debate on antisemitism in the Labour Party. In this way antisemitism virtually stopped being only about the 'perception of Jews', as the IHRA definition formulated it, let alone about actual discrimination, exclusion, exploitation as well as attacking and murdering Jews, but about what Jews perceive to be antisemitism.

I am a great believer in encompassing the situated gazes of all the participants in social encounters in approaching a determination of what is 'the truth' in any social encounter (e.g. Yuval-Davis, 2015; Yuval-Davis et al., 2018, 2019). However, such intersectional dialogical epistemology is very different from a relativist one, which gives ultimate validity to each situated standpoint and ignores the overall context and power relations as well as any possible validity for the other situated gazes.

I do not have space here to enter into a detailed critique of some versions of identity politics which tend to homogenise all members of a certain social category or grouping and thus collapses individual and collective constructions of identity, social categories, and social groupings. In such a context, people can come out with declarations that 'as a woman', 'as a Black', 'as a Jew', this is what they feel, this is how they define the situation. In transversal politics (Cockburn and Hunter, 1999; Yuval-Davis, 1997, 2006), which have developed as an alternative to such identity politics, activists see themselves as advocates, rather than representatives of identity groups

Not all Catholics are represented by the Pope. As a member of 'Women Against Fundamentalism' I worked closely with the feminists from 'Catholics for Free Choice' who successfully resisted the attempts of the Vatican from excluding them from the list of recognised NGOs at the UN conference in Cairo in 1994 on Population and Development.

As Jews, thankfully, we do not have any one religious or political hierarchy which claims to represent us all, except the Israeli government, of course. However, it is still the case that most of world Jewry are not the citizens of Israel and even if and when we are, we have the right to declare – as American activists have recently been declaring on placards at anti-Trump demonstrations – 'Not in My Name!'.

As socialist feminists, we have always pointed out that being socially oppressed and discriminating against others are not mutually exclusive. That the same working-class heroic men, fighting the class war at work and in the streets, can come home and beat their wives, and advertently or inadvertently have also benefited from being part of colonising and imperial nations. Elsewhere (Yuval-Davis, 2017) I have differentiated between support of all victims, whatever their politics and values, from our positionings as human rights defenders, and transversal solidarity, which is an alliance across borders and boundaries, among all of us who share the same emancipatory values.

Sadly, the victims of racisms can themselves become the perpetrators of racism. Therefore, while we should not be afraid of confronting and fighting against antisemitism and other forms of racism, we should also not be afraid of criticising the victims of racism, individually and collectively, when such a critique is due.

The overall context: the rise of contemporary right-wing antisemitism

These days, probably more than ever, it is important to differentiate between antisemitism and critique of Israel. Significantly, the most important pro-Israeli lobby in the USA is run today by antisemites – the Christian Evangelists. The usual logic which has driven many antisemitic people throughout the years – including some Nazis (Brenner, 1983) – to support Zionism and Israel, has been that if all Jews migrate to Israel, then their own society will be 'cleansed' of Jews. The Evangelists have an additional motivation – according to them Jesus will come back only after all the Jews return to the Holy Land. Then, all those Jews who would not have converted to Christianity by that time, will be annihilated (Haija, 2006).

This inherently antisemitic ideology has not prevented the state of Israel or the settlers on the West Bank from receiving huge contributions from the Evangelists, each side seeing the other as their unwitting instrument to achieve their own goals.

The fact that it is the Christian Evangelist lobby rather than the Jewish lobby which is the largest pro-Israeli lobby in the USA has come to media headline recently after the director of the ADL – the Anti-Defamation League – protested against Nigel Farage's (former leader of the extreme right UKIP party and then leader of the Brexit Party) conflation of the Jews and the pro-Israeli lobby, defining it, rightly, as constructed within the old antisemitic myth of the Jews as the puppet masters of world politics, a myth which was mostly developed by the famous forgery 'The Protocols of the Elders of Zion', which was first published by the Tsarist Russia secret police in 1903. Ironically ADL is largely responsible for the conflation of antisemitism and critique of Israel, by promoting the notion of a 'new antisemitism' throughout the years.

Nigel Farage is not the only extreme right winger who reiterates antisemitic rhetoric. At the time when there is so much focus on antisemitism in the Left, there is a rise of extreme right antisemitism in a way which has not been seen for many years. It is not the focus of this chapter to explain why this has happened. I would argue, however, that this is connected to what I've called elsewhere (Yuval-Davis, 2018) 'the double crises of governability and governmentality' under neoliberal globalisation. These crises have caused the transformation of multiculturalism as the main governance technology of controlling diversity and discourses on diversity into what we've called (e.g. Yuval-Davis et al., 2018, 2019) 'everyday bordering' accompanied and reinforced by the rise of autochthonic political movements. The focus of both these top-down governance technologies and bottom-up politics, which are dominated by senses of fear and precarity, are political projects of belonging, which aim to 'free' contemporary state and society from all those 'who do not belong' to the nation. They should not be entitled to public resources or even be allowed to live in the country.

While the main focus of these political projects is usually 'the migrants', 'refugees and asylum seekers', 'the Muslims', and 'the terrorists', gradually neo-Nazi ideologies, including antisemitism, have become more salient as well.

What is most shocking, however, is the fact that Netanyahu, the Prime Minister of Israel, in return for support of Israel, has been giving 'absolutions', in the style the Pope used to do to 'sinning' Catholic kings. He has given 'absolutions' to such extreme right heads of state as Hungary and Poland, let alone Donald Trump, the US President.

An important reminder of the difference between antisemitic discourses and critique of Israel has been the recent murderous attack on the Jewish synagogue in Pittsburgh in the USA in which 11 people died. The attacker, an extreme right-wing, white activist, a supporter of Trump, was not interested in Israel as the Jewish state or the Palestinians as its victims. On the contrary, he blamed the Jews for being responsible for bringing Muslims and other undesirables to the USA. The particular synagogue he attacked, the Tree of Life, supports refugees to settle in the USA.

Even more shocking than the attack itself, or Donald Trump's late and lukewarm condemnation of the attack, has been the response of Netanyahu who was later in his condemnation even than Trump. Notably, as the *New York Times* reported, the Israeli ambassador to the USA was the only official on site to welcome Trump's controversial visit to Pittsburgh.

Unlike his responses in similar attacks which took place in France several years ago, Netanyahu neither renounced the rise of antisemitism in the US nor reiterated his invitation to those Jews hurt by the attack to immigrate to Israel. Such radical Jews, who, following humanitarian values as well as their construction of Judaism, campaign for the rights of refugees, are those that Israel, in its recent legislation, is forbidding from even visiting Israel.

Socialist feminists should follow the popular refusal of Jews and others in Pittsburgh to reduce antisemitism and the fight against it to the support of Israel and its policies as well as its exclusionary ideological foundations. The fight against antisemitism is about the fight against all forms of racialisation and oppression.

References

Abdo, N., Yuval-Davis, N., 1995. 'Palestine, Israel and the Zionist Settler Project' in Stasiulis, D., Yuval-Davis, N. (Eds.), *Unsettling Settler Societies: Articulations of Gender, Race, Ethnicity and Class*. Sage, London, 291–322.

Al Jazeera, 2018. 'The Lobby Series'. www.aljazeera.com/investigations/thelobby/.

Back, L., Solomos, J., 2013. *Theories of Race and Racism: A Reader*. Routledge, London; New York.

Barth, F., 1998 [1969]. *Ethnic Groups and Boundaries: The Social Organization of Culture Difference*. Allen and Unwin, Bergen.

Brenner, L., 1983. *Zionism in the Age of the Dictators*. Croom Helm, London.

Casillo, R., 1988. *The Genealogy of Demons: Anti-Semitism, Fascism, and the Myths of Ezra Pound*. Northwestern University Press, Evanston, IL.

Cockburn, C., Hunter, L., 1999. 'Introduction: Transversal Politics and Translating Practices'. *Soundings* 12 (Spring): 88–93.

Goldberg, D.T., 2009. *The Threat of Race: Reflections on Racial Neoliberalism*. John Wiley & Sons, Oxford.

The Guardian, 2018. 'Corbyn in Antisemitism Row after Backing Artist Behind "Offensive" Mural'. www.theguardian.com/politics/2018/mar/23/corbyn-criticised-after-backing-artist-behind-antisemitic-mural.

Haija, R.M., 2006. 'The Armageddon Lobby: Dispensationalist Christian Zionism and the Shaping of US Policy towards Israel–Palestine'. *Holy Land Studies* 5(1): 75–95.

Hakim, J., 2015. 'Affect and Popular Zionism in the British Jewish Community after 1967'. *European Journal of Cultural Studies* 18(6): 672–689.

Hancock, A., 2011. *Solidarity Politics for Millennials: A Guide to Ending the Oppression Olympics*. Springer, Dordrecht.

IRHI, 2016. 'Definition of Antisemitism'. www.holocaustremembrance.com/working-definition-antisemitism.

Kimmerling, B., 2002. 'Jurisdiction in an Immigrant-Settler Society: The "Jewish and Democratic State"'. *Comparative Political Studies* 35(10): 1119–1144.

Klug, B., 2003. 'The Collective Jew: Israel and the New Antisemitism'. *Patterns of Prejudice* 37(2): 117–138.

Léon, A., 1972. *The Jewish Question: A Marxist Interpretation*. Pathfinder Press, New York.

Lerman, A., 2013. 'The New Antisemitism'. Paper presented at the *Anti-Jewish and Anti-Muslim Racisms and the Question of Palestine/Israel Symposium*, LSE, 17 December.

Marx, K., 1844. On the Jewish Question. www.marxists.org/archive/marx/works/1844/jewish-question/. Accessed: 24 September 2019.

Masalha, N., 2000. *Imperial Israel and the Palestinians: The Politics of Expansion*. Pluto Press, London.

Pappe, I., 2007. *The Ethnic Cleansing of Palestine*. Oneworld Publications, Oxford.

Rattansi, A., 2007. *Racism: A Very Short Introduction*. Vol. 161. Oxford University Press, Oxford.

Sand, S., 2010. *The Invention of the Jewish People*. Verso Books, London.

Shohat, E., 1988. 'Sephardim in Israel: Zionism from the Standpoint of Its Jewish Victims'. *Social Text* 19/20: 1–35.

Tobias, H.J., 1972. *The Jewish Bund in Russia from Its Origins to 1905*. Stanford University Press, Stanford, CA.

Weisel, E. 2001, 'Jerusalem in My Heart'. www.nytimes.com/2001/01/24/opinion/jerusalem-in-my-heart.html.

Wistrich, R.S., 1977. 'The SPD and Antisemitism in the 1890s'. *European Studies Review* 7(2): 177–197.

Yuval-Davis, N., 1984. 'Zionism, Antisemitism and the Struggle against Racism'. *Spare Rib* (September): 9–14.

Yuval-Davis, N., 1997, *Gender and Nation*. Sage, Los Angeles, CA.

Yuval-Davis, N., 2006. 'Human/Women's Rights and Feminist Transversal Politics' in Marx Ferree, M., Tripp, A.M. (Eds.), *Global Feminism: Transnational Women's Activism, Organizing, and Human Rights*. New York University Press, New York, 275–295.

Yuval-Davis, N. 2013. 'Antisemitism, Islamophobia or Racism? Anti-Jewish and Anti-Muslim Racisms and the Question of Palestine–Israel'. *Open Democracy*, 24 December.

Yuval-Davis, N., 2015. 'Situated Intersectionality and Social Inequality'. *Raisons politiques* 2: 91–100.

Yuval-Davis, N., 2017. 'Recognition, Intersectionality and Transversal Politics' in Rayman, P., Meital, Y. (Eds.), *Transformative Recognition: Israel/Palestine and Beyond*. Brill, Boston, MA, 157–167.

Yuval-Davis, N., 2018. 'Autochthonic Politics, Everyday Bordering and the Construction of "The Migrant"' in Fitzi, G., Mackert, J., Turner, B.S. (Eds.), *Populism and the Crisis of Democracy*. Vol. 3: *Migration, Gender and Religion*. Routledge, London, 69–77.

Yuval-Davis, N., Anthias, F., 1992. *Racialized Boundaries: Race, Nation, Gender, Colour, and Class and the Anti-Racist Struggle*. Routledge, London; New York

Yuval-Davis, N., Wemyss, G., Cassidy, K., 2018. 'Everyday Bordering, Belonging and the Reorientation of British Immigration Legislation'. *Sociology* 52(2): 228–244.

Yuval-Davis, N., Wemyss, G., Cassidy, K., 2019. *Bordering*. Polity Press, Cambridge.

PART IV

SOLIDARITIES

16 | WOMEN IN BRAZIL'S TRADE UNION MOVEMENT

Patrícia Vieira Trópia

In Brazil, since the 1980s, there has been a new approach on studies about labour, following the perception that 'the working class has got two genders' (Souza-Lobo, 1991). Since then, issues related to the intensification of women's work exploitation and the lack of pay equity, labour, and politics have been discussed. It is also evident that these issues were largely driven by the performance of women struggles within and beyond the workplace. The gender relations category has become central to understanding working relationships and, especially, to highlighting the perverse forms of domination that exist in large fields of social life. *However, the subject of the working women, feminism, and activism has been much less attractive.* Brazilian society went through deep changes in the 1990s due to the restructuring of capitalism – reorganisation of production, automation, robotics, fiscal adjustment, social spending reduction, economic opening, and privatisation of state enterprises. All those changes affect the class structure and job market with the increase in informal employment and in unemployment. Women, who traditionally were placed in low-qualified and low-paid jobs, had their working, health, and life conditions deteriorating. There has been an increased participation of women in the informal labour market, subcontracted housework, part-time and temporary work.

Since the 1980s the most progressive trade unions in Brazil have been trying to attract women. In 1986 the creation of the National Commission for the Issues of Working Women within the largest Brazilian federation – the Central Workers Union – is an example of this change. Although in the 1990s unemployment reduced the number of unionised members, the trade unions, trying to reverse this decrease, began to attract and stimulate female membership by implementing quotas policies with regard to their board compositions. Since the Labour Party obtained state power, some progress has happened. For example, after the parliamentary dispute in 2015 household workers obtained the legalisation of some rights. The objective of this chapter is to present the main struggles, forms of action, and claims of Brazilian activist women in the trade union movement.

Introduction

During the 1990s, civil society activism grew across Latin America, particularly in Brazil. There are several reasons that explain the origin of social movement's activism. It is possible to identify, however, neoliberalism as a common origin to all of them (Galvão, 2008). The activism of social movements resulted, fundamentally, from the recognition that neoliberal capitalism – which guarantees the interests of financial capital – had produced adverse effects in popular sectors and for the middle class. These movements are encouraged by: economic demands (for better wages, in defence of employment, against unemployment); political demands (in defence of citizen's rights); and social demands (youth movements for public transport politics, for instance).

This struggle is against economic oppression. It was increased by regressive neoliberal policies, the withdrawal of rights, and social oppression, as well as provoked by the maintenance of ethnic and gender inequalities, that flourish in the scenario of income concentration.

In Brazil, many social movements have emerged with those characteristics over the last three decades, such as the Factory Occupation Movement, the Homeless Movement (Movimento dos Trabalhadores Sem Teto – MTST), the Affected by the Dams Movement (Movimento dos Afetados por Barragens – MAB), the Agriculture Producers Movement (Movimento dos Produtores Agrícolas – MAP), the Unemployed Movement, the Peasant Women Movement (Mulheres da Via Campesina) and the Landless Workers Movement (Movimento dos Trabalhadores Rurais Sem Terra – MST).

Particularly in the 1990s, the social contradictions, which exist historically in Brazil, became more visible. One of its effects was the increase of women's activism in social movements, both in the countryside and in the cities, in reaction to the humiliating precarisation of work, and resulting in the search for an alternative to overcome it.

The objectives of this chapter are (1) to analyse women's performance in Brazilian trade unionism since the 80s; (2) to present Brazilian activist women's main struggles, forms of action and claims in the trade union movement; and, finally, (3) to indicate some structural and ideological limits of 'trade union feminism' in Brazil.

Women's performance in Brazilian trade unions: 'the new unionism'

The considerable participation of women in trade unionism is a growing phenomenon in Brazil. Between 1998 and 2006, the participation of women in the labour market in Brazil grew 37 per cent. Nevertheless, in the same period, the number of women workers affiliated to some unions grew 69 per cent. In 1998, women represented 35 per cent of all workers (formal and informal) associated to some unions. In 2006, women corresponded to 40 per cent. In 2006, women were an absolute majority in the following economic sectors: domestic work (90%), education (74%), health and social security (79%), textile and clothing (56%), and the financial system (52%). However, in domestic employment the number of affiliated members was only 2 per cent, and in education, the financial system, textile and clothing industry around one-third of the women were affiliated (Central Única dos Trabalhadores – CUT, 2008).

However, on average, women earn 30 per cent less than men.

The position of women on the union boards have also shown improvements: although in 2001 35.5 per cent of the unions had no women on their boards, 35 per cent of the unions had up to 25 per cent women on their boards, and 29.4 per cent of unions had more than 25 per cent women on their boards.

Women's path in Brazilian trade unionism is similar to that experienced by the female workers and trade union activists in other countries, such as France, England, Italy. These countries have seen an increase of trade union activism among women since the 1960s due to the massive access to the labour market and the development of feminist struggles in contexts of radical movements like in May 1968 in France (Beroud, 2016) or Italy's 'Hot Autumn' of 1969 (Frisone, 2016).

In Brazil, until the 1980s, most of the studies on the labour movement ignored women's presence, relegating them to marginal positions both in the establishment of the working class (Souza-Lobo, 1991) and in the trade union movement (Neves, 1992).

Women were, in fact, more invisible than absent.[1]

This perspective began to change when the composition of the labour market was modified and 'new characters walk[ed] onto the stage' (Sader, 1995: 5), including the 'new trade unionism', a trade union trend that was active in rights' claiming, and responsible for the biggest strike wave globally at the end of the 1980s. In the 1970s, women's struggle arose, guided by the belief that union action directed towards the working class should consider not only productive relations but also reproductive ones.[2]

Beyond the feminist movement, women's participation was meaningful in the occupations of urban areas – a fight for land – in local communities and in movements for health and transport improvement (Souza-Lobo, 1991). According to Sader (1995), women in the 1970s, with the support of the progressive Catholic Church started to organise and fight for political autonomy and particularly by creating nurseries in poor neighbourhoods, an essential condition for their economic independence. Finally, women (mothers, daughters, grandmothers), many of them left-wing activists during the military regime (Merlindo and Ojeda, 2010), started a campaign in favour of political amnesty, organised by the Feminine Movement for Amnesty and, later, the Brazilian Committee for Amnesty.

If, in the 1970s, women accounted for 18.5 per cent of the economically active population (EAP), in the late 1980s they corresponded to 35.5 per cent of all workers. In ten years, female employment in industrial activities had grown 181 per cent (10.9 per cent per year), at a higher rate than traditional female working sectors like services provision and social activities (especially education) (Humphrey, 1983). Women's work spread among other industrial branches and large contingents of women joined the metal-mechanical industry, exactly to develop activities in production itself.

Women would become, however, a distinguished segment of the working class. The burden of overloaded domestic responsibilities (home, children, parents, siblings) weighed heavily on the female workforce, underscored by the prevailing conception that women's social role is the reproduction of life.

The wage level for women was much lower even in equivalent occupations; it was evident that a concentration of women was in unskilled or semi-skilled jobs and women were subjected to patriarchal capital power. That is to say, the nature of exploitation and forms of oppression in employment were strongly conditioned by obligations of women in relation to reproduction. According to Neves (2006: 257), women's access to industrial work occurred in the form of 'excluded insertion', because they occupied the less qualified functions and had less opportunity to occupational mobility.

Research that emerged in the 1970s in Brazil had the merit to denounce 'that the female presence in the unions was practically non-existent' (Neves, 1992: 136). Souza-Lobo (1991) objected to the current use of the masculine in the analysis on the working class, which spoke of male workers when actually referring to female workers. Strictly, it was about stating that the practices, representations, and conditions of work, employment, and unemployment of female workers were not equal to the male workers and that, therefore, the class relations would be sexed (Hirata and Kergoat, 1994, 2007).

Women's inclusion in industrial employment, especially in large metallurgical enterprises of São Bernardo do Campo in the 1970s and 1980s, helps us understand the first trade union initiatives they had.

In the late 1970s, women's rights activism appeared in a more organised way at the 1st Congress of Metallurgical Female Workers in São Bernardo, when mobilised female workers discussed the government proposal to abolish night work, claimed for nurseries in the workplace, denounced the harassment of managers, and argued against wage inequality (Souza-Lobo, 1991). The organisational and participative experience of women working in metallurgy spread to other trade unions, industrial sectors, and regions, and it embodied a grassroots nature in a wider movement, and at the same time, introduced a heterogeneity of views on political democratisation. There was, also, the multiplication of 'mothers clubs, community associations with significant women participation, nursery campaigns, the fight against wage and professional differentiations, and the complaint of a double working day and violence against women' (Neves, 1992: 137).[3]

Research shows that in the mobilisation of women activists constant references were made to 'feminist movements' as well as to the Catholic Church, which, under the influence of Liberation Theology, played a unique role by stimulating the debate on liberation from oppressive relations and collective and 'autonomist' participation (Sader, 1995: 202).

The contact between the CUT women's movement with feminist organisations, especially academic ones, would have been 'essential' to the female trade union activists to start reflection on their condition and fight for their rights.

However, this relationship between academic feminism and feminist workers is not without conflicts. It means that (1) a proportion of workers and lower-class housewives (some of them with a traditional Catholic background) were resistant to some of the questions brought up particularly by academic feminists (such as abortion, contraception, sexuality, etc.); (2) the superior attitude of some academic feminists gave them the reputation of 'the owners of the truth' among women who took part in grassroots organisations (Araújo and Ferreira, 1998).

The workers began to claim greater participation in trade unions through the creation of Women's Departments (Souza-Lobo, 1991), which had the function of bringing into union organisations debates on prejudice in the labour market, gender inequalities, and the need to expand women's participation in factories and in the board of directors (Cappellin, 1994; Araújo and Ferreira, 1998).

In general, research indicated that the trade unions had a crucial role in the confrontation of the different forms of exploitation and oppression in the factories, although the wide range of claims, expressed by women in conferences or within their struggles, were reduced to the maternity subject (Souza-Lobo, 1991).

Some research argues that women, precisely because they have been under-represented in traditional trade unions, especially in leadership positions, could be the source of trade union renewal (Kirton and Healy, 2003; Briskin, 2006).

New unionism is a trend of Brazilian unionism, which emerged in the late 1970s, declaring itself class-oriented, autonomous from political parties, and independent of the state. It proposed to take the lead in the defence of eliminating the exploitation of labour by capital and the real possibility of construction of a new society. The result of the unions' action guided by the 'new unionism' was an increase in the wave of strikes, wage levels, and the crises of the military regime. During this process the women's role – strictly involved in the strikes or in solidarity with strikers – was visible.

Women's performance on the unionist agenda in the 1980s and 1990s

During the 1980s and the early 1990s, there was an increase in the debate on gender relations, including broader demands on behalf of working women on the unionist agenda, as well as an opening for these women in the decision making on union boards (Araújo and Ferreira, 1998; Ferreira, 2005; Nogueira, 2011; Delgado, 1996).

Among the main outcomes, the most important was the creation, in 1986, of the National Commission for the Issues of Working Women (CNMT) and many Women Committees in the unions affiliated to the Central Workers Union (CUT) (Delgado, 1996). In 2003, women created the National Office for the Issues of Working Women in CUT (SNMT/CUT).

In the 1990s the debates over positive actions in CUT become more significant, resulting in the adoption in 1994 of a quota system through which unions were forced to appoint women in at least 30 per cent of union leadership positions. Since 2015, at least 50 per cent of union leadership positions were going to be filled by women.

An important change in relation to the 1970s was the debate about abortion. In 1991, women from CUT approved the campaign against criminalisation of abortion, because in Brazil the practice of abortion is a crime. Women from CUT assume that the criminalisation of abortion also reflects a class inequality considering that the majority of women who die from unsafe abortions are poor, black, peasant, housewives and favela residents.

However, if feminism 'arrives at the shop floor' and it is re-appropriated by a growing number of women trade union activists, the CUT still remains resistant to the insertion of policy on decriminalising abortion among their main battle flags and claims.

Under what circumstances did these changes happen in the 1990s?

In the 1990s, Brazil began suffering the effects of capital restructuring, such as the demands to increase productivity and international competition, as well as the development of public transport systems and information circulation, all of which impacted both the industrial and the financial sectors. During this period there was significant investment in technological innovations and new ways of organising production, particularly in the role of the third sector and an increase in the geographic mobility of businesses.

Apart from all those changes, the implementation of neoliberal policies impacted working conditions and the market, which therefore had an effect on: increases in unemployment, outsourcing, and informalised labour; decreases in wages; the reduction of rights; and the introduction of new working relations such as temporary working contracts, temporary breaks in contracts, and the third sector (Pochmann, 2004; Harvey, 1992, 2004; Leite, 2009).

The impact of these changes was distinct for men and women in the three different economic sectors. Among bank clerks there was an increase in female participation in total employment and an expansion in promotions to management positions, yet this expansion occurred in professions such as telemarketing, attendants, and typists, whose contracts were predominantly outsourced and therefore precarious (Segnini, 2000).

Regarding the chemical and metallurgical industries, although there have been major changes in quantitative terms, unemployment and outsourcing intensified the differences between men and women. They were often out of reach of regulatory mechanisms of labour relations. Furthermore, they experienced a reduction of their wages, as well as a deterioration in employment relations and working conditions.

For the chemical and metallurgical industries, the integration of women occurred in small and medium-sized businesses as well as in repetitive, routinised occupations (assembly, quality inspection, and packaging). They are often subject to the control of managers and have the lowest wages (Ferreira, 2010).

This scenario was reflected in the trade union struggle, leading trade unions in Brazil to a defensive position. The temporary or permanent loss of jobs that impacts the number of affiliates leads unions to review their practices as they seek to attract new segments to their bases, including the women sector.

On one hand, the advancement of women's participation in the unions is real as far as it broadens the specific demands of workers in CUT's discussions. But on the other, the recession and unemployment forced the leadership to take a propositional unionist stand, in which it is necessary to be flexible, pushing women's claims and demands into the background.

According to Ferreira (2010), women's demands included: strategies to prevent RSI (repetitive strain injury); health support for workers who have already developed RSI; mechanisms to prevent wage inequity; as well as access to professional development, training, and better work positions. Furthermore, they also demanded an improvement in the quantity and quality of women's participation in the daily working of the unions, particularly in regard to leadership positions.

Moreover, in concrete terms, trade unions had to face the recession to fight neoliberal ideology and unemployment, thus prioritising the fight for the preservation of employment and labour rights that were threatened, and thereby undermining the implementation of women's specific resolutions and proposals. The collective agreements of the period prioritised economic issues, particularly related to job retention and the replacement of wage losses. Social causes concerning working conditions, safety, labour relations, and benefits were also slightly enlarged (Araújo et al., 2001).

Employers eventually refused their requests regarding RSI, sexual harassment, and the expansion of child-care rights although trade unions have tried to negotiate them. Consequently, these issues did not become part of collective agreement clauses.

The National Women Treasury Office at CUT and the Women's committee for banks, chemicals, and metalworkers trade unions were active in denouncing prejudice, sexual violence against women inside and outside work, as well as in the struggle to expand women's rights, such as the extension of maternity leave, child-care assistance, and stability during the gestation period.

Women's performance at the unionist agenda in the 2000s: advances and limits

In the 2000s, since the Labour Party came to power, there was a reconfiguration in class structure. Firstly, the Labour Party encouraged measures of a neoliberal nature, guaranteeing the interests of international financial capital. However, economic policy changed during the second mandate of Lula's government. Some developmental measures aimed to encourage and support industrial capital and agribusiness.

Some political actions implemented by the Lula and Dilma Rousseff governments have impacted positively on the poorest sectors and historically excluded population – the Growth Acceleration Plan; growth of Gross Domestic Product (GDP); increases in income, minimum wage, and formal employment; expansion and diversification of external trade policy; protectionist industrial policy, especially during the crisis of 2008–2009; changes in educational policy (REUNI) and on science and technology policy.[4] As a result of the adoption of credit enlargement policies, minimum wage recovery, confrontation of informality, and income transfer programmes – such as the Bolsa Família Program – a change in the level of popular consumption and social reproduction of the poorest families has taken place, including that such programmes are articulated to the health and education systems. Although class inequality in Brazil has not been affected, two labour market indicators help us to understand the action of activist women in this context: the formalisation of the labour market and the increase in the minimum wage.

Within the debates around the formalisation of the labour market and the confrontation of class, race, and gender inequalities, discussions around the domestic job market in Brazil have been growing. In fact, in 2008, the process on the PEC of domestic workers began. PEC is a Project of Constitutional Amendment that aims to ensure equality of treatment between domestic workers and other workers in Brazil.

In 1992, only 16.5 per cent of female domestic workers had a registered job, while in 2006 the percentage of registered work rose to 26.3 per cent. Only one in every four domestic workers had a formal employment contract. In this sector, women constitute 80 per cent of workers, but only 2 per cent are affiliated to trade unions.

The campaign for the regulation of domestic work was headed by feminist women in the National Congress and the National Federation of the Household Workers (CUT). After a dispute, in 2015, the household workers obtained the legalisation of rights. The legalisation of rights did not come without conflict. Indeed, there was a conservative reaction from large sectors of middle class of Brazilian society.

The rise to power of the Workers Party produced, in turn, resistances and ruptures in trade unionism.

Outraged with the performance of CUT's leadership regarding the social security reform and labour reform proposed by Lula's government, several unions, especially public servant unions, decided to leave CUT. Social security reform, approved in December 2003, changed some of the rights of public servants, establishing higher earning limits and ceasing the right to receive the same income as non-retired workers. This Social Security Reform especially affected traditional professions occupied by women such as teachers and nurses. During this government, women were most affected by the rise of outsourcing.

Shortly afterwards, these dissidents created the National Coordination of Struggles (CSP-Conlutas), a *sui generis* organisation that aggregates and represents both the unionist and social movements around an anti-neoliberal and socialist project, including formal and informal workers, rural and urban unemployed, students, urban movements, opposition trade unions, unionist leadership minorities.

The CSP-Conlutas, a 'far left' union federation on the syndicalist spectrum, has attracted, more and more, women from the trade union movement and from social movements.

During the First Congress of Conlutas, in 2008, 35 per cent of the delegates were women (Trópia et al., 2013). In 2015, women constituted 40 per cent and in 2017, 39.7 per cent of delegates.

An interesting fact about the profile of these women is their marital status: 55 per cent of them were not married. Developed with union activists, my research shows that, while activist men are mostly married, activist women are usually single because marital obligations tend to hamper the political involvement of Brazilian women in unionism (Carvalho and Trópia, 2014; Trópia et al., 2013). Most women were in the age group 31–68 years old, although it should be highlighted that 32 per cent of them were 15–24 years old. The educational level is relatively high: 70 per cent were graduates or post-graduates.

An important aspect of the occupational status of women surveyed is that the majority was inserted into the formal labour market (57.6%), especially in the public sector (36.8%), and urban private sector (16%), while 24.8% of them were students.

The economic sectors where women took part were: education (32.8%), processing industry (4.8%), services (4.8%), and health (2.4%). Within the education sector, teaching was the most widespread profession. The contractual situation is mostly stable. The average income, in 2017, among women is approximately 560 euros/month.

The ideological political profile of these women is an important factor in understanding their pivotal role in left-wing trade unionism. Among these women, 58 per cent were affiliated to a political party, of which the Unified

Socialist Workers (PSTU) was the most favoured. An interesting aspect is that when asked about their voting in the first round of presidential elections in 2006, the majority claimed to have supported the only female candidate, former Senator Heloisa Helena (PSTU), who was eventually defeated by Lula from the Partido dos Trabalhadores (PT).

The majority of women surveyed had previous political experience, such as attending union meetings and student congresses. Among women who represented the union movement in the Conlutas' Congress, 38 per cent took part in union leadership and 40 per cent in union opposition. This reveals that Conlutas' women are very active in the way they engage with the unionist movement.

CSP-Conlutas created a Women Working Group in 2004, with the aim of organising the struggle of women against all forms of oppression. The main objective was 'to provide impetus for discussion, to propose policies and actions that emphasise the central intervention of the women fight and its claims, in order to contribute to the process of organising their fights' (Souza, 2016: 81–82).

In 2008, this group created the Fighting Women's Movement, aiming to spread the feminist agenda inside Conlutas and to politicise the struggle at the base of the unions and popular organisations (Carvalho and Trópia, 2014). The claims of the Fighting Women's Movement are: general wages increase – Equal Pay for Equal Work!; guarantee of full care for pregnant women in prenatal and childbirth stages; maternity leave of six months – but looking to extend that to one year – for all female workers and students, without granting tax exemptions for companies; recognition of the certificate of accompanying children as a child benefit; full-time, free, and high-quality day care for all children of the working class; birth control to avoid abortion; legal, secure, and free abortion to avoid death!; immediate revocation of Medida Provisória 557/2011, which criminalises women; women's autonomy over their own body; against the requirement to obtain consent from husbands in order to perform sterilisation; the end of violence against women; implementation and expansion of the Maria da Penha Law; punishment of attackers; construction of refuges; racial quotas in universities; criminalisation of homophobia; the end of outsourcing that affects mainly women; in defence of public welfare and women in retirement.

Although the Fighting Women's Movement is a movement inside a left Federation Union, with a socialist programme, under the influence of Marxist and Trotskyist ideas, our research shows that the dissemination of the feminist agenda among affiliated unions does not always happen. The female activists of the Fighting Women's Movement have faced many difficulties in attempting to discuss, present, and spread their ideas and claims among unions.

Conclusion

In relation to female participation in trade union daily activism and in leadership positions, it is legitimate to ask: which obstacles have blocked women from engaging in greater activism in the trade union movement. Madeleine Guilbert (1966) states that three obstacles hinder women's unionisation and activism:

1. the use of female work was controversial and undervalued – used by capital as a strategy to reduce the cost of labour in general and to compete with men's work;
2. the position occupied by women in the labour market – low-skilled jobs, precarious jobs in small businesses are structural limits to activism because it requires a more stable insertion;
3. the deep inequality in the division of domestic work between men and women.

We add the following obstacles to women's activism in trade union movement.

The lack of value of domestic work (work at home, child care etc.) enhances the difficulties that activist women have when taking on trade union or political tasks, in addition to the triple shift (paid work + domestic work + activism) (Afshar and Barrientos, 1999).

The idea that a 'union is no place for women' promotes mistrust of female workers in the union, which results in their enclosure in the domestic space (Araújo and Ferreira, 1998: 56–67).

The claims of women are often seen as secondary or even diversionist; the unions hardly organise themselves to guarantee material conditions for the development of activist women's work (Delgado, 1998), remaining still a sexist culture.

A dominant view in several unions on the far left is that specific women's claims 'would break the unity of the class'.

An important aspect of trade union female activists is that most were politically formed by the progressive sectors of the Catholic Church and less under the influence of libertarian and communist ideas.

In conclusion, it has been noted that women are organising themselves within the trade union movements. This struggle is not carried on without contradictions because, beyond the conflict against capital (land, industrial, commercial, or financial), women face the domination of patriarchy in capitalist society.

Finally, feminist activism will be central to face the rule of the ultra-conservative president Jair Bolsonaro, who in his speeches naturalises wage inequalities between women and men and makes apologies for rape. In economic and social terms, his government will deepen social inequalities, putting on hold many feminist achievements.

Notes

1 In the early 2000, Bernardes (2007) published a book about women and their 'invisibility in the politics'. She discovered that the first female affiliated to the Communist Party in Brazil was Rose Bittencourt who for 'seven years worked in a factory lines in Petropolis, Rio de Janeiro' (Benardes, 2007: 134). She became a combative union leader, taking part in the struggles of the Workers' Peasants Bloc (BOC). In 1930, Rose was delegated to the World Women's Congress in the Soviet Union, where she represented the Brazilian working women.

2 The range of new unionism embraces, beyond the retaking of strike action, the huge growth of middle-wage workers and services sector trade unionism, the advancement of rural trade unionism, the rise of the trade union federations, attempts to consolidate the organisation of workers in factories, increases in the unionisation rates.

3 According to Souza-Lobo, until the 1980s, women's movements remained on the fringe of every form of institutionalisation. Only since 1982 have organisations specifically for women been created, such as the Feminine Condition Council in São Paulo, the National Council on Women's Rights, other Women Condition Councils, and the first commissions of women in trade unions and political parties.

4 I thank FAPEMIG for supporting the research 'Middle Class and Politics in Dilma Rousseff's Government (2011-2014)'.

Bibliography

Afshar, H., Barrientos, S. 1999. 'Introduction' in Afshar, H., Barrientos, S. (Eds.), *Women, Globalization and Fragmentation in the Developing World*. Macmillan, London, 1–17.

Araújo, A.M.C., Ferreira, V.C., 1998. 'Construindo um espaço: a participação das mulheres no movimento sindical (1978–1988)'. *Revista de Sociologia e Política* (Curitiba) 10/11: 55–81.

Araújo, A.M.C., Cartoni, D., Justo, C.R.M., 2001. 'Reestruturação produtiva e negociação coletiva: a experiência recente dos sindicatos dos metalúrgicos, dos químicos e dos bancários de Campinas'. *Revista Brasileira de Ciências Sociais* 16(45) (February): 85–112.

Bernardes, M.E., 2007. *Laura Brandão: a invisibilidade feminina na política*. Centro de Memória da Unicamp, Campinas.

Beroud, S., 2016. 'Trabajo y gênero: perspectivas de investigación sobre los sindicatos en Francia' in Trópia, Patrícia Vieira et al. (Eds.), *Mulheres trabalhadoras (in) visíveis*. Fino Traço, Belo Horizonte, 65–78.

Briskin, L., 2006. 'Victimisation and Agency: The Social Construction of Women Union Leadership'. *Industrial Relations Journal* 37(4): 359–378.

Cappellin, P., 1994. 'Viver o Sindicalismo no Feminino'. *Estudos Feministas* (Rio de Janeiro) 2(1): 271–290.

Carvalho, P.d.S., Trópia, P.V., 2014. 'Mulheres militantes da Conlutas: construindo o feminismo de esquerda e classista'. Anais do V Seminário Trabalho e Gênero, November.

Central Única dos trabalhadores (CUT), 2008. *Igualdade é o máximo, cota é o mínimo – as mulheres no mundo sindical*. São Paulo.

Delgado, M.B.G., 1996. *A Organização das Mulheres Na Central Única dos Trabalhadores – A Comissão Nacional sobre a Mulher Trabalhadora*. Master's dissertation, PUC - São Paulo.

Delgado, M.B.G., 1998. 'Mulheres na CUT: um novo olhar sobre o sindicalismo' in Borba, Ângela, Faria, Nalu, Godinho, Tatau (Eds.), *Mulher e política; gênero e feminismo no Partido dos Trabalhadores*. Fundação Perseu Abramo, São Paulo, 209–224.

Ferreira, V., 2005. 'Sindicatos: espaços para a atuação das mulheres? Um estudo sobre a participação das mulheres em sindicatos filiados à Central Única dos Trabalhadores num cenário de reestruturação produtiva (1986–1999)'. Master's dissertation, IFCH- UNICAMP, Campinas.

Ferreira, V., 2010. 'Gênero, sindicalismo e poder nos anos 90: Analisando os impasses da participação das mulheres em sindicatos filiados à Central Única dos Trabalhadores num cenário de reestruturação produtiva'. *Anais do VII seminário do trabalho*, Unesp, Marília – SP.

Frisone, A., 2016. 'Gendering the Class Struggle: Trade Union Feminism in Italy in the 1970s' in Marín Corbera, Martí, Domènech Sampere, Xavier, Martínez i Muntada, Ricard (Eds.), *III International Conference Strikes and Social Conflicts: Combined Historical Approaches to Conflict*. CEFID-UAB, Barcelona, 826–838.

Galvão, A., 2008. 'Os movimentos sociais na América Latina em questão'. *Revista Debates* (Porto Alegre) 2(2) (July–December): 8–24.

Guilbert, M., 1966. *Les femmes dans l'organisation syndicale avant la guerre de 1914*. Editions du CNRS, Paris.

Harvey, D., 1992. *A condição pós-moderna*. Edições Loyola, São Paulo.

Harvey, D., 2004. *O novo imperialismo*. Edições Loyola, São Paulo.

Hirata, H., Kergoat, D., 1994. 'A classe operária tem dois sexos'. *Revista Estudos Feministas* 2(1): 93–100.

Hirata, H., Kergoat, D., 2007. 'Novas configurações da divisão sexual do trabalho'. *Cadernos de Pesquisa* 37(132): 595–609.

Humphrey, J., 1983. 'Sindicato um mundo masculino'. *Novos Estudos CEBRAP* 1. São Paulo, April.

Kirton, G., Healy, G., 2003. 'Transforming Union Women: The Role of Women Trade Union Officials in Union Renewal'. *Industrial Relations Journal* 30(1): 31–45.

Leite, M.d.P., 2009. 'O trabalho no Brasil dos anos 2000: duas faces de um mesmo processo'. Paper presented at the workshop 'A informalidade revisitada', ABET/UFCG/Fundação Joaquim Nabuco, Recife, December.

Merlindo, T., Ojeda, I. (Eds.), 2010. *Direito à memória e à verdade: Luta, substantivo feminino*. Editora Caros Amigos, São Paulo.

Neves, M.d.A., 1992. *Relações de gênero e sindicalismo*. Meeting of ABEP, Unicamp. www.abep.org.br/~abeporgb/publicacoes/index.php/anais/article/download/589/569. Accessed: 10 April 2015.

Neves, M.d.A., 2006. 'Trabalho e gênero: permanências e desafios'. *Sociedade e Cultura* 9(2): 257–265.

Nogueira, C., 2011. 'Anotações sobre a auto-organização das mulheres da Via Campesina no Brasil e do MST'. *Revista Pegada* 12(1): 34–41.

Pochmann, M., 2004. *Reestruturação produtiva. Perspectivas de desenvolvimento local com inclusão social*. Vozes, São Paulo.

Sader, E., 1995. *Quando novos personagens entram em cena*. Paz e Terra, Rio de Janeiro.

Segnini, L., 2000. 'Desemprego, terceirização e intensificação do trabalho nos bancos brasileiros' in Rocha, I.B. (Ed.), *Trabalho e gênero: mudanças, permanências e desafios*. Editora 34, São Paulo, 187–210.

Souza, A.P., 2016. *As mulheres e o feminismo no movimento sindical: um estudo das experiências do ANDES-SN*. Master's dissertation, Federal University of Juiz de Fora.

Souza-Lobo, E., 1991. *A classe operária tem dois sexos*. Brasiliense, São Paulo.

Trópia, P.V., Galvão, A., Marcelino, P., 2013. 'A Reconfiguração do Sindicalismo Brasileiro nos anos 2000: as bases sociais e o perfil político-ideológico da Conlutas'. *Opinião Pública* 19(1): 81–117.

17 | ARGENTINEAN FEMINIST MOVEMENTS

Debates from praxis

Ana Isabel González Montes

Introduction

This text is the product of the fruitful dialogue with a number of feminist activists and scholars. My first point of departure is that it is necessary to get to know each other, in order to build bridges between feminists in the Global North and the Global South in such a troubled world. Like most feminists in Argentina, I am convinced that feminists around the world should unite to stand up against predatory capitalism. This article analyses the historical development of feminism in Argentina and intends to characterise our society in order to find the keys to meeting the challenges identified by feminist struggles today (for further reading see Cieza, 2010; Trinchero, 2000).

History shows how many times transgressive practices, even without the benefit of feminist theory, have driven significant advances in women's social and political status. Today, new practices and theoretical developments emerging from the feminist tradition converge with those transgressive practices, like a sort of genealogy, enriching the analysis and promoting new paths. Mass mobilisation in the demand for autonomy and equality progressively assumes a feminist identity that questions patriarchy, racism, and capitalism and recovers our historical roots, even those that are most contradictory and conflictive.

The framework gives an overview, in a critical and unorthodox way, of the contributions of Marxist historical materialism and the formation of social classes in shaping the Argentinean state, and uses concepts inspired by the Gramscian tradition, such as hegemony, the construction of common sense, or the concept of the historical bloc to account for class alliances at different historical moments and praxis as an axis of historical development.

This work is structured in three sections: historical background; then a short description of feminist struggles today, focusing on consensus and differences; concluding with some suggestions of specific problems for dialogue between feminists in the Global North and the Global South.

Recovering our historical genealogies

As Latin American feminists, we believe that, just as we use self-reflection as a methodology to scrutinise the 'glass ceiling' imposed on us by our gender socialisation within capitalist patriarchy, we must also be able to provide self-critical analyses of our own history as a country and region, the setting in which our feminist practice is developing.

Just as to shoot an arrow it is necessary to pull the bowstring back, as Argentinean feminists we are reviewing our own history and reclaiming that of the women who preceded us in the struggle for freedom and equality. There is a saying, "When you do not know where you are going, look where you come from'. This search for genealogies is inspired by an intersectional perspective on the conceptualisation of women, their experiences and numerous struggles.

The construction of the Argentinean nation-state

Argentina, as a modern nation-state, was consolidated into such at the end of the nineteenth century on the basis of what a number of scholars conceptualise as 'the republican genocide'. Until 1862, two-thirds of the territory were controlled by Indigenous Peoples. Internal civil wars took place between the landowning sectors of Buenos Aires, allied to British imperialism,[1] and the *caudillos* (leaders) of the province.

Thus, Argentina was integrated into the international context as a primary agro-exporter. During this period, its landowning oligarchy allied with British and French capitalists, to whom they donated land and also the labour of Indigenous and *gauchos and mestizos* (children from marriages between Spanish and Indigenous) labour, who worked in conditions of semi-slavery.[2] Argentina also began exporting wool from Patagonia to supply the looms of England's textile industries.[3]

Indigenous youths were captured and sent to work in the sugar mills, the *caciques* (Indigenous leaders) and elders were imprisoned, and women and children were reduced to working in the households of rich families. Of course, as always with the subjugation of peoples, sexual violation and sexual slavery of women was the norm as well as stealing Indigenous children.

Argentina's external debt began and, along with it, economic dependency. Argentina became a country of the periphery, and this led its dominant classes to become minor partners of the central countries' capitalist classes.

Argentine capitalist development shows two historical trends: one on the basis of urban paid labour relations in production; its workers were mainly, but not only, European migrants. The other is based on an overexploited labour force, comprising mostly the Indigenous People and their *mestizo* (combined European and Native American) descendants, especially with regard to the rural and extractive industries. We hold this to be the model of postcolonial capitalist development: modern capitalism develops on the basis of a servile and overexploited labour force and the plundering of natural resources in peripheral countries, and continues doing so.[4] An analysis of the development of capitalism in the central countries and the class struggle would be incomplete and misleading if it failed to take into account the relationship of these issues with the peripheral countries' domination and colonialism.

In the 1880s, a republican state of oligarchic landowning character was consolidated via the Junkers (members of the Prussian landed nobility). They rewrote the history of Argentina, denying the existence of Indigenous Peoples, and stating that 'Argentines descended by ship'.[5] Since then, the hegemonic collective imaginary, shared by all social classes, is that Argentines are white and more European than the rest of Latin Americans. This negationism built a strong racist matrix of the whole society, keeping in line with the Eurocentric frames. Everything that comes from Europe is understood as good; everything native is vile. There were important mechanisms to cement this collective imagination: the schools, the mandatory military service, and the media, among others. A paradigmatic example is the newspaper *La Nación*, which was founded by Bartolomé Mitre in 1870 and which today continues to be the leading conservative daily paper. General Mitre was president of the nation and ideologue of the War of the Triple Alliance. In 1976 *La Nación* and its main competitor, the centrist *Diario Clarín*, in alliance with the military dictators took over the company *Papel Prensa* (the largest supplier of newsprint in Argentina), kidnapping and torturing several members of the Graiver family.[6] With this crime against humanity they planned to build a monopoly in order to control freedom of expression.[7]

The first feminists

Between 1890 and 1930 there was a large migration from the poorest European areas (Italy, Spain, Poland, etc.) to Argentina, to settle in what we know as the '*pampa gringa*', mainly in urban areas. This population's access to land was very limited. However, it was to experience upward social mobility, and soon would enjoy access to public universities.

It was in this period, at the beginning of the twentieth century, that the first movements and organisations of women who identified as feminists appeared. These groups were driven by educated women, mostly doctors or educators, usually migrants of European origin and socialists, and developed in cities such as Buenos Aires, Rosario, or Cordoba.[8] In 1910 the First International Feminist Congress, summoned by the Association of University Women, took place in Buenos Aires.

Some socialist doctors, such as Alicia Moreau de Justo, whose father had participated in the Paris Commune, were concerned about the health, in particular with regard to venereal disease, of women who worked as prostitutes. Communist and anarchist women were also organised and played a strong social and political role, through their demands for better working and living conditions. For example, the anarchists led the 'strikes of the *conventillos* [urban tenements]', for better housing.

The central themes of these first feminists' agendas were the situation of women in education, and their civil and political rights, most specifically women's suffrage. A very important achievement of this period was the reform of the Civil Code in 1926 (Law 11.357 Women Civil Right). Until that reform, women's legal status had been on the same footing as that of the Indigenous population and the mentally disabled, categories that were considered minor. However, these significant milestones were enjoyed mainly by urban middle-class women; they did not reach most of the countryside, especially Indigenous and poor rural women.

There were clear differences among women, where racist hierarchies separated them, even among women in the poorest strata of the working classes. Eurocentric and racist thought prevailed even inside leftist political parties.[9] Indigenous and black women had fought against Spanish colonialist domination in South America in the eighteenth and nineteenth centuries, but this fact was erased from history and forgotten until recently.[10]

When women won their public space

Industrial development took place in the 1940s and 1950s, as part of a process of import substitution and national industrialisation, in the period of the Second World War and the decade following it.

In 1946 the political and social phenomenon known as Peronism arose. It is a very complex and difficult period to understand. We do not use the term *populism* to describe the Peronist period: *populism* is used to characterise so many different historical phenomena that it ends up confusing rather than clarifying things. In addition, in the European context, it often has negative and pejorative connotations, different to the use that is given to it in Latin American scholarship.

During this time, in terms of social and political classes, a new historical bloc emerged that replaced the hegemonic bloc of the liberal and pro-British landowning oligarchy.

This new historical bloc was based on the alliance of the organised working class (CGT),[11] the national business bourgeoisie (CGE),[12] a nationalist (anti-imperialist) sector of the Armed Forces and an assortment of social groups such as internal migrants. These internal migrants[13] were called 'little black heads' by the urban middle classes. Some members of the Radical Party,[14] a few communists and several trade union anarchists supported Peronism, which became known as '*hecho maldito del país burgués*' (a damning historical event for the bourgeois country).[15]

It was during this period that the Argentinean welfare state was established, expanding social and economic rights. In particular, the majority of its labour laws were enacted (with respect to holidays, working hours, bonuses, child labour, women's working conditions, maternity leave, social protection, etc.). Many of these measures had been taken in response to previous petitions by socialists, anarchists, and communists. This was not the case concerning the citizen rights of the Indigenous population.

During the course of the two Peronist governments a substantial redistribution of economic resources occurred: 52 per cent of the gross national product, which was produced by the agro-export sector, went to the proletariat. For the first time, the Indigenous People were acknowledged as citizens and granted identity documents. Before this, they had not been accorded that status. According to juridical criteria, they did not exist.

In terms of feminism and the social and political status of women, the Peronist period presents a great paradox. With a patriarchal and anti-feminist discourse, it was also an era in which working women had huge political prominence and obtained important social, labour, and political rights.

The figure of Eva Perón, 'Evita', was the most controversial: the most hated by the upper classes and the most loved by men and women workers.

Evita, using a discourse based on 'loyalty to the leader', and appealing to the status of women as mothers and wives, and against 'feminists', carried out transgressive practices for the time. She was born out of wedlock, and grew up to be a low-status actress who then married an army officer twice her age.[16] This quote from her speech in 1947 illustrates how paradoxical she could be in talking about women's self-liberation while constantly referring to Perón's words:

> Just as the workers could only save themselves and, as I have always said, repeating Perón's words, that only the humble will save the humble, I also think that only women will be the salvation of women. (Perón, 1951)

In 1947 the law in favour of women's suffrage was passed. In 1949 Eva Perón, along with other political leaders, formed the Peronist Women's Party, against some male elements of the Justicialist Party. Many lower-class women commanded by Evita toured the country organising other women and encouraging them to participate in the Women's Party.

In the elections of 1951, the first time that women were allowed to vote, 23 women were elected as national deputies, six as national senators, and a total of 109 as provincial legislators.

Likewise, Evita participated strongly in government decisions, and maintained a direct and good relationship with the people (*el pueblo*) and the most combative sectors of the CGT, while fighting those who were considered opportunists and traitors to the *descamisados* ('shirtless', i.e. the very poor).

These practical experiences proved decisive for Argentine women, who won their public space and never left it again.

Although Juan Domingo Perón was initially supported by the Catholic Church, at the end of his second term he put in place measures that pitted the conservative sector of the Catholic Church against the government. These measures were aimed at creating legal equality for legitimate and illegitimate children,[17] they included the law on divorce, the suppression of compulsory religious education, the elimination of subsidies to denominational schools, and the law on prophylaxis that promoted the sanitary control of brothels. In addition, in the legislative, the law on separation of church and state awaited its sanction.[18]

The Argentine Communist Party (PCA), directed along Stalinist lines by its leader Victorio Codovila, of Italian origin, opposed the transformations carried out by the government of the Justicialist Party. The PCA's right-wing allies in the Democratic Union were supported by United States imperialism. The women, who at that time defined themselves as feminists, belonged to the middle classes. They opposed Perón's laws, even the law which granted women the vote. While they initially supported this legislation, they knew that the vote of poor women and workers would lead to a success of Peronism, which was something they rejected. The fiction writer Victoria Ocampo, a member of the oligarchic upper class, was a renowned exponent and spokesperson of this kind of feminism. Their official argument was that they rejected the vote because it was granted by an authoritarian government. However, it was going to be voted in a democratically elected Congress. Unfortunately, socialist and communist feminists of European origin could not understand the social, economic, and political changes taking place, and racism, elitism, and their class interests prevailed over solidarity.

The strong resistance of the middle classes and the Left against Peronism was sustained by criticisms concerning the vertical and statist character of its measures and its cult of personality, political persecution, and patriarchal frames.

We agree with some of these criticisms. However, racism led the Left and the middle and upper classes to call Peronist supporters 'little black heads' and 'zoological alluvium'.[19]

The racism and elitism of the upper and middle classes prevent them, until today, from accepting that the majority must enjoy the same rights. Instead of accepting them as autonomous political subjects, the upper and middle classes denounce the majority as objects of demagogic manipulation.

The issue of authoritarianism is something that should be reviewed both in our past and present history. Every time a democratically elected government takes measures in favour of the people (*el pueblo*), it is called authoritarian. But the Right and so-called 'democratic' republicans do not use that term to name neoliberal governments that suspend the rule of law, hold political prisoners, and proscribe the mayors any political force. Undoubtedly, during the Peronist government there were political detainees and some restrictions of freedom of expression, but nothing that was comparable with the repression and persecution that came afterwards. Here it is necessary to draw a distinction between the public policies, redistribution of wealth, experiences of life and struggle developed by the popular sectors and the people, and the Peronist ideology and the role of the leader, although a lack of space prohibits a detailed examination of these here. This confrontation between socialism and middle-class feminism against the Peronist popular masses was to have important consequences later. It also confronts us with the dilemma of practice vs discourse. The women of the French Revolution had already voiced this: 'Freedom, how many crimes are committed in your name?'

The turbulent years

In 1955 a military coup[20] expelled the second Peronist democratically elected government from political power. Just before the coup, the Air Force bombed the Plaza de Mayo, killing more than 400 people, including children. Many of the union leaders were imprisoned or blacklisted, as were the leaders of the Women's Party.[21] In 1956 many Peronist leaders were shot without trial. The Partido Justicialista (Justice Party) was banned until 1973.

Between 1955 and 1973 there was a series of weak civilian governments and military coups. These military coups opened the economy to foreign capital, now mostly American and European, and were resisted by organised workers.

This dynamic was accompanied by an increasingly intense popular mobilisation, whose main protagonists were workers and university students. The government's repressive responses became correspondingly fierce, and resulted in arrests, torture, and selective disappearances of people. Later, in the context of a strengthening union, peasant and student political organisations that included armed resistance in their agenda were created. Some of these guerrilla organisations were Marxist and others belonged to the Peronist Left.

In the most critical period of political turbulence (1968–1976) there arose another paradoxical situation. Women had strong participation in various student, labour, and political organisations, including armed organisations, and this generated important changes in social practices of gender relations in that generation. Such a rupture with forms of the traditional monogamous family, which included contraception, abortion (illegal), the relatively shared parenting of children, the advancement of women in the university environment, etc., took place without theoretically and analytically questioning patriarchal relations (with few exceptions). Of course, patriarchal gender relations would continue to exist in the public and domestic spaces, especially in the trade union organisations, and also in the Left parties and armed organisations. Motherhood was another important sphere where women had huge difficulties in trying to make changes. The social construction of motherhood that forces women to devote all their time and energy to their children collided with time and dedication to political commitment and brought subjective suffering to women activists.[22] Nonetheless it was a time of rupture.

During that period, the women who self-identified as feminists were a minority, from the middle class and inspired by United States and European feminist theorists. In general, most of these had no political involvement in the mobilisations and struggles over issues such as social justice, political sovereignty, economic independence, the seizure of power and socialism.

The two most well-known organisations were Unión Feminista Argentina (UFA) and Movimiento de Liberación Femenina (MLF).

State terrorism

On 24 March 1976, a genocidal coup d'état took place, its objective being the destruction of all popular resistance and the reorganisation of social relations, including industrial social relations. The military junta sought to discipline society and the labour force into accepting the imposition of a neo-liberal economic model, articulated with international financial capital. The civil bloc that accompanied the Armed Forces was composed of businessmen who – while remaining linked to the agro-industrial sector – were already minor partners with transnational financial capitalism, the leadership of the Catholic Church, and some members of traditional political parties. This dictatorship, with the support of the CIA, coordinated a plan to exterminate the Left, broadly speaking, both in Argentina and in South America with what was called the 'Condor Plan'.

The only ones who dared to publicly confront the dictatorship were the Mothers and Grandmothers of the Plaza de Mayo. They began to wear a white headscarf, symbolising the diaper they had wrapped their babies in, babies who now, years later, were their 'disappeared' (*desaparecidos*) sons and daughters. Transgressive public practices by women again appeared without a link to the theoretical questioning of patriarchy; these women, mostly housewives, went out on the streets and were the first to challenge and resist the bloodiest of all the dictatorships suffered by our country.[23]

Times of convergence? Contradictory synthesis?

When democracy was gained in 1983 by popular mobilisation and defeat of the Junta in the Malvinas War, new feminist streams were created and established. It was a time of convergence of historical political experiences and feminist theoretical reflections. Many women who returned from exile brought feminist theory with them, and those who had remained in the country during the dictatorship had reflected and questioned vertical patriarchal structures within the left-wing organisations in which they had participated.

Many issues that affected women had seen more advances in concrete practice than in the formal regulations themselves. That is why, when the functioning of the National Congress recovered, the women members of the political parties represented in it, several of them now feminists, together with other feminists from the middle class, fought and obtained, not without difficulty, laws with respect to child custody (1985), divorce (1987), domestic violence (1994), and a female quota for the election of deputies and national senators (1991).

The first National Women's Meeting (ENM: Encuentros Nacionales de Mujeres) was held in 1986 in the City of Buenos Aires. It was promoted and organised by women, many of them former political activists from the 1970s, and most of them middle class who had embraced feminism during the dictatorship, either in internal or external exile. These meetings were crucial as a mechanism for the dissemination and discussion of the problems facing women across the country and the development of a massive feminist praxis. They have continued to take place every year since then. The number of women participants has grown from 1,000 to 80,000 currently.[24] The venue of the meeting moves from south to north, east and west to cover the great geographical area of the country. The ENM has no permanent organisational structure, and the meeting is organised each year by a provisional and local committee. The meetings are autonomous, nobody funds them, and their methodology is based on horizontal, non-hierarchical workshops where women's experiences are discussed and shared, recognising the value of different knowledges. It is from these shared experiences that a collective, although not uniform, critique against patriarchy and its current manifestations develops.

The National Campaign for the Right to Legal, Safe and Free Abortion was articulated at the heart of these reunions, the first time that a public strategy on this subject became so widely known.

Only when the National Meetings (EN) exceeded 10,000 women did the Left parties,[25] in particular the Trotskyists, who are very strong in Argentina, and conservative sectors of the Catholic Church begin to pay attention and to participate in them. Women were sent by the Church exclusively to oppose the demand for the legalisation of abortion.[26]

After 34 years without dictatorships, with an important baggage of experiences and feminist struggles associated with the striving for Memory, Truth and Justice, judgements against genocide, demands for better living conditions, and protests against the external debt caused by transnational and neoliberal capitalism, we consider that qualitatively important steps have been taken towards equal rights for women and sexual diversity in Argentina.

Argentina's feminisms today can be characterised in general by: a growing participation of youth from the middle-class and university sectors, which are today predominantly on the Left and not any more guided by racist ideologies and elitist attitudes towards poor and Indigenous populations; a growth of popular organisations led by key feminist women; a significant development of the topic of sexual diversity and gender identities;[27] and a strong public visibility. A number of parties of the Left, whose active elements are mainly young people, have incorporated the slogan, 'There is no socialism without feminism', and many men are beginning to self-identify publicly as feminists. The Mothers of the Plaza de Mayo and HIJOS[28] also support feminist struggles. The presence in universities of feminist scholars and women's studies has been institutionalised. CONICET[29] has had a woman as president, and today some faculty directors are women, some of them with a strong feminist agenda.

Peasant women, migrant women from Paraguay and Bolivia, and Indigenous women define their feminism and participate, integrated within the political and popular organisations (Classist Combative Movement, National Indigenous Peasants Movement, Tupac Amaru Neighborhood Association, Confederation of Workers of the Popular Economy, Organisations of Women with African Heritage, etc.). These organisations demand territory, natural resources, social and economic rights, and respect for ethnic identities. All have incorporated gender equality issues, respect for sexual and gender diversity, and in them the leadership of women is strong.

On the whole, Indigenous women who participate in organisations of Indigenous Peoples consider gender complementarity as a feature of their gender identity. Respect for culture, territory, and *buen vivir* (good living) are their main topics of struggle and mobilisation. Some of their leaders participate in the feminist debates calling for a specific feminism with particular and distinctive contents. A fundamental element of this feminism is its community collective orientation, the non-separation of community and territorial claims for the equal status of women. It is interesting to note that at the last Latin American Feminist Meeting in Montevideo, November 2017, there were several workshops for Indigenous and women of African background.

There are two fundamental aspects to highlight here. When spaces of democratic participation are opened and the impunity of the military dictatorship is challenged and faced with the works of Memory, Truth and Justice, the historical memory and our own genealogies are also recovered: this includes the women who fought for the independence and the struggles of the Indigenous and black women for freedom and against servitude and slavery. The other aspect of today's feminist movements is the pre-eminence of feminist media. In this sense, the active incorporation of young women journalists into the feminist movement, those who formed the collective Ni Una Menos (Not One Less), has been fundamental for the call to the massive marches of 8 March and the call for the International Women's Strike on 3 June. These new irruptions have been of vital importance for the extensive visibility of feminism.

However, gender relations have not yet been transformed to a great degree and throughout the country. In trade unions,[30] in state institutions and public policies or in traditional political parties, the issue of gender inequalities is still treated separately from party politics by gender or equal opportunities officials. In the northern provinces of the country, the problem is even more serious. Also, Catholic conservative women and Evangelist women strongly oppose the legalisation of abortion, and indeed any change oriented towards social justice. These sectors are very developed in our country and continue to be racist and discriminatory. And the risk of regression with respect to the historical conquests is always present. More recently, fundamentalist movements, both Catholic and Evangelical, have emerged in the public arena, aggressively questioning not only the legalisation of abortion, but also Comprehensive Sexual Education (ESI), which is legally obligatory for all schools in the country since more than a decade ago.

As has happened before in our long history of struggle for freedom, equality, and autonomy (both for women and in society at large), patriarchal power responds with violence, in this case through increasingly cruel and brutal femicides. The repressiveness of the neoliberal state has used its might to increase punitiveness in general against all types of crime. But feminism has countered such tactics, arguing that social relations must be changed, but not by increasing legal penalties, as that always ends up punishing the poorest and most unprotected people. Feminists constantly point out that the application of justice in our society is strongly sexist, classist, and racist.

The feminist movement today: agreements and disagreements

It could be argued that there exists today a feminist movement with discrete feminisms within. In this section we will analyse some, though not all, of the different currents that make up the feminist movement presently prevailing in Argentina. We shall refer to the organisations that have a presence in the mobilisations in the streets and develop activities of women's organisation in different social sectors and challenge the powers of the state (executive, legislative, and judicial) but also engage with other social spaces such as the mass media or educational institutions.

It seems that concrete demands and street mobilisations unify feminists. Theoretical approaches and practices differ substantially and divide them. We are going to use a political criterion to identify two big blocs in order to analyse feminist organisations: those that are identified as 'national and popular' and those that are identified as 'Left'.[31] We do not ignore that there are other possible and equally valid criteria for the analysis.

Demands and agreements

As we have already seen, the right to legal, safe, and free abortion is one of the slogans that unify the struggles of all feminist currents. The National Campaign for the Right to Legal, Safe and Free Abortion is supported by all national and popular organisations, the Left, and social organisations.

Since the campaign started, strategies for the legalisation of abortion have been designed, varying from simple protest to proposals for action, challenging institutions. These strategies have resulted in important achievements. The campaign questions a fundamental aspect of the structure of our state: the relationship between the Catholic Church and the state. Feminists demand the separation of church and state and the right to free abortions in public hospitals.[32] Part of the strategy is to provide judicial follow-up to cases in which non-punishable abortions are penalised. The judicial cases are accompanied by large demonstrations throughout the country.[33]

The defence of the rights of sexual and gender diversity has also unified feminist currents. In the past, the only destination for many transgender persons was prostitution. With their organisation they have started to access education and other forms of paid work. Among other things, they demanded and were granted a job quota in public institutions. Some feminist organisations are highly engaged in the subject, while others simply support the cause.

Protests against gender violence and femicide unify all social sectors, bringing together men and women of different social classes and generations. Initially, this was the subject that invoked large demonstrations by the organisation Not One Less. Later, the tragedy surrounding transvesticide was added to the campaign. Femicide and transvesticide show, in the most brutal way, the power relations of the current patriarchy.

In our society, women as a whole have advanced much more in relation to our rights than most men have in accepting them. The relations of gender inequality are challenged, and this includes the traditional model of masculinity. Today, young women practice greater sexual freedom, while many men maintain the traditional belief that they are entitled to sexual violence against women. However, there are also young men developing new forms of masculinity.

The large mobilisations against gender violence have also allowed issues such as domestic violence and sexual harassment in the Catholic Church, football, mass media, and other areas, to come to light.

That patriarchal relations of violence are constitutive of capitalist relations is an implicit agreement among almost all feminist currents.

Feminist struggles against the trafficking of people for sexual exploitation is another important issue of agreement in the feminist struggle. Although it is analysed in the context of gender violence, it is also linked to the national and international capitalist market of people-trafficking. Argentina has an internal trafficking market in women and girls, and it is a host country to victims of international trafficking (Dominican and Paraguayan women) and an exporter of women bound for Europe, Arab countries allied to the West, or Japan. In general, prostitution is analysed not as a choice but as one of the most violent mechanisms of gender oppression, aggravated by the framework of capitalism, that turns everything into a commodity in the pursuit of profit. In Argentina, exploitation through prostituting of others is a crime, not the exercise of prostitution in itself.

However, AMMAR (Asociación de Mujeres Meretrices de Argentina: Association of Women Sex Workers in Argentina), considers prostitution a paid employment and the members designate themselves as sex workers. They claim the right to call themselves as they wish and that their empowerment as sex workers restores their dignity and removes their stigma. They also claim the need for protection and social security for sex work. AMMAR is part of the Argentine Workers' Central Union (CTA). They believe that feminists have turned their backs on prostitutes and that all measures aimed at closing public places where prostitution is practised lead to a greater clandestinisation of their work and thus favour pimps. Some former members of AMMAR criticise this organisation for receiving international funding, on the basis that this imposes unwanted conditions: They also refuse to call pimps businessmen as AMMAR suggests. Several women who left AMMAR to begin studying want to generate alternative sources of work for their former colleagues. One other aspect to be highlighted is the recent emergence of organisations of young university women who oppose abolitionism, basing their arguments on women's right to autonomy and deciding on their bodies. They criticise the conservative feminist morality that rejects prostitution.

We believe that this debate has two distinct angles: one linked to personal autonomous decisions within the framework of limited job options and gender inequality and oppression of women, and the other that takes into account the political economy of sex within the framework of the capitalist system and market where hypersexualisation yields great profits by transforming sex, among other features of human life, into merchandise, thus covering up multiple means of oppression.

Disagreements

The main disagreements arise from the ascriptions and political identities of the feminist organisations, social insertion, language, and analytical categories used, but mainly from their relation to the state in the period of the Kirchnerist governments (from 2003 to 2015).

National and popular feminism

The national and popular organisations of the twenty-first century emerged, as a resurgence, from the widespread movement of leftist Peronism destroyed by the repression of the dictatorship. But it resurfaced by watering the underground parched riverbeds of denied, silenced stories, subaltern stories, stories repressed not only by the most concentrated economic powers, but also by the cultural hegemony that wanted to make Argentina a white European country.

The national issue stems from an anti-imperialist conception, from an opposition against transnational financial capital and the idea of Patria Grande (the big homeland), which strives for a South American homeland without borders between peoples. It has nothing to do with right-wing nationalisms.

In general, these currents – which due to their practice can be framed within popular, neo-Marxist feminisms[34] – emphasise the concrete historical identities and the recovery of memory. Memory in Argentina means memory of the struggles, resistance, and violations of human rights that were suffered by those struggling at the hands of dictatorships and dominant blocs. Memory unites us with the rest of Latin America.

This sector had a greater articulation with public policies during the Kirchnerist governments. The construction of socialism was not then an issue, although redistribution of wealth, the extension of citizen rights for all sectors of the population and cultural changes were of great concern. During 2003–2015 the main problem was transforming the state from within. All the organisations of the national and popular field supported the Kirchner policies. Some considered Cristina Fernández de Kirchner a natural leader, while others gave their support critically.

Some of the Kirchnerist policies were:

- *Economic policies*: disengagement from the IMF (International Monetary Fund); tackling the external debt; refusal to pay the vulture funds, and the approval given by the UN to a convention against international usury; autonomous technological development, including satellite sovereignty. Support was given to the development of small and medium industry and cooperatives, to encourage the internal market.
- *Human rights policies*: impetus given to the trials against the genocides; searching for the children appropriated by the dictatorship as a state policy; migratory law, that recognised migration as a human right; a law about audiovisual communication services based on the right to information and free expression, distinguishing it from that of freedom of enterprise, which sought to end the monopoly of the media.
- *Gender policies*: several laws related to sexual and reproductive rights; retirement law as a right given to housewives and as a way to make visible the value of domestic work; law for private home service workers, most of whom were poor women; the first laws against trafficking in Argentina, and the law of protection against gender violence; the creation of the Council for Gender Policies in the Ministry of Defence; policies related to the recognition of rights of sexual diversities, including equal marriage and the right of adoption for homoparental families. The social policies of cooperatives were very important as job opportunities for transsexual women and economic independence for women victims of gender violence.

The main criticisms of the Kirchnerist government made by the feminists of the national and popular field were related to the productivist and extractivist model and the need for more force in the application of policies. President Cristina Fernández did not support abortion, but said that if Congress approved the bill to legalise abortion she would not veto it.

A big disadvantage was the inability to build an organised political force sufficiently developed to face the real economic power and forces of the Right.

Feminism within parties of the Left

At the beginning of democracy, autonomous feminist organisations prevailed in leftist feminist circles, whose leaders came mostly from the revolutionary organisations of the 1970s, organisations related to the Communist Party and various groups related to the Revolutionary Communist Party, with a Maoist orientation. With the passage of time this changed. Today the largest Marxist-Feminist groups are Trotskyists (Bread and Roses from the Workers' Socialist Party [PTS-Partido de los Trabajadores]) and The Reds.

They proclaim that the struggle is against capitalist exploitation and patriarchal oppression. They promote the figures of Clara Zetkin and Rosa Luxemburg. They participate actively in the strikes, stoppages, and social movements of the working class, and the movement of recovered factories. They also participate in all mobilisations for women's rights and in the national campaign for the right to abortion

Lately, since gaining some representation in the National Congress and provincial legislatures, they have begun to pay more attention to legislative issues. They believe that all governments are equally exposed to capitalist exploitation, and during the Kirchner period they maintained a strong opposition and criticism of the government.

The Workers' Party (PO – Partido Obrero), Trotskyist and the most sectarian of all, insists on considering feminism as bourgeois. For them, the struggle is for socialism, and only that will emancipate women. They see 'machismo' (a non-academic description of patriarchy in Latin America) as part of the capitalist superstructure. However, they have begun to attend the National Women's Meetings to try to recruit women and to downplay party politics.

The challenges for feminists in the present political landscape

Today the political landscape of our country and Latin America has completely changed due to the triumph of neoliberal right-wing governments. Dilma Roussef and Cristina Fernández de Kirchner were presidents who carried out policies in favour of women and the popular sectors. One was dismissed by means of an impeachment full of irregularities and the other was defeated in elections. Both were stigmatised and discredited by the hegemonic mass media, a stigmatisation that was framed in gendered codes.

The social bloc that sustains the government of Cambiemos (the coalition created in 2015, led by Mauricio Macri) is based on the agro-export sector, a historical ally of conservative political convictions, the sector of transnational corporations and the financial sector. The first government measures tended to favour the following three categories: (i) devaluation and removal of taxes on agrarian exports; (ii) exchange deregulation, financial deregulation, and rate hikes for the financial sector; and (iii) raising and dollarising tariffs for energy transnationals. The high interest rate, the widespread dismissal of workers in the public and private sectors, and the irrational rise in tariffs for domestic utilities (water, gas, and electricity) destroyed real wages and popular consumption, and unemployment increased dramatically.

Financial speculation being the main economic policy, the opening to the vulture funds and the elimination of measures to protect national production have led to a brutal flight of capital and the fall of our economy into the abyss within just two years.

In order to maintain this model of speculation, the government turned to the IMF, who responded with its recipe for budget adjustment. This indebted the country and seriously affected the labour and social achievements obtained during the previous government. The cabinet ministers of Cambiemos are businessmen and CEOs of transnational companies. This puts them in a serious conflict of interest with their public function and is punishable under Argentinian legislation.

All social and economic policies aimed at greater equality and wealth redistribution are being dismantled, as well as those linked to technological and scientific development. In the same way, public health and education are progressively deteriorating.

This model is maintained by criminalising social protest and using judicial persecution as a mechanism of political persecution. There is harassment of judges who act according to the law and who are then replaced by judges who violate the right of the presumption of innocence and use preventive and arbitrary detention as a method of political persecution. Judicial independence is violated and it seeks to influence judicial decisions using the mass media to condemn people before any kind of fair trial: this is known as 'lawfare'.[35] As a result of this practice, today in Argentina we have 25 political prisoners, the first since the recovery of democracy in 1984, and many people prosecuted for the protests carried out against these policies. Five women from the Tupac Amaru Neighborhood Association have been imprisoned for over two years. Tupac Amaru was the largest popular organisation in the country, with great capacity to mobilise against all kinds of injustices. That is why the government tries to destroy it by imprisoning its leaders. All of them are women of humble origin.[36]

The repressive policies are also directed towards Indigenous Peoples who claim their territories and towards immigrants.[37] Attacks against transsexual persons and Senegalese migrants have also intensified.[38]

Economically concentrated powers, allies of the transnational financial capitalists and media monopolies, obstruct any attempt to deepen democracy and the redistribution of wealth, an indispensable condition for better outcomes in transforming class and gender relations.

Today the challenge for Argentine feminists is to confront neoliberal regressive and repressive policies while keeping our specific agenda alive. While we fight against the policies of structural adjustment, against the IMF and the indebtedness that condemns our country to misery, we have to continue our battle for our autonomy, legal abortion, and against the different forms of gender violence, among other concerns. On these issues we are all in agreement. However, in political mobilisations, unity is not achieved.

Ideologies and political identities divide us. The much-needed unity of action on the diversity of ideas is not achieved and should be a fundamental task for those of us who believe that the destruction of patriarchy is an important component of the destruction of the current neoliberal capitalism within the framework of our concrete and specific historical reality.

Final open reflections

Similar reflections would be necessary when thinking about building bridges between feminists from the Global South and the Global North.

Today as yesterday, we consider that we cannot understand the development of capitalism without taking into account the relations of domination between the countries (central and peripheral), such as colonialism, in the past, and the new forms of domination and extraction of natural resources. In this sense it is necessary to remember the concrete historicity of social relations of production and of the relations of exploitation and domination. With globalisation, it is not possible to analyse the social classes disconnected from the articulations of the productive forces and relations of production within the countries and their articulation with the central and peripheral countries and the international division of labour.

Transnational financial capitalism generates new forms of domination. To seize a country's natural resources causes massive forced and violent population displacements and migration. War is part of patriarchal capitalism. Marxist feminists need to look beyond our national and regional borders in a globalised world. Solidarity with those who are forced to migrate needs to be accompanied by a firm stand against armament and wars that seek to strip people of their natural resources with the excuse of defending freedom and democracy. None of this is achieved by bombing and massacring civilians.

Feminists today face several types of fundamentalism, not only religious fundamentalism, which in Latin America comes from the most conservative parts of the Catholic Church and the Neo-evangelical churches. The other great fundamentalism is that of neoliberalism.

To make transformations effective, a concrete knowledge of historically located social relations is necessary. In our subaltern societies, gender and ethnic relations are constitutive of the relations of production and exploitation. That is why the struggle against patriarchy is inextricably linked to the struggle against capitalism in its current phase of neoliberalism. Starting from the concrete historical experience means to recognise the historicity of the categories of analysis and to be able to unravel the concrete material, symbolic, and cultural power relations in each society.

Knowing and sharing our different genealogies allows us to build our own concrete and changing identities with which women can identify, and from there to try to understand the genealogies and identities of other people in other struggles.

In this way, the necessary empathy that leads to a common fight can be generated. Each subalternity must be able to criticise its own subalternity in order to transform it. As Fabio Frosini once said in a seminar I attended, 'in order for the universal not to be mere ethnocentrism implies translatability into each particular language so that it can be understood by these other languages and experiences'.

This requires a lot of listening and understanding of the specific contexts in which feminists from different regions of the world have to act.

Who knows today what socialism is? We only know that it has to be based on our own collective solidarity and on the equality of gender, class, and ethnicity – the bedrock of feminist values.

To start building our utopia we have to ground it in our own concrete, conflictive, contradictory, and painful histories. All voices and histories must be heard and accorded the same value and respect. Building bridges and making our histories by dialoguing between each other.

The philosophy of praxis should be based on the concrete actions of gendered human beings who seek to transform the reality that oppresses them.

Notes

1 They fuelled the War of the Triple Alliance (Brazil, Argentina, and Uruguay, 1865) against Paraguay in its attempts to achieve autonomous development.

2 Some descendants of those who had appropriated Indigenous lands by committing genocide are now in government with Mauricio Macri. Their grandfathers and fathers had supported the various military dictatorships.

3 This era is very well described by Friedrich Engels in *The Condition of the Working Class of England*.

4 It suffices to look at the photographs in the Iquitos Museum, Perú, showing Henry Ford and Harvey Samuel Firestone, in their impeccable jackets and pressed white trousers, surrounded by Indigenous People who would not long survive the industrial exploitation of their natural resources to manufacture car tyres. We ask, is it so different today?

5 Recently President Macri repeated publicly, without embarrassment, that 'in Argentina, we are all descendants from Europe'.

6 They have owned the principal newspaper *La Nación* ever since.

7 Members of the current government have revitalised and reinforced the denial by repudiating the genocide inflicted by the previous dictatorship.

8 Two notable socialist organisations were the Feminist Socialist Center and the National Feminist Union.

9 Some anarchists tried to integrate in other ways. Several of them went to live and work in the countryside with the poorest *peones* and rural workers.

10 Just to mention two of them: Juana Azurduy: born in Alto Perú (present-day Bolivia), she commanded troops against the Spanish army; and Remedios del Valle: a camp-follower turned soldier, she proved a canny war strategist, and was formally appointed as colonel by the first independent government, but was never able to receive her retirement pension because she was a woman and black.

11 Confederación General del Trabajo (General Confederation of Labour): unified all industrial trade unions.

12 Confederación General Económica (General Economic Confederation): unified medium-sized national enterprise.

13 Many families, due to the lack of local development and the dispossession of their lands, migrated from the provinces to the cities, where they joined the industrial working class.

14 Created by Hipólito Yrigoyen, it represented the professional urban middle class. Yrigoyen was overthrown by a conservative military coup in 1930.

15 These words were spoken by John William Cooke, a left-wing Peronist, by which he meant that, once people experience living in dignity, they will always fight to return to that.

16 At that time there was a regulation in the Armed Forces stating that an officer's future wife had to be subjected to an investigation about her social belonging. This regulation was eliminated only when Defense Minister Nilda Garré created the Council for Gender Policies in the Ministry of Defence in 2007.

17 Law 14,367 (1954) eliminated classifications among children born out of wedlock (adulterine, illegitimate, or incestuous), and conferred on them all the rights that until then had been accorded only to those born inside wedlock.

18 Many of these achievements were then derogated by the military coup in 1955. And some of them, such as the divorce law, would be obtained only after the last dictatorship; others are still part of the feminist movement's demands, one being the separation of the Catholic Church and state.

19 Dark-skinned people emigrated from the provinces were described as animals from the zoo and the term alluvium (flood) was used because there were thousands participating in political meetings.

20 This military coup was called Liberation Revolution.

21 Some of them were detained for up to five years without trial.

22 Recently a group of women survivors of jail and clandestine concentration camps worked around rape and sexual harassment. It proved very difficult. But when they tried to talk about motherhood, and their relationship with their children, it was much harder to address the issue. The separation from their children was more painful than other forms of torture. It remains an open wound for many activists in Latin America.

23 In honour of truth we must say that two of them were indeed feminists: Lita Boitano and Laura Bonaparte.

24 The Argentinian population today is 41 million.

25 The women of the Argentinian Communist Party and the Revolutionary Communist Party participated from the inception of the National Women's Meetings.

26 Some nuns from the progressive sector of the Catholic Church, who worked in poor neighbourhoods, participated from the beginning as a personal decision to criticise the patriarchal structure of the Church.

27 The National Plan against Discrimination (2005) implemented by the National Institute against Discrimination, Xenophobia and Racism protected the visibility of this problem. The Law of Equal Marriage provided legality and legitimacy (Law 26.618 / 2010).

28 Hijos por la Identidad y la Justicia contra el Olvido y el Silencio: Sons and Daughters for Identity and Justice Against Forgetting and Silence. These are the sons and daughters of the disappeared.

29 Consejo Nacional de Investigaciones Científicas y Técnicas: National Scientific and Technical Research Council.

30 It is interesting to note that, both in the Central de Trabajadores Argentinos (CTA: Argentine Workers' Central Union) and in the General Confederation of Labour (CGT), advances are being made by feminist young women in union leadership who are building a women's trade unionist bloc.

31 The use of quotation marks is because many of us who ascribe to the 'national and popular' field also consider ourselves leftists. For us, being on the Left means fighting to transform society. And those who fight most bravely are not necessarily Marxists, although some are.

32 The slogans are: 'Sex education to decide'; 'Contraceptives, not to abort'; 'Legal abortion to not die, We give birth'; 'We decide'; 'Legal abortion in the hospital'; 'Get your rosaries from our ovaries'.

33 Some victories have been achieved, such as the liberation of Belén, a young woman who was being prosecuted and imprisoned in the province of Tucumán after being accused of killing her foetus, when in fact she had had a miscarriage (*aborto espontáneo*: spontaneous abortion).

34 National popular and Marxist feminists differ in terms of their methods of analyses and concrete political and historical identities.

35 It is being applied in the case of Lula Da Silva, the Vice President of Ecuador, and to pursue political opponents in Argentina.

36 These women are Milagro Sala, Mirta Guerrero, Mirta Aizama, Gladys Díaz, and Graciela López.

37 In this scenario we already have two murdered: Santiago Maldonado and Rafael Nahuel.

38 See Law 25.87/2004, which stipulates the human right to migration, which has now been changed by a simple presidential decree.

References

Cieza, D., 2010. *Argentina ante el bicentenario: la sociedad, el estado y los actores en un país conflictivo*. De la Campana, La Plata.

Perón, E., 1951. La Razón de Mi vida. Cap. LIII(53) El Partido Peronista Femenino. Ediciones Peuser, Buenos Aires.

Trinchero, H., 2000. *Los dominios del demonico: civilización y barbarie en las fronteras de la nación*. Editoria EUDEBA, Buenos Aires.

18 | MARXIST FEMINISM FOR A GLOBAL WOMEN'S MOVEMENT AGAINST CAPITALISM[1]

Ligaya Lindio McGovern

Introduction

The neoliberal economic project to aggressively further expand capitalism globally has posed a challenge to women's movements around the world. Alongside capitalist global expansion is the propagation of a neoliberal ideology that consequentially exacerbates poverty, class, and gender inequalities within the nation-states, within regions, and between the North and the South (Lindio-McGovern and Wallimann, 2012; Ally, 2012). These consequences serve global capitalism as they provide the ground to embed capitalism: without the cheap labour of the working class and the super-exploitation of women on a global scale capitalism will collapse. This context provides an opportunity to rethink paradigms that shape thought and action in the politics of resistance of global women's movements against capitalism. Since the embedding of global capitalism requires an ideology (in this case neoliberalism) to justify its practice, a counter-frame of resistance becomes important in responding to the challenge. This chapter argues that the Marxist-Feminist frame needs to be taken back from the margin to the centre as a framework of analysis and guide in shaping movements to liberate women from class and gender oppression/exploitation in the context of global capitalism. This is not entirely a new prescription, for there had been debates in the past that proposed the Marxist-Feminist frame – as seen in the works of Angela Davis (1981), Heidi Hartmann (1979), Jacklyn Cock (1980), and Martha Gimenez (1975). What might be somewhat new is the search for the art of resistance that helps us identify the common ground on which we can bind packets of resistance here and there in order to confront transnationally the course of this global neoliberal force in order to change it.

The Marxist-Feminist frame as an analytical frame for a global women's movement

Analysis of the context of global capitalism in which women's (as well as men's) lives are enmeshed must precede collective transnational action of women's movements in order to locate what binds and divides women on a global scale. The Marxist-Feminist perspective has the potential as an analytical frame to be useful in making visible the threads that bind and divide women and divide men and women in the context of global capitalism buttressed by imperialism and militarism. The creation of divisions plays an important role in the maintenance of global capitalism, which is why it is important to make them visible in order that a protracted struggle to tackle it from all fronts can be coordinated transnationally.

Central in the premise of the Marxist-Feminist frame is to locate the position of women in the mode of production and relations of production and in the organisation of social reproduction. Production and social reproduction are two sides of the same coin. The capitalist mode of production and the social relations that perpetually reproduce this mode are the target for change. The analytical task of locating the position of women in the mode and relations of production, is not merely so women can move up in the capitalist ladder as implicit in the Liberal Feminist frame, but rather in order to examine/identify the intricate ways the stratification of women and men in the capitalist mode of production maintains such system, with the ultimate goal of changing the system towards a non-capitalist alternative. The importance of this analytical task cannot be overemphasised in starting and maintaining a transnational women's movement against global capitalism.

The super-exploitation of women's labour in the capitalist mode and relations of production

Women's productive and social reproductive labour play a central role in maintaining the capitalist system. When in the 1970s the Women in Development (WID) thought (that derived from the Liberal Feminist frame) promoted the idea that development must integrate women in the productive labour market without questioning the capitalist nature of development, this was a way to make women participate more in maintaining the capitalist system (Lindio-McGovern, 1997; Boserup, 1970). What it did was to stratify the labour market based on gender and class by making women's labour cheaper than men's, and creating a corporate hierarchy where men predominate and retain their higher status within the corporate bureaucracy. The few middle-class women who may break the glass-ceiling create the faulty myth that the capitalist corporate ladder is something that women can aim for, thus rechannelling and neutralising efforts to change and challenge the capitalist system. Meanwhile, class divisions between women in the capitalist relations of production are created and maintained as the majority of women integrated into the capitalist relations of production are working-class women who provide super-exploited labour in global assembly lines from the garment sweatshops in New York to electronics and garment assembly lines in the Philippines, Bangladesh, Indonesia, Malaysia, Mexico, etc. To maintain these global assembly lines, a culture of consumerism and materialism is promoted among the middle-class and wealthy men and women, especially in the Global North, bringing them into the commodity chains as consumers in the global consumption market.

As more women are integrated into the capitalist labour market, new relations of reproductive labour ensue. The social reproduction of the next generation of workers is essential for the maintenance of the capitalist system, just as it was necessary for the maintenance of slavery. In new social relations of reproductive labour, a new class of super-exploited and disposable migrant domestic workers is created. The predominant group of migrants are women from poorer to richer countries, thus stratifying the global reproductive labour market based on class, nationality, ethnicity, gender, race, and citizenship. The maintenance of this global reproductive labour force must not put stress on capital, so it must be largely privatised, placing the burden for wages mainly on families, and to be super-cheap it has to be a migrant woman from a Third World country or a poor woman within the country. In fact, a new class of entrepreneurs has emerged in the trading of migrant domestic workers, making the women profitable commodities for exchange – the more they can trade, the larger is their profit with minimal capital investment (Lindio-McGovern, 2012).

What then does centring Marxism-Feminism within this context mean? It means that the central goal of women's movements globally is to transform radically the capitalist mode of production and social reproduction, think and create new systems of production and social reproduction where the goal is not simply to maximise profit that trickles up. The common ground for a global and transnational women's movement should be this. If global capitalism divides women and men as it thrives on class and gender stratification, then what will bind women globally and bind men and women transnationally is the struggle against global capitalism to seek non-capitalist relations of production and reproduction. Such women's movements must go beyond simply driving for larger women's labour force participation in the capitalist system as an indicator of women's liberation. It is a movement that rallies around 'working class women's politics' (Gimenez, 2012) that transforms systems that are inherently exploitative of women's labour.

The Marxist-Feminist frame shaping women's movements

Is there a women's movement that has embraced, and still does, the Marxist-Feminist frame? Yes. The MAKIBAKA, the revolutionary women's movement in the Philippines, is an example. MAKIBAKA (Malayang Kilusan ng Bagong Kababaihan, Free Movement of New Women), the acronym is a Filipino word which literally means to struggle, was founded in April 1970 (see Taguiwalo, 2009). The 1970s was the period when a critical political awareness grew among students attributing the roots of the socio-economic problems of the country to imperialism, feudalism, and bureaucrat capitalism. MAKIBAKA grew out of the student's movement organisation, Kabataang Makabayan (KM, Patriotic Youth) that had a women's bureau. There were women student activists, such as Maria Lorena Barros who became one of MAKIBAKA's founding chairs, who saw the need for setting up a particular all-women's group that would define the role of women in the struggle and address the woman issues in a semi-feudal, semi-colonial, and patriarchal Philippine society. They envisioned that a women's organisation separate from the youth organisation will bring more women into the revolutionary struggle and will channel the struggle to a level that seeks to address the structural inequality in Philippine society and 'articulate the women's question within the broader framework of national and class oppression' (Ledesma, 2015: 15). According to Ledesma the International Spokesperson of MAKIBAKA, the formation of MAKIBAKA 'is a major landmark in the history of the women's movement in the Philippines' because it 'articulated the oppression suffered by women and the need for women's liberation through participation in the nationalist struggle'.

Central in the change agenda of MAKIBAKA is the transformation of the feudal, semi-feudal, and capitalist modes and relations of production. Land to the tiller to eliminate the landlord system, coupled with communal relations of production is central in its concept of agrarian reform, economic development, and politics of change. MAKIBAKA participates in the broader national liberation struggle of the Philippine revolutionary movement for self-determination in shaping the country's economic and political development that has been stunted by what it calls 'capitalist and imperialist globalisation'. Its concept of 'class' locates women in the feudal, semi-feudal and capitalist relations of production in the Philippines, and therefore in its view the liberation of women is linked to the transformation of gendered class systems embodied in the modes and relations of production.[2] At the height of martial law in the Philippines under Ferdinand Marcos's dictatorship in the 1970s that clamped down on political activists, MAKIBAKA inevitably decided to operate underground when one of its leading founding members, Lorena Barros, who propagated the slogan, 'A woman's place is in the revolution', was killed by the military in battle. Such experience demonstrates the powerful alliance among the forces of global capitalism, imperialism, and militarism: capitalism is expanded globally under neoliberal regimes through the implementation of neoliberal policies that control the political economies of periphery nations for the benefit of the core (modern imperialism) and militarism that provides the repressive instruments to violently suppress dissent directed at transforming economic systems that maintain the wealth and power of the 'transnational capitalist class' (Sklair, 2001, 2002; Robinson, 1996) that benefits most from such economic system.

Under the current Duterte authoritarian regime and rising fascist dictatorship, MAKIBAKA confronts a misogynist counter-insurgency state violence when Duterte uttered a public statement to the military to 'shoot' women revolutionaries in their 'vagina because when they have no more vaginas they will become useless'. Such a violent, sexist statement reflects a violent ideological battle against the growing consciousness of women that a woman's place is in the struggle. Such a statement comes at a moment in history of Philippine resistance when women's participation in the revolutionary movement remains undefeated and growing. Instead of bowing down to Duterte's misogynist fascism more women have joined the New People's Army, a revolutionary army that they see is needed to defend the people against the oppressive violence of the Armed Forces of the Philippines. Duterte's and the previous governments' counter-insurgency against the revolutionary movement and any group that advocates a radical socio-economic reform is meant to preserve the neoliberal regime and the socio-economic-political structures that concentrate wealth and power in the small landed and corporate elite. Landlords have gained political power through control of the legislature or acquisition of government positions, or through the use of paramilitary forces to defend their land.

Such system thrives on gender and class inequalities, and therefore women's revolutionary resistance threatens the preservation of the capitalist system that co-exists with the concentration of ownership and control of land in the small landed class, consequently producing a mass of landless peasants and agricultural workers in the Philippines. This kind of system enables transnational capital to embed itself in the Philippine political economy. As landlords convert use of lands to circumvent land reform dislocating peasants and agricultural workers, a massive supply of cheap labour is produced creating the preconditions for transnational capital to profitably thrive in the Philippines in conjunction with the extraction and plunder of its resources and environment. Those who are not absorbed in the formal economy create informal services for survival or they become a labour market for export to richer countries as cheap reproductive workers, service workers, factory workers, agricultural workers, health workers, and seafarers. Thus, the global circuit for the mobility of cheap labour for capitalist enterprises and its social reproduction (referring here to the maintenance and reproduction of cheap labour) is constructed, although it may not be immediately visible to the casual observer.

Applying the Marxist-Feminist frame in the context of global capitalism aggressively entrenched by neoliberal ideology and neoliberal practices and policies of global structures – such as the transnational corporations and other superstructures like the IMF, WTO, NAFTA, the TPPA (TransPacific Partnership Agreement) – will provide a counter-ideology and alternative organisational practice to the neoliberal economic project. Change requires a repertoire of dialectics between the power holders of the status quo and the oppressed and the exploited. The Marxist-Feminist frame can guide thought and action in shaping a global women's movement in the context of global capitalism.

An emerging transnational women's movement, the International Women's Alliance (IWA), has the potential of playing a significant role in this process. A global alliance of women's movement organisations, institutions, alliances, networks, and individuals from countries in Europe, the Middle East, Africa, Asia Pacific, Latin America, North America, and Oceania, IWA was founded with the leadership of Filipino women in August 2010 in Montreal, Canada, which I attended. One of the central issues IWA included in its discourse during the founding conference is 'capitalist imperialism'. Its first objective reflects a politics that challenges the alliance of capitalism and imperialism: 'to build a global women's movement by uniting, mobilising and organising women from all parts of the world in the struggle against imperialist aggression, war, occupation and intervention and capitalist domination and exploitation'. The third objective shows that IWA's political action of mobilising and organising women must be informed with a profound understanding of how women's oppression and exploitation is linked to imperialism and capitalism: 'to deepen understanding on the root causes of women's oppression and exploitation and the role of imperialism and capitalism, as well as social institutions, in perpetuating reactionary values and in preventing the realization of women's equality and freedom' (International Women's Alliance, https://iwa2010.org/about/our-alliance/). As the founding organisation, GABRIELA (General Assembly of Women for Rights, Integrity, Equality, Leadership, and Action), the progressive coalition of the women's organisations in the Philippines (the majority of whom are grassroots, working-class women) that takes a critical stance against neoliberal globalisation, played a significant role in organising IWA. Liza Largosa Masa, who became an elected Congresswoman of GABRIELA Women's Party in the Philippines, was IWA's first founding chair. The current chairperson is from Pakistan. To date, IWA as a transnational women's movement, comprises about 100 organisations of women workers, peasants, and rural women, urban poor, migrants, Indigenous and minority nationalities, youth, professionals, academicians, and other marginalised and poor women from different countries. Its focus on grassroots women speaks about its class orientation. One can see here the influence of GABRIELA, as the founding member organisation of IWA, whose organisational strategy is oriented towards working-class women who experience more the exploitative dynamics of capitalism and imperialism buttressed by militarism. It shows, as well, that transnational women's movements and alliances against capitalism do not just spring out of the blue. They are rooted in nation-states where global capitalism embeds itself and articulated in specific ways as it constantly seeks how women's and men's labour could be used cheaply.

GABRIELA, that is national but also transnational, was founded in 1984 during the Marcos dictatorship. As a grassroots-based alliance, GABRIELA has more than 200 organisations, institutions, desks, and programmes based in communities, workplaces, and schools throughout the Philippines. It also has chapters in various continents of the world – in Europe, Asia, North America, and Oceania. The acronym is in honour of Gabriela Silang who fearlessly took leadership in the revolution against Spanish colonialism in the Philippines to pick up the role her revolutionary husband, Diego Silang, left after he was killed. Her spirit and action continue to inspire a militant women's movement in the Philippines against imperialism.

GABRIELA recognises how the Philippine pre-colonial mode of production transformed into feudal and capitalist modes under colonial rule and how it shaped the class-gender structure of Philippine society. Way back in the 1980s GABRIELA produced publications that were critical of capitalist globalisation and capitalist imperialism that bolsters it. In its education and consciousness-raising events and seminars it incorporates a critical stance on capitalism and the semi-feudal system that feeds it. It organises working-class women and poor women to mould their collective power. In some ways this reflects the Marxist-Feminist frame integrated in its ideology and influencing its organisational politics. While this frame is reflected in GABRIELA's national and international politics, it is also reflected it its local politics of member organisations. For instance, Amihan, a peasant women's movement organisation under GABRIELA organises peasant women across the Philippines since peasant women and rural women comprise the bulk of grassroots women in the Philippines. Formed in 1986, Amihan (named after the soothing north-easterly wind that comes during harvest season) initially had six provincial chapters, but has grown to 32 provincial chapters across the three major regions of the Philippine archipelago – Luzon, Visayas, and Mindanao. Amihan reflects a Marxist-Feminist frame in its conceptualisation of genuine land reform. Contradicting the government's pro-landlord Comprehensive Agrarian Reform Program (CARP), Amihan's alternative land reform programme, contained in the *Amihan Praymer*, is based on the principle of 'free land to the tiller'. The programme will eliminate the landlord system or feudal economy that creates a large class of poor landless peasants by implementing free distribution of land to landless peasants collectively or in special cases individually, and that landlords who are not despotic will be allowed to own land only if they till the land themselves without the use of tenancy or waged agricultural workers. The ideology and process of implementing agrarian/land reform, Amihan advocates, must be sensitive to the particular situation of peasant women, like peasant women must have equal rights with men in the ownership/titling of land and that they should have equality with men in decisions related to land. It also addresses the blurring of domestic labour and farm work in the case of women who do not get paid for work like preparing the meals of farm workers and tenants while working in the fields. In the context of long-standing government indifference to implementing genuine land reform, Amihan has participated in collective land occupations of idle lands in order to make them productive both for subsistence and for contributing to food security. For a more detailed discussion about Amihan and its alternative land/agrarian reform programme see Lindio-McGovern (1997). But such action – although actually a grassroots initiative on land reform – has been met with military repression, demonstrating the alliance of the neoliberal state with the class that benefits from feudal and semi-feudal modes of production. The co-existence of a feudal or semi-feudal economy and capitalist mode of production in the Philippines benefits transnational capital, as the large landless peasantry can provide cheap labour in the agribusiness of transnational corporations and expulsions from land conversions further facilitates the embedding of global capitalism in the Philippines, such as the expulsions of Indigenous communities from their ancestral lands by corporate mining (see Lindio-McGovern, 2018) and landlords converting their lands for transnational corporations' ventures.

Neoliberal policies of economic liberalisation that unfetter the movement of capital across national borders, privatisation that opens new spheres of capitalist ventures around the world, and deregulation that dismantles protection for labour to create a disposable, controllable, and cheap workforce are interlocking global forces of 'capitalist imperialism' (Lindio-McGovern, 2011). These complex intersecting forces, embedded locally in nation-states and controlled largely by supra-national structures, offer a context in which women's movements rooted in different nation-states can forge transnational women's movements to challenge global capitalism. But it would require a master frame around which to rally women of all classes and nationalities. The Marxist-Feminist frame has the potential as a master frame to bind women transnationally as global capitalism that generates classed and gendered inequalities hurt women and families, and as the exploitation of women's productive and reproductive labour results in the families' limited access to resources and opportunities on a global scale. The increasing privatisation of child care that coincides with the increased participation of women in the capitalist labour force hurts families in the Global North and South. Migrant women and local women's groups and labour unions can unite through forming alliances under this frame since the cheapening of migrant labour is a way for capitalism to depress the wages of local workers. However, migrant women need to organise among themselves both in the host countries and beyond borders to harness their collective power. An example of this is movement organisations of migrant workers, mostly composed of migrant domestic workers, such as the Asian Migrant Coordinating Body (AMCB), the International Migrant Alliance (IMA), and Migrant International (IM). All these movement organisations address cheap and unsubsidised reproductive labour that maintains and reproduces the capitalist system on both the local and international scales.

Conclusion

The foregoing discussion shows that there are indications of the potential of the Marxist-Feminist frame as a master frame for a transnational women's movement to challenge global capitalism frontally and systemically, while embedded in a certain locale, like the nation-state. Global capitalism embeds itself in particular ways in nation-states as it depends on neoliberal governments to implement neoliberal policies that will facilitate the global expansion of capitalism. But global capitalism needs the other side of the same coin to maintain and reproduce itself – the cheapening of social reproductive labour that will be provided mainly by women, not only on the national but also on the global scale. The cheapening of productive labour for the maximisation of profit requires not only an army of cheap workers to run the machines of factories or provide the service work of service organisations, but also the creation of cheap reproductive workers. The complexity of these dynamics requires an analytical frame to study and make explicit its intricacies. Applying the Marxist-Feminist frame would be a central task in this requirement.

But centring the Marxist-Feminist frame would also require giving it an organisational form in order to make it influence political change, under neoliberal regimes where the expansion of global capitalism is entrenched by fascism and militarism. Forming alliances of transnational women's movements united around the master frame of challenging and transforming global capitalism and the nuanced ways they are embedded in neoliberal policies of national economies would be an important step. While the task is long and arduous, its potential is hopeful as exemplified by the existence and persistence of social formations such as GABRIELA and IWA, including the formation of the Marxism-Feminism Conference in Vienna. Embracing this hope and articulating it in our research and political action is hope in itself.

Notes

1 An earlier version of this paper was presented at the Marxism-Feminism Conference held in Vienna, Austria on 7–9 October 2016 at the Institute of Fine Arts Vienna.

2 Professional women and academicians can take this kind of class orientation since they are not immune from the impact of the crisis of capitalism as demonstrated by the worst global economic crisis of 2008. The academia is increasingly corporatised and it has been a knowledge circuit for the maintenance of capitalism and reproduction/propagation of its ideology of neoliberalism that propels global capitalism.

References

Ally, S., 2012 [2009]. 'Globalization and Regional Inequalities – Regional Divisions of Reproductive Labor: Southern African Migrant Domestic Workers in Johannesburg' in Lindio-McGovern, L., Wallimann, I. (Eds.), *Globalization and Third World Women: Exploitation, Coping and Resistance.* Syracuse University Press, Syracuse, NY, 15–33.

Boserup, E., 1970. *The Women's Role in Economic Development.* George Allen and Unwin, London.

Cock, J., 1980. *Maids and Madams: A Study in the Politics of Exploitation*. Ravan Press, Johannesburg.

Davis, A., 1981. *Women, Race and Class*. Random House, New York.

Gimenez, M., 1975. 'Marxism and Feminism'. *Frontiers: A Journal of Women's Studies* 1(1): 61–80.

Gimenez, M., 2012. 'Global Capitalism and Women: From Feminist Politics to Working Class Politics' in Lindio-McGovern, L., Wallimann, I. (Eds.), *Globalization and Third World Women: Exploitation, Coping and Resistance*. Syracuse University Press, Syracuse, NY, 35–48.

Hartmann, H., 1979. 'The Unhappy Marriage of Marxism and Feminism: Towards a More Progressive Union'. *Capital and Class* (Summer): 1–33.

Ledesma, C.K. 2015. 'Women in Revolution: Maria Lorena Barros and MAKIBAKA'. www.ndf.org/women-in-revolution-maria-lorena-barros-and-makibaka/. Accessed 9 December 2018.

Lindio-McGovern, L., 1997. *Filipino Peasant Women: Exploitation and Resistance*. University of Pennsylvania, Philadelphia, PA.

Lindio-McGovern, L., 2011. 'Neoliberal Globalization in the Philippines: Its Impact on Filipino Women and Their Forms of Resistance' in Polakoff, E., Lindio-McGovern, L. (Eds.), *Gender and Globalization: Patterns of Women's Resistance*. de Sitter Publications, Whitby, Ontario, 33–56.

Lindio-McGovern, L., 2012. *Globalization, Labor Export and Resistance: A Study of Filipino Migrant Domestic Workers in Global Cities*. Routledge, London; New York.

Lindio-McGovern, L. 2018. 'Corporate Mining, Sustainable Development and Human Rights of Indigenous People in the Philippines'. Paper presented at the International Sociological Conference, Metro Toronto Convention Center, Toronto, Ontario, 15–21 July 2018.

Lindio-McGovern, L., Wallimann, I., 2012. [2009]. 'Introduction. Neoliberal Globalization and Third World Women: Exploitation, Coping and Resistance' in Lindio-McGovern, L., Wallimann, I. (Eds.), *Globalization and Third World Women: Exploitation, Coping and Resistance*. Syracuse University Press, Syracuse, NY, 1–14.

Robinson, W.I., 1996. *Promoting Polyarchy: Globalization, US Intervention and Hegemony*. Cambridge University Press, New York.

Sklair, L., 2001. *The Transnational Capitalist Class*. Blackwell, Oxford.

Sklair, L., 2002. *Globalization, Capitalism and Its Alternative Visions*. Oxford University Press, New York.

Taguiwalo, J.M. 2009. 'The Formation of MAKIBAKA'. https://redbrandog.wordpress.com/2009/09/20/the-formation-of-makibaka/. Accessed 9 December 2018.

19 | MARXIST/SOCIALIST FEMINIST THEORY AND PRACTICE IN THE USA TODAY

Nancy Holmstrom

In the United States today we see an exciting revival of feminism. The election of Donald Trump brought to the surface the most egregious and blatantly offensive forms of sexism, from reports of his extra-marital affairs to his predatory and crude language ('grabbing pussy'). It is worth noting that this kind of behaviour is not new, even at the highest level of American government. President John F. Kennedy was notorious for his affairs and even orgies in the White House. But in those days, almost half a century ago, when abortion was mostly illegal, LGBTQ rights did not exist, (indeed 'LGBT' was not yet coined), the women's liberation movement was not yet on the horizon, such behaviour was hidden, and JFK's sexual misconduct is still only rarely discussed publicly in the United States. In today's day and age, however – especially because it is combined in a contradictory and misogynist way with Trump's alliances with social conservatives who oppose abortion, even birth control and same sex marriage (all of which are now legal) – this blatant predatory sexism is just too much!

Therefore, ironically, one silver lining in Trump's election to the presidency is that it has ignited a new women's movement. At Trump's inauguration in January 2017, the Women's March in Washington DC protesting Trump was the largest march *in the history of the United States*, with sister marches taking place throughout the country. The organisers and most speakers were liberal and white, which was reflective of the crowd, many (or perhaps most) having been supporters of Hillary Clinton. However, the rally also included more radical voices, in the crowd and on the platform, in particular Angela Davis. In an electrifying speech stressing the racism and genocidal violence at the heart of US capitalism, she connected fights to save the planet, for clean water at Standing Rock and Gaza, and pledged collective resistance to hetero-patriarchy, racism, and xenophobia. She warned, 'Those who still defend the supremacy of white male hetero-patriarchy had better watch out ... This is just the beginning and in the words of the inimitable Ella Baker, "We who believe in freedom cannot rest until it comes"'. On International Women's Day the International Women's Strike (IWS), connected to protests around the globe, held a large rally and march in New York City. Marches again took place in 2018 one year from the inauguration and on International Women's Day. Innumerable articles in the press show women getting involved in electoral politics for the first time and the predictions that they would help change the makeup of Congress has borne fruit. Meanwhile the #MeToo movement against sexual harassment has exploded in the media and shows no signs of letting up, with some extending it to #WeToo.[1] The question remains as to how radical this new feminist movement will be. Certainly it will be mixed, as feminism has always been – but as I will discuss later in the chapter, there are reasons to be optimistic about its radical potential and the direction it is likely to take.

Varieties of feminism

In the 1960s and '70s in the heyday of the women's liberation movement in the United States, when 'feminism' was too tame a word, mainstream feminists in the US were social welfare feminists, as is typical in Europe. They supported abortion rights of course, and equal pay for equal work, as do all feminists, but they also supported public childcare and welfare. Gloria Steinem and *Ms.* magazine are examples. But in the era of capitalist restructuring, and the employers' offensive, the movement declined, and at the same time that so many activists were moving into careers and families, American politics was moving to the right, into neoliberalism – and it took mainstream feminism with it. So instead of collective social provision, we heard about individual responsibility and self-sufficiency. The Clintons' welfare 'reform', which for the first time in 50 years denied poor women with children the resources they need, exemplifies this change – and Gloria Steinem's support for Hillary Clinton, despite all that Clinton has done against the interests of the majority of women in the world, is a sad example of the rightward evolution of mainstream feminists. Some people have expressed surprise when I have said this, as they are thinking exclusively of gender-specific issues, like abortion, where Clinton takes pro-choice feminist positions. But women are *not only impacted by issues that are uniquely or primarily gender-related.* Clinton's support for her husband's welfare 'reform', her support for the war in Iraq, for harsh criminal justice policies, and her failure to support universal medical care, not to mention her pro-Wall Street positions – all these have done great harm to women. Men have been harmed by these policies too, to be sure. Oftentimes women were disproportionately harmed, but not always. Either way, however, women have been harmed – and it is essential that we understand 'women's interests' in this broad way.

Recently American socialist feminists Hester Eisenstein (2010) and Nancy Fraser (2009, 2017) have criticised 'feminism' for its accommodations to capitalism. Although much of their critiques are valid, this way of posing it is very misleading (Brenner, 2017). It erases the political-economic causes of the rightward move of US politics and collapses the many varieties of feminism into its most powerful version. It is hardly surprising that liberal feminism, which is not anti-capitalist, is hegemonic today – indeed it has always been. What is new is the way feminist ideas have been deployed in combination with conservative nationalist forces (never known for support of feminism) in favour of imperialism and against immigrant men, particularly Muslims (Farris, 2017).

Nevertheless, there has always been a more radical anti-capitalist feminist current in the United States, and it has been engaged in all kinds of struggles for many decades, with some modest success, as I shall discuss later in the chapter. Some of us call ourselves Marxist, socialist or materialist feminists, others call themselves black feminists or anarcho-feminists, ecofeminists, or some other name. Personally, though I am a Marxist, I usually choose the label 'socialist feminist', just because it is the most inclusive of the terms and is less likely to be misunderstood, at least in the United States. (In Europe with social democratic parties so discredited, perhaps this is not so.) So, for the purposes of this chapter I will use 'socialist feminism' to include all of these more radical versions of feminism, some of which are Marxist and some not. As I define it, all socialist feminists see class as central to women's lives, yet at the same time none would reduce sex or race oppression to economic exploitation (Holmstrom, 2002). All socialist-feminist politics have an anti-capitalist edge, not merely anti-neoliberal capitalism.[2] As we will see throughout this chapter, women of colour have played an important role pushing feminist movements to the left; some identify as socialists, others do not but given that most black women are working class or poor, black feminists tend to be more radical than the average white feminist.

Which word we choose to identify ourselves *largely* depends, I think, on the political context we're in, and the debates in which we're involved, as well as how we understand these categories. So, the same label may not mean the same analysis – and different labels may not mean different analyses. For example, Margaret Benston (1969: 13–27) was one of the first Marxists to analyse women's domestic labour, back in 1969. She considered herself a Marxist, used Marxist categories, wrote in *Monthly Review*, a Marxist publication, and is described as a Marxist feminist. In fact, however, her analysis was more like that of feminists of the 1970s who were calling themselves '*Socialist* Feminist' precisely in order to distinguish themselves from Marxists. Hilary Wainwright calls herself a feminist socialist (Wainwright, 2015) rather than a socialist feminist in order to signal her interest in bringing insights from feminism into the socialist movement and into visions of socialism. She's been arguing this since the 1970s and recently expressed her frustration that she still has to make the same argument.

Varieties of socialist feminism: one system or two

Sometimes these different labels do signal different theoretical analyses of women's oppression and capitalism. Interestingly, however, as I shall discuss in the conclusion, these different theories need not entail different politics.

What are called 'dual systems theories' of women's oppression in capitalism were developed in the 1970s in response to the appalling sexism in much of the left, new as well as old, and to 'Marxist' theories which ignored or dismissed women's oppression. In the United States, Heidi Hartmann referred to the 'unhappy marriage of Marxism and feminism in which Marxism subsumed feminism' (Hartmann, 1979), contending that to understand women's oppression in capitalism, we must theorise it in terms of another system, patriarchy, existing before and after capitalism. Though unfortunately few American activists follow developments outside the United States, it happened that across the ocean, similar dual system theories were developed, most notably by Christine Delphy. They accepted Marx's critique of capitalism but contended that it must be supplemented *and significantly revised* in order to understand women's oppression.

It is easy to show that sexism – and racism – increase the rate of exploitation in Marx's sense, as women and racial minorities are typically confined to the lowest paid work or paid less for the same work. But dual systems theorists say this benefits male workers as well as capitalists and should be seen as a function of patriarchy as well as capitalism – and that these two kinds of inequalities have equivalent importance. (Notice that the oppression or exploitation is part of the material base if one wants to speak in those terms.) Many feminist critics also charge that it was sexist of Marx to focus so exclusively on wage labour in capitalism and to ignore all the unpaid labour done by women in the home, again very material. Indeed, they find it particularly insulting that, according to Marx's analysis, this labour is not 'productive' labour. Surely, they contend, much of this labour is absolutely necessary for the reproduction of the work force, both biologically and in the sense of getting the worker to the factory door every day. Hence it is not only necessary for life in general, but for capitalism as it provides the basis for all work. Other feminist critics like Christine Delphy (1984; Delphy and Leonard, 1992), however, reject this focus on capitalism; instead they theorise a domestic mode of production alongside capitalism in which men exploit women's labour.

I will address these two points in turn. It was not sexism, nor an oversight, I contend, that led Marx to exclude household labour from his category of productive-in-capitalism, though of course it is productive in a general sense; production of people is obviously essential in all times and places and modes of production. Marx restricts the definition of productive labour as he does in order to 'express[es] precisely the specific form of the labor on which the whole capitalist mode of production and capital itself is based' (Marx, 1963). Hence the concept is the key to understanding the 'essence' of capitalism, and to understand the limits to which it can be reformed. As Rosa Luxemburg said: from the standpoint of capital,

> The dancer in a café, who makes a profit for her employer with her legs, is a productive working woman, while all the toil of the women and mothers of the proletariat within the four walls of the home is considered unproductive work. [This] sounds crude and crazy but it is an accurate expression of the crudeness and craziness of today's economic order. (Luxemburg, 1912: 21)

Note that the labour of a male carpenter who works for the state is equally unproductive in this sense.

Though domestic labour does not produce surplus value, capitalism and the constraints it poses are still important for understanding its persistence. The more labour done in the home for free, the less capitalists have to pay labour; hence their desire to push it onto the individual family. This helps to explain why women in the United States were able to win legal equality, but why caretaking is still largely a private responsibility.

But men also benefit from women's unpaid labour in the home, feminists rightly insist. Even if most men do not benefit from this gender system since it benefits capitalism, they certainly benefit in the short run. They have a shorter workday! And even though domestic labour does not produce surplus value, this does not mean that women are only oppressed in the home, but not exploited. As Delphy points out, exploitation is a broader concept than extraction of surplus value. Marx himself said clearly that this is simply the form that exploitation takes in capitalism. The unpaid surplus labour women have no choice but to do in the home[3] is exploited labour. Whether it is husbands, or men in general, or both capitalists and men who exploit domestic labour is too complicated to resolve here, but I am inclined to say that there is *no one* answer to this question. Rather, it depends on the details of the family, in particular just how much nonwage work a woman does and whether or not this is on top of wage work – which most women in developed capitalist countries are doing. So I think a theory of a domestic mode of production is less plausible today if it ever was. Marxists need not claim, however, that capitalist class relations are the *only* important social relations, or indeed the only class relations that exist in capitalism. In fact, other modes of production, e.g. slavery, have often coexisted with capitalism, and hierarchies based on race/ethnicity and nationality have thrived within capitalist societies. So, even if the idea of a distinct patriarchal mode of production, with men and women forming two classes is not, as I shall argue, the best way of illuminating sexism and capitalism, it is not inherently inconsistent with Marxism.

What is a 'system'?

What *would* require a significant revision of Marxism is the claim that these two systems of capitalism and patriarchy are of equal explanatory weight for understanding our current system, its history, and its trajectory. While this can be further researched, the idea raises a number of thorny methodological issues:

1. If it is necessary to postulate a distinct system of equal importance to understand how sexism works within capitalism, then why only two systems? In addition to these two, there is racism, there is heterosexism, ageism, ableism. Racism in particular has played a critical role in the history of US capitalism, but all are relations of power and unjust privilege. Does it mean we should theorise them as systems? This leads to the question:

2. What exactly constitutes a system? While I have no definitive answer, capitalism is clearly a system; its constitutive elements give it powerful tendencies that work across time and place, whatever their variations. A necessary condition for the transition from feudalism to capitalism in England centuries ago was the separation of producers from their means of subsistence and the amassing of wealth by others; today we see the same process of primitive accumulation in Russia and China as they have transitioned from the Soviet system to versions of capitalism (Holmstrom and Smith, 2000: 1–14). Descriptions of factory conditions in the developing world today could be taken directly from Engels's descriptions from the nineteenth century. The drive to turn everything into a commodity has penetrated areas of the globe, of our bodies, and our minds, in ways few could have imagined. Most significantly, the need to develop the productive forces, to grow, to accumulate on an ever-expanding basis is so powerful that it now threatens the very basis of human life on this planet.[4] Now that's a system!

I do not see sexism having anything like this kind of explanatory weight. What we see are *descriptions* of multifarious ways in which sexism operates in capitalism and in other modes of production, how it has changed, even lessened within capitalism, but persists. While it has some autonomous causal efficacy, struggles against it have succeeded *only within the terms set by capitalism*. Thus, we now have women at the highest levels of society, but the majority are disproportionately poor and becoming poorer. (Increased class differences are even more pronounced in the case of race in the US.) For understanding capitalism, it is essential to see how deeply sexist – and racist – it is, but this does not entail that sexism and racism constitute 'systems' in anything like the sense in which capitalism is a system.

3. If we do take them as distinct systems, involving two sets of classes, men and women, and capitalists and workers (or more to deal with race), how these 'classes' interrelate is complicated. Some women exploit both other women and also men – both in capitalist terms and in familial terms – and as I indicated, the class divide is increasing. How do the classes formed by capitalism and patriarchy (and racism) interrelate? Sex and race hierarchies definitely exist, but it is clearer in my opinion to see them as existing *within* socio-economic classes rather than as distinct *kinds* of classes (thus, for example, within the working class, whites tend to be better off than

blacks, men better off than women). These hierarchies can therefore create conflicts of interest among working-class men and women and between black and white workers, even though they would all benefit from an end to capitalism (an implication that is controversial among Marxists). Keep in mind, however, that gender inequalities today are significantly less in the US than class inequalities, as two recent sex-discrimination lawsuits reveal. A bond-saleswoman at Morgan Stanley sued because her salary of over a million dollars/year was much lower than her male colleagues'; women at Walmart sued because their annual salary was $1,100 lower than the men's, but the average pay for *all* Walmart employees is only $10/hour. Despite these gender inequalities, the woman bond salesperson was still really rich, and the male Walmart worker quite poor.

Intersectionality

The popular concept of 'intersectionality' might seem to answer the question of the relationship among these different kinds of oppressions. The term 'intersectionality' is credited to Kimberlé Crenshaw (1989: 139–167), an African American law professor who introduced it in 1989, but the idea has been around for longer; we see it in socialist women in the nineteenth century who focused on working women's distinct struggles, and it is found in Marxist feminists like Alexandra Kollontai. But most importantly in the United States, the concept goes back to the groundbreaking Combahee River Collective Statement[5] of 1977. Drafted by a group of radical black feminists, it brought together not only sex and class but race and sexuality. They wrote from their specific identities as black lesbians of working-class origin who had found the male-dominated black liberation movement (especially its nationalist wings) (Mullings, 2002: 313–335) and the mainstream white feminist movement unwelcoming or downright hostile. Though they collaborated well with socialist feminists they wanted to make clear what they thought was their unique perspective – and they did. Their manifesto argued that black women's unique experience of oppression was erased as they were put into either the category of race or of sex; nor can these two identities simply be 'added on' because they are so interrelated. The manifesto made the radical claim that because these multiple kinds of oppression are so interwoven, it will be impossible to free oneself from one without dismantling them all. Explicit socialists, they insisted that a socialist revolution must also be a feminist and anti-racist one. They identified as Third World women, expressing solidarity with anti-imperialist struggles and they suggested that their position at the bottom might be used to 'make a leap into revolutionary action. If Black women were free, it would mean that everyone else would have to be free since our freedom would necessitate the destruction of all the systems of oppression' (Taylor, 2017: 23). The radical Black Feminism of the Combahee River Collective Statement has been extremely influential in current movements, as I shall discuss later. Thus, the concept of intersectionality is extremely valuable for understanding the specificities of the position of American black women, but also more broadly, as an analytic and strategic insight. In political practice it is extremely important to emphasise the intersection of different kinds of oppression, or else we risk the false counter-position of class politics and what are dismissively labelled 'identity politics'. Since working-class women's lives and oppression do not begin at the door to the factory or office (likewise for non-white working-class men) socialists wanting to organise working-class women and men of differing race/ethnicities have to recognise this, and they increasingly do so, though there is still much room for improvement.[6]

However, turning back to the abstract question of one system or two (or more) systems, the concept of intersectionality in itself does not *explain* on a theoretical level exactly *how and why* different kinds of oppression relate as they do. Moreover, the notion of intersectionality does not commit us to two or more systems, as we could just as well be exploring the intersection of *different aspects of the one system of capitalism*. In fact, talk of a *distinct system of patriarchy* tends to obscure the integration of sexism with capitalism and to encourage people treating them as distinct autonomous systems. Thus, for example, Ann Cudd, my co-author of the recent book *Capitalism For and Against: A Feminist Debate* (Cudd and Holmstrom, 2011), blames patriarchy for women's lower pay and absence of childcare – but not capitalism, though it is obvious that capitalists benefit from the lack of childcare and from women having lower salaries. My concern is that if we proliferate systems of equivalent importance that we lose explanatory coherence and end up with simple pluralism.[7]

Nevertheless, there are several reasons why dual or triple system models are more attractive to many than a unitary model. As discussed, there is the political importance of an intersectional approach, the fear – based on all too many historical examples – that sex and race oppression will be subsumed by class, and the fact that sex oppression and race oppression *seem* distinct, and are experienced as distinct, from class oppression. For these reasons theorists have continued to work to develop intersectional theories, which are seen by many to support dual or triple system analyses. A recent sophisticated version is that offered by French theorist Danièle Kergoat (2009) who wants to capture the interplay, the dynamic social and historical character of gender, race, and class rather than seeing them as abstract and distinct elements that are added together in a geometric way. To do so, she borrows the term 'consubstantiality' from theological debates regarding the unity and difference of the three elements of the Trinity. Gender, race, and class are each held to be a relation of production involving exploitation; thus, there is no difference of substance between the three (problematic assumptions, but I will ignore this). By co-forming and mutually determining one another, they constitute a unified system of three systems of equivalent importance. The theory of consubstantiality is an intriguing attempt to understand differences within a unity, which makes it a definite improvement over additive models and would be attractive to many American socialist feminists though, regrettably, few are familiar with work done in non-English-speaking countries. However, the unity provided by the concept of consubstantiality is not really a coherent one because given the equal importance of the three, their unity cannot provide an explanation of *how, when, and why* the elements interact as they do. The relation is ultimately mysterious, like the Trinity, as Cinzia Arruzza wittily puts the point (Arruzza, 2014)

A framework model: one non-reductive system

If we conclude, then, that a two- or three- (or more) system model cannot give us the coherence and unity we want in order to understand the system in which we live, then we need to find a one-system model that can accommodate differences. The system in which we live is capitalist and patriarchal and racist and heterosexist …, but to leave it at that description does not tell us how and why they all work together – and how this is different from simple pluralism. Instead of a multi-system model, I think we need a model that gives primacy of explanation to capitalism, but – and I stress this – which is not reductive. There are different ways of expressing this: recall Engels's 'Letters on Historical Materialism' where he clarifies that all he and Marx ever said was that the economic was *'ultimately decisive'* or determining *'in the long run'*, etc. Such phrases help to dispel misinterpretations of the theory, but they do not get us very far. Better, I think, is what has been called the framework model, based on Marx, in which explanation is contextualist, rather than atomist.[8] The idea is that different modes of production like capitalism and feudalism have structures that make possible different causal relations. Capitalism is then understood to be the context or framework within which other relations of oppression operate, with more or less salience in different times and places. So this gives capitalism a primacy in explanation, but it does not rule out other causes. Rather, in fact, it helps to explain *how and why other causes operate* – both material and non-material causes. Thus, while capitalism did not create male dominance, it uses it; capitalism's essential nature allowed for male dominance to lessen in certain ways but sets obstacles to its complete eradication. In the 1960s and '70s, political and economic conditions led many more women to higher education and the paid work force, and lowered fertility rates. Inspired by the civil rights movement which had successfully challenged allegedly biologically based subordination and led to anti-discrimination laws, women now had both the impetus and the opportunity to join together to challenge the patriarchal gender order. While they succeeded in dismantling restrictions on abortion, discriminatory laws, and policies in the public and the private sphere, nevertheless women still do the bulk of the caretaking labour today. (This will be explored further in later sections of the chapter.)

Analogous questions regarding capitalism and racism have arisen among black radicals, who range from nationalists (analogous to Radical Feminists) to liberals and social democrats to Black Marxists, like C.L.R. James. Although James was known for his powerful critiques of racism and colonialism and his defence of Black Power, he accepted something like the one-system framework model I have proposed, as seen in this quote from his masterwork *The Black Jacobins*: 'The race question is subsidiary to the class question, and to think of imperialism in terms of race is disastrous. But to neglect the racial factor as merely incidental, is an error only less grave than to make it fundamental' (James, 1963: 283).[9]

Variations within one-system theories: wages for housework and social reproduction feminism

Earlier in the chapter I defended Marx's restriction of the concept of productive labour to labour that produces surplus value, since that is the key to profit, which is the goal of capitalist production. Forms of labour that do not produce surplus value are less central to capitalism and therefore to Marx's theoretical work since his aim was to explain why capitalist societies do what they do. Nevertheless, feminists are absolutely correct to complain that productive-for-capitalism is a very limited notion of productive labour, in Luxemburg's words, a 'crude and crazy' concept reflective of the crude and crazy system that is capitalism. They are also correct to argue that this narrowness obscures the work of household and community maintenance, labour caring for children, the elderly, and all others unable to take care of themselves, all of which are necessary foundations for capitalism; indeed, it is the labour that makes all other labour possible. As this work is still done largely by women, women's productive contribution to society is obscured in capitalism. This kind of labour is increasingly commodified in developed capitalist countries (caregivers in for-profit nursing homes and day care centres or working in the home but for private agencies, cooks, servers, and on and on) and hence it would be included as productive-in-capitalism. However, much caring labour is not for pay. It is done for free, out of love. By and large feminists do not want it to be commodified, but to have the material support and respect that it deserves.

The wages for housework movement (Dalla Costa and James, 1975), which originated in Italy in the 1970s, had followers in the United States and in recent years has enjoyed renewed interest, partly due to the influence of Silvia Federici's important book *Caliban and the Witch* (Federici, 2004). Adherents claimed that non-waged housework actually produces surplus value, even though it was not directly employed by the capitalist because housework produces the labourers and gets them to the workplace ready for work. However, I have argued elsewhere against this[10] that it is problematic to use Marxist categories but to change them in this way. These concepts are technical theoretical ones that, like any scientific term, e.g. molecule, can only be understood within the terms of the theory as a whole. Housework is definitely necessary for the production of surplus value, but that does not mean it produces surplus value. These are two different concepts. As already said, Marx's theory was designed to illuminate exactly what drove the capitalist system, namely profit, and it relies on getting as much as it could of what was necessary for free, like household labour or like water, for that matter.

I suspect that underlying the wages for housework movement's conflation of labour *necessary* for production of surplus value with labour that *produces* surplus value might be a strategic assumption: if housewives' labour produced surplus labour, just as much as workers' labour at an auto plant, then housework and struggles around unpaid domestic labour should not only be equally valued, but should be an equally central part of working-class struggle. However, this would not automatically follow. Consider guards in profit-making prisons. They produce surplus value but they would not therefore be an important focus of socialist strategy. So, production of surplus value is not sufficient. Nor is it necessary, as today's struggles of public employees demonstrate.

Nevertheless, even if the theory behind the wages for housework movement is mistaken, they are certainly correct in pointing to the importance of work, done mostly by women, which is outside wage work. Marxist feminists have begun to explore how to theorise the complete story of labour in capitalism, an approach that has been called social reproduction feminism. The general idea is that the Marxist analysis of a mode of production has to be expanded to include all the socially necessary labour required for that mode of production, both production and species production. Lise Vogel is credited as the first, at least in English,[11] to use the phrase in her work reviewing the history of Marxist theorising on women's oppression in 1983 (Vogel, 1983). She starts with the contradiction at the heart of class societies between class exploitation and the need to reproduce the next generation. Exactly how this is worked out depends on class struggle. Within capitalism Vogel located women's ongoing oppression in their special responsibility for the renewal of labour power, that is their role bearing and raising children and the household labour that goes along with it. While her analysis remained at an abstract level, Johanna Brenner and Barbara Laslett (2000: 59–82) used a social reproduction approach in a more concrete historical way. Their conception is of a single system of species reproduction, which always involved a division of labour, but one that takes different forms related to changes in the capitalist economy. Neither the relations of production nor those of reproduction are given by nature but are the result of gender and class struggles. Using this approach, they explained how women's political organisation was able to challenge the gender order in the 1960s and '70s, whereas they had been unable to do so earlier. The organisation of social reproduction at the turn of the century, in particular the lack of opportunities in the paid workforce, made marriage women's 'best career option', even for women who had jobs. Thus, when reforms were won in the 1930s, they were premised on the male breadwinner model of the family; so, for example, women-dominated jobs were excluded from fair labour legislation. Even left organisations that supported civil rights failed to support working women who protested against these policies, much less to question the gendered division of labour in the home.

In the 1960s and '70s, however, when political and economic conditions led many more women to higher education and the paid work force, and lowered fertility rates, women had both the impetus and the opportunity to join together to challenge the patriarchal gender order. Today with even more women in the work force, a lot of the work of social reproduction has been commodified and many women employ other women as nannies and maids and elder caregivers while the majority of American women have been doing a 'double day' for the past few decades. The responsibilities of men in the family and of the state have, nevertheless, become objects of struggle both on the political and on the personal level. Thus changes in the organisation of social reproduction within the framework of capitalism have both advanced and retarded women's emancipation, at different times and in different ways.

Recently a number of Marxist feminists are using this social reproduction framework (Bhattacharya, 2017). Some have connected it to the International Women's Strike, as I will discuss in the next section. Demands have been made by feminists in the United States to support caregiving as a public good, as it is in many countries with stronger social democratic traditions. These are crucial demands to make but they should be recognised as transitional demands in the sense that they are not winnable under capitalism but rather point us towards a different society. A society that gave equal value to non-waged caring labour would be socialism, not capitalism, a mode of production that aimed at the satisfaction of need not the maximisation of profit.

Socialist feminism in practice: varieties of intersecting struggles

This section discusses the varieties of ongoing struggles and how socialist feminists approach them. There may not be much connection with the theoretical differences among socialists feminists discussed above, as I have found over the years that such abstract differences do not necessarily entail *political* differences. Socialist feminists tend to agree on the best approaches to political organising even when we don't share the same abstract model. Moreover, the connection between theory and political strategy is not as direct as some assume; as just discussed above, for example, production of surplus value is neither necessary nor sufficient for being at the centre of socialist organising. Good socialist strategy depends on many factors, which are not timeless. The framework model I've outlined would stress the need for coalitions between different groups up against the constraints of capitalism, but would go beyond coalitions, attempting to integrate the issues. However, the same is true for those who accept a dual or multi-systems model. In the remainder of this chapter I will discuss the hopeful signs of a new radical women's movement in the United States today and the distinct approaches socialist feminists take, whatever abstract model they adhere to.

Socialist Feminists are involved in all kinds of struggles, some explicitly gendered, others not. In all cases, it's the struggles of working-class women that socialist feminists focus on, whether the struggles are on the job, in the community – wherever. What defines socialist feminists is both the politics they articulate and the way they organise themselves and articulate those politics (Brenner and Holmstrom, 2013: 266–287). It goes without saying that we support all struggles for women's legal rights, but that is far from enough.

The paradigmatic gendered struggle for legal abortion was won in the US in 1973 but socialist feminists and black feminists pressed to go beyond an individual right to choose. The concept of reproductive rights was developed in the late 1970s by socialist feminists in the United States with prodding from women of colour who wanted protection against sterilisation abuse and the social changes that would support their decision to have children: childcare, maternity leave, welfare, decent medical care, housing, and education. This would seem obvious in countries with a strong social democratic tradition, but not in the US. Most activists, pushed by women of colour, have come to prefer the terms reproductive freedom or reproductive justice because they bring to the fore that social and economic changes are required for all women, working class and women of colour, to be able to control if and when they have children and to be able to raise them in dignity and health (Silliman et al., 2004; Roberts, 2015). Exemplifying an intersectional approach, this approach pushes towards an anti-capitalist politics because unlike legal abortion, these demands challenge capitalist profits. We never won these in the United States, and where they were won, neoliberalism has brought continual attacks on these benefits.

Another crucial gendered struggle in this period is against sexual harassment known as the #MeToo movement which has since spread to the #WeToo movement. It started with complaints against powerful men in Hollywood and then television, then the arts and advertising and athletics and also in politics. Most of these men were celebrities, as were many of those making the charges, and so they got incredible publicity, encouraging more women to break their silence about their own harassment, and educating masses of Americans on how pervasive the problem was. It had a powerful shaming effect and some of the perpetrators actually lost their jobs. All this would have been a significant victory in itself. But more significant was the spreading of this movement to the millions of more vulnerable low-wage women who cannot rely on shaming a celebrity because the perpetrators were their foremen, their supervisors, or their coworkers. They are often women of colour, many immigrants, some dependent on tips, all of which adds to their vulnerability. This became known as the movement from #MeToo to #WeToo because individual solutions were less possible for women in these positions. Though Hollywood celebrities raised 13 million dollars for a legal defence fund to help poorer women (the Time's Up movement), what women workers need most are organised collective remedies, to prevent abuse in the first place. The most inspiring example of how this could work is the Fair Food Program (FFP) of the Committee of Immokolee Workers (CIW), farmworkers in Florida who had faced not only sexual harassment, but rape, violence, wage theft, and slavery-like conditions when they started organising 20 years ago. The FFP is a worker-led, workplace-monitoring programme which has been called by the United Nations expert on human trafficking 'an international benchmark' (CIW.online.org; Kaufmann, 2018). They held a five-day fast and a march in New York City in the spring of 2018 to bring attention to Wendy's, the one major fast food restaurant that has not signed onto the FFP. Whether or not CIW activists are explicit socialists, the CIW exemplifies the kind of bottom-up working women's movement that socialist feminists champion.

In contrast to reproductive rights, against sexual harassment, and labour struggles, environmental struggles do not seem gendered nor to have anything to do with class. What could be more universal than the need for clean air and water? But this does not mean it is not a women's issue – as women are half the human race! So just as feminists argued that women's rights are human rights, it is equally true that human rights are women's rights. Moreover, there is often some gender dimension even if it's not explicit. The United Nations Population Fund says that women in developing countries are particularly impacted by climate change, directly because of the difficulty of meeting their family's needs, and indirectly, by the wars engendered by scarce resources. Women are often the leaders of grassroots environmental movements, disproportionately taking place in non-white and poor communities, hence known as environmental justice struggles. Socialist feminists strongly support these intersectional struggles, as they stress that the roots of the environmental crisis lie in capitalism's inherent drive to expand production.

People throughout the world have heard of the new radical black movement called Black Lives Matter, founded in 2013 to protest the acquittal of a white 'neighborhood watch' volunteer for killing Trayvon Martin, a 17-year-old black high school student. It might seem surprising to include #BLM in my account of socialist feminist organising, but I do so because it was founded by three black women influenced by black feminism whose politics are explicitly intersectional. While focused on police killings of black people, they put at the centre of their politics people marginalised by traditional civil rights and black liberation organisations: women, queers, and the disabled; they reject dominant black male leaders, an orientation to church associations, and the Democratic Party and have a de-centralised structure. Some activists felt that there was not sufficient focus on the black women also killed by the police so they started 'Say Her Name' to complete, but not to compete with, BLM. Internationalist in their perspective, BLM called attention to the connections between urban police departments in the US and the state of Israel. The Platform for Black Lives that arose from BLM, states that state violence is not limited to police shootings, but includes the under-investment in black communities which has been devastating to their health and well being. Calling for a range of economic initiatives under community control, it is a model of progressive thinking. Another black woman-led organisation is Critical Resistance founded by Angela Davis and Ruth Wilson Gilmore, that opposes the prison industrial complex ('the carceral state') from a feminist, anti-racist, and anti-capitalist perspective. It is allied with INCITE, an anti-gender violence organisation, which opposes the law-and-order feminism typical of work in this area. Instead, they connect interpersonal violence to state violence and propose transformational, restorative strategies rather than punitive ones.

Finally, there is also a revival of labour militancy – which is centred on occupations that are dominated by women. In West Virginia teachers had endured abysmally low salaries and impossibly high health care costs, as had other public employees. Teachers organised outside their unions starting with a secret Facebook page that built a network of teachers that later had the strength to undertake the strike, even though public employee strikes are illegal in the state. It is interesting, but unsurprising, to know that the teachers who initiated the Facebook page were organised socialists, members of the IWW (Industrial Workers of the World) and DSA (Democratic Socialists of America). Though the teachers who responded were not socialists, by the end of the strike, undoubtedly many more would answer to that label. West Virginia is a complicated place politically. Although the state voted for Trump, it was Bernie Sanders who won the Democratic Party primary and most importantly, West Virginia has a long tradition of radical coal miner union organising which the teachers clearly built on. They included demands for other school personnel and helped families disadvantaged by the strike (even feeding children who depended on free school breakfasts and lunches).

Their organised strength, supported by parents and the broader community, helped them to win a 5 per cent across-the-board raise for all public employees against powerful odds. Facing the same conditions of underfunding, teachers in Oklahoma followed West Virginia with a nine-day strike, this time led by the union. They won some gains, but not their demand that the funding be through taxes aimed at the rich. The union (against some members' resistance) decided they should go back to work and focus on electing better state legislators. As I write, teachers in Arizona, another Republican state, who have endured underfunding for decades, are considering a strike. Voters in these states may elect Democrats next year, but the radical potential seen in West Virginia will not be realised unless people break from both the Republicans and the Democrats.

The success of the West Virginia teachers had an important precedent in the 2012 teachers strike in Chicago led by the Chicago Teachers Union. Its progressive leadership had a history of working with parents, starting with the fight against school closings. Their strike demands for smaller classes, better services for students, mostly poor and minority, against the standardised testing that was dominating the lives of both the teachers and the students served to unite teachers, students, and parents. The teachers argued that their own demands for job security versus threats of privatisation were also in the interests of students. As a result, their strike was widely supported by parents and students. The movement against school closings brought together a diverse group, including gay socialist feminists and black community activists, not all of whom supported gay rights. Rather than tackle their differences directly, they worked in solidarity, recognising that the parents should be in the leadership of the struggle. Over time, that kind of solidarity is the best way to overcome distrust and change minds. Public employees combining with those they serve is a huge step forward and hopefully can be emulated in other sectors.[12] Too often workers and consumers are pitted against one another. And workers with some benefits and protections are pitted against those who lack them. Public employees are especially vulnerable to this kind of divisive anti-working-class ideology in the United States because it is tax payers who pay their salaries, and fewer and fewer workers in the private sector have union protections.

These struggles all illustrate a point made by Hilary Wainwright in the *Socialist Register* 2017 volume on Revolution. 'In many diverse locations, grassroots trade union and community alliances have been a driving force in the defense and improvement of public services or utilities in the face of privatization' (Wainwright, 2017: 94). Some are theorising this as an instance of social reproduction feminism and are hoping that the International Women's Strike (IWS) organisation will be able to play an important role. Certainly, Americans are facing what can be called a crisis of social reproduction, so perhaps that will prove to be a useful way of bringing together diverse struggles. But socialist feminism has always stressed that working women's lives do not begin and end at the workplace and so it is necessary to bring together issues affecting their lives in their families and their communities. Education is the battleground today but health care could be tomorrow, as the majority of Americans now favour some kind of universal medical care and even some Democrats are finally willing to take up this demand which had been central to Bernie Sanders' campaign. In fact, the labour struggles around education and health care are all bound up together as one of the key issues in recent strikes was teachers' inability to meet rising health-care costs.

Self-organisation

These struggles exemplify certain core principles of socialist feminism, as Johanna Brenner and I discussed in the *Socialist Register* of 2013 (Brenner and Holmstrom, 2013: 266–287). A core principle of socialist feminism is self-organisation; in Eleanor Marx's words, *women's emancipation must come from themselves*. But at the same time, they cannot do it alone, but only in coalition with others, so socialist feminists work to build inclusive movements, connecting workplace and community, waged and unwaged work, caring labour recognised as labour.

Whatever the issues, socialist feminists pay attention to the structure and process of the groups in which they work. Differences of power and privilege along sex/gender lines are particularly intimate and subtle. So, transforming this power requires the transformation of ourselves and our relationships – an insight associated with the women's liberation movement. One way to address this problem is to allow – or better yet, to encourage – women's caucuses, whether in unions, social movements or left groups. The Occupy Wall Street movement, which contributed to the radicalisation of American young people, protested against domination by the 1 per cent, and stressed a horizontal process. Nevertheless, the idea of separate spaces for women and people of colour met some resistance in Occupy, which is sad. Leftists should note that more than 100 years ago, Marx and Luxemburg supported organising men and women both together, and separately; Alexandra Kollontai's work in the Bolshevik government along with autonomous women's committees prevented women's jobs from being given automatically to returning soldiers rather than allocated according to need and led to historic gains for women, such as equal pay and eliminating the status of 'illegitimacy', Most of these gains were rolled back under Stalin where no self-organisation was permitted.

The growth of social media and young tech-savvy activists has opened new possibilities for self-organisation-from-below. As already mentioned, it was a secret Facebook website that the teachers in West Virginia used to organise for a strike. As widely reported the Arab Spring owed a great deal to social media organising and they even reached out in support of demonstrators in

Ferguson, Michigan, showing the exciting possibilities for global organising and solidarity. This of course is the reason that authoritarian regimes attempt to control it so tightly, China being the prime example. But for democratic movements and governments, social media can be used not only to organise but as an instrument of governing. An inspiring example of the possibilities – and challenges – can be seen in Barcelona today where a city government that emerged from grassroots movements uses on-line citizen input into its decisions (Charnock and Ribera-Fumaz, 2018: 188–201).

In the United States today, there is a new openness to socialism.[13] What we are finding in the current period is that the sufferings caused by neoliberal capitalism, along with racism and sexism exacerbated by the economic crisis, are boiling over. Add to that the pure ugliness and meanness of the Trump White House, along with the bankruptcy of both the Republican and the Democratic parties, and people are just disgusted. Working-class people, whatever their political ideologies, are fed up. From the Occupy movement to Black Lives Matter to the Bernie Sanders's campaign, to new labour organising, we begin to see the possibility of a new radical left. While union membership has declined, community-based workers' centres have become increasingly important, especially among immigrants. For example, 'Make the Road by Walking', based in New York City and environs, provides legal services, organises around workplace justice, immigration, environmental issues, stopping the 'school-to-prison pipeline', and seeks to build the capacities for leadership of their members. Where unions are illegal, sometimes other organisational forms have taken their place, as in the CIW (Coalition of Immokolee Workers) discussed earlier. Organising logistics workers at Amazon is in the works, as it is at Walmart (the largest employer in the US). Domestic workers have been organised and have influenced legislation (though enforcement is difficult). There is an ongoing campaign, mostly extra-union, for a living wage called 'Fight for Fifteen' ($15 an hour minimum wage). Since the Sanders campaign, all left groups have seen some growth. But by far the most dramatic has been the growth of the Democratic Socialists of America (DSA), currently the largest socialist group in the US since the 1930s: 50,000 plus members, most of them young. Their statement of About DSA starts with their commitment to democracy as both means and end. The following conveys the flavour of their politics:

> We are socialists because we reject an international economic order sustained by private profit, alienated labor, race and gender discrimination, environmental destruction, and brutality and violence in defense of the status quo.
>
> We are socialists because we share a vision of a humane international social order based both on democratic planning and market mechanisms to achieve equitable distribution of resources, meaningful work, a healthy environment, sustainable growth, gender and racial equality, and non-oppressive relationships. (www.dsa.org)

From this statement and from my descriptions of the diverse movements above, readers will appreciate why I think that it is more likely than ever in the past that this emerging radical movement will incorporate core insights of socialist feminism.

Notes

1 It is worth remembering that the very term 'sexual harassment' was not created until Catherine MacKinnon's (1979) groundbreaking work *Sexual Harassment of Working Women* and not recognised by the US Supreme Court as a violation of anti-discrimination law until the mid-1980s.

2 As with any continuum, it is not always clear how to draw the lines. For example, Iris Marion Young, whom I knew for decades, saw herself as a socialist feminist but is included as a liberal feminist in an encyclopaedia entry.

3 For a powerful demonstration that women do not freely choose their lot, see Mathieu (1990).

4 See works by Marxist ecologists such as Ian Angus, John Bellamy Foster, Michael Löwy, Andreas Malm, Richard Smith, Chris Williams.

5 The Combahee River Collective Statement originally appeared in Eisenstein (1979). It has been reprinted many times, most recently in Taylor (2017). One of its members, Barbara Smith, is credited with founding the academic field of Black Feminism and retains her commitment to socialism.

6 For further Marxist discussion of intersectionality, see Brenner (2002: 336–348). A recent symposium on intersectionality in the Marxist journal *Science & Society* (2018) takes a more critical stance on the very concept of intersectionality.

7 Iris Marion Young (1997: 95–106) made something like this point.

8 This is developed by Fisk (1989: Chapters 2 and 3).

9 The Black Marxist tradition is less well known than other varieties of black radicalism in the United States, but it was substantial and still is, as documented in a recent collection: Johnson and Lubin (2017). It is alive and well today in such younger writer/activists as Cedric Johnson, Touré Reed, Keeanga-Yamahtta Taylor, and others.

10 There were many Marxists and feminists who contributed to what was called 'the domestic labor debate'. For my own contribution see Holmstrom (1981: 186–211).

11 Frigga Haug has a similar approach if I understand her correctly. Unfortunately, few Americans follow work in German and the translations of Haug's work are not the clearest for American readers. See Haug (2015a, 2015b) and in this volume.

12 For example, transit workers' unions could reach out to riders about common interests, like better staffing. Hilary Wainwright (2003) has several examples like this.

13 Surveys differ in the exact numbers, but they are consistent in reporting significantly more positive attitudes overall towards socialism than in the past and differences in attitudes varying according to age, with millennials being much more positive than their elders.

References

Arruzza, C., 2014. 'Remarks on Gender'. *Viewpoint Magazine*, September.

Benston, M., 1969. 'The Political Economy of Women's Liberation'. *Monthly Review* 21: 13–27.

Bhattacharya, T. (Ed.), 2017. *Social Reproduction Theory: Remapping Class Re-centering Oppression*. Pluto Press, London.

Brenner, J., 2002. 'Intersections, Locations, and Capitalist Class Relations: Intersectionality from a Marxist Perspective' in Holmstrom, N. (Ed.), *The Socialist Feminist Project*. Monthly Review Press, New York, 336–348.

Brenner, J., 2017. 'There Was No Such Thing as "Progressive Neoliberalism"'. *Dissent*, 14 January.

Brenner, J., Holmstrom, N., 2013. 'Socialist-Feminist Strategy Today' in Panitch, L., Albo, G., Chibber, V. (Eds.), *Socialist Register 49: The Question of Strategy.* Merlin Press, Pontypool, Wales, 266–287.

Brenner, J., Laslett, B., 2000. 'Gender and the State' in Brenner, J., *Women and the Politics of Class.* Monthly Review Press, New York, 59–82.

Charnock, G., Ribera-Fumaz, R., 2018. 'Barcelona en Comú: Urban Democracy and "The Common Good"' in Panitch, L., Albo, G. (Eds.), *Socialist Register 54: Rethinking Democracy.* Merlin Press, London, 188–201.

Combahee River Collective Statement, in Eisenstein, Z. (Ed.), 1979. *Capitalist Patriarchy and the Case for Socialist Feminism.* Monthly Review Press, New York, 362–372.

Crenshaw, K., 1989. 'Demarginalizing the Intersection of Race and Sex: A Black Feminist Critique of Anti-discrimination Doctrine, Feminist Theory and Anti-racist Politics'. *University of Chicago Legal Forum* 1: 139–167.

Cudd, A., Holmstrom, N., 2011. *Capitalism For and Against: A Feminist Debate.* Cambridge University Press, Cambridge.

Dalla Costa, M., James, S., 1975. *The Power of Women and the Subversion of the Community.* Falling Wall Press, Bristol.

Delphy, C., 1984. *Close to Home: A Materialist Analysis of Women's Oppression.* Hutchinson, London.

Delphy, C., Leonard, D., 1992. *Familiar Exploitation.* Cambridge University Press, Cambridge.

Eisenstein, H., 2010. *Feminism Seduced: How Global Elites Use Women's Labor and Ideas to Exploit the World.* Routledge, New York.

Farris, S., 2017. *In the Name of Women's Rights: The Rise of Femonationalism.* Duke University Press, Durham, NC.

Federici, S., 2004. *Caliban and the Witch.* Autonomedia, New York.

Fisk, M., 1989. *The State and Justice.* Cambridge University Press, Cambridge.

Fraser, N., 2009. 'Feminism, Capitalism and the Cunning of History'. *New Left Review* 56 (March–April): 97–117.

Fraser, N., 2017. 'The End of Progressive Neoliberalism'. *Dissent,* 2 January.

Hartmann, H., 1979. 'Capitalism, Patriarchy and Job Segregation by Sex' in Eisenstein, Z. (Ed.) *Capitalist Patriarchy and the Case for Socialist Feminism.* Monthly Review Press, New York, 206–247.

Haug, F., 2015a. 'Gender Relations' in Mojab, S. (Ed.), *Marxism and Feminism,* Zed Books, London, 33–75.

Haug, F., 2015b. 'The Marx within Feminism' in Mojab, S. (Ed.), *Marxism and Feminism,* Zed Books, London, 76–101.

Holmstrom, N., 1981. '"Women's Work," the Family and Capitalism'. *Science and Society* 45(2): 186–211.

Holmstrom, N. (Ed.), 2002. *The Socialist Feminist Project.* Monthly Review Press, New York.

Holmstrom, N., Smith, R., 2000. 'The Necessity of Gangster Capitalism: Primitive Accumulation in Russia and China'. *Monthly Review* 51(9) (February): 1–14.

James, C.L.R., 1963. *The Black Jacobins.* 2nd edition. Vintage, New York.

Johnson, G.T., Lubin, A. (Eds.), 2017. *Futures of Black Radicalism.* Verso, New York.

Kaufmann, K., 2018. 'What Farmworkers Can Teach Hollywood about Ending Sexual Harassment'. *The Nation,* 24 January.

Kergoat, D., 2009. 'Dynamique et consubstantialité des rapports sociaux' in Dorlin, E. (Ed.), *Sexe, race et classe. Pour une épistémologie de la domination.* Paris: PUF.

Luxemburg, R., 1912. 'Women's Suffrage and the Class Struggle' in Holmstrom, N. (Ed.) (2002), *The Socialist Feminist Project.* Monthly Review Press, New York, 20–21.

MacKinnon, C., 1979. *Sexual Harassment of Working Women.* Yale University Press, New Haven, CT.

Marx, K., 1963. *Theories of Surplus Value I.* Progress Publishers, Moscow.

Mathieu, N., 1990. 'When Yielding Is Not Consenting'. *Feminist Issues,* Spring.

Mullings, L., 2002. 'Mapping Gender in African-American Political Struggles' in Holmstrom, N. (Ed.), *The Socialist Feminist Project.* Monthly Review Press, New York, 313–335.

Roberts, D., 2015. 'Reproductive Justice, Not Just Rights'. *Dissent* (Fall). *Science & Society* 82(2) (April 2018).

Silliman, J., Gerber Fried, M., Ross, L., Gutierrez, E.R. (Eds.), 2004. *Undivided Rights: Women of Color Organize for Reproductive Justice*. South End Press, Cambridge, MA.

Taylor, K. (Ed.), 2017. *How We Get Free: Black Feminism and the Combahee River Collective*. Haymarket Books, Chicago, IL.

Vogel, L., 1983. *Marxism and the Oppression of Women: Toward a Unitary Theory*. Rutgers University Press, New Brunswick, NJ.

Wainwright, H., 2003. *Reclaim the State*. Verso, London.

Wainwright, H., 2015. 'Why I Became a Feminist Socialist'. *Jacobin*, 28 December.

Wainwright, H., 2017. 'Radicalizing the Party-Movement Relationship: From Ralph Miliband to Jeremy Corbyn and Beyond' in Panitch, L., Albo, G. (Eds.), *Socialist Register* 53: *Rethinking Revolution*. Merlin Press, London, 80-101.

Young, I.M., 1997. 'Socialist Feminism and the Limits of Dual Systems Theory' in Hennessy, R., Ingraham, C. (Eds.), *Materialist Feminism*. Routledge, New York, 95-106.

20 | SOLIDARITY IN TROUBLED TIMES

Social movements in the face of climate change

Kathryn Russell

We may be fast approaching the precipice of ecological collapse, but the means to derail this train wreck are in the making as, around the world, struggles against the destruction of nature ... are growing and building momentum. Today we are riding a swelling wave of near simultaneous global mass democratic 'awakening', an almost global mass uprising. This global insurrection is still in its infancy, still unsure of its future, but its radical democratic instincts are, I believe, humanity's last best hope. (Smith, 2016: 163)

In *Green Capitalism: The God that Failed*, from which this compelling quote is taken, economic historian Richard Smith makes a convincing argument that the capitalist paradigm is incapable of pulling us back from climate disaster because its imperative for growth entails deepening the very contradictions that are causing the crisis in the first place. He offers concrete examples of failed efforts at 'greening' capitalism and argues for building the sort of human relationships that make radical change possible and organising for aggressive efforts at centralised planning and regulations to lower carbon emissions rapidly. When the productive forces of oil, gas, and coal are shut down, working-class people, women, people of colour, and those in poverty are most impacted by the loss of jobs and tax revenue. Broad social movements will need to be built that include all stakeholders, progressive activists, scientists, academics, government officials, and others working against climate change. In the US, coalitions seeking what is called a *just transition* from fossil fuel economies to a renewable energy future offer the sort of hope Smith seeks. They bring together radical trade unionists, environmentalists, and social justice activists (see Section 1). Four unions in the US who are part of the global network Trade Unions for Energy Democracy provide an inspiring example of the sort of stance that needs to become more widespread in the labour movement. The United Electrical Workers, the New York State Nurses Association, NEJB Unite Here, and National Nurses United put forward the following statement:

> As progressive unions, we are committed to working with legislators on the national and local levels to develop policies needed so that workers whose jobs will be affected are ensured a just transition. We are also committed to developing the kind of policies needed for the U.S. to make its rightful contribution to the global effort to limit warming to less than 1.5°C, a target supported by nearly every country in the world under the Paris Agreement. We welcome the ambitious clean energy and emissions targets adopted by many states and cities – but ambition must be matched by implementation.[1]

Many scholars have clearly explained how the 'train wreck' of capitalism, as Smith calls it, has disrupted the regenerative powers of humans and nature that constitute an ecosystem, a wide-ranging and multilayered network of internal relations constantly changing and rooted in the interpenetrating history of the earth and humanity. The reproduction of life and society involves an immense span of conditions that are at the same time social and 'natural', but they are all relations of power. In his book *The Discovery of Global Warming*, Spencer Weart calls climate an erratic beast that we are poking with a stick (2008: 118). Who would doubt that in the face of severe wildfires, storms, drought, and floods that the natural world does not have its own form of power?

Our ecological crises are many sided. Capital's voracious need for accumulation drives the consumption and production of ever more fossil fuel through dangerous and extreme methods. For example, the massive energy company TransCanada is mining tar sands from precious Boreal forest land in Canada for heavy oil. From a life cycle perspective, producing crude oil from tar sands is 81 per cent more carbon intensive than producing it through average conventional oil.[2] Tar sands production contaminates water supplies, threatens wildlife habitat, lays waste to the land, leaves toxic pools of sludge, and disrupts Native American communities.[3]

Social movements struggle the world over for control of the basic necessities of life: air, water, and soil. We need to move to renewable energy forms that are distributed democratically in decentralised locations and that are locally controlled through people who freely associate themselves to protect their lives and direct the development of their communities. The capitalist imperative of constant economic growth, however, holds the entire ecosystem, including human civilisation, hostage. Historically ossified divisions of labour and hierarchical relations of production, white supremacy, war, and patriarchy divide humanity and threaten the integrity, stability, and beauty of the ecosystem. Such is the 'train wreck' that has disrupted the ecosystem's regenerative powers. It is matched, however, by a political commitment and moral sense that now, as perhaps never before, we must work across class, religious, racial, or ethnic lines to build intersectional coalitions that are transnational.

New relations of production and divisions of labour that can heal the contradictions between humans and nature will emerge as geothermal, wind, water, and solar energy sources are developed. The concept of a *just transition* is one such way alliances of labour, social justice activists, and environmentalists address the need to create sustainable forms of life. I will recount two such efforts in Section 1, when I describe a Common Bound conference in the US in 2016 and a local Ithaca, New York coalition that I was part of from 2015 to 2017. Both show how activists who struggle together to develop local, collective, and democratic control over energy production and distribution are challenging old divisions of labour based in a capitalist, white, male-dominated fossil fuel economy. As they resist the destruction of the ecosystem and build new social relations, emotions like love and moral outrage form a bond that holds them together.

Can love really be a revolutionary force? To answer that question, in Section 2, I will turn to a Marxist-Feminist theory of human nature and social ecology. This paper will move from the concrete to the very abstract, from my participatory research in grassroots movements for social justice and green energy to considerations at a high level of abstraction about human nature, practical material activity, and radical epistemology. I will incorporate arguments presented by Ann Ferguson and Rosemarie Hennessey (2015) who suggest that the practice of 'solidarity love' in an *affective* economy is a revolutionary form of expending human material energy. I will support their analyses and then, in Section 3, argue that calls for love, solidarity and resistance can be a force for revolutionary change only if they are channelled with an abolitionist epistemology and the sort of love that fuels moral outrage. When humans constantly have to witness the harms capital causes as it chases about the globe to find ever more sources of valorisation, they can become increasingly conscious of the need for radical change. The form of knowing embedded in their awareness can invoke a moral imperative leading to more revolutionary resistance to capital.

Section 1. A just transition: fighting for collective control over energy production and distribution

> An economic transition is needed that shifts global economic growth patterns towards a low emission economy based on more sustainable production and consumption, promoting sustainable lifestyles and climate-resilient development while ensuring a *just transition* of the workforce.[4]

Environmental activism in the United States has been heightened by the sense of urgency posed by climate change. Polls continually show that citizens acknowledge that the weather is 'out of whack': floods, droughts, storms, and fires are devastating communities and news reports are filled with claims by climate scientists that disruptions are happening faster than they expected. 'Carbon and methane are seizing physical territory, sowing havoc and panic, racking up casualties, and even destabilizing governments', said noted climate activist Bill McKibben in the *New Republic* on 8 August 2016. People's understanding of the reality of climate change and the possibility of impending disasters deepened as news spread about the October 2018 Intergovernmental Panel on Climate Change report from Incheon, Republic of Korea.

> A landmark report from the United Nations' scientific panel on climate change paints a far more dire picture of the immediate consequences of climate change than previously thought and says that avoiding the damage requires transforming the world economy at a speed and scale that has 'no documented historic precedent'.[5]

Many people I have met in grassroots environmental groups in the United States recognise that capitalism's requirement for growth is incompatible with the health of the ecosystem, the safety of the climate and the security of food, water, health, and economic prosperity. In this section, I will discuss organising for a just transition from fossil fuel dominance to green economies by talking in Section 1a) about the diverse array of social forces at a conference in Buffalo, New York in the summer of 2016 and in Section 1b) about the Coalition for Sustainable Economic Development (CSED), a local alliance of labour, environmental, and social justice activists in my town of Ithaca, New York.[6] I was active in both as a community union organiser from the Tompkins County Workers' Center.[7] Bringing labour and environmentalists together addresses the contradiction between capitalist production and the healthy reproduction of the ecosystem.

Labour and environmentalists have discovered new affinities that can give us hope by organising to ensure that conversion to a peaceful, lower emission and cleaner economy is achieved without disproportionately harming communities dependent on military contracts and toxic, dangerous production. In the US, many of these connections take place within the BlueGreen Alliance or the Labor Network for Sustainability.[8] Unionists have organised around environmental issues in the work place since the 1970s under such leaders as Tony Mazzocchi of the Oil, Chemical and Atomic Workers union, who was instrumental in bringing workers into the peace movement. In the 1990s as the Cold War ended, some union members began to focus on the idea of a just transition as citizens demanded corporate and governmental cleanups of chemical pollution and opposed nuclear energy and continued military buildup. 'If the production method has to be changed, trade unions demand participation in the decision making, justice in the decisions made, protection from the changes made and adaptation to local needs' (Murillo, 2013: 36). In recognition of the need to account for working-class and frontline community impacts, environmentalists call for *climate justice*, the latter word incorporating the idea that promoting resiliency, adaptation, and mitigation in the face of climate change cannot ignore ethical demands that the solutions be fair to all stakeholders.

Much has been written about what a just transition would entail, but the idea is not without controversy. Rich Trumpka, president of the American Federation of Labor and Congress of Industrial Organizations, famously remarked that it was simply an invitation to a 'fancy funeral'. Some climate activists feel that the complexities of addressing broad, far-reaching working-class needs would take too much time, delaying the urgent action needed to lower carbon emissions immediately. Covering these debates and enumerating what changes are necessary for a just transition to take place is beyond the scope of this paper. However, I have found that the phrase's rhetorical obviousness is useful in conceptualising what must be considered as fair when a group goes up before government officials or when one is trying to bring unity to a diverse group of grassroots community members. Potential meanings are voiced in a given local situation when coalitions practising a sort of 'transversal politics' strive to find agreement about how to meet different needs in the face of possible conflicts of interest (Hill Collins, 2000; Yuval-Davis, 1999). The organising that took place in CSED is a case in point (see below).

Many factors, too many to list here, are frequently brought into play in struggles over what would constitute a just transition. From my experience, these points are suggestive of a working-class perspective: genuine, transparent discussion and collaboration between all groups of an impacted community; strategic planning for good, stable jobs with living wages and safe working conditions to replace those that are lost; apprenticeship programmes to build skills and worker capacities; guarantees that local labour will be hired; sufficient pensions for those who choose to retire; ensuring the right to organise; and state support for school districts that will suffer from loss of tax revenue and for property owners whose tax rates might increase in the face of the loss of local businesses.

Thus, partnerships are growing among climate activists and workers, albeit slowly. Moreover, it is remarkable that many activists in these movements explicitly use the feminist concept of 'intersectionality' to weave together an environmental narrative and a narrative of justice. It is important to ask, however, if these liaisons can sufficiently challenge capital and go beyond identity politics and a recognition of mutual self-interest by deepening awareness of the connections between climate disruption and all forms of capitalism, even green ones. These dynamics provide fertile ground for Marxist-Feminist analyses.

Section 1a. 'System change, not climate change'

In the summer of 2016, several progressive members of CSED attended an important conference organised by the New Economy Coalition, a US-based national alliance of progressive groups who fight for social justice. They describe themselves as follows: we are 'a network of organizations imagining and building a future where people, communities, and ecosystems thrive. Together, we are creating deep change in our economy and politics – placing power in the hands of people and uprooting legacies of harm – so that a fundamentally new system can take root'.[9] That summer they brought over 900 activists together for a conference called 'Common Bound' with the following call:

> This conference is about transforming the system. It's about radical solutions that are rooted in love, solidarity, and liberation. It's also about dismantling the systems of oppression – like white supremacy, capitalism, and patriarchy – that stand in the way of pushing back against the worst parts of a broken system and building up powerful, inspiring alternatives to replace it.

Naming the system 'white supremacy, capitalism, and patriarchy' is indeed potentially revolutionary, and their rhetoric of 'love, solidarity, and liberation' is powerful. But can the energy of solidarity love concretise into a material force effectively challenging capital? In Section 2, I will argue that we can conceptualise how love *can* be revolutionary if we use a Marxist theory of human nature, a phenomenological theory of alienation, and a materialist feminism. In Section 3, I will claim that love can have such a weight as long as it is channelled with a spirit of abolitionism and moral outrage. An abolitionist ethic and an epistemology of love can rise over and above the crushing despair caused by witnessing the beginning of ecological collapse accompanied by political polarisation and the realisation that government and corporations are only offering concessions that actually promote the problems we already face.

Conferences like Common Bound are history marking but also history making, because grassroots activists have the opportunity to build new, concrete solidarity relationships. The 'swelling wave of near simultaneous global mass democratic "awakening"' Richard Smith describes (above) happens primarily in specific local and regional spaces. There, these relationships can be repeatedly solidified, deepened, and moved forward. They represent radical democratic theory and practice in the making.

The historic victory of getting a statewide ban on fracking[10] in New York State empowered these alliances, making continued struggle for more centre-left coalition work possible. The movement against fracking revealed that many state environmental regulations were actually written by gas and petroleum industry lawyers, a revelation that furthered people's distrust in the state's Department of Environmental Conservation. On a daily, concrete basis, grassroots environmental activists fight to shut down coal-driven power plants, proposed natural gas storage facilities, the dumping of fracking waste in landfills and on our roads, and to prevent the build out of natural gas and oil infrastructure.

In large part, the fossil fuel resistance movement seeks to abolish the use of carbon-based sources as our main supply of energy. Many now unite around a revolutionary call for the *abolition* of fossil fuels, not just regulation. 'System change; not climate change' is not an empty slogan but a need and goal felt deeply that guides people's orientation to what should be done. More and more people are moving to acts of civil disobedience. For example, in New York, 657 arrests[11] were made at the gates of Crestwood Corporation, a storage and infrastructure provider for natural gas products. The group called We Are Seneca Lake organised this direct action campaign.

> We Are Seneca Lake is an ongoing, citizen-based, grassroots campaign that seeks to protect Seneca Lake and the surrounding region from gas storage expansion by Texas-based energy company, Crestwood Equity Partners

(formerly Crestwood Midstream). Crestwood's intention is to repurpose the crumbling salt mines underneath Seneca Lake's hillside into massive, unlined gas tanks for three highly pressurized products of fracking: methane (natural gas), and propane and butane (LPG, or Liquefied Petroleum Gases) and to turn the Finger Lakes into a fracked gas transportation and storage hub for the entire Northeast. Our intention is to direct the future of our community down sustainable, renewable pathways.[12]

I was among those arrested at the Crestwood gates. I experienced the abolitionist spirit incorporating the passions of both love and outrage. Young and old fought for years to get rid of Crestwood; we were ultimately successful in stopping their plans for development along the shores of Seneca Lake.

The 2016 conference Common Bound drew together hundreds of activists not only from New York but also from 41 other states, five Canadian provinces, and 22 countries including Malaysia, Nigeria, Cuba, El Salvador, and Spain. They represented a centre-left alliance, a convergence that might grow to be part of the 'global mass uprising' mentioned above by Smith. The following list of attendees is striking: the Malcolm X Grassroots Movement, Black Lives Matter, the Institute for Policy Studies, the American Sustainable Business Council, Natural Capitalism Solutions, the New System Project, Labor Network for Sustainability, 350.org, Code Pink, Food First, the Caring Economy Campaign, Black Youth Project 100, the Post Carbon Institute, and the US Federation of Workers' Cooperatives. Over 30 of us from Ithaca, New York attended. We were associated with the Coalition for Sustainable Economic Development (CSED), the Multicultural Resource Center, SURJ (an English acronym that means Showing Up for Racial Justice), We Are Seneca Lake, Fossil Free Tompkins, and the Campaign for Renewable Energy. As we try to create a new system of energy production that works with rather than asserts power over the planet, we are a small but typical part of the global network of activists fighting for a paradigm shift in energy production and use.

The Common Bound conference took place just as the country had been rocked by the shootings of two black men by police – Philandro Castile and Alton Sterling. The first day, carloads of people went to a local Black Lives Matter protest to acknowledge their solidarity with black communities, whose neighbourhoods are militarised by trigger-ready police forces armed to the teeth by surplus military equipment. The national militarised state is thus mirrored locally. The conference signalled how progressive activists in North America have taken up the notion of intersectionality, which Black, Latina, and lesbian feminists brought to the forefront in the 1980s. Recent developments in Queer Studies and transgender activism have been indispensable in this regard too. In my experience, the idea of intersectionality is used across categories of gender, race, ethnicity, class, and sexuality as a way of expressing solidarity and of marking the moral outrage we feel over the multifaceted and deep structural ways corporate domination, a fossil fuel economy, and constant war direct the course of our history.

Section 1b. Local organising for sustainable development in the face of neoliberalism

A good example of a centre-left alliance working for a just transition to a green economy was the Coalition for Sustainable Development (CSED) in Ithaca, New York. For the first time in that community, an alliance of environmentalists, social justice organisations, business leaders, leaders from the unionised building trades council, and elected officials came together. The unions involved all had statements on sustainability, and at the time, three were members of the BlueGreen Alliance at the national level. We built a coalition that included labourers, plumbers and pipefitters, electricians and carpenters, retired professors, energy experts and lawyers. Our unity was sparked early in 2015 when a controversial urban development plan was slated to receive tax breaks, the sort of corporate benefits the neoliberal model doles out to businesses. CSED's principle of unity stated,

> We believe we can no longer pursue business-as-usual when it comes to economic development in our county. The problems we face as a community and society are significant: the planet's future health is endangered, economic inequality is worsening, racial and ethnic divisions are still being exploited, and the shared visions that bind us together as humans are threatened. (CSED, 2014)

CSED fought for nothing less than a new economy. We openly articulated our collective understanding that green growth would bring good new jobs, more than the old, fossil-fuel-driven division of labour did.

From 2015 to 2017 CSED grew in size and importance, changing the terms of public discussion over tax policy and development. We argued that tax relief should not be given simply to attract new business but should also include community benefits. Companies receiving tax abatements[13] should comply with high standards for energy efficiency, hire local labour at living wage rates, and employ a diverse workforce. We brought together unions active in collective bargaining and introduced climate change into the agenda of local unions. We united people who had been community activists for decades. We counteracted the stereotype common among workers that marks environmentalists as capital's ally and the tendency for environmentalists to see labour's needs as an obstacle that can be ignored. We all recognised that sound, energy-efficient, and better buildings would have to be built by highly skilled labour organised and trained by the unions.

Radical social movements are built day by day through forging personal relationships which, among activists, can be a form of solidarity love. In that sense there are many ways that CSED was a progressive force for change especially if we take seriously the important role that emotions and affective relationships play in radical or reformist organising. We formed friendships through our meetings, the gatherings we organised, and even our emails. We had fun, we picnicked together, we laughed together, we argued. Plumbers and professors hugged each other. We congratulated each other on the victories we won, and we exchanged deep smiles around the room in recognition of each other, since we knew we would not have accomplished them alone. We broke down suspicions and stereotypes. Environmentalists demonstrated they could be relied on to struggle for workers' rights because we were in the same local protests. They, in turn, learned to understand workers' need for jobs with real dignity more empathically.

Such cognitive shifts show how emotions and empirical knowledge can be woven together through close, ongoing personal relationships. People internalised and identified with the stories we shared about what specific families were facing in their material lives, and we recognised in each other the emotions we felt when our needs were unmet. An *affective* element moved knowledge from remotely abstract – something one may have read about – to concrete.

Despite the connections we built, we constantly ran up against austerity measures and the business-as-usual policy of neoliberalism that so threatens the ecosystem and hampers the expansion of human creative productive capacities, specifically the transformation to a renewable energy economy. Under such dogma, all local spaces are held hostage by capital. This model is piece-by-piece, where individual businesses compete for tax abatements, and lax and rarely enforced government standards are part of a permitting process manipulated by the colluding forces of government and industry. We pushed against this model in favour of more centralised, future-oriented planning for energy use. Instead of a rational, aggressive model of addressing climate change, moreover, local activists were forced to deal with one development project at a time. It felt like we fought carbon molecule by carbon molecule, investigating every detail of project specifications, constantly bringing pressure to bear on decision makers to limit greenhouse gas emissions on one aspect of a project at a time.

One such case was the Maplewood Project, a development venture sponsored by Cornell University, an internationally recognised Ivy League institution known for its liberal approach to education and its well-earned reputation in combatting climate change. The plan for Maplewood was to create over 800 new housing units for graduate students. This endeavour provided a special opportunity for our organising efforts because it was not only a private developer that was building housing for profit, but it included Cornell University, which has a special need to popularise its image as a progressive institution.

Moreover, the knowledge required to effectively challenge the Maplewood developers or educate the community and government was collectively constituted. We brought together progressive Cornell faculty, climate scientists, geologists, engineers, professional staff, and students. We built relationships of trust and solidarity in order to explain how the project would prevent the county's goal of achieving a 20 per cent cut in carbon emissions. A retired lawyer researched legal powers the lead agency actually had under state government recommendations requiring a concrete plan to limit emissions in an Environmental Impact Statement. Since folks from the building trades had constructed the original project, only they knew how shoddy the former buildings were, and they could visualise the process of bidding by general contractors and subcontractors along with timeline of demolition and a process of hiring a labour force. We talked to neighbourhood residents who would be impacted and who could help us push Cornell to implement its greenhouse gas emissions reduction target of 100 per cent by 2035.

We were ultimately only minimally successful. Our efforts did cause local officials to significantly change their scoping agreement, for example, by requiring the developer to identify and quantify potentially significant increases in energy use and to both mitigate or propose reasonable alternatives to their energy design. The buildings were outfitted with air source heat pumps instead of fracked methane gas brought from Pennsylvania, a state just to the south of us loaded with fracking fields. Despite our pressure on Cornell and the developer to hire local union labour, they brought in unorganised workers, even some from out of state.

The example of CSED illustrates how alarming consequences for the climate crisis follow from neoliberalism, because of the lack of a federal or state-level mandatory plan for cutting down on carbon emissions. Though our county government did have an enviable greenhouse gas reduction policy and had begun to be serious about measuring the carbon dioxide and methane emitted locally, there was no enforcement. Officials and planners operated the way they were used to operating – 'business as usual'. Accustomed to giving industry and Cornell University what they have always given them, namely what they wanted, city and town planners were even unaware of the power they did have according to the New York State Department of Environmental Conservation. We had to educate the officials involved instead of being able to rely on government employees to accomplish that task; there was no money to hire experts. Because of cut backs, all social services and government agencies were short staffed and had little funds. Such a neoliberal quagmire can foster no paradigm shift in energy production and use.

In CSED meetings we did not paper over our differences. We practised what Yuval-Davis, following a theory originating in Italian feminism, calls 'transversal politics' (1999). We all recognised that the union officials had a responsibility to care for the short-term interest of their members, just as the environmentalists had a desire to care for the long-term interest of the life forms they saw as threatened by global warming. We were respectful, however, of each other's varying social positions. That was easier because we shared many values: social equality, energy efficiency, sustainability and transparency of democratic decision making. We all rejected the hostility to any growth sometimes found among radical environmentalists. We shared a commitment to unity in struggle, and we protested city or county decisions we regarded as incompatible with our vision of sustainable development.

Individually, CSED members were rooted in different social sectors and positions, as trade union officials, retired academics, professionals, or racial justice advocates. We had various social, political, and personal identities. I have been rooted in academia as a professional philosopher, for example, but as a representative from the Tompkins County Workers' Center, I shifted back to my working-class origins and advocated for working-class perspectives as well as I was able to, consulting frequently with leadership from the Center. Moreover, the building trades are part of the North American model of unionised male workers. Given the fossil-fuel-driven division of labour that is stratified by race and gender and the fact that the environmental movement is overwhelmingly white and professional, personal relationships within CSED were often tenuous and sometimes conflictual. The previous years had seen many of us divided over the closing of a local coal-fired power plant. New owners proposed repowering the plant with fracked methane gas, which would seriously increase local carbon emissions. Workers who were represented by the International Brotherhood of Electrical Workers (IBEW) were afraid they would lose their jobs and community members felt threatened with the loss of tax revenue. At a public forum, the IBEW workers and community allies showed up in force in identical orange T-shirts paid for by the power company. They were outnumbered, however, by those of us in the abolitionist Fossil Free Tompkins group who came with hundreds of cards signed by people who were against fracking and thus the repowering plan.

To analyse the revolutionary potential of groups like CSED, however, we can look to Nora Räthzel and David Uzzell's book *Trade Unions in the Green Economy: Working for the Environment* (2013). On their terms, we can label CSED an empowerment group: they point out that in *Reform and Revolution*, Rosa Luxemburg theorised that revolutionary sorts of reforms are movements that propose alternatives which make 'transformative agendas visible and achievable. They should sow the seed of alternative forms of working and living in practice' (Räthzel/Uzzell, 2013: 9). CSED revealed the inadequacy of current forms of government and business. It pushed for a just transition to an economy run on renewable fuels. It illuminated forms of social change needed to move to a renewable economy while taking workers' local needs seriously. Räthzel and Uzzell say, a strategy that links the 'green jobs' campaign with a trade union programme that makes use of workers' skills and knowledge to explore and design ways in which industries ... can be converted, would constitute such a strategy of 'revolutionary reformism'. (2013: 9)

The example of CSED shows that activists from across class, race, and ethnic lines can effectively struggle in friendship and solidarity. We had a common recognition that production and development for profit stands in the way of making collective progress. We acknowledged that green jobs would make use of workers' skills and knowledge to design ways in which industries and services could become sites producing socially useful and environmentally sound products. Our organising around tax giveaways, buildings, and infrastructure made visible the greed of developers and revealed how city, county, state, and federal government were at their service, putting profit over people and entrenching policies that were bad for all of us. Collective transversal groupings such as ours can work against the idea that climate disruption can be resolved through individualist solutions like buying green and recycling and by changing particular business practices and energy policies piece by piece. Local alliances like CSED could create new forms of production with a socially owned, decentralised, and democratically controlled renewable energy sector. Plumbers and electricians had a desire to exercise their skills in developing solar power and energy-efficient buildings. We all wanted to expand our skills and knowledge base in order to develop a new economy.

Nevertheless, from my point of view, the CSED example supports the argument that climate disaster cannot be resolved without the sort of national planning blocked by capitalist relations of production. A neoliberal austerity budget fails to provide legal assistance for service recipients, local sustainability officers, professional educators, or, for that matter, state-subsidised local urban and regional planners. Grassroots activists must spend their own time studying the intricacies of environmental impact statements and compare them to state regulations and initiatives, then pressure local developers and planners on a case by case basis.

Section 2. Solidarity love, a theoretical approach

In a beautiful piece of writing labelled posthumously by scholars as 'On James Mill', Marx uses his theory of alienation to speculate about what genuinely human relations would be like under a truly communal system of production. He calls forth the concept of *love* to capture the depth of a potential free relation between two human subjects.

> Let us suppose that we had carried out production as human beings ... I would have been for you the mediator between you and the species, and therefore would become recognised and felt by you yourself as a completion

of your own essential nature and as a necessary part of yourself, and consequently would know myself to be confirmed both in your thought and your love.[14]

Obviously, Marx is not simply talking about romantic love in the quote above. He is applying Hegel's phenomenological theory of the relation between subject and object – two subjectivities consciously recognising themselves in each other in a way that is genuinely human. In the *Economic and Philosophical Manuscripts* Marx calls this a form of 'species-love'. It links the two subjects so that their capacity to be fully human connects them and completes them. Love mediates the two humans in a way that is non-alienating.[15] In this section, I want to leave aside the essentialism Marx employs in the quote above and focus on the idea that love can be a positive and historically progressive force. A Marxist-Feminist methodology can pick up on Marx's employment of the concept of love in fruitful ways.

An effective social ecology would include questions such as these:

1. Why and how have the regenerative powers of humans and nature been devalued and destroyed?
2. How have intersections of gender, race, and class formed historically under capitalist patriarchy and white supremacy?
3. How might divisions of labour change to release creative powers of new relations of production?
4. What would have to change in human practice to develop an ecological realisation that we should participate in the ecosystem rather than dominate it, to recognise that we are not alone, that the climate system is speaking to us in ways we must attend to?
5. What is the role of emotion (love, outrage, fear, etc.) in correcting the historical path of climate disruption?

Taking a Marxist-Feminist look at questions 1 and 2, we note that the slave-based mode of production in the development of US capitalism devalued and destroyed human regenerative powers as it historically constructed gender, race, and class as intersecting relations of power. A racialised division of labour was created and maintained by white male violence. Since West Africans knew how to grow rice, cotton, and indigo in a climate like Virginia and the Carolinas, they had the form of labour power needed by planters who came from Northern Europe. They were also knowledgeable about iron production. These powers were redirected into an exploitative division of labour, devalued as a way of life controlled by them, and concentrated as surplus value in a class of mostly white men. The caring labour and childbearing capacity of African women were appropriated to reproduce the agrarian slave-based production system and a white patriarchal family. The cotton grown by slave men and women made Southern plantation owners wealthy and provided the raw material for Northern white male industrialists to organise the first forms of factory production – textile mills where the first workers were white women. Moreover, in the early colonies some white women were privileged because they were given land by British joint stock companies whose goal was the formation of the heterosexual patriarchal nuclear families deemed necessary for the formation of a colonial settler state. A masculine form of white productive labour could be reproduced and stabilised, and female care work could be privatised.

Race, class, and gender exploitation in this history are intersectional because they are already a part of each other materially and structurally. This is the sort of perspective that Angela Davis uses to argue that racialised police violence in the US is part of the prison industrial complex and the militarised nation state. In her compelling book *Freedom Is a Constant Struggle*, she argues that the hyper-masculine forms of police violence seen today stem from the history of the white male overseer. Thus, white supremacy, patriarchy, and capitalism intersect because the historical constitution of each ties them to one another. Davis (2016) argues, 'the greatest challenge facing us as we attempt to form international solidarity and connections across national borders is an understanding of what feminists often call intersectionality. Not so much intersectionality of identities, but intersectionality of struggles' (2016: 140, 145). It is important to acknowledge her emphasis on *struggles* that are intersectional because they are organised forms of solidarity in activism. Her approach is not a form of pluralism, as found in liberal individualism which sees intersectionality as multiple senses of oneself and inseparable parts of one's experience, already existing always within one person.

A Marxist-Feminist social ecology can use a theory of intersectionality to show that, as humans, we do not stand as a unity in our relations with nature. Mainstream environmentalists are often saddled with a dualist ecology since they tend to see humans at large as the source of environmental crises; humanity stands opposed to nature. Many also have an apocalyptical view that human civilisation, as a whole, will come to an end. They do not go beyond modern Eurocentric philosophic universalism, and they lump everybody together without accounting for stratified privileges and disadvantages that necessitate a more careful analysis of 'blame and gain' as well as differential degrees of vulnerability. We know that privileged nations and classes have a stranglehold on the development of rapid and serious responses to climate disaster. Critical race theory, feminism, and Marxism do not make overly abstract generalisations about humanity but are able to see people as differentiated by race, nationality, ethnicity, sexuality, class, and other relevant factors. Marxist feminism can see identities across differences and thus avoid seeing intersectionality as aggregative (Russell, 2005).

We can view gender as a form of race, race as a form of gender, or class as a form of either gender or race. Gender carries race and class within itself. Consider the problem of men's violent control of women through sexual assault. A Marxist-Feminist rejection of pluralism, universalism, dualism, or essentialism can account for the fact that rape is not a one-dimensional thing that happens to women as such; it does not designate events of a homogenous kind. Rape unfolds out of a set of preconditions having overlapping contexts. We can classify acts as patriarchal sexual violence without losing sight of the many different expressions they can have in multiple, even contradictory, types of settings. Sexual violence is not automatically a simple antagonism of men against women because the women involved can be on opposite sides of class, national, or racial power struggles. For example, in the invasion and occupation of Iraq, the threat of rape kept Baghdadi women inside their homes at the same time as it kept US female soldiers obedient in their regiments – they even avoided drinking water for fear of having to leave their barracks at night. Though these women were supposedly enemies in war, they experienced male sexual violence as a way of forcing compliance. We can see other contradictions in the cluster of relations constituting rape if we remember that in the Jim Crow South, white men and women bonded together to charge a black man with rape in order to justify lynching him. Thus, one set of acts denoted as male sexual violence can include incompatible interests and tensions between the perpetrators and targets of these acts (Russell, 2007).

Under white supremacist, capitalist patriarchy, ossified, hierarchical divisions of labour in the fossil fuel economy hamper the development of the types of human powers needed for a renewable energy economy. In addressing question 3, above, we can already see that new relations of production are arising out of the depletion of fossil fuels, natural disasters, and the recognition of the many dangers caused by the exploitation of nature. Like Hegel, Marx argues that our passions or desires motivate our activity and provide the material force that constructs history and regenerates our form of life. Humans have an array of powers corresponding to needs that are satisfied through conscious material activity. Our practical actions form an internal relation with the objects that satisfy these needs. Harnessing the sun or wind for energy will not destroy them for they cannot be used up. Using them as renewable forces of production to satisfy the object of our need for, say, electricity will change the nature of our needs and the actions we go about to satisfy them. We have the capacity and aspiration to engage in activities that are transformative, and out of these passions and desires, new divisions of labour and relations of production will be created. Thus, we can also recognise the beginning of an answer to question 4. As we pay serious attention to what the climate system is saying, we can engage in dialogue with other parts of the environment not rooted in our own self-interest, participating in energy production by employing the sun and wind. Thus, we learn that we are only another aspect of the ecosystem and we have to change our behaviour, particularly our carbon intensive mode of production. At some point in the future perhaps we will learn too how to regenerate our lives more successfully and how not to interfere so much with the reproduction of flora and fauna.

Furthermore, in thinking about question 5, we note that human beings have the power to love and to empathise. As Marx suggests in the quote I used at the beginning of this section, we find loving relations particularly satisfying and we seek them out. These emotional needs can be seen to form an affective, or caring, economy made up of social relations of power, either those expressing power *over*, which are dominative, or power *with*, which are solidarity relationships. Both can take place privately or in public. We have daily material needs based in the body: needs for sustenance and shelter as well as emotive needs rooted in connections involving an exchange of human energy. Ann Ferguson and Rosemarie Hennessey (2015) agree with authors Gibson-Graham, and Hardt and Negri that global resistance movements create a 'transformative anti-capitalist revolutionary love' generating a collective power that can undermine 'global capitalism and its intertwined domination systems of patriarchy, racism and imperialism' (Ferguson, 2015: 258). They move deeper into the network of social relations constituting revolutionary love than the former authors do, however, to offer materialist feminist analyses of emotional relationships. There is a difference between the energy 'territorialised' by capitalism, imperialism, and racial and sexual divisions of labour and the collective energy formed within revolutionary forms of solidarity. The latter 'deterritorialises' energy bound up in relations that drain our human potential to become freely associated social producers of our own lives.

Ann Ferguson argues in her article 'Feminist Love Politics: Romance, Care, and Solidarity', that humans do not only have physical material needs but we also have 'social needs for love, affection, sexual connection, and a sense of belonging in relation to social groups' (Ferguson, 2015: 250). She asks what sort of group politics we need in order to change the economic, political, and ideological strictures that bind us. She argues that the sort of paradigm shift needed 'to break down the gender and racial divisions of affective and caring labor will have to come first from the pre-figurative practices of movements for social justice' (2015: 252). These give rise to what she calls 'solidarity love' that refocuses surplus energy and satisfies feminist needs for political identification and affiliation that would correspond to the dream of a more equitable and sustainable world. This refocused social energy can offset energy lost in apolitical relations in one's family or in couple love relationships. Ferguson maintains that progressive and leftist social change movements are forming new kinds of solidarity relationships that break down divisions and create bonds of mutual support across race, class, and nationality. This revolutionary love is a productive force that can break up old social relations of production and reproduction. It is a material force that can act against alienation.

Furthermore, caring for others has an intrinsic material value that resists appropriation. Ferguson argues,

> [C]aring body-based labor tends to resist the de-territorializing that is involved in other types of commodity production because of the non-alienable value in the work relationship due to the mutually experienced pleasure or wellbeing produced in the caring labor process, *even when* other aspects are exploited. (2015: 259)

Affective energy is not only produced in activities such as feeding someone or otherwise directly caring for them, but is also released through the emotional bonding that takes place in friendships or working together on social causes. In 'Bread and Roses in the Commons', Rosemarie Hennessey theorises that the transformative force of solidarity love forms a surplus energy that can be theorised 'in materialist terms as the passionate reason that accompanies the conversion of unmet need and living labor into organised resistance for a common cause' (2015: 265). Moreover, caring for the natural environment also releases energy that can be profoundly satisfying for people as well as protective or healing of ecological systems. We can have solidarity orientations towards non-human animals and plants and even land. This is the sort of emotional connection spoken of by conservationist Aldo Leopold when he encourages us to 'think like a mountain', because 'Only the mountain has lived long enough to listen objectively to the howl of a wolf'.[16] The ecosystem includes humans and all forms of life as well as nonliving entities. It is a web of subject–object relations that are internal to each other. As Leopold says, we are simply elements of the land community.

As people try to develop wind, water, and solar energy sources, new relations of production are developed. Workers in the building trades such as those involved in CSED, especially those who are unemployed, have socially useful labour power and surplus material energy thrown off by neoliberal macroeconomic policies and alienating, capitalist relations of production. People in frontline communities abandoned by the coal, oil, or gas industry form an exploitable reserve army of labour, but one which could be drawn into progressive forms of production using the sorts of energy creatively released by serious engagement in transformative social change movements. Their labour could be drawn into new productive relations that build on their desire to utilise their human powers, their skills, and their knowledge in progressive, pre-figurative ways. Activists fighting for just transitions form an important historical, material force pushing for these sorts of new relations of production.

Section 3. Conclusion: an abolitionist epistemology of moral outrage

> We are dealing with a vast, interdependent world that is interconnected in unprecedented ways. But there are unbearable things all around us. You have to look for them: search carefully … If you spend a little time searching, you will find reasons to engage. The worst attitude is indifference. 'There is nothing I can do; I get by' – adopting this mindset will deprive you of one of the fundamental qualities of being human: outrage. Our capacity for protest is indispensable, as is our freedom to engage.[17]

Appeals to the power of love and solidarity such as those I mentioned at the beginning of this chapter, are not simply rhetorical. They represent a material force powerful enough to attract people to social movements, connecting with each other deeply. In a Hegelian Marxist sense, the power of love connects two or more subjectivities through practical material activity that can transform history. They call into play the emotional energies that can prefigure the sort of human relationships needed to shift to a renewable energy economy. Progressive social change movements form new kinds of solidarity relationships that can refocus the surplus energy lost in oppressive relations in one's family, community, or work. Thus, they satisfy needs for political identification and affiliation that would correspond to the dream of a more equitable and sustainable world.

Activists who struggle together to develop local, collective, and democratic control over energy production and distribution are challenging old divisions of labour based in a male-dominated fossil fuel economy. As they resist the destruction of the ecosystem, emotions like solidarity love and moral outrage play a large part as the bond that holds them together or drives them apart. Above, the famous quote from Hessel attributes outrage to the quality of being uniquely human. The Zapatistas refer to this energy as 'dignified rage'. I would argue that the passion incorporated in nonviolent direct action includes a sense of moral outrage that intensifies the love power that Ferguson and Hennessey address. Our transformative efforts are thus even more effective in 'reterritorialising' the energies sapped by oppressive relationships.

Tim DeChristopher, who founded the Climate Disobedience Center, is known for disrupting a Bureau of Land Management oil and gas auction in December of 2008, by posing as Bidder 70 and out-bidding oil companies for pieces of land in national parks in the state of Utah. He was sentenced to two years in federal prison in July 2011 for this act of civil disobedience. He read this statement at his sentencing:

> I want you to join me in standing up for the right and responsibility of citizens to challenge their government. I want you to join me in valuing this country's rich history of nonviolent civil disobedience … This is not going away. At this point of unimaginable threats on the horizon, this is what hope

looks like. In these times of a morally bankrupt government that has sold out its principles, this is what patriotism looks like. With countless lives on the line, this is what love looks like, and it will only grow. The choice you are making today is what side are you on.[18]

DeChristopher's orientation can be captured epistemologically as a form of passionate reason. As such, it arises from the surplus energy generated from unmet needs and is transformed into resistance. Abolitionist ecological epistemology provides a critical stance. It takes a side and thus is a standpoint epistemology. It is fed by love and outrage. Activists like DeChristopher are not simply using a utilitarian cost–benefit analysis to spur others to action. Outrage is not compelled by an argument that harming the environment and perpetuating an oppressive system can be weighed against, for example, the usefulness of bringing in jobs by mining the tar sands and building pipelines to profit from exporting oil and gas. The epistemology of abolitionism and love corrects and extends utilitarian cost–benefit analysis. It is a moral philosophy of critical solidarity and liberation. Truth entails resistance.

This sort of standpoint provides a critical corrective force that makes love a criterion of truth. In the struggle against fracking for oil and natural gas, activists formed arguments illustrating this sort of epistemology. The nature of the evidence against fracking involved empirical truths surely, but not merely empirical. For activists, emotional, moral, and cognitive commitments are bound tightly together, making the belief that fracking is wrong *practically* self-evident. The moral outrage with which these truths are held dear feeds the degree to which these truths are enlivened; we *feel* their truth through a combination of logical and moral intuition. Together these truths justify nonviolent civil disobedience. Here is an example of a sort of passionate reasoning process:

The argument:

a) Empirical demonstration of fracking dangers.
b) Moral invocation of a need to avoid harm.
c) Stance that social relations of power inhibit reform and successful regulation.
d) Thus, fracking must be banned.
e) State authorities will not permit any peaceful disruption of fracking.
f) Thus, we adopt a moral imperative for civil disobedience.

An argument like this link truth and goodness. We can only capture it epistemologically through a theory of knowledge that is robust enough to embrace passionate moral outrage. Within an abolitionist context, labelling the truths as self-evident is an *outlaw* use of the phrase, subversive and creative. A moral and social responsibility entailing nonviolent civil disobedience follows from the recognition of truth.

Another example of a loving abolitionist outrage could be seen in the mass uprisings in 2016 during the occupation of Freedom Square in Chicago confronting police violence and during the occupation of land in North Dakota to stop the tar sands oil pipeline threatening the water supply of the Standing Rock Sioux nation and the 17 million people who lived along the Missouri River. The Chicago occupiers were confronting a police compound where prisoners had been tortured and denied the right to visit with attorneys and loved ones. One organiser told of children receiving dance lessons, educational workshops, and of serving communal meals in a space where people were defending their own lives with the spirit of 'love and abolitionist ideology'. Activists in both encampments signalled their linked struggles and their solidarity, recognising that their liberation was inextricably connected. Both occupations were forming intentional communities where the caring labour usually done in families was organised collectively and led by women (Hayes, 2016).

The nonviolent direct action in North Dakota opposed the completion of a pipeline designed to carry flammable and toxic oil from fracking fields, ultimately going all the way to Texas for profitable export. It was a struggle to protect the commons – the land, the water supply, and sacred ancestral burying grounds. The noted environmental group headed by Bill McKibben 350.org posted this headline: 'Love, Solidarity and Resistance'. They said, 'We know that we are all connected, that our fights are connected, and that to win, we need to join together. Reject the Dakota Access Pipeline and stop all fossil fuel leasing in the Gulf of Mexico'.[19]

Interestingly, the tribal women of the Brave Heart Society, White Buffalo Calf Woman Society, and Stone Boy Society issued an open letter to then-President Obama calling on him to stop the pipeline and its related violence as well as the threats to women that usually develop with fracking and pipeline construction. 'Man camps' that house workers provoke increased alcohol and drug consumption as well as sex trafficking. The women said that 40 per cent of those being trafficked were Native women. They condemned the violence occurring in strong terms:

> A war of 'bio-politics' [is] being waged on indigenous homelands all across the Americas. Bio-politics occurs when human life processes are managed under regimes of authority over knowledge, power and 'subjectivation'. In other words, our indigenous bodies, which are essentially a direct reflection of Mother Earth, have been and continue to be controlled by corporations and governments that operate for profit without regard for human life.[20]

Therefore, not only is the Dakota pipeline struggle forming pre-figurative affective communities and defending the commons, but it is also protecting Native women's reproductive rights, caring rights which are 'intimately connected to the struggle for cultural survival and control over their land base' (Silliman et al., 2004: 106). Therefore, an abolitionist ethic of solidarity love took place in black people's struggle against police violence and in Native American resistance to the fossil fuel industry's appropriation of land. Both communities struggled for self-determination against profound repression and state sanctioned forms of masculine hegemonic violence. The creation of the US settler state and American empire required the dehumanisation of both peoples through commodification, forced displacement, or genocide, forms of oppression still manifested today.

In conclusion, I want to suggest that an ecological epistemology would intensify the moral outrage accompanying abolitionist forces of solidarity love. Sandra Steingraber, an ecologist and winner of the Goldman Award who has served jail time for her arrest against fracking infrastructure with We Are Seneca Lake, is a powerful leader whose words unite many:

> We are all musicians in a great human orchestra, and it is now time to play the Save the World Symphony. You are not required to play a solo, but you are required to know what instrument you hold and play it as well as you can. You are required to find your place in the score. What we love, we must protect. That's what love means. From the right to know and the duty to inquire flows the obligation to act.[21]

We use both passion and reason in ways that could enable us to move away from the brink of climate chaos and that could intensify our movements against white supremacy and patriarchal capitalism. During a just transition to non-alienating relations of production in a green economy, our epistemology ought to be a moral philosophy of critical solidarity with other humans and the whole ecosystem. Revolutionary love and a commitment to truth entail resistance.[22]

Notes

1 http://unionsforenergydemocracy.org/statement-on-4th-u-u-national-climate-assessment/. 30 November 2018.

2 Environmental Defence (2014) *Reality Check: Tar Sands and Climate Change*. https://environmentaldefence.ca/report/report-reality-check-climate-change-and-the-tar-sands/. April 2014.

3 www.nrdc.org/stories/dirty-fight-over-canadian-tar-sands-oil. 31 December 2015.

4 www.labor4sustainability.org/uncategorized/just-transition-just-what-is-it/. (Emphasis added.)

5 www.nytimes.com/2018/10/07/climate/ipcc-climate-report-2040.html.

6 Ithaca, NY was once home to the Cayuga Indians and sits south of Cayuga Lake making it a beautiful tourist area in the Finger Lakes region of New York. It has a population of 31,000 which doubles in size during the school year because of internationally ranked Cornell University and Ithaca College. It is 70 per cent white and the eighth most expensive place to live in the US (Economic Policy Institute). It is one of the best college towns to live in and historically much more liberal; it is surrounded by a conservative rural area, however, of struggling small family farms and agribusiness. Tompkins County is really two counties. While a portion of

the population thrives, many more face low wages, growing inequality, erosion of middle-class jobs, housing costs through the roof, and the institutionalisation of a low-wage service economy. This is a serious economic challenge not only for the one-third to one-half of the population not receiving a living wage.

7 See http://tcworkerscenter.org.
8 See www.bluegreenalliance.org, and www.labor4sustainability.org.
9 https://neweconomy.net/about.
10 High-volume hydraulic fracturing, also known as fracking, involves blasting millions of gallons of chemical-laced water thousands of feet underground to crack shale and release natural gas trapped inside it.
11 '657 arrests have been made at the gates of Crestwood since the We Are Seneca Lake campaign began. 404 different Seneca Lake Defenders have been arrested. In addition, at least 144 Seneca Lake Defenders have successfully blockaded for an entire day without being arrested' (www.wearesenecalake.com/seneca-lake-defendes/).
12 We Are Seneca Lake, Finger Lakes, New York. 2016. www.wearesenecalake.com/.
13 In the US, tax abatements are given to corporations such as developers to lower the local taxes they have to pay as an enticement to locate in a particular community.
14 www.marxists.org/archive/marx/works/1844/james-mill/.
15 Other thinkers have seen love as a relation that connects human beings in special ways, such as critical theorist Erich Fromm. In this paragraph I am simply using the quote from Marx as a springboard for my own thoughts.
16 'Thinking Like a Mountain'. www.uky.edu/OtherOrgs/AppalFor/Readings/leopold.pdf.
17 Stéphane Hessel, 'Indignez-vous!' http://indignez-vous-indignacion.blogspot.com/p/english.html.
18 www.peacefuluprising.org/tims-official-statement-at-his-sentencing-hearing-20110726.
19 https://350.org/from-standing-rock-to-the-gulf.
20 http://indiancountrytodaymedianetwork.com/2016/09/09/obama-hear-our-cry-lakota-women-call-president-stop-violence-165737.
21 www.americanswhotellthetruth.org/portraits/sandra-steingraber.
22 www.truth-out.org/news/item/37378-from-nodapl-to-freedomsquare-a-tale-of-two-occupations.

References

CSED, 2014. 'Principles of Unity'. *Published online*, March 2014.
Davis, A., 2016. *Freedom Is a Constant Struggle: Ferguson, Palestine, and the Foundations of a Movement*. Haymarket Books, Chicago, IL.
Ferguson, A., 2015. 'Feminist Love Politics: Romance, Care, and Solidarity' in Jónasdóttir, A.G., Ferguson, A. (Eds.), *Love: A Question for Feminism in the Twenty-First Century*. Routledge, New York, 250–264.
Hayes, K., 2016. 'From #NoDAPL to #FreedomSquare: A Tale of Two Occupations'. *Truthout*, 25 August. www.truth-out.org/news/item/37378-from-nodapl-to-freedomsquare-a-tale-of-two-occupations.
Hennessey, R., 2015. 'Bread and Roses in the Commons' in Jónasdóttir, A.G., Ferguson, A. (Eds.), *Love: A Question for Feminism in the Twenty-First Century*. Routledge, New York, 265–281.
Hill Collins, P., 2000. *Black Feminist Thought: Knowledge, Consciousness, and the Politics of Empowerment*. Routledge, New York.
Marx, K., 2000 [1844]. 'On James Mill' in *Karl Marx: Selected Writings*. 2nd edition. Edited by David McLellan. Oxford University Press, Oxford, 124–133.
Murillo Martin, L., 2013. 'Making the Environment a Trade Union Issue' in Räthzel, N., Uzzell, D. (Eds.), *Trade Unions in the Green Economy: Working for the Environment*. Routledge, New York, 29–40.

Räthzel, N., Uzzell, D., 2013. *Trade Unions in the Green Economy: Working for the Environment*. Routledge, New York.

Russell, K., 2005. 'Multiculturalism as Solidarity: Globalized Resistance' in Anton, A., Schmitt, R. (Eds.), *Toward a New Socialism*. Lexington Books, Lanham, MD, 463–482.

Russell, K., 2007. 'Feminist Dialectics and Marxist Theory'. *Radical Philosophy Review* 10(1): 35–56.

Silliman, J., Gerber Fried, M., Ross, L., Gutierrez, E.R., 2004. *Undivided Rights: Women of Color Organize for Reproductive Justice*. South End Press, Brooklyn, NY.

Smith, R., 2016. *Green Capitalism: The God That Failed*. World Economics Association Books, Bristol.

Yuval-Davis, N., 1999. 'What Is "Transversal Politics"?' *soundings* 12: 94–98.

Weart, S., 2008. *The Discovery of Global Warming: A History*. 2nd edition. Harvard University Press, Cambridge, MA.

INDEX

#MeToo movement, 307, 318–19
#WeToo movement, 318–19
11 September 2011 attacks, 231, 232

abalone, 153
abandonment, 242
abolitionism, 332, 333, 344–7
abortion, 267, 282, 284, 285, 287, 289, 292, 306, 307, 314; criminalisation of, 268; legal, campaigning for, 318; right to, 290
Achinstein, B., 169,
actor-victim thesis, 31–2
Adam, Barbara, 46
Adam, Marie, 237
Adivasi people, 222
Adorno, Theodor, 231
affective energy, production of, 343
Africa, gendered life in, 197
Agamben, Giorgio, 3, 233, 246; *Homo Sacer*, 241
agency: of women, 190; rationalised, 176
agential realism, 51
aggrievement among workers, 129
agrarian reform *see* land reform
Aguilar, Delia, 66
Akhlaq, Mohamed, murder of, 224
Alarcón, Roberto, 'La Huelga', 124, 125
alienated labour, theory of, 16
alienation: in Marx, 41; theory of, 338–9
alikreukel, collecting of, 155
Althusser, Louis, 32
ama de casa (homemaker), 194
Amazon, organising at, 323
Ambedkar, B.R., 4, 214, 224, 227; 'Annihilation of Caste', 222, 223; 'Castes in India', 223; conversion to Buddhism, 216, 218–24; *The Buddha and His Dhamma*, 226
Amihan movement, 302–3
Anand, S., 222
Anderson, Perry, *The Indian Ideology*, 212, 224
Anti-Defamation League (ADL), 258
anti-racism, 239
anti-semitism, 249–60; and the Left, 252–3; new, 258 (use of term, 251); rightwing, rise of, 257–9

apartheid, 153, 160, 164, 254, 255; town planning under, 193
apocalyptic views, 340
'apparent antithesis', 115
Arab Spring, 322
Argentina: construction of nation-state in, 277–8; feminist movements in, 4, 276–95; military coup in, 282, 283; viewed as white European country, 288; women's movement in, demands and agreements in, 286–8
Argentine Workers' Central Union (CTA), 288
Arruzza, Cinzia, 314; 'Remarks on Gender', 70–2; 'Three Theses', 82
Arya Mahila Sabha, 217
Asian Development Research Institute, 24
Asian Migrant Coordinating Body (AMCB), 303
Asosiación de Mujeres Meretrices de Argentina (AMMA), 287
assemblage, 55, 56, 65
assembly line work, 187; global, 297; womens work on, 198
Association of University Women (Argentina), 278
Aung San Suu Kyi, 23
austerity, 176, 335, 338
Australian Aboriginal peoples, seasonal walk of, 46
Austria, position of migrants in, 238
authoritarianism, issue of, 281
Autonomia Operaia, 113
autonomy, of womens bodies, 272, 288
awareness sessions, 26

Babri Masjid, destruction of, 225, 228
Bai, Lakshmi, 216
Baker, Ella, 306
ban, 241; as prohibition, 240; two regimes of, 246
Banaji, Jairus, 77–8
bandanas, worn by fisherwomen, 161–2
Barcelona, on-line citizen input in, 323
Bare Life, 241, 242
Barth, F., 250

Basavanna, 228
Basavanna reform movement, 227–8
Bauböck, Rainer, 95
Bauer, Bruno, *The Jewish Question*, 211
Beauvoir, Simone de, 71
Bebel, August, 252
Beck, Ulrich, 48
becoming human, 243–6
beef, eating of, 223, 224
Beer, Ursula, 93
Behar, Katherine, 60, 62, 63; *Object-Oriented Feminism*, 59
Behari Medhavi, Bipin, 217
Being, ontological ground of, 61
Belgrade, pride parade in, 234
Bennett, Jane, *Vibrant Matter*, 55
Bennholdt-Thomsen, Veronika, 91
Benston, Margaret, 308
Berlant, Lauren, 66
Berlin Wall, 244; fall of, 231, 232, 244
Bharatiya Janata Party (BJP) (India), 213, 222, 223, 228
Bhattacharya, Tithi, 106, 116, 118, 167
Billion Women Rise, 19
binaries, 52, 53, 127; moving beyond, 58; of gender, imposition of, 81
biopolitics, 232, 245, 346
bios, 241, 242
birthing, 44, 124, 139, 170, 179, 316
black clothing, wearing of, 161–2
Black Lives Matter, 319–20, 323, 333
black women, 313, 320; as caretakers of nature, 146; double burden of, 202; in industrial employment, 196–8
blogs: outside of traditional union remit, 135; used in struggles, 133–6, 138, 140
blue economic justice, 159–63
blue economy, 144–66; as African Renaissance, 149; as blue imperialism, 150; as site of economic growth, 148; concept of, 152; constructions of illegality in, 152–4; divergent stances on, 148; use of term, 147
BlueGreen Alliance (USA), 330, 334
Bolsa Familia program (Brazil), 270
Bolsonaro, Jair, 273
borders, 239; at Tijuana, 238; militarisation of, 237; violence of, 238
Boycott, Divestment and Sanction movement, 249
Braidotti, Rosi, 51, 53, 54, 55, 56, 57, 66–7
Brave Heart Society (USA), 346

Brazil: feminist movements in, 3; restructuring of, 263, 268; trade union movement in, 263–75
Brazilian Committee for Amnesty, 265
Brecht, Bertolt, 37; *Flüchtlingspräche*, 30–1; learning from, 30–1; *The Good Woman of Szechwan*, 29; *The Seven Deadly Sins*, 29
Brenner, Johanna, 316, 322
Briskin, Linda, 116
Buchanan, A., 89
Buddhism, 223, 226; see also conversion, to Buddhism
Burawoy, Michael, 128, 168, 170, 181–4, 191
Burma, 24; genocide in, 23
Byzantine Empire: as imperial state, 78–9; position of eunuchs in, 70–87; use of term, 73

Caithanya, Raja, 224
Caixeta, Luznir, 237
Cambiemos coalition (Argentina), 290, 291
Campaign for Renewable Energy (USA), 333
Cape lobster, 153
capital: indifferent, 71; regulation of, 24, 26
capitalism, 58; contradictions within, 10, 180; reading of, 314; requirement for growth, 330; state-managed, 172
capitalist imperialism, 303; use of term, 301
capitalist ontology, as market freedom, 58–64
carbon emissions, reduction of, 330
carceral state, 320
care, 109, 111, 124–6, 135, 343; among women workers, 137, 196–8; as labour, 170; commodification of, 140, 315; concept of, close to concept of ethics, 183; crisis of, 4, 37, 167–86 (conceptualisation of, 179–81; potentials of, 181–4); decommodification of, 180; for life, 28; in the workplace, making of, 142; insurance for, 97; professionalisation of, 173; professions of, 128; state's withdrawal from, 97; struggles of, 126–8; theories of, 5
care giving, as public good, 317
care sector, women's work in, 3
care work, 4; as quasi-market, 95–7; borne by female relatives, 97; commodification of, 183; definition of, 199; exploitation of, 88–101; flight from, 198–200, 202; in Germany, 95–7; lay nature of, 97; misrecognition of, 170; privatisation of, 340; seen as private responsibility, 310; unpaid, not considered by Marx, 92–4; world chain of, 237

care workers: mobilisation of, 177; sense of responsibility of, 177
Carina, a welder, 199
caring: as production, 204; during strike action, 132, 133; for the natural environment, 343; labour of (done by women, 315 (by African women, 339); organised collectively, 346); practices of, 28-9, 37; rationalities of, 176; rights regarding, 346-7; satisfaction of, 202-4
Carr, Brian, 244, 245
cash for care programmes, 97
caste system, 214, 223, 224; challenging of, 218, 219, 222, 225, 227
Castile, Philandro, killing of, 333
castration, banning of, 73
Catholic church, 257, 265, 266, 267, 273, 280, 284, 285-6, 292
Catholics for Free Choice, 257
Cebile, a car worker, 196, 197
Central Workers' Union (CUT) (Brazil), 263, 267, 268, 269, 271
Chakravarti, Uma, 216, 225-6
'Chalu Udupi' campaign (India), 224
Chandoke, Neera, *State and Civil Society*, 214
Chandra Sen, Keshab, 217
Chatterjee, Partha, 245
Chemnitz: events in, 241; formerly Karl-Marx-Stadt, 243
Chicago, strike of teachers in, 321
Chicago Teachers Union, 321
child care, 14, 111-12, 127, 158, 159, 170, 179, 192, 194, 199, 269, 272, 315, 316, 318; absence of, 313; assistance for, 269; free day care, 272; free school meals, 320; in public sector, 193; of waged workers, 134; privatisation of, 303; public, 307
child custody, 283
child minders, 199, 200
childbirth *see* birthing
China, 311; control of social media in, 323; Cultural Revolution, 25; mud schools in, 23
Christian Evangelists, 257-8, 285-6
Christianity, 220, 241, 243, 257
Church of England Mission, Pune, 218
citizenship: attainment of, 244; biopolitical, 233; necropolitical, 233; of European Union, 233
Civil Code (Argentina), reform of, 279
civil disobedience, 332, 344, 345

civil rights movement, 314
civil society, as space of contestation, 214-16
class, 42, 105, 110, 119, 147, 163, 193, 203, 300, 312, 340, 341; centrality of, 308; increasing differentiation in, 311; interrelations of, 311
class consciousness, 11
class struggle, 182, 183
Classist Combative Movement (Argentina), 285
climate change, 211, 329, 338; effects of, on fishing communities, 159, 160; movements relating to, 327-49
Climate Disobedience Center (USA), 344
climate justice, 330
Clinton, Hillary, 306; critique of, 307
closure, 88, 89
Coalition for Sustainable Economic Development (CSED), 330, 333, 334, 335, 336, 337, 338, 343
coalitions and alliances, 328, 331, 338
Cock, Jacklyn, 296
Codovila, Victorio, 281
Colebrook, Claire, 66
Collins, P.H., 18
colonial matrix of power, 245
colonialism, 292
Combahee River Collective Statement, 312
Committee of Immokolee Workers (CIW) (USA), 319, 323
Committee on Values of the World Economic Forum, 26
commodification, 61, 62, 128, 181, 311, 347; of care, 140, 183, 315; of environment, 144; of land and water, 141; of property, in fishing communities, 151; of social reproduction, 317; of women, 60; *see also* de-commodification
commodities, fictitious, concept of, 181
common, use of term, 35
Common Bound conference, 328, 331, 332, 333
common sense, 276
commons, 35; feminist, 141; protection of, 346
Communist Party of Argentina (PCA), 281
Communist Party of India (Marxist) (CPI-M), 225
Comprehensive Agrarian Reform Program (CARP) (Philippines), 302
Comprehensive Sexual Education (Argentina), 286
Condor Plan, 283

INDEX | 353

Confederation of Workers of the Popular Economy (Argentina), 285
Congress of Metallurgical Female Workers (Brazil), 266
Congress Party (India), 219, 228
CONICET organisation (Argentina), 285
Connell, Raewyn, 75, 81, 189
conservation, top-down policies in, 149
Constantine IX Monomachos, 78, 81
construction, process of, 33
constructionism, 40-1
consubstantiality, use of term, 313-14
consumerism, culture of, 297
contagion, idea of, 242
contraception, 267, 282
contradiction, 82
conversion, 227; to Buddhism, 218-24; to Christianity, 218, 222, 225-6
Cooper, Melinda, 238
cooperatives, of women, 150
Corbyn, Jeremy, 252
Cornell University, 335-6
cosiness, of strike action, 125
cotton, growing of, by slaves, 339-40
Council for Gender Policies (Argentina), 289
cow politics, in India see Gau Rakshaks
Crenshaw, Kimberlé, 65, 312
Crestwood Corporation, 332-3
critical race theory, 340
Critical Resistance movement, 320
Cudd, Ann, 313
cultural turn, 51
Czarniawska, B., 173

Dabolkar, Narendra, murder of, 227
Dakota Access Pipeline, 346
Dalit people, 218, 219, 220-1, 222, 223, 224, 227, 229; burning of, 225
Dalla Costa, Mariarosa, and Selma James, *The Power of Women and the Subversion of the Community*, 113-14
da Silva, Luiz Inácio (Lula), 270, 271, 272
Davis, Angela, 249, 306, 320; *Freedom Is a Constant Struggle*, 340
debt, 284, 292; distribution of, 246; national, 289
DeChristopher, Tim, 344-5
de-commodification, of care, 180
de-growth, 144
dehumanisation, 244, 246

Deleuze, Gilles, 51, 55, 245
Delphy, Christine, 71, 110, 309, 310
democracy, 25; commitment to, 323
Democratic Socialists of America (DSA), 320, 323
Democratic Union (Argentina), 281
Department of Agriculture, Forestry and Fisheries (South Africa), 160, 161, 163; protests at, 162
Depressed Classes, conference of, 219
deregulation financial, 291
Derrida, Jacques, 245
detraditionalisation, 47
devaluation of labour power, 95, 96, 97, 98
development, discourse and practice of, 147
Dharmashastras, 217
dialectics, 41, 42-3, 54; as method, 27; attack on, 53-8
Dickens, Peter, 40-1, 44, 45, 48
die-ins, at hospitals, 177
Diehl, Charles, 74
Dietze, Gabriele, 240, 246
differences of power and privilege, 322
differing, within capitalism, 57
dignity, use of word, 26
Dimitrakaki, Angela, 126
Dingpolitik, 52
direct action, 113
disappeared persons, 283
discrimination, 65-6, 97, 98, 246
disembedding, concept of, 40
division of labour, 42, 47, 54, 175, 220, 339, 342; domestic, 273; gendered, 13-14, 30, 191; in caring practices, 37-8; in fossil fuel economy, 337, 341; in Gandhi, 223; in home, 317; industrial, 40, 45, 47; modernist, 44, 47-8; old, challenges to, 328; post-Fordist, 232; racialised, 339; social, 58
divorce, 280, 283
Doctors Without Borders, 246
Dolphijn, Rick, with Iris van der Tuin, *New Materialisms*, 56
domestic labour, 45, 48, 110-11, 266, 315; and labour theory of value, 91-4; as man's job, 201; blurred with farm work, 302; does not produce value, 116; in Marx, 309; of fisherwomen, 154; of women, 195 (invisibility of, 170); seen as unproductive, 310; unpaid, 13, 93, 127; valuing of, 289; *see also* household workers

domestic labour debate, 42, 91, 92
domestic mode of production, theorisation of, 310
double movement, in Polanyi, 181
double oppression of women, 112, 114, 197, 203
dual (and triple) systems theory of women's oppression, 71, 72, 82, 117, 309
dualisms, avoidance of, 52, 56
Duterte, Rodrigo, violence of, 299–300
Dunayevskaya, Raya, 4
Durkheim, Émile, 41, 47

Eastern Europe, humanisation of, 245
Ebert, Teresa, 53, 55
ecofeminism, 144, 145, 146; as Marxist sociology, 40–50; as politics, 163–4; as sociology of knowledge, 42; Marxist, 145–7
ecological crises, 328
ecological modernisation, 47
ecology: dualist, 340; feminist, 5
economic crisis, of 2008, 51
education, 25, 270, 322; of women, 217, 278 (in universities, 282, 317)
effeminacy, theorisation of, 83
Eisenstein, Hester, 307
El-Tayeb, Fatima, 244
elderly, care for, 179; in Germany, 95–7; regulation of, 97
Elena, a car worker, 195
Emana, a car worker, 197–8
emotion, 16, 124–6; among workers in struggle, 134; of strikes, 125; role of, 339; see also traditional feelings
emotional labour, 127
empathy, 342
empowerment, of women, 29, 58
Encuentros Nacionales de Mujeres (ENM) (Argentina), 284
'end of work', 203
energy see renewable energy
energy production and distribution, control over, 329–38
Engels, Friedrich, 28, 105, 111, 311; 'Letters on Historical Materialism', 314
enlightenment, 16
entrepreneurship, 190
Environmental Impact Assessments (EIA), 336, 338
environmental justice, 319
epistemic advantage, 18

epistemology, training in, 25
equal pay, 322
equality: for legitimate and illegitimate children, 280; of women, in decision-making, 302
equilibrium, in Marxism, 108
Erlöv, I., 176
Essed, Philomena, 246; *Racism in Europe*, 239
ethics, professional, 183
ethnic cleansing, 234
eunuchs: and class society, 75–6; and the state, 79; as clergymen, 80; emasculation of, 73; indicative of contradictory variations, 83; ineligible as emperors, 78; position of, in Byzantine Empire, 70–87; prejudices against, 79–80
European Union (EU), 236; constitution of, 238; humanisation project of, 244; whiteness of project, 239; Schengen border, 238
Eusebius, a eunuch, 81
Evangelical Christianity, 292
exchange, ideology of, 63, 64
exchange-value, 58, 62, 90
exclusion, 88, 89, 97, 98, 246; technologies of, 250
exploitation, 65, 88–101, 231, 246, 247; as concept, 96 (broadening of, 98); feminist approach to, 92; Marx's use of term, 90, 91, 94; of elderly care work, 96; primary, distinct from secondary, 90; relation with exclusion, 97–9
export processing zones (EPZ), 187
extended case method, 191
externalisation of control costs, 176
extractive industries, 149, 292

Facebook, used for organising, 133, 138, 320, 322
Factory Occupation Movement (Brazil), 264
Fair Food Program (FFP) (USA), 319
falling rate of profit, tendential, 179
family, 193, 197; male breadwinner model of, 317; nuclear, 202, 340; pressures on, 180; reduced size of, 171; women's desire for, 196
fantasies, distribution of, 246
far-right groups, rise of, 231
Farage, Nigel, 258
Farris, Sara R., 126

INDEX | 355

fascism, 3; in Europe, 231–48; postmodern, 234–6; use of term, 235
fear, distribution of, 246
Federici, Silvia, 99; *Caliban and the Witch*, 315; *El patriarcado del salario*, 141; *Wages Against Housework*, 113–14
femicide, 240, 286, 287
Feminine Movement for Amnesty (Brazil), 265
feminisation of work, 98, 188, 189
feminism, 225, 226, 232–4, 282, 340; academic, 267; autonomist, 112, 113–15, 119; black, 15, 312; class-based, 66; genealogies of, 276–7; in austerity, 67; indeterminate, 57; indigenous, 147; liberal, 57, 297, 307; market feminism, 62; neo-liberal, 51–69; new materialist, 4, 52, 53, 57, 64; political subjects of, 237; red, 53, 64–8; second-wave, 19; seen as bourgeois, 290; socialist, 1, 110–12, 256–7, 259, 308–10 (in practice, 317–22; use of term, 308); transversal, 56; varieties of, 307–8; vitalist, 53; white, 312; within Left parties, 290; *see also* ecofeminism, Marxist feminism, object-oriented feminism *and* trade union feminism
feminisms, hyphenated, 15
feminist movements in authoritarian states, 3
Ferguson, Ann, 329, 343; 'Feminist Love Politics', 342
Ferguson, Michigan, demonstrations in, 323
Ferguson, Susan, 117, 126, 127
Fernández de Kirchner, Cristina, 290
fertility rates, lowering of, 317
Fessing, Eric, 237
Fight for Fifteen campaign, 323
Fighting Womens Movement, in CSP-Conlutas, 272
financial capitalism, 291, 292
financialisation, 1, 169, 179, 239; public sector workers within, 177–9
Fine, Ben, 106, 108
First International Feminist Congress, 278
fish farming, harmful nature of, 163
fisheries: displacement of, 152; overfishing of, 160; regulation of, 160–1; small-scale, regulation of, 151; sustainable management of, 159; women's knowledge about, disregarded, 160
fisherwomen: as 'women who fish', 156; demonstrations by, 161, 162; household

livelihood activity of, 156; power and activism of, 159–63; underpaid activities of, 155–8; unpaid work of, 158–9
fishing, narrowness of term, 156
fishing industry in South Africa: as industrialised whiteowned sector, 153; commercial, 161; informal, 153; permits, 162; quotas in, 153; regulation of, 161; small-scale, women's work in, 144–66
flat ontology, 51–69
flexibility, in employment, 140
Fordism, 189, 231
Former Yugoslavia, 239, 240
Fortress Europe, 237
Fortunati, Leopoldina, 113, 115
Fossil Free Tompkins organisation (USA), 333, 337
fossil fuel economy, 328, 334, 347; campaigning against, 332; challenging of, 344; transition from, 327
Foucault, Michel, 3, 232, 245
Four-in-One-Perspective, 38
fracking, 333, 336; banning of, in New York State, 332; campaigning against, 345, 347; violence entailed in, 346
framework model, 314–15
France, 242, 245
Franchise Commission (India), 220
Fraser, Nancy, 168, 170, 179–80, 183, 307
free transport, allowed by workers, 131
freedom, 63; as market freedom, 62; for women, 65–6
Freedom Square, Chicago, occupation of, 346
French Revolution, 223, 282
Frosini, Fabio, 293
funding machine, 22–6

Gaby, a car worker, 194
Gandhi, Indira, 214, 227
Gandhi, Mahatma, 219, 220, 221, 222, 223; murder of, 224
Gau Rakshaks, 223, 224
gay rights, 321
Gaza, 306
gender, 56, 66, 68, 72, 105, 110, 119, 163, 192, 203, 263, 285, 300, 312, 340, 341; as instrument of labour, 57, 58; as language construct, 59; diversity of, 287; dyadic, imposition of, 81; in Africa, 197; in Marx, 35;

Marxist feminist writings on, 109; policies regarding, 289; position of eunuchs in Byzantine Empire, 70–87
gender bias, 48
gender equality, 37, 187, 193; as gender segregation, 198–200, 201
gender performativity, 3
gender regimes, 201–4; challenging of, 198; concept of, 189; in the workplace, 187–207 (varieties of, 192–8)
gender relations: as sites of struggle, 57; at work, 5
gendered stratification of labour market, 297
General Assembly of Women for Rights, Integrity, Equality, Leadership, and Action (GABRIELA) (Philippines), 301, 304; organising activities of, 302
General Confederation of Labour (CGT) (Argentina), 280
genocide, 235, 250, 284, 289
German, Lindsey, 13
Germany, 29, 253; care work in, 95–7; immigration to, 241
Gibbon, Edward, 74
Giddens, Anthony, 40
Gimenez, Martha, 296; *Marx, Women and Capitalist Social Reproduction*, 105
Gita, V., 225
gleaning of inshore produce, 155, 156, 158, 159
Global Southern Lecture series, 249
global warming, reduction of, 327
globalisation, 128, 231; gendered processes of, 203; resistance to, 49
Godhra train incident (India), 225
Godse, Nathuram, 224
Goodman, J., 144
governmentality, 237, 245; crisis of, 258; genealogy of, 233
Gramdan movement (India), 226
Gramsci, Antonio, 10, 25, 189, 276; view of civil society, 215–16
'Great Derangement', 227
green economy, 144, 148
greenhouse gases, reduction of, 336
greening of capitalism, 327
Grosz, Elizabeth, 56
growth, hostility to, 337
Guattari, Félix, 55
Guilbert, Madeleine, 273

Guilland, Rodolphe, 74
Gustafsson, R.Å., 178, 180
Gutiérrez Rodriguez, Encarnación, 238

Habermas, Jürgen, 42
hagiography, 80
Hakim, Jamie, 251
Haldon, John, 77–8; *A Social History of Byzantium*, 78; *The State and the Tributary Mode of Production*, 77–8
hand, drawing of, 137–8
Haraway, Donna, 12, 18, 62
Harding, Sandra, 17; *The Science Question in Feminism*, 12–13, 15
Hardt, Michael, 342
Harijan Sarva Sewa Sangh, 220, 221
Harman, Graham, *The Road to Objects*, 59
Hartmann, Heidi, 13–14, 71, 296, 309
Hartsock, Nancy, 11–12, 14, 17, 18, 19
Harvey, Alan, 77
Harvey, David, 47–8, 183
Hasselbladh, H., 172, 173
Hatzaki, Myrto, 76
Haug, Frigga, 1, 146; *Der im Gehen erkundete Weg*, 32; *Sexualisierung der Körper*, 32
headscarf-wearing, control of, 240
health, of women, 278
health system: crisis of, 29; womens work in, 199
Hegel, G.W.F., 18, 61, 214, 215, 339, 341, 344; parable of master and servant, 10, 11
hegemony, 10, 276
Heinrich, Michael, 107
Hekman, Susan, 17
Helena, Heloise, 272
Hennessey, Rosemarie, 329, 342; 'Bread and Roses in the Commons', 343
Hermin, a fisherwoman, 150, 153, 154, 160, 162, 163
Herrin, Judith, 75
Hessel, S., 344
hierarchies of sex and race, 311–12
HIJOS organisation (Argentina), 284
Hilarion, a eunuch, 81
Hill Collins, Patricia, 15
Hindu Code Bill (India), 226
Hindu religion, 212, 217, 219, 220, 221
Hindutva, 213, 222, 228, 229; rise of, 224–6
history, entering into, 32–3
holocaust, 254

home, as prison, 30
Homo Sacer, 241
Hopkins, Keith, 80
Horgan, Goretti, 66
hottentot, 155
household, concept of, 196
household labour *see* domestic labour
household workers: equality for, 270; rights of, 263
households: multiple wage earners in, 194; rationalisation of, 171
housewife, concept of, 115
housing, 278
human rights, 25, 26; as womens rights, 319; protection of, 244; violations of, 289
humanity-nature question, 40–1
Hunter Education Commission, 217
hunter-gathering mode of production, 46
Hypatia journal, 18
hyper-individualisation, 236

identity politics, 244, 249, 256–7, 313, 331
impersonal, is political, 59
INCITE organisation, 320
Independent Jewish Voice, 254
Independent Labour Party (India), 221
India, 4, 26; Constitution of, 219, 221, 227, 229; viewed as Hindu Nation, 212, 213
'indifferent approach', 82
Indigenous Peoples, 44, 46, 92, 147, 277, 279, 284, 346; children of, stolen, 277; existence of, denied, 278; expulsion of, 303; recognition of, as citizens, 280; women, 285
industrial production, 89; Departments I and II, 107
Industrial Workers of the World (IWW), 320
industrialisation, 171, 340
inequality, 312; mechanisms of, 88; of wages, 269
Inez, a car worker, 195
insecurity, of employment, 132, 133, 136
Institute of Critical Theory (Berlin), 1
institutional ethnography, 191
Intergovernmental Panel on Climate Change (IPCC), 329
International Brotherhood of Electrical Workers (IBEW), 337
International Development Association of Sweden (SIDA), 23

International Holocaust Remembrance Alliance (IHRA), 251, 256
International Labour Organisation (ILO), 187
International Migrant Alliance (IMA), 303
International Monetary Fund (IMF), 289, 291, 292
International Women's Alliance (IWA), 4, 301, 304
International Women's Day, 306
International Women's Strike, 124, 285, 306, 317, 321
intersectionality, 5, 117, 119, 312–14, 331, 333, 339; of struggles, 317–22, 340
iron, production of, 339
Islam, 220, 228
Islamophobia, 212
Israel, 249–60, 320; claim to representation of Jews, 253–5; critique of, 3; invasion of Lebanon, 249; nationality law, 255; support for, 254

Jackson, Cecile, 48
Jaffri, Ehsan, 224
James, C.L.R., *The Black Jacobins*, 315
Jat-pat-Todak Mandal, 222
Jerusalem, 256
Jewish Bund, 253
Jews for Justice for Palestinians, 254
Jews: as scapegoats, 252; question of nationhood, 254; right to return to Israel, 253
Jónasdóttir, Anna, 16
Johnston-Arthur, Araba Evelyn, 238
judges, harassment of, in Argentina, 291
Junkers, 278
just transition from fossil fuels, 327, 329–38, 347; concept of, 328
Justicialist Party (Argentina), 280, 281, 282
Justinian II, 78

Kabataang Makabayan (KM) (Philippines), 298
Kalburgi, M.M., murder of, 227
Kalpana, K., 225
kanban system, 176
Kandasamy, Meena, *The Gypsy Goddess*, 226
Kandidatos, a eunuch, 81
Keezhvenmani, massacre at, 226
Kennedy, John F., 306
Kergoat, Danièle, 313
Kirchner governments (Argentina), 288, 289

Kleinmond (South Africa), 150-2, 157, 158, 160, 163
knowledge: regimes of, 41; situated and plural, 12-13, 18
Kollontai, Alexandra, 4, 110, 312, 322; 'Communism and the Family', 112
Komnenoi dynasty, 74
Kothari, Rajna, *The State Against Democracy*, 214
Kourany, Janet, 18
kreef, 155, 159
Krul, Matthijs, 118
Krupskaya, Nadezhda Konstantinova, 110, 112; *The Woman Worker*, 111-12
Kuefler, Matthew, *The Manly Eunuch*, 75
Kuhn, Thomas, 17

labour: as category, 34; indifference to, 34; productive, 41-2; reproductive, 41-2; *see also* local labour
Labour Network for Sustainability (USA), 330
Labour Party (Brazil), 263, 270
Labour Party (Partido dos Trabalhadores) (PT) (Brazil), 272
Labour Party (UK): antisemitism in, 256; definition of term anti-semitism, 251
labour theory of value, 68, 88, 89, 92, 94, 115, 118; and domestic work, 91-4, 95; as viewed by feminism, 89, 93
labour unions *see* unions
Lacan, Jacques, 71
Lampedusa, deaths of migrants, 232-3
land reform, 299, 302-3
'land to the tiller', 299, 302
landlords, power of, 300
Lankesh, Gauri, 228; murder of, 227
Largosa Masa, Liza, 301
Lash, Scott, 47
Laslett, Barbara, 316
Latin American Feminist Meeting (2017), 285
Latour, Bruno, 52
lawfare, 291
layoffs of workers, 197; at Veolia company, 129-30
Leacock, Eleanor Burke, 54; *Myths of Male Dominance*, 61
LeBaron, Genevieve, 126
Ledesma, a MAKIBAKA organiser, 299
Lenin, V.I., 37
Leo III, 76

Leopold, Aldo, 343
Lesedi, a car worker, 192-3
'let live and make die', 232
Letta, Enrico, 232
LGBTQ community, 23, 234; rights of, 306
Liberation Theology, 266
Libya, 241; refugee camps in, 246
life, as threatening force, 66; as zoe, 51; capture of, 237; deading of, 237; production of, 38, 146
life activity of women, 12, 16
life-affirming positivity, 57
Lindio-McGovern, Ligaya, 303; with Ann Cudd, *Capitalism For and Against*, 313
Lingayats, 227-8
lobsters, catching of, 154, 157-8
local labour, hiring of, 331, 336
Lorena Barros, Maria, 298, 299
Lotta Feminista (Italy), 113
love, 16, 344, 345; as progressive force, 339; as a revolutionary force, 329; for the familiar and the old, 38; power to love, 342; revolutionary, 332, 342-3; *see also* solidarity love
loyalty to company, requirement of, 131
Lugones, Maria, 244, 246
Lukács, Georg, 10; *History and Class Consciousness*, 9
Luxemburg, Rosa, 4, 110, 112, 290, 309-10, 315, 322; Reform and Revolution, 337; re-reading of, 34-7; *The Junius Pamphlet*, 36; *Trümmer*, 36; writings on the women question, 111
Luxton, Meg, 126

machismo, 290
Macri, Mauricio, 290
Mahadevi, Akka, 227-8
Mahars, 220, 221
'Make the Road by Walking', 323
Malayang Kilusan ng Bagong Kababaihan (MAKIBAKA) (Philippines), 298-300
Maldonado-Torres, Nelson, 245
Malvinas War, 283
Manoramabai, daughter of Pandita Ramabai, 218
Manu Smriti, 216; burning of, 219
Mao Zedong, 25
Maplewood Project (USA), 335-6
Marcos, Ferdinand, 299, 301

INDEX | 359

marginalisation, 98, 246; of fisherwomen, 154–5, 163; of women, in waged work, 204
marginalism, 88
Maria, a car worker, 199, 200
Maria da Penha Law (Brazil), 272
marine resources, conservation of, 148
marketisation, 182; of forces of production, 181–2
marriage, 214, 289; as women's career option, 317; inter-caste, 220; same-sex, 306
Martin, Trayvon, killing of, 320
Marx, Eleanor, 322
Marx, Karl, 11, 18, 24, 27, 41, 52, 53, 54, 57, 58, 61, 62, 68, 105, 114, 115–20, 144, 309, 316, 322, 341, 342, 344; and gender relations, 35; and social reproduction theory, 105–23; *Capital*, 9, 34, 35, 90, 105, 106, 109, 113, 118, 188 (Vol. 1, 106; Vol. 2, 106–7); 'Contribution to the critique of Hegel's Philosophy of Law', 211; *Critique of the Gotha Program*, 168; does not consider care work, 92–4; *Economic and Philosophical Manuscripts*, 339; feminist critiques of, 92; *Grundrisse*, 35, 105; legacy of, 28; male bias of, 93; 'On James Mill', 338–9; 'On the Jewish Question', 211, 215, 252; re-reading of, 34–7; read against the grain, 88–101; views of (on civil society, 214–15; on productive labour, 315; on religion, 212–13); with Friedrich Engels (*The Communist Manifesto*, 34; *The German Ideology*, 9, 90; *The Holy Family*, 10); *see also* domestic labour, in Marx
Marxism, 2, 13, 17, 18, 22, 42, 47, 55, 77, 82, 89, 145, 147, 167, 179, 224, 225, 234, 272, 282, 308, 312, 316, 332, 340; academic demise of, 88; concept of exploitation in, 89–91; critique of religion, 211–12; gender blindness of, 13
Marxist feminism, 1, 24, 55, 70–2, 81, 82, 83, 91, 93, 97, 98, 105, 108, 116, 125, 127, 141, 144, 164, 167, 168, 184, 189, 231–48, 288, 292, 302, 312, 316, 317, 331, 341; as analytical frame, 296–8; as transformative power, 27–8; binary category of, 127; conferences of, 22 (*12 Theses*, 27; first, 1–2; second, 2; third, 2; fourth, 2, 304); contradictions in, 27–39; definition of, 2; framing of, in women's movements, 298–303; in the Philippines, 4; in USA, theory and practice of, 306–26; in world perspective, 296–305; need for, 2–5; profit fixation in, 94–5; views of religion, 211
Mary, a fisherwoman, 162, 163
masculinities, 75; new forms of, 287
Massey, Doreen, 189
materialism, 43, 45, 49; dialectical, 56; embodied, 44–5; historical, 54 (and Byzantine history, 76–8); new, 51, 52, 53, 55; *see also* feminism, new materialist
maternity leave, 269, 272, 318
matter of corporeality, 51
Max QDA systems, 191
Maya, a car worker, 192
Mazzocchi, Tony, 330
Mbembe, Achille, 232, 233, 241, 243
McKibben, Bill, 329
McNally, David, 119
McNay, Louis, 190
McRobbie, Angela, 190
Mear One, 252
Medida Provisória 557/2011 (Brazil), 272
Meiksins Wood, Ellen, 71, 82
Mellor, Mary, 40
memory, in Argentina, 289
Memory, Truth and Justice (Argentina), 285
memory work, 37; collective, 32
men: control of offspring by, 15; dominance by, 17, 314 (in black liberation movement, 312; in fossil fuel economy, 328; in marine industry, 149); empowerment of, 16; in positions of power, 318; predominant in corporate hierarchy, 297; responsibilities of, in family, 317; seen as defining working class, 266; white, middle class, as decision makers, 48
Merkel, Angela, 243
Messis, Charis, 76
mestizo people, 277
meta-industrial class, 45–7, 48, 49, 145
methodology, 191–2
Mexico: restructuring of, 194–5; Volvo factories in, 187–207 *passim*
Microsoft, 24
Mies, Maria, 15, 40, 42, 91
Migrant International (IM), 303
migrant labour, as slavery, 238
migrants, 92, 124, 239, 258, 291, 301; as labour export, 300; female, in care sector, 97; illegal, employed in care sector, 96; in

Austria, 238; integration of, 242; internal, in Argentina, 279; invisibility of, 245; mainstreaming the integration of, 242; men as, 308; perceived animality of, 242; political issue of, 22–3; women as, 298, 303
migration, 1, 25, 26, 192, 231, 292; as a human right, 289; from Mexico, 194; gendered experience of, 194; into Germany, 241; of fish, patterns of, 159; of Jews to Israel, 257; to Argentina, 277
Miliband, Ed, 252
militarisation, 237
Milošević, Slobodan, 234, 235
Minkie, a fisherwoman, 155, 156
misogynism, 218
Mitropoulos, Angela, 238, 246
Mladić, Ratko, 234
mode, meaning of, 55
mode of assemblages, 55
modernism, 14
modernity, 47
modes of production, 314, 316
Mohandesi, S., 170, 172–3, 175
Mohanty, Chandra Talpade, 244
Mojab, Shahrzad, 1, 19
Mol, Arthur, 47
monistic universe, 55
moral economy, 196–7; of the workplace, 132
moral outrage, 334, 344–7
Moreau de Justo, Alicia, 278
Morgan Stanley, 312
Morris, Rosemary, 81
Mose, Kirstine Nordentoft, 237
motherhood, social construction of, 282
Mothers and Grandmothers of the Plaza de Mayo, 283, 284
Mount Athos, 78, 81
Movimento dos Productores Agricolas (MAP) (Brazil), 264
Movimento dos Trabalhadores Rurais Sem Terra (MST) (Brazil), 264
Movimento dos Trabalhadores Sem Teto (MTST) (Brazil), 264
Movimiento de Liberación Femenina (MLF) (Argentina), 283
Müller, Heiner, *Zement*, 29–30
Mulheres de Via Campesina (Brazil), 264
Mulinari, Paula, 'Where is the strike...', 125
Multicultural Resource Center (USA), 333
multiculturalism, 239

Murphy, Michael, 127, 141
Muslims: attacks on, 225; hostility to, 308; rights of, in India, 224
mussels, collecting of, 155, 158
Mutts, of the Lingayats, 227–8
Myanmar *see* Burma
Myrdal, Alva, 171–2

Nandy, Ashis, 43
Narmada Valley struggle, 222
nation-states, 236, 304; Argentinian, 277–8
National Campaign for the Right to Legal, Safe and Free Abortion (Argentina), 284
National Commission for the Issues of Working Women (Brazil), 263, 268
National Coordination of Struggles (CSP-Conlutas) (Brazil), 271, 272
National Democratic Alliance (NDA) (India), 227
National Federation of the Household Workers (Brazil), 270
National Indigenous Peasants Movement (Argentina), 285
National Nurses United (USA), 327
National Office for the Issues of Working Women (Brazil), 268
nationalism, 225
nature: commodification of, 42; feminine relations to, 44; humanising of, 49; in Marx, 145; living differently with, 43; mediated by women, 45; women in, 152–4
Nazism, 243, 250, 257
necessary labour, 109
necrocapitalism, 232–4, 241–3
necropolitics, 3, 232, 236, 239, 240, 242, 243
negativity of oppositional critique, 57
Negri, Antonio, 342
Nehru, Jawaharlal, 219, 221
NEJB Unite Here (USA), 327
neoliberalism, 51–69, 167–86, 202, 231–48, 264, 270, 281, 283, 290, 292, 293, 296, 300, 303, 307, 318, 335; impact on working conditions, 268
Netanyahu, Benyamin, 258
Netherlands, racism in, 239
New Economy Coalition (USA), 331
New People's Army (Philippines), 300
New Public Management (NPM), 176
new unionism, in Brazil, 264–7

New York State Department of Environmental Conservation, 336
New York State Nurses Association, 327
night work, abolition of, 266
Nnaemeka, Obioma, 197
normality: capitalist, 188–9, 204; of fascism, culture of, 235
'Not in My Name', 225, 257
'Not One Less' (Argentina), 285, 287
nuclear weapons, tested by India, 227
nurseries, 265; in workplace, 266
nurses, 174, 176; exit of, 177; falling numbers of, 199

Obama, Barack, 346
object-oriented feminism, 51, 59, 60, 61, 62
objectification, 60
Obolensky, Dimitri, 78
O'Brien, Mary, 16; *The Politics of Reproduction*, 15
Ocampo, Victoria, 281
Occidentalism, 240
Occupy movement, 19, 24, 25, 322, 323
oeconomia, meaning of, 79
Ogawa, R., 169
oil companies, out-bidding of, 344
Oklahoma, strike of teachers in, 321
Olga, a car worker, 192–3
Olivia, a car worker, 195
one-system theories, variations within, 315–17
ontologies, new, 52
operaismo, 113
Operation Phakisa (South Africa), 149, 162–3
oppositional consciousness, 17
oppression, analysis of, 117
Oran, S.S., 168
Órban, Viktor, 242
Organisations of Women with African Heritage (Argentina), 285
Orientalism, 74, 77, 82
Oslo agreement, 255
Ostrogorsky, George, 77
Other, 239, 244, 245; role of, 246; sterilisation of, 236; transforms into *Homo Sacer*, 243; violence against, 240
outsourcing, 268

Pakistan, 213
Palestine, 249–60
Palestine/Israel, two state solution, 255
Palestinians, 3
Pansere, Givind, murder of, 227
Papić, Žarana, 240; *Europe after 1989*, 234–5
paradigm shift, 17
parenting of children, 45; shared, 282
part-time work, 129, 188
Partido de los Trabajadores (PTS) (Argentina), 290
Partido obrero (PO) (Argentina), 290
passion for one's work, 135; *see also* women, pride in work
Patel, Sardar, 221
Patlagean, Evelyne, 80
Patria Grande (Argentina), 288
patriarchy, 2, 12, 13, 15, 16, 70, 71, 72, 116, 126, 140, 170, 211, 216, 225, 239, 276, 280, 281, 282, 283, 286, 292, 310, 313, 331; as legal principle, 76; Brahmanical, 217, 218; in Byzantine Empire, 76, 82–3; shifting, 235; struggle against, 117, 292–3; views regarding women on boats, 156
patriotism, 345
Pauli, Gunter, 147
pensions, 331
performative metaphysics, 51
periwinkles, gathering of, 158
Perón, Eva, 280
Perón, Juan Domingo, 280, 281
Peronism, 279, 280, 288; opposition to, 281
Peronist Women's Party (Argentina), 280
Peterson, K., 176
Petit, Santiago López, 235
petitions, during strike actions, 136
phallocratic institutions, 11, 12
Philippines, womens organising in, 298–303
Phule, Jotiba, 219
Phule, Savitri, 219
Pierre, J., 174–5
pimps, termed businessmen, 288
Pittsburgh, attack on synagogue, 258–9
place, significance of, 189–90
Platform for Black Lives, 320
Plaza de Mayo, 282
poaching of fish, 163; as assertive action, 154
Polanyi, Karl, 169, 170, 181–4; *The Great Transformation*, 181–4
Polanyian analysis, 167–86
police *see* violence, of police
political prisoners, in Argentina, 291
Portugal, 22

post-Fordism, 189, 232
post)humanist position, 4, 51, 55, 56, 57, 58, 59, 64, 65, 66
postmodernism, 14, 231, 235
Potere Operaio, 113
poverty, of women, 311
power, 17–19
pre-figurative practices, 342, 346
precariat, 168
precarity, 128, 188, 231, 264, 268
precautionary principle, 47
prenatal care, 272
preservative love, 16
pride in work *see* women, pride in work
primitive accumulation, 311
private property, abolition of, 211–12
privatisation, 236, 303, 321; of care work, 340; of child care, 303; of collective infrastructures, 141; of ocean resources, 160; of reproduction, 203, 298; of welfare state, 175
production, 297; forms of, 28; of life, 204; of means of life, 38, 204; re-imagining of, 170–4; relationship with reproduction, 182; social, 164; social relations of, 52; *see also* industrial production
productive labour: concept of, 98; in Marx, 315
professions, 168–9, 174; breaking occupational unity of, 169; disciplining of, 184; in welfare, 169; mobilisation of, 177; of care, 128
profit-fixation, in Marxist feminist debates, 94–5
proletariat, 9, 10, 14, 30, 77, 168, 169, 215, 216, 280, 310; seen as male, 11; women, 111
property rights, of women, 226
prostitution, 278, 287
Protocols of the Elders of Zion, 258
Puar, Jaspir, 65
Public Administration Act (1985) (Sweden), 174
public sector: continuous change in, 175; industrial management techniques in, 178; reducing the size of, 174; restructuring of, 167–86
Pune Pact, 220
Puniyani, Ram, 225

Queer Studies, 333
Queer theory, 5

quota systems: for election of parliamentarians, in Argentina, 283; for union membership, 263; in Brazilian unions, 268; in fishing industry, 162

race, 71, 105, 119, 147, 163, 193, 202, 203, 244, 246, 310, 312, 340, 341
racial-state, 236
racialisation, 54, 235, 239, 244, 245, 246, 250, 259
racism, 2, 231, 250–2, 257, 276, 278, 279, 284, 286, 309, 311, 315; anti-Jewish, 250; entitlement racism, 239; in Netherlands, 239; not talked about, 245
radical immanence, 56
Radical Party (Argentina), 279
Ram, Lord, 228
Ramabai, Pandita, 4, 216–18, 227; care for child widows, 218; conversion to Christianity, 218, 222, 225; founds institution for widows, 217; *Stri Dharma Niti*, 218; *The High Caste Hindu Woman*, 218
rape, 273, 319; gang rape, 229; genocidal, 240; not a one-dimensional thing, 341; of Muslim women in Balkan wars, 240; threat of, in Iraq, 341
Rashtriya Swayamsewa Sangh (RSS) (India), 212, 224, 228
rationalism, 228
rationality, concept of, 182–3
Räthzel, Nora, 146; with David Uzzell, *Trade Unions in the Green Economy*, 337
realism, 40–1
reciprocity, discourse in South Africa, 197
Reds, The (Argentina), 290
Reena, a fisherwoman, 153, 158
reflexive inquiry, 13
refugees, 236, 237, 238, 239, 243, 258; and necrocapitalism, 241–3; as non-citizens, 244; banning of, 246; European crisis of, 241; Jewish, 255; Palestinian, 255; perceived as superfluous, 242; violence against, 242
relations of production, 317; new, 341, 343
relations of ruling, 11
religion: abolition of, 211; as private sphere, 211; as resistance, 211–30; freedom from, 226; freedom of, 226; Marxist critique of, 211–12; protest potential within, 213; reform of, 216; right to practise, 212
religious education, compulsory, 280

renewable energy, 327, 328, 333, 341–2, 343
rent-seeking, 88, 89
reproduction, 46, 94; autonomous, 170; biological, 15, 38, 109; carried out by women, 45; definition of, 170; Marxist feminist approaches to, 110; of capital, 3, 106–9; of labour power, 94; of systems, 167; re-imagining of, 170–4; retheorisation of, 141; relations of, 127; relationship with production, 182; social, 3, 41–2, 49, 110, 119, 125, 128, 133, 140, 141, 159, 194, 297, 298 (as concept, 71; as site of struggle, 171, 177, 182; cheapening of labour of, 304; commodification of, 317; crisis of, 171, 321; inherent tendency to crisis, 179; internalised, 171; privatisation of, 203; relationship with production, 203; use of term, 126; *see also* social reproduction theory)
reproductive freedom, 318
reproductive justice, 318
reproductive labour, 142; invisibility of, 47; of women in fisheries, 158; threefold problem of, 115; undervaluing of, 167
reproductive rights, concept of, 318
Republika Srpska, 240
resistance, 329; art of, 296; engages truth, 345; everyday, 128; forms of, at work, 126; theory/strategy for, 48–9
retirement rights of housewives, 289
revolution: socialist, 312; womens place in, 299
Revolutionary Communist Party (Argentina), 290
Ringrose, Kathryn, 75, 79–80
Rodwin, a fisherman, 152–3, 162
Roetner, John, 91
Rohingya people, 23, 24
Roma, deportation of, 238
Romanos I, 80
Rosetta, female persona in history, 33
Round Table Conference (India), 220
Rouse, Joseph, 18
Rousseff, Dilma, 270, 290
Rowina, a fisherwoman, 157–8, 160, 161
Roy, Arundhati, 222
RSI, prevention of, 269
Rudén, Janne, 136
Ruddick, Sara, 16, 45
Russia, 239, 311; situation of women in, 111

Russian Revolution, 216
Ryan, Michael, 18

Saad Filho, Alfredo, 106, 108
saffron, dressing in, 228
Said, Edward, 74
Salleh, Ariel, 40, 144
Sánchez Ferlosio, Chicho, 124
Sanders, Bernie, 320, 322, 323
Sanskritisation, 220
Sarah, a fisherwoman, 150, 160, 161
Sardar Sarovar Dam, struggle against, 222
Sarris, Peter, 77
Save the World Symphony, 347
Say Her Name campaign, 320
Sayer, Sean, 42
Scheduled Caste and Scheduled Tribe (Prevention of Atrocities) Act (India), 229
Scheduled Castes Federation (India), 221
school closures, campaigning against, 321
science: introduced into production, 34; not value-free, 13
Scott, James C., 128
seafood, gathering of *see* gleaning of inshore products
Second International, 110, 112
secular state: concept of, 224; need for, 213
secularism, 211, 225
self-organisation, 322
Sen, Samar, 22
separate spaces for women and people of colour, 322
Serbia, 235
Service and Communication Union (SEKO) (Sweden), 125, 135
Setalvad, Teesta, with Javed Anand, *Communalism Combat*, 224
sexism, 71, 231, 286, 300, 306, 309, 311
sexual difference, 240; codes of, 56
sexual harassment, 269, 277, 307, 319; in Catholic Church, 287
sexualisation, 54
sexuality, 60, 267, 312, 342; diversity of, right to, 289; freedom of, 61, 287
Shastri Dongre, Anand, 216
shifts, extra, working of, 131–2
Shiva, Vandana, 15, 40, 43, 45
Shivamaran, Mythili, 226
Showing Up for Racial Justice (SURJ) (USA), 333

sick leave, of workers, 131, 132
Signs journal, 17
Sikhism, 220
Silang, Diego, 302
Silang, Gabriela, 302
silencing of women, 11
Simon Commission, 220
sitting by the phone, for jobs, 137
situated imagination, 18
Sivamaran, Mythili, 225
slavery, 91, 250, 277, 298, 310, 319; in USA, 339
sleeping patterns of workers, 134
Smith, Dorothy, 17, 18, 19, 191; *The Everyday World as Problematic*, 11
Smith, Richard, 332; *Green Capitalism*, 327–8
snoek, 155, 157
social democracy, crisis of, 36
social media, 322; control of, 323; role of, 126
social movements, 264, 342, 344; in relation to climate change, 327–49; inclusivity of, 327; relation with workplace struggles, 128
social protest, criminalising of, 291
social reproduction feminism, 315–17
social reproduction theory (SRT), 105–23, 167, 183–4
Social Reproductive Frame (SRF), 127
Social Security Reform (Brazil), 271
socialism, 23, 31; openness to, 323
socially necessary labour time, 95
Sohn-Rethel, Alfred, 40
solidarity, 124–6, 133, 135, 137, 140, 200, 292, 293, 327–49, 334, 336, 338, 340, 344, 345; in strike action, 142; *see also* strikes, solidarity strikes
solidarity love, 329, 335, 342; theoretical approach to, 338–43
Sonnenfeld, David, 47
South Africa, 255–6; Volvo factories in, 187–207 *passim*; women's fisheries work in, 144–66
Southborough Committee on Franchise, 220
sovereignty, 241; genealogy of, 233
speaking in tongues, 218
Spinoza, Baruch, 51, 55
Spivak, Gayatri Chakravarty, 43; *Can the Subaltern Speak*, 24; *Three Women's Texts*, 24; *In Other Worlds*, 24; *Outside in the Teaching Machine*, 24
Srebrenica, genocide in, 234
Sri Guru Bababudan Swamy Dargah, 228

Sri Narayana Guru, 219
Srinivas, brother of Pandita Ramabai, 217
St Helena Bay (South Africa), 151
Standing Rock, water campaign, 306, 346
standpoint theory, 9–21; feminist, seen as relic, 17; gendering of, 10–12
state, as illusory commons, 28
Steenberg Cove (South Africa), 150–2, 158
Steinem, Gloria, 307
Steingraber, Sandra, 347
sterilisation: abuses of, 318; husbands' consent for, 272
Sterling, Alton, killing of, 333
Stoetzler, Marcel, 18
Stone Boy society (USA), 346
strategic essentialism, 43
strike guards, 139
strikes, 124–43, 197, 267, 278, 320–1; of public employees, illegal, 320; of teachers in West Virginia, 320–1; public support for, 137, 138; right to strike, 169; solidarity strikes, 138, 139; wildcat strikes, 135; *see also* International Women's Strike
subalternity, 26
subject: under capitalism, 234; women as, 32–3
subject/object relationship, 339
subjectivisation, gender and, 190
subjugated standpoints, 12
subjugation, in sphere of intimacy, 167
subordinated subject, 32
subsistence approach, 16, 91, 92, 93
subsistence farmers, 48; women as, in India, 45
subsistence farming, 3, 45, 91
subsumption, 24, 127; of life to capital, 232
suckling, 44
suggestions box, 130
surplus, socially produced, 90–1
surplus labour, theft of, 55
surplus-life, 52
surplus value, 94–5, 98, 116, 118, 310, 315, 316, 318; in field of housework, 315–16
surveillance, 237
sustainability, 159; concept of, 164; ethics of, 67
sustainable development, local organising for, 334, 334
Sustainable Development Goals, 148
Sweden: gender equality in, 198–200; healthcare sector in, 168–86; renewal of welfare sector in, 174; strikes in, 125–6; Volvo factories in, 187–207 *passim*

Swedish Medical Society, 183
swimming, learning of, 156
Symeon the Sanctified, 80-1
system, definition of, 310-12
'system change, not climate change', 331-4

talk, need for, in struggles, 132
talking back to power, 11
Tamil Buddhist Movement, 223
tar sands, mining of, 328, 345, 346
tariffs for domestic utilities, 291
tax relief for corporations, 334, 335
teachers, in West Virginia, strike of, 320-1, 322
Teitelman, E., 170, 172-3, 175
temporary and part-time contracts, 125, 129, 132, 136; limitation of, 139
Terlinden, Ulla, 45
Thassar, Pandit Iyothee, 223
Theophylact, 80
Therborn, G., 168-9, 177, 179
Times Up movement, 319
Tompkins County Workers' Center (USA), 330, 337
Torrant, Julie, 52
Tougher, Shaun, 74, 80
Toyota company, 176
trade union feminism, 264
trade unionism, new, 265
trade unions *see* unions
Trade Unions for Energy Democracy (USA), 327
traditional feelings, 30
trafficking of people, 287, 319; laws against, 289; of Native women, 346
TransCanada company, 328
transform!Europe, 2
transgender community, 249, 287, 333
translatability of languages, 293
TransPacific Partnership Agreement (TPPA), 300
transportation to work, 193
transsexual persons, 289; attacks on, 291
transversal politics, 256-7, 331, 336, 338
transvesticide, 287
Travellers in Support of the Strike (Sweden), 125, 136
tributary mode, 70-87
triple burden of women, 163, 203
Tristan, Flora, 4
Trotskyism, 284, 290

Trump, Donald, 227, 242, 306
Trumpka, Rich, 330
Trust for Community Outreach and Education (TCOE) (South Africa), 149
truth, 17-19; absolute, 17; linked to goodness, 345
Tupac Amaru Neighbourhood Association (Argentina), 285, 291
turbo-fascism, 233, 234-5, 240
Tzimiskes, John, 81
Tzinzilokas, Kosmas, 78

Unemployed Movement (Brazil), 264
unemployment, 202, 241, 245, 264, 268; in Brazil, 263; of black women, 196
Unified Socialist Workers Party (PSTU) (Brazil), 271-2
Unión Feminista Argentina (UFA), 283
union membership, decline of, 128-9
unionisation, of women, obstacles to, 273
unions, 133, 134, 135, 137, 138, 139, 182, 336, 337; absence of strategy among, 132; attacks on, 169; declining membership of, 323; in Brazil, women's involvement in, 263-75; in public sector, 169; lack of information from, 139; male dominated, 141; marginalisation of women within, 204; new membership of, 269; of coal miners, 320; organising around environmental issues, 330, 334; women on boards of, 265; *see also* new unionism
unitary theory of social reproduction, 71-2, 115-20, 314-15
United Electrical Workers (UEW) (USA), 327
United Nations (UN), 255
UN Conference on Population and Development, 257
UN Conference on Sustainable Development, 147-8
UN Higher Commissioner for Refugees (UNHCR), 240
UN Population Fund, 319
United States of America (USA), 281, 282; socialist feminist movements in, 3, 306-26
University of Coimbra, 22
unpaid labour, 140, 155-8; of fisherwomen, 158-9, 164; of women, 127, 172, 302, 309, 310, 315
unproductive labour, 92, 94, 310; of women, 112
untouchability, 223, 226; challenging of, 219, 220, 221, 223

Urry, John, 42
Uygur Muslims, 23

Vajpayee, Atal Bihari, 227
value, production of, 112, 116
varna, 222–3
Vemula, Renuka, 223–4
Vemula, Rohit, suicide of, 223
Veolia company, 129; lack of care for workers, 129; strike at, 125–6
victimhood, 249
victims, support for, 257
Victoria's Secret, 63
violence: against black people, 320; against women, 266, 272, 286, 287, 299–300; domestic, 283; entailed in fracking, 346; gendered, 16, 292, 320; hyper-militarised, 240; military, gendered, 240; of police, 346, 347; of the state, 320; sexual, 240, 269, 341
Vogel, Lise, 105, 108–9, 110, 119; *Marxism and the Oppression of Women*, 71, 115, 116, 117
Volvo company, 130; seen as worst employers in Global South, 204; women's work in, 3, 187–207
votes of women, 279, 280, 281
vulnerability, 340; social, use of term, 98

wage labour, 66; abolition of, 53; industrial, 91; productive, 89, 91
wage-dumping, 97
waged work of women, 58, 187–207, 264–7, 273, 298; as bank clerks, 268; 'can do it', 195; in formal labour market, 271; in informal market, 263; in public sector, 172; industrial, 193, 194, 202
wages, 114, 192, 194, 197; equality of, 272; family wage, 14; household dependence on, 170; industrial, 200; inequality of, 273; minimum wage, 270; of women workers, 172, 266 (low, 188, 313); reduction of, 269
Wages for Housework, 110, 315–17; *see also* domestic labour debate
Wainwright, Hilary, 308, 321
Walby, Sylvia, 71
Walmart, 312; organising at, 323
war, gendered nature of, 16
water, access to, 219, 220, 306, 346; struggles over, at Chowdar Tank (India), 219
Waterman, Peter, 127

We Are Seneca Lake campaign, 332–3, 347
wealth, concentration of, 128
Weart, Spencer, *The Discovery of Global Warming*, 328
Weber, Max, 65
Weeks, Kathi, 14, 18–19
Weisel, Eli, 256
welders, women as, 199
welfare: invasion of capital into, 178; labour regulation in, 178
welfare regimes, 172
welfare state, 198; as *Gesellschaft*, 173; in Argentina, 279
Welma, a fisherwoman, 155, 158
Werlhof, Claudia von, 91, 93, 95
West Bank, Jewish settlement in, 255
West Virginia, strike of teachers in, 320–1, 322
Westphal, Florian, 246
Wheeler, Mahawa Kaba, 149
White Buffalo Calf Woman Society (USA), 346
white people, better off than black people, 311; *see also* feminism, white
white supremacy, 331–2, 339, 340
widows, support for, 217–18
Wilson Gilmore, Ruth, 320
Wolf, Christa, 33
women: as caretakers of nature, 146; as heroines, 31; as social construction, 37; as targets for environmental policy, 161; as transformative force, 31; as victims of war, 16; caring practices of, 29; caucuses of, 322; claims of, seen as secondary, 273; commodification of, 60; common experience of oppression, 31; commons of, 203 (illusory, 28–9); constant struggle for recognition, 195; employment of, in industrial sector, 265–6; identify with work, 190; in health care system, 199; in men's jobs, 201; in nature, 152–4; in waged work *see* waged work, of women; invisibility of, 265; labour of, super-exploited, 297–8; liberation of, 32; linked to nature, 145; not permitted on boats, 156; on trade union boards, 265; pride in work, 195, 196, 202–4 (contradictions of, 200–1); reforming position of, 216; seen by men as competitors, 201; subjectivities of, 190; waged work of *see* waged work, of women; white, as beneficiaries of

colonialism, 340; work of (in fisheries, 144–66; seen as unproductive, 112); *see also* domestic labour
women activists, marital status of, 271
Women Against Fundamentalism, 257
Women in Development (WID), 297
women of colour, 318–19
Women Working Group, in CSP-Conlutas, 272
Women's Departments, in Brazilian trade unions, 267
Women's March (USA), 249, 306
women's movement: global, 296–305; new, in USA, 318; Second, 31
women's movements, 278; goals of, 298; new, 306–7; transnational, 301, 304
Women's Party (Argentina), 282
work, 16; liberating nature of, 203
work-life balance, 203
working class, 62–3, 172, 241, 337; concept of, 115; disciplining of, 184; in Marx, 215; industrial, 19; organised by welfare state, 182; reproduction of, 119; two genders of, 263

working class women: lives of, 322; politics of, 298; struggles of, 318; *see also* proletariat
working day, in Marx, 114
World Bank, public sector studies of, 168
World Social Forum, 19
World Wildlife Foundation (WWF), 148, 150, 152, 159
Wriedt, Vera, 237

Xenophon, 81

Yemen, malnutrition in, 243
Young, Iris, 109, 117
Yugoslavia, former, 234
Yuval-Davis, Nira, 18, 336

Zapatistas, 344
Zetkin, Clara, 4, 110–11, 112, 114, 290; 'Social Democracy and Womens Suffrage', 110
Zionism, 253, 254, 257; as settler colonial project, 255; critique of, 251; popular, 251, 256
zoe, 241, 242
Zuma, Jacob, 149

www.ingramcontent.com/pod-product-compliance
Ingram Content Group UK Ltd.
Pitfield, Milton Keynes, MK11 3LW, UK
UKHW021834230226
468319UK00006B/424